THE PUBLIC SPEAKER'S TREASURE CHEST

A COMPENDIUM OF SOURCE MATERIAL TO MAKE YOUR SPEECH SPARKLE

by

Herbert V. Prochnow

THORSONS PUBLISHERS LIMITED
Wellingborough, Northamptonshire

Third Edition (revised and enlarged) 1977
Tenth Impression 1984

Original American edition published by
Harper and Row Publishers Inc., New York

ISBN 0 7225 0974 X

Printed and bound in Great Britain

THE PUBLIC SPEAKER'S TREASURE CHEST

Contents

Preface

The first edition of this book and a revised edition have met such a gratifying response over the years that the authors have been encouraged to bring out a new, revised and further enlarged edition. This volume contains many new items and almost 5,000 in all to assist a speaker or toastmaster.

There is included for the first time a chapter with more than 100 quotations for special days or events. There are many new items in various parts of the book.

The book has been written primarily for two groups of persons—the many men and women who must occasionally make an address, introduce a speaker, or preside at a meeting; and the large number of persons who would like to improve their conversation. In addition, there are individuals not in these groups who may find the humorous stories, epigrams, witticisms, quotations, amusing definitions and illustrations entertaining and of interest.

At the beginning of the book there are two chapters that show how to prepare a speech and how to make a speech sparkle. It is hoped that the reader will be able by a study of these chapters to grasp the essential steps in the preparation of any speech. Many illustrations have been included to be helpful.

To make the book also a compendium of source material that may be used on many occasions in speeches and conversation, there are approximately 5,000 humorous stories, epigrams, similes, amusing definitions, quotations from literature and from modern sources, pertinent proverbs, interesting incidents from famous lives, humorous and witty verses, quotations for special days and events, and unusual phrases. These materials are the practical tools by which speeches and conversation are made fascinating and colorful. Books have been published which contained humorous stories; other books have presented similes or quotations. In this book, however, an effort is made to show in a single volume not only how to write a good speech, but also to present an abundance of material which will assist in the preparation of speeches and the improvement of conversation. The range is from the simplest humorous story to the more difficult tools of effective speech. The public speaker has here instantly available a treasure chest of all types of speech materials.

The most commonly used medium of making speeches and conversation more interesting is humor. There are times when a humorous story, well told, will strikingly illustrate a point or definitely relieve a tense moment in discussion or argument. At other times a short, barbed epigram, subtly introduced, is helpful. Sometimes a witty definition is of assistance. But humor must never be dragged in or consist merely of a series of irrelevant jokes. It must be to the point, clearly told, and without any "that reminds me" introduction.

Quotations from the Bible and from literature are important speech materials because they frequently represent the most unusual, thoughtful, and classic expressions great men have made on significant subjects.

The simile is used by far too few men and women. Yet it is a simple and serviceable tool of speech. An occasional simile adds distinct character to utterance and to writing.

There are also the infinite number of interesting incidents which may be obtained from the stories of famous lives. In them one finds illustrations of achievement, tragedy, patience, adversity, persistence, and all the experiences of human life. The wider one's reading in this field, the richer one's conversation and speech. Finally, by careful reading one acquires the knowledge which permits unusual phrases, such as those in Chapter IX, to be made a part of daily conversation or for prepared or extemporaneous speeches. Eloquence may be one of the products of wise use of the increased knowledge which comes from reading good books. Repeated study and daily use of the source materials in this book will return rich rewards.

This book has grown in part out of the practical experience of addressing many hundreds of business and banking conventions, associations of commerce, Rotary, Kiwanis, Lions, and Optimists clubs, high school and college commencements, professional societies, and other organizations. To the extent that it serves to make speeches and conversation more effective and interesting, it will have served its purpose.

H.V.P.
H.V.P., Jr.

CHAPTER

I

How to Prepare Your Speech

Cicero, a great Roman orator and philosopher, once said, "Before beginning, prepare carefully." This is sound advice for anyone who is to make a speech or introduce a speaker.

Epictetus, the Stoic philosopher, once said, ":No great thing is created suddenly, any more than a bunch of grapes or a fig. If you tell me that you desire a fig, I answer you that there must be time. Let it first blossom, then bear fruit, then ripen."

One may say with equal truth that few if any great speeches are created suddenly. The ideas they contain almost invariably grow out of years of experience. And the actual preparation of a speech generally requires many hours of concentrated thought and hard work, if it is to be a significant contribution on any subject.

Someone once asked Senator Daniel Webster how long he had worked on his great "Reply to Hayne." Webster said, "Twenty years." He had had about five days for preparation, but he had formulated his ideas on the subject over many years. No significant address is made without great effort and sustained thought.

The unpardonable sin in public speaking is the sin of inadequate preparation. The experienced speaker understands how to organize and prepare an effective address. He uses a number of relatively simple tools of speech which greatly assist him, and which anyone may readily learn and use.

Cicero said there were five essentials in public speaking: (1) determining exactly what one should say; (2) arranging the material in the proper order and with good judgment; (3) clothing the speech in well-chosen words and carefully phrased sentences; (4) fixing the speech in mind; (5) delivering it with dignity and grace. It will be helpful always to keep in mind these five essential steps which embrace the whole subject of public speaking.

When we proceed to the actual preparation of the speech itself, we find there are three simple divisions in almost every speech: the introduction, the body or discussion, and the conclusion or summary. The introduction should clearly state the subject to be discussed so that the audience may thoroughly understand it. The body of the speech or discussion should be a carefully prepared, logically arranged statement of the ideas which the speaker wishes to convey. It is advisable to divide the main body of the speech into several parts: generally, two, three, or four. Each of these parts should make a complete unit in itself so the audience will find it easier to keep the essential ideas of the speech clearly in mind. Finally, in the conclusion, the speaker usually should summarize in a few brief sentences the two, three, or four ideas he presented in the main body of the speech. This plan of dividing a speech into an introduction, body, and conclusion is the most desirable form for most occasions, and for most speakers, and any deviation from it should come only after one has gained considerable experience in speaking.

Having taken what may be called a panoramic view of a speech, we are ready to present in considerably more detail the exact steps necessary for its preparation. Not all persons prepare speeches with the same thoroughness and exacting attention. Consequently, not all persons give equally good speeches.

The steps here outlined as necessary in preparing a speech are designed to be comprehensive and of assistance both to the beginner and to the more polished public speaker. With experience, some of the steps may perhaps be eliminated or modified, but finished public speaking is a high art, and it requires something more than slipshod and careless preparation.

A distinguished former senator, Arthur H. Vandenberg, an able speaker, once advised us that in his opinion "scrupulous and painstaking preparation is indispensable. When brilliance and force are extemporaneous in a public address, they are the exception that proves the rule." Every conscientious speaker is acutely and sensitively aware of the serious nature of his responsibilities. Therefore, many speakers will spend from a half-hour to as much as one or two hours in preparation for each minute they expect to speak. A fifteen-minute speech would mean a minimum of seven and one-half hours of preparation.

When one addresses an audience of one hundred people for thirty minutes, it is the equivalent of taking 3,000 minutes of one person's time. That means fifty hours, or more than six days of eight hours each. It would be little short of criminal deliberately to waste one person's time for six working days. Yet that is precisely what happens when a speaker without complete and thorough preparation takes the time of an audience of one hundred persons. If the audience is larger, the waste of time is proportionately greater. Should a person receive an invitation to address a meeting and know that he will not have time to make proper preparation for the occasion, he should decline the invitation. To accept it would be unfair to the audience and harmful to himself and the institution or business he represents. And yet, everyone of us has had the painful experience of hearing many speeches which showed little or no preparation and were a waste of time to the listeners.

An invitation to speak is a distinct honor. It may mean that a group of persons believe the speaker has exceptional knowledge in a field, or command of some phase of a subject, superior to that of many others who would like to receive his ideas. It may mean that others believe he has the ability to analyze and interpret a subject to the enlightenment of his audience. And in some instances it may mean that the speaker has the extraordinary ability to inspire others to greater achievement in life. No speaker who seriously contemplates these possibilities and the responsibilities they carry will ever appear before any audience poorly prepared. He will strive earnestly to fill each address with constructive ideas, logically arranged, and eloquently presented. Too many speakers are unpardonably casual about the preparation of their speeches. To paraphrase Ben Jonson, any fool may talk, but only a wise man, thoroughly prepared, can give a great speech.

The outline which follows presents in a rather definitive form the steps almost every speaker will find it helpful to take in preparing a speech:

Steps in Preparing a Speech

I. Determine the exact subject of the speech so that it is clear in the mind of the speaker. If the speaker himself has a hazy conception of the nature of his subject, if his mind is foggy or fuzzy, and if he does not see clearly the outlines and limitations of his topic, how can he expect to leave his audience other than confused?

II. Think through the whole subject to be certain that he has formulated his own ideas and conclusions. In most cases, these ideas and conclusions will be predicated upon his own study, observation, and experience.

III. Read exhaustively all the speeches, pamphlets, and books on the subject of his speech. It may be necessary to take some notes. This work is not as difficult as it may appear. No wise person will ordinarily agree to speak in a field about which he knows nothing. Nor will an intelligent chairman of a program committee invite a speaker who is ignorant of his subject. Consequently, in preparing his address, the speaker will already be intimately acquainted with much of the material available on the topic. But he must be certain that he has a comprehensive understanding of the entire subject and is familiar with the most recent studies in that field. A superficial or shallow understanding of the subject may lead to disaster before an intelligent audience.

IV. Outline the speech into its three principal divisions and any minor subdivisions as follows:

A. Introduction.

B. Main body of the speech or discussion, perhaps divided into two, three, or four subdivisions.

C. The conclusion or summary.

V. Write out the speech after it has been fully outlined. Long-experienced speakers may find it possible simply to outline an address and speak from the outline. But the person who is striving for perfection should, in the beginning at least, write out each speech in its entirety. Otherwise, there is almost certain to be looseness in the structure of the speech. A mother who was criticizing an inadequately prepared speech of her own son said, "Jim, you may call that a speech, but I call it simply running off at the mouth." The failure of beginners particularly to write out a speech results in sloppiness of expression. Writing a speech tends to give preciseness and exactness in wording. Most persons may find it easier to write a speech longhand and then have it typed.

The late Senator Robert A. Taft once advised us that he prepared his addresses by the following method:

I jot down a number of ideas. Then I arrange those ideas and work them out in greater detail, so that the notes may cover as much as two foolscap pages. Then I dictate the address. Then I correct the first draft and have it written. Sometimes there is a second correction.

I should judge that it may take me eight hours to prepare a thirty-minute address, assuming that I do not have any extensive reading or research.

Of course sometimes it is not possible to prepare an address fully, but it is much better to do so even if you intend to speak extemporaneously.

Dr. Harry Emerson Fosdick gave us the following instructive and interesting explanation of the procedure he used in preparing his sermons:

I always write out my sermons in full in advance. To the best of my recollection, after nearly forty years of preaching, I have never preached a sermon that was not written out fully. I do not see how any one can keep his substance serious, and his style flexible and varied unless he writes in full. At any rate, for myself there is no other method that is conceivable.

As for delivery, that I handle in varied ways; sometimes having the manuscript before me and reading freely; and sometimes drawing an outline from it and speaking from the notes.

With regard to the time spent on an average sermon it is very difficult to reckon that. How can one reckon the long period during which a sermon matures, oftentimes unconsciously germinating from some seed of an idea planted long before? All that I can do is to deal with the actual writing process, and not at all with the hours spent on the theme that contributed the substantial material to the sermon, and that there is no way of clocking. I would estimate that I spend a half hour in writing for each minute of the sermon.

No one can read the statements of these two eminent men without being impressed with the seriousness with which they assume the responsibility of speaking to an audience and the thoroughness with which they prepare their addresses.

Writing the Introduction

The two parts of an address most difficult to prepare are the introduction and the conclusion. Both must be relatively short. Both must be worked out with the greatest care.

In the introduction, the proposition to be discussed must be trimmed to its precise proportions. Sometimes, with experience, the introduction may be eliminated, particularly if the title clearly conveys the nature of the topic. However, it is almost always necessary to use an introduction, and seven possible methods of beginning an address are presented below with illustrations:

I. *Announce the subject directly in the first sentence or paragraph.*

Illustrations

Secretary of State Dean Rusk used the following brief introductory statement:

I welcome this opportunity to talk with this distinguished group of American business leaders. I shall talk about the contribution of American business to furthering the key foreign policy objectives of the United States. I should like to see the business community focus its unique skills and resources on this great task.

General Curtis E. LeMay, Chief of Staff, United States Air Force—

It is a distinct pleasure for me to return to Chicago before this club once again, and I must say I am very happy and pleased to see such a large crowd here for lunch today in spite of the sloppy weather. Mr. Bard, I think this must be due to your leadership.

John F. Kennedy accepted the Presidential nomination with this concise opening paragraph:

With a deep sense of duty and high resolve, I accept your nomination. I accept it with a full and grateful heart—without reservation—and with only one obligation—the obligation to devote every effort of body, mind and spirit to lead our party back to victory and our nation back to greatness.

Richard Cardinal Cushing introduced the question he was discussing directly in the opening paragraph of an address on "The Recognition of Red China":

The controversy over the recognition of Red China has lasted for 10 years and attained greatest publicity and, indeed, success at recent meetings of the United Nations. The question is, Should other nations and especially the United States diplomatically recognize the present regime on the mainland of China?

In one short paragraph, in fact, in one short sentence of only a few words the speaker was into his subject.

II. *Tell a story of human interest, "paint a picture," or give an illustration.*

Each one of the examples which follow is different, but each one introduces the subject with an interesting word picture.

Illustrations

Monroe E. Spaght, president of the Shell Oil Company, speaking on "International Education to Create a Better Understanding"—

A century and a half ago, Charles Lamb, the famous English writer, was walking along a London street with a friend. And he stopped and pointed.
"Do you see that man over there?" he said, "I hate him."
"Hate him?" his friend said, "How can you hate him? You don't even know who he is."
And Lamb said: "Precisely."
We have all seen tragic examples of this very kind of hate born of ignorance—both within our country and without and beyond. In certain languages the word for "enemy" is "stranger." The problem comes down to *"precisely"* that alluded to by Charles Lamb. *We don't know* our fellow man!

And I suggest that you and I must make it our *business* to correct this. I believe our one great hope is the dissemination of knowledge. That is why, when the International Institute of Education and through them, you good people asked me to come today to Chicago to talk about international education, I accepted with no reservation.

No sense of crisis prompted my decision to talk on this subject. The Institute is in no particular trouble. We come together today simply as businessmen, to discuss a subject that is, I feel, directly related to our business.

The future position of America in this changing world is dependent in part on how well we know other people, and how well they know us. Perhaps the vehicle through which this can best be accomplished is international education, and I suggest that companies which now recognize their responsibility to domestic education should recognize their overseas opportunities as well.

Jenkin Lloyd Jones, editor of the *Tulsa Tribune*—

I am very glad you got that plug in about my meteoric career from a reporter to an editor in eight short years. I have been asked on many occasions by journalism school students how that was done, and I am happy to tell them that I think I owe it all to superior diligence, considerable natural ability, and a father who owned the newspaper.

A couple of years ago I was passing through my old college town with my pretty daughter, and I stopped at my fraternity house to take her through the old card room.

This card room, I explained, was the house holy-of-holies. Each generation of the brothers carved their names in wooden table tops, and when the wood could hold no more the tops were hung along the wall to be regarded reverently by the undergraduates. I was anxious to show my daughter my name in the mouldering oak. It, undoubtedly, was the Kilroy in me. So, I took her into the fraternity house and led her up to the card room. But we couldn't get in. They had turned it into a kennel for the house dog.

As I turned away with burning cheeks it suddenly occurred to me that the boys had been pretty smart. Names are not to be worshipped. There is no particular inspiration in reading headstones in a graveyard or thumbing through the telephone directory. The comfort of the house dog is certainly of more legitimate concern than the collection of dusty initials.

For a name deserves to be remembered only in relation to the effect its owner had upon his times. In this, the world's great rascals like Alcibiades and Warren Hastings and Adolf Hitler have a genuine claim to fame. But the only name that deserves reverence, whether famous or not, is attached to that person who in greater or lesser degree in accordance with his talents and opportunities changed things for the better.

The name on the wooden table top means no more than the name carved deeply into marble on an expensive cemetery mausoleum. These are merely manifestations of Kilroyism. The fact that Kilroy was here is of no importance. The question is: did anything happen because Kilroy was here?

Dr. Edward R. Annis, former president of the American Medical Association—

When you talk about some of the crowds that I have spoken to, it reminds me of an invitation I had in South Miami not long ago. A lady called me and said, "Dr. Annis, now that you have made the big time on television and all that, how many people do you have to have before you make a speech?" I said, "Well, I still insist on two—but I will be one of them." I will talk to anybody who will listen, because I think it is important.

On this occasion, my daughter Barbara, who is sixteen, asked me, "Daddy, can I come with you?" I was a little surprised that she wanted to go. Sixteen-year-old girls have other things to do. Later when we got there I found the reason was, we were down at the other side of Coral Gables, and many of her girl friends were going with the mothers because this gave them a chance to get together.

As I was being introduced by an over enthusiastic patient of mine, a member of the club, with the information supplied by one of my secretaries, and with the usual exaggerations, about half way through, Barbara touched me, and said, "Daddy, is she talking about you?" and I said, "Well, I think so." And as only teenagers can do, because they see through all this camouflage, she shrugged her shoulders and raised her arms and said, "Big deal."

I was introduced in Des Moines last year, and they said, "You know, Dr. Annis, it isn't very often we let Democrats talk out here." I said, "Well, I appreciate the opportunity of speaking here. I just want to ask you a question. Where do you think you Republicans would be without us Southern Democrats?"

Dr. Heinz L. Krekeler, member of the European Atomic Commission—

It is a distinct honor and a great privilege for me to have been invited today as your speaker. It is the second time I have been invited to speak to this distinguished audience, and I feel when you invite somebody for the first time to be a speaker, you take a calculated risk. When you invite them for the second time, it is your known risk.

President Harry D. Gideonese of Brooklyn College—

Robert M. Hutchins, my former chief at the University of Chicago, used to say that it was a college president's principal duty in life to afflict the comfortable. This might well serve as my text for these remarks to an honors assembly.

President James G. Gee of East Texas State College—

In a setting of the present, let us picture William Wordsworth, then poet laureate, sitting in his English home and evaluating the outcomes of the French Revolution. On that occasion, he is reported to have cried out in ecstasy: "Great was it to have lived in that day. But to have been young was very heaven." Of course, the poet was probably taking a somewhat romantic and idealistic view in thinking of the improvements in the rights of man which had resulted from that fierce struggle. It seems that he might have elected to overlook the scenes of carnage, mortal conflict, wanton sacrifice of human life, and uncounted miseries suffered by untold thousands in bringing about the fruition he was admiring.

In this day and hour of our time, *we* might take on the romantic and idealistic view of the poet and perhaps temporarily push aside the fateful and inexorable realism seemingly now required of this nation and of all her patriotic, purposive and worthy citizens.

The hour is not in the future; rather, the *present,* when all must accept and perform their proportionate share of duties and responsibilities, within the extended limits of our several individual abilities, if we may reasonably expect to preserve our cherished American way of life.

Glenn E. Hoover, emeritus professor of economics, Mills College—

Of all the ways in which man differs from other animals, his predilection for making and listening to speeches is perhaps the most significant.

When our aboreal ancestors first began to gabble with each other, our species was cut off, irrevocably, from the rest of the animal kingdom. And so it is that both you and your speaker are again the common victims of a very ancient custom.

Howell Appling, Jr., Oregon Secretary of State—

I am highly complimented that I should be asked to come here today . . . to be with you on this occasion . . . and to talk with you about some things that may be of interest to you. And I must say that I am glad to see ladies in the audience today because what I intend talking with you about involves some decision-making and, regardless of what we men may prefer to think about it, a lot of the decisions these days are made by the ladies.

I remember a young farm boy one time who went to his father and he said, "Dad, Lucy and I are planning on getting married and we're having a little trouble agreeing on who's going to be the boss. Now I know you've faced the same question yourself and I'd appreciate a little advice on it."

And the father said, "Well, son, there's no doubt about it; this is a matter that is going to affect your and Lucy's happiness for a great many years to come, so I tell you what you do. You get the old wagon out and load a hundred White Leghorn pullets on it and hitch the grey mare and the black mare to the wagon, and head out down the road. And I tell you what you do. You stop at every house and inquire who the boss is and if the wife says she is, give her a chicken, and if the man says he is give him one of the mares and when you run out of either one, you'll have the answer.

Well, the boy thought that was a pretty good idea so he started out and about nightfall he found himself with just one chicken. Naturally he still had the two mares, and he had just one more house to call on.

So he knocked on the door and explained his problem and asked who the boss was and the man said, "Why, I am, of course." Well by that time, that surprised the boy, but he said, "All right, come on out and pick out your mare." Well, the man looked the horses over very carefully for spavines and lameness and all the other things and opened their mouths and looked at their teeth to see how old they were. Finally, he said "Well, I guess I'll take the grey." All this time the wife had been looking at him kind of hard-eyed from the porch, and in one of those calm, stern tones she yelled over and said, "Henry, you'd better take the black." At which Henry said, "Well, I guess I'll take the black." And the boy said, "Mister, you'll take a chicken!"

III. *Use a statement that excites attention, arouses curiosity, surprises the audience, or is particularly informative.*

Illustrations

President Robert F. Goheen of Princeton University, used this introduction at opening exercises for Princeton University—

Gentlemen of the Freshman Class, this service of worship is traditional for the beginning of the academic year at Princeton. It affirms the unity of the university and the high aspiration of mind and spirit which constitute its essential life and endeavor down through the years.

The custom of having the President speak at these Exercises calls to mind the story of the college president who, in a conversation with a young alumnus said: "By the way, did you ever hear me preach?" "Frankly, sir," the young man replied unflinchingly (and borrowing from Charles Lamb), "I never heard you do anything else."

I shall continue to try to avoid that reputation, but I am especially glad to have the opportunity to talk seriously to you as you begin your university careers.

Leo Cherne, executive director of the Research Institute of America, beginning an address before the Congress of the International Society for the Welfare of Cripples—

Bringing health to those who are sick, surcease of pain to those who are suffering, and medical rehabilitation to those who are crippled are the only forms of aid which the citizens of great nations can extend to less privileged people without the possibility of misunderstanding. When an individual who suffers is helped and is helped directly as a single human being, then, and only then, the ultimate and central principle of all religious faiths and man's highest ethical concepts is applied.

I do not wish to be misunderstood. Today much more than half of the world is in the most urgent need of various kinds of help. Huge parts of the earth urgently require the kind of rehabilitation which is not individual. Economic, technological, scientific, monetary, fiscal, managerial, military, and educational needs exist which are almost beyond measurement. Their very magnitude, their urgency provides much of the soil of misunderstanding and the charge of self-serving manipulation.

John L. Burns, president of the Radio Corporation of America, begins an address on "The Endless Frontier"—

No one who has just witnessed, as I have, the exhilarating aerial exploits of the Canadian International Air Show could possibly depart without the conviction, first, that space travel is not too many harvests away, and, second, that it might be fun to have a ticket on the first manned ship to explore the cosmos.

This urge for space travel seems to be spreading. I recently read that more than 300 people have volunteered. A man in San Francisco offered to send his wife! A man in London, who found a parking ticket on his car, wrote the judge that he had volunteered for space travel and wasn't certain he'd be available for a court hearing!

Dr. Louis M. Orr, past president of the American Medical Association, begins an address before a graduating class at Emory University—

I was truly pleased when President Martin invited me, on behalf of the trustees and faculty of your university and mine, to deliver the commencement address. At the same time, I was somewhat awed by the responsibility of delivering such an address from the position of a returning alumnus.

A situation like this usually implies a kind of model for success who is going to tell you to go and do likewise. I am much better qualified, I can assure you, to discuss the mistakes I have made and to warn you against doing likewise.

However, I do want to talk about *you* and the *mere fact of existence.*

An engineer in one of America's largest companies has described a human being this way:

"Man is a complete, self-contained, totally enclosed power plant, available in a variety of sizes, and reproducible in quantity. He is relatively long-lived, has major components in duplicate, and science is rapidly making strides toward solving the spare parts problem. He is water-proof, amphibious, operates on a wide variety of fuels; enjoys thermostatically-controlled temperature, circulating fluid heat, evaporative cooling; has sealed, lubricated bearings, audio and optional direction and range finders, sound and sight recording, audio and visual communication, and is equipped with an automatic control called a brain." Thus ends his description.

The engineer's picture of a human being is significant, I think, for what he has omitted. He did not tell us what sets his "robot" apart from such mechanical marvels as man-made moons in the sky, factories run by electronic brains, and engines powered by atoms. He does not tell us what goes beyond the mere fact of its existence and turns it into a human being.

The meaning of being human is a big, broad subject. But for our purpose, let me put it this way: Science will never be able to reduce the value of a sunset to arithmetic. Nor can it reduce friendship or statesmanship to a formula. Laughter and love, pain and loneliness, and challenge of accomplishment in living, and the depth of insight into beauty and truth . . . these will always surpass the scientific mastery of nature.

Senator J. W. Fulbright, speaking before the Graduate School of Banking at the University of Wisconsin—

I am honored to be invited to address this seminar of bankers and, I assume, some professors. Having been a professor in my youth and having had a banker for a father, I have a sentimental affection for both professions.

Often on the Senate floor after hours of monotonous debate, I long for the peace and quiet of the academic life, but every month when the bills pour in I wish that I had followed in my father's footsteps.

I am still a member of the Banking and Currency Committee of the Senate, but the bankers have so few problems these days there is little for the Committee to do. I cannot remember when a banker has lobbied me for any measure—apparently their problems are solved. I cannot say the same for our foreign relations.

Richard J. Babcock, president of Farm Journal, Inc., begins with an interesting illustration—

When a Connecticut Yankee comes to Missouri to speak on the subject of agriculture, surely one must wonder if this isn't carrying coals to Newcastle. Perhaps not necessarily so. Way back in 1877 when a forward thinking man by the name of Wilmer Atkinson began to publish a little farm paper called the *Farm Journal* it was dedicated, as he said, "to serving the interests of farm families within a day's ride of Philadelphia."

Farm Journal is still published for farm families who live within a day's ride of Philadelphia. Thanks to the jets, that day's ride now includes the 900-odd farm families who read *Farm Journal* in each of our two newest states, Alaska and Hawaii, as well as the 3,000,000 subscribing families who live in the 48 contiguous states.

IV. *Tell a humorous story that is definitely related to the subject or to the situation under which the speaker is addressing the audience.*

No story must be used simply to introduce humor. However, a good humorous story, well told and relevant, may provide an excellent introduction. If a speaker can tell a humorous story on himself, the audience enjoys it especially. Observe how frequently this device is used by actors entertaining over the radio. Over 1,000 humorous stories of all kinds and suitable for many occasions are presented in Chapter IV.

General Laurence S. Kuter begins with this story—

I find that this club is full of former or reserve fighter pilots and aircraft artillery commanders. In this group of experts, I am to tell you of a subject which many of you know very well which leads me to the old story of the intoxicated man running through the park at night and seeing in a reflecting pool before him the moon and saying, "What's that?" And his friend said, "Well, that is the moon." He said, "Then what in the world am I doing up here?"

Herbert V. Prochnow, beginning a commencement address at the University of Wisconsin—

It is a heartwarming experience to be invited to speak in my home state, at my alma mater, and among friends, where one's faults are forgiven, one's eccentricities are looked upon as evidence of a sturdy individualism, and one's accomplishments are generously magnified. Mark Twain once said, "When I was fourteen years old my father was so ignorant I hated to have the old man around. But when I was twenty-one, I was surprised to see how much my father had learned in only seven years." The passing years bring wisdom, but they also bring humility. They bring less self-assurance, but they bring a larger sense of the abiding values of life.

The opening comments of Secretary of Commerce Luther H. Hodges are preceded by the final observation of the chairman of the luncheon meeting at which Mr. Hodges spoke—

Gentlemen, I give you the all round man, a man who started his business career as a secretary and who today is still a secretary, Luther H. Hodges.

The Hon. Luther H. Hodges: Thank you, Mr. President. I suppose you could say I didn't get very far, very fast. I started as a secretary and finished as a secretary. It reminds me of a story I heard about a fellow who had had some real warfare in World War II. He had been tired out, battle fatigue, and he had been drinking wine, too much of it in fact, in a French restaurant. He was looking out the window and he saw a wedding party come up, and he said to the Frenchman who couldn't speak English, "Who's that?"

And he said, "Je ne sais pas."

Well he kept drinking and about three hours later a funeral procession came up and he said, "Who's that?"

And the Frenchman said, "Je ne sais pas."

And he said, "He didn't last long, did he?"

In his closing comments a chairman presented the distinguished explorer, Sir Edmund Hillary, who responded as indicated—

Gentlemen, our honored guest, keeper of the bees, conqueror of mountains, explorer of icy wastes, bearer of light to the dark corners of the world, Sir Edmund Hillary.

Sir Edmund: After that magnificent introduction by your president, I really feel almost bashful about speaking at all. I must tell you, Mr. President, I have never had a better and possibly a more inaccurate introduction.

Not all speakers can introduce humor at the beginning of an address as spontaneously as George Bernard Shaw did when he appeared before a London audience which had applauded him vociferously. He stepped to the front of the platform ready to give his speech. The crowd was calling wildly for him. As the roar subsided, and in that tense moment of silence, just before he began, a voice from the balcony cried "Blah!" That would have finished many speakers. But not Shaw. He looked up and said calmly, "Brother, I agree with you fully, but what can two of us do against so many?"

V. *Ask a challenging question.*

A thought-provoking question, directly to the point of the address, focuses the attention of an audience immediately upon the subject.

Illustrations

A former Secretary of Commerce, Frederick H. Mueller, begins an address—

Mr. President, Distinguished Guests, Gentlemen:

"It was the best of times, it was the worst of times, it was the age of wisdom, it was the age of foolishness, it was the epoch of belief, it was the epoch of incredulity, it was the season of Light, it was the season of Darkness, it was the spring of hope, it was the winter of despair, we had everything before us, we had nothing before us."

Every student has read that introduction to *A Tale of Two Cities* by Charles Dickens.

He was describing other times. Yet, any reader of today's headlines and today's political speeches might conclude that history is repeating itself, for current talk also swings in sharp contrasts.

The important question about present conditions is simply this? What is the truth?

Dr. Lee A. DuBridge, president of the California Institute of Technology, speaking on "Adventures in Space"—

Now that the space age is in its third year, it has become obvious that space activities are here to stay and that every thinking American should have some comprehension of what it means to shoot objects off the earth into space; of what some of the possibilities and impossibilities are for venturing into space; of what the reasons are why we should undertake such ventures; and of what some of the questions and problems are which we should like to investigate.

We begin with the question of "what is space?" Are we "flying through space" in an airplane at an altitude of 10,000 or 20,000 feet above the earth's surface? No, for in an airplane one is being supported by the lift of the earth's atmosphere on the wings, and therefore he is clearly not yet in "empty space." For our purposes tonight, let us say that space begins beyond the atmosphere at a distance of about 200 miles above the surface of the earth. From here on out, space is very empty indeed.

Dr. James R. Killian, Jr.—

Today the United States is the most powerful, the wealthiest, the most technologically advanced nation in the world. Will we tomorrow still be showing the vitality, the productivity, the creativity, the resources of moral and cultural strength which are required for this leadership? In this period of rapid changes in the affairs of men and nations, in this time of relentless challenge to the United States, do we have those qualities of adjustment, those characteristics of the "adaptive society" which are requisite to meet the accelerating rate of change which is the overriding characteristic of our time?

General Thomas S. Power, speaking before the Economic Club of New York City—

Soviet Russia, which ten years ago seemed as unlikely a challenger to our leadership as Communist China may seem today, almost overnight developed into a major threat, not only to our over-all supremacy but to our very survival. For the Soviets had achieved the capability to undertake what neither Lenin nor Stalin ever dreamed would be possible—a devastating attack on the United States.

It is, therefore, well to ask ourselves three pertinent questions. First, is our national policy of deterrence still feasible and desirable? Second, if we decided that it is, can our present and projected military posture support that policy adequately? And third, with continued advances in military technology, will we eventually reach a point where a policy of deterrence is no longer possible?

Dwight D. Eisenhower poses two questions—

Tonight I want to talk with you about two subjects: One is about a city that lies 4,000 miles away.

It is West Berlin. In a turbulent world it has been, for a decade, a symbol of freedom. But recently its name has come to symbolize, also, the efforts of imperialistic communism to divide the free world, to throw us off balance and to weaken our will for making certain of our collective security.

Next, I shall talk to you about the state of our Nation's posture of defense and the free world's capacity to meet the challenges that the Soviets incessantly pose to peace and to our own security.

VI. *State facts which show the importance of the subject to the welfare of the audience.*

Illustrations

Reginald Maulding, President of the Board of Trade in the British Cabinet, speaking before the Economic Club of New York City on "Trade Policies for a Free World"—

The subject on which you ask me to speak is "trade policies for a free world." I take it that what you have in mind is the part that trade policies will play in securing the fundamental objectives of the free world, namely, the preservation of peace and the safeguarding of national and individual freedom. This is indeed a subject very close to my own heart because I believe that in facing these problems today trade policies are of quite overriding importance.

There was a time when it could be said that most wars arose from trade rivalries. Now I believe the opposite is true. The absence of a proper basis for competitive international trade is more likely to contribute to the continuation of friction and difficulties between nation and nation. We can expect lasting peace only if it is based on proper human understanding between nation and nation, between people and people throughout the world. This cannot be realized in a world divided by trade barriers. The free flow of goods and services, of travelers and work, people and capital between one country and another is, in my judgment, the greatest guarantee of the kind of international understanding upon which alone our hopes of peace can securely rest. Moreover, it is only in a world where trade moves freely that the peoples now living in grinding poverty can hope to see themselves and their successors achieving decent standards of living.

Congressman John W. Byrnes of Wisconsin, speaking before the American Farm Bureau Federation—

I'd like to point out this morning what I believe are some alarming developments in our national internal life and to suggest the role that you can play in helping our nation to meet these challenges.

As I do so, I hope I can avoid either the undue optimism of a Pollyanna or the unwarranted pessimism of a modern Cassandra. Rather, I hope to approach my theme with the attitude the modern farmer goes about his business, bringing to my task the same practical outlook, the same careful weighing of assets and liabilities and the same refusal to be governed by either false hope or fearful gloom.

At the start, I should make clear that I am basically an optimist. In the past few months, I have had the opportunity to travel the length and breadth of our land, once again, I was reassured by what I saw. We live in a marvelous country. As one leaves the hothouse atmosphere of Washington and goes out among the people, one cannot help but be deeply impressed by the basic strength of our country. That strength is reflected in our abundant resources, in their dynamic development, and, above all, in our energetic, freedom-loving, and God-fearing people.

I have no fear for the future of such a nation and such a people. I believe they can meet and conquer any problem once they understand the nature of the problem and its significance.

It is in this area, the area of recognizing our problems, of understanding them and of choosing the right solutions, that we face our greatest challenge, and it is here where my basic feeling of optimism is tempered by a few nagging doubts. They are brought on by a number of warning signals in our economic and political life which we cannot afford to ignore any more than can the farmer when he finds the first evidence of disease in his livestock.

As a prospering, highly developed nation, we face the same danger which has confronted every successful nation or civilization since history began. Our danger is that, as we enjoy our strength and prosperity, we neglect, and thus weaken, those very institutions and principles which made us strong and prosperous and free. Our danger lies in complacency, selfishness, ignorance, and irresponsibility.

VII. *Begin by a significant quotation or idea from some other person.*

Illustrations

H. Bruce Palmer, president of the Mutual Benefit Life Insurance Company, speaking on "Inflation Control"—

America's No. 1 problem is what I would discuss with you today—the problem which Bernard Baruch, that preeminent financial advisor to American Presidents of both political parties, calls "the most important economic fact of our time—the single greatest peril to our economic health." This problem is the primary cause of our mountainous national debt. It is the reason for our high tax rates and record expenditures in what is called a time of peace. It is the force which has put our price structure on stilts and eroded the purchasing power of the dollar. I am talking about inflation.

Mr. Baruch's diagnosis of this disease also is worth considering. He says: "The inflation of our time flows from the selfish struggle for special advantage among pressure groups."

On one occasion Newell Dwight Hillis stated in an introduction to an address on "Conscience and Character," "Von Humboldt said that every man, however good, has a yet better man within him. When the outer man is unfaithful to his deeper convictions, the hidden man whispers a protest. The name of this whisper in the soul is conscience."

Devereux C. Josephs, former chairman of the board of New York Life Insurance Company, speaking before the New York State Bar Association—

I am delighted to be with you for dinner tonight for a number of reasons. I have a great respect for lawyers—their crisp minds and orderly process of thinking. I always hope that by association some of it will rub off on me. . . . This occasion also gives me a chance to share with you a concern I have about the rosy future that the prophets have pretty generally been projecting. Incidentally, I have tried to disassociate myself from them ever since I read in Samuel Butler's Notebook the dictum: "The lions would not eat Daniel, they would eat most anything but they drew the line at prophets." However, the future is where we will spend the rest of our lives and we had better be aware of it.

The question is often asked, "Should you ever apologize in opening a speech?" The answer is "No! never apologize in opening a speech." Do not say, "I did not have time to prepare." The audience is the best judge of that condition. Why should you tell them that this occasion did not mean enough to you to consider serious preparation? Do not say either, "I don't know how to talk," or "I have nothing to say." If not, why did you accept? Surely you would not willingly bore an audience. Moreover, these statements are a reflection upon the judgment of the program committee which invited you to speak. What the audience wants is not apologies. They want the best speech —and not even the second best speech—you can possibly give with thorough preparation.

There are some introductions which seem to be in the nature of apologies, which, however, are not apologies of the kind we have described. They may be statements indicating that the speaker feels himself humble in the face of his responsibilities. They may even be sincere compliments to the audience. The listeners do not object to that kind of introduction. It is one thing actually to be unprepared and quite a different matter to be fully prepared, but humble when you contemplate the responsibilities of giving a good address. Introductions of this character follow:

A business executive addressing the Erie, Pennsylvania, Association of Commerce on "The Problems of Management"—"I should be much less than frank if I did not tell you that I know there are men in this audience eminently better qualified to speak on this subject than I am, men who could bring to this discussion far richer experience, infinitely greater wisdom and more mature reflection." The gray-headed business executives in that audience liked that statement. The speaker was not posing as a know-all. By his sincerity, they knew he proposed to give them the best thinking on the subject at his command.

The late Dr. Glenn Frank, president of the University of Wisconsin, speaking on "The Statesmanship of Business and the Business of Statesmanship"—-

Of one thing I am sure, and that is that you did not invite me here under any delusion that I am a businessman, or that I know anything you do not know about the mystical secrets of office procedure, or high finance. It would, therefore, be a sterile presumption on my part to try to discuss with you any of the technical aspects of business organization or financial procedure. You do not, I am sure, expect me to do that. And I have no desire to assume the glib omniscience of the after-dinner speaker who can solve everybody's problem but his own within the limits of thirty minutes.

The classic example of a speaker who seemed to deprecate his ability was Mark Antony when he said,

> I am no orator, as Brutus is,
> But, as you know me all, a plain blunt man,
>
> . . . .
>
> For I have neither wit, nor worth, nor words,
> Action, nor utterance, nor the power of speech
> To stir men's blood; I only speak right on.

Writing the Body of the Speech

The body is the substance of the speech. Fill it with facts and figures. They speak in a singularly convincing fashion. In addition, the facts and figures presented consecutively throughout the body of the address must march directly to the conclusion the speaker hopes to establish. The listeners should never have to say, "What in the world did the remarks the speaker made on (this or that subject) have to do with his conclusion?"

The listener must receive something definite that he can carry away with him. What a pitiful spectacle a speaker makes when he becomes mired through an entire address in generalities and abstractions. Let us assume that the speaker has taken for his subject the hazards of operating a retail business. He says, "The retailer is engaged in a very hazardous business. His profits are small and his future is uncertain." Those are generalities. He might have said, "The retailer is engaged in a very hazardous business. The best studies available by the mercantile credit agencies indicate that the average retail store lives sixty-six months. In one middle western city, for example, there are 1,200 retail stores. Thirty of these stores go out of business every month—three hundred sixty stores die yearly. Thirty-two new stores are established monthly—many of them to lose their capital in a few months." Every audience likes the speaker who digs out new facts, new figures, new material relating to their interests. No matter how skillful he may be with words, no speaker can satisfactorily paint and prop up a speech lacking substance. The speaker who will make a reasonable effort to build substance into his address is certain to be acclaimed by his audience. Out of every ten speakers, seven are almost certain to fail to make a serious effort to get worthwhile facts for an audience, two will do a fair job, and one will make a comprehensive and exhaustive study of the subject. Even a little effort will place a speaker among the first three out of ten. A little more effort will leave him just one real competitor out of ten speakers on the average two-day convention program.

Specifically, what guiding principle can be set down for the preparation of the body of the speech? There are at least five as follows:

I. *Know the subject thoroughly.*

Strange as it may seem, few men are masters of their fields. The author has made a number of studies in the field of selling. With the assistance of college students of business administration, he has made tests of the knowledge which sales persons in various lines possess relative to the goods they sell. Certainly one would assume that a hat salesman, a shirt salesman, a hardware salesman, would have considerable knowledge of the field in which each of them sells. However, these tests in a number of lines reveal that out of ten sales persons, six or seven know practically nothing about the goods they sell, two or three know a little and one person is well informed. And yet these persons are supposed to make convincing sales speeches. Enthusiasm in selling and in speaking grows out of knowledge. A person who does not know his subject has nothing about which to enthuse. Unfortunately, not a few speakers are compelled to play around in the suburbs of their subject because they are ignorant of it.

Illustrations

Dr. You Chan Yang, Korean Ambassador to the United States, gives some interesting facts about Korea—

The Republic of Korea has accomplished a modern educational miracle. In a nation that had 80 per cent illiterate in its own language, illiteracy has been reduced to 6.8 per cent—one of the most favorable figures in the world.

Among children aged 6-11, 96 per cent are enrolled in school.

Elementary and Middle Schools are within walking distance of practically every child in Korea; High Schools are accessible to all.

Seventy-eight colleges, in fifty-five universities, have an enrollment of some 90,000 students.

Higher education has "taken hold" for girls as well as boys. Ewha University, enrolling 5,800, is the largest women's university in the world, and Korea's traditional men's universities have gone coeducational.

William Allen White, editor of the *Emporia Gazette,* was probably the best-informed person in the United States on the functions and operations of a country town newspaper. Note how vividly he analyzed the foundation of the country town newspaper in this excerpt from an address broadcast over the Columbia Network.

The American country town paper rests entirely upon the theory of the dignity of the human spirit. It is democracy embodied. It emphasizes the individual. For instance, here is an item: "John Jones is in town today with the first load of hay from the third cutting of alfalfa." That item is the alpha and omega of small town journalism. It dignifies John Jones. It dignifies labor. It dignifies small business. And now, Mrs. Jones has the first forsythia out in her Emporia garden—that's a news item. We're glorifying Mrs. Jones. We're glorifying the human spirit, making the Joneses proud to be Joneses, to cut themselves hay; to have a beautiful individual garden. Upon that glorification rests the American country newspaper, and, incidentally, the American democracy.

Roy G. Lucks, president of California Packing Corporation—

Canned and packaged foods have been responsible in large part for a revolution in retailing. They also have played a role in a much broader revolution.

Two or three generations ago, the work of preparing three meals for the family occupied about five and a half hours every day. The same three meals today can be prepared in about ninety minutes' work. That is a net saving in time of four hours per day.

To put it another way, the food preparation which used to require about 2,000 hours a year now can be done in about 550 hours—a net savings of 1,450 hours, or about two solid months every year.

A businessman describing a pair of pliers—

These pliers are hand-forged and hand-finished. They are made of high-carbon steel. If I could break one of those handles, I could show you a grain of steel as fine as the grain of a file. Ordinary pliers work loose at the pivot. The pivot wears, and after it's worn it jams. That's because the holes are punched. The holes in these pliers aren't punched, they're drilled. Take a good firm grip on the handles. Notice how they fit your hand—how they stick? See those little button-like things on the handles, with the little holes in the center? That's the suction grip idea. When you're working around your car with those pliers and the handles become greasy, they won't slip. Notice the finish. Ordinary pliers rust. The nickel plating chips off. The nickel on those pliers will stick; and that's because they are made perfectly smooth and clean, and then plated. Those pliers will last a lifetime. They're guaranteed.

Competitively, what chance has an ordinary salesman who does not know the product against this businessman who does? Simply no chance! In speaking, knowledge brings confidence and confidence brings enthusiasm.

II. *Use facts, figures, and illustrations.*

It is worth repeating again and again that illustrative matter filled with illuminating facts and figures is the most persuasive and interesting material for the body of speeches. Figures frequently have an eloquence that cannot be captured in phrases.

Illustrations

President Tom E. Shearer of the College of Idaho, speaking on "The Road from Here to There"—

Let us suppose that one of you wants to be a writer—a good writer, financially successful and critically approved. You may well find that the road from here to there, if you manage to negotiate it, is a long and tortuous one.

Take the case of the late Kenneth Roberts, author of that very successful novel—*Northwest Passage*. He tried to explain how he got "there" in his book *I Wanted to Write.*

He had been a very successful magazine writer commanding large amounts for articles from magazines of wide circulation. But he wanted to write fiction. So, acting upon the advice of his friends he severed his secure magazine connections, packed up his research materials, and with a $1,000 advance from a publisher, headed for Italy to write an historical novel.

Here is the road he took to get from "here" to "there." As he began his first novel, *Arundel*, he said:

"I hung a schedule on the wall beside my bed: It read 'Write a chapter every four days: Write one and one-third pages (1,500 words) every day for 120 days.' My heart," he says, "sank whenever I looked at it."

He began writing *Arundel*, after much research, in January 1929, and finished, under a grueling schedule, at the end of June. After a year of sales and with unusually good reviews—the book managed to sell only 9,266 copies. The financial return to the author was only a trifle more than he had been receiving for one magazine article. After continuing to pour out his energies on other novels, for *eight more years*, he finally hit the market with a critically acceptable and financially successful book— *Northwest Passage*.

Mr. Taylor used another interesting illustration in his address—

International politics is in the limelight today. You may dream of becoming a statesman of high position. Perhaps you would like to achieve such stature that, upon your passing, the President of the United States would be moved, in behalf of the whole nation, to say this about you:

"The lifetime of labor for world peace is ended. His countrymen and all who believe in justice and the rule of law grieve at the passing from the earthly scene of one of the truly great men of our time.

"Because he believed in the dignity of men and in their brotherhood under God, he was an ardent supporter of their deepest hopes and aspirations. From his life and work humanity will, in the years to come, gain renewed inspiration to work even harder for the attainment of the goal of peace with justice. In the pursuit of that goal he ignored every personal cost and sacrifice, however great.

"All Americans have lost a champion of freedom."

I would remind you that the idea for the "there" which that man, John Foster Dulles, achieved, was born in the determination of a very young man to one day be the Secretary of State. I remind you also that he was a Phi Beta Kappa, a man scoring the highest marks in his professional law training; and that, as he moved on step by step, ultimately to arrive "there" he was never satisfied. He was a man who could say "time is the most valuable thing in life, and I don't want to waste it."

It was a long road indeed from that Presbyterian minister's home to the place where it could be said of John Foster Dulles, "In all the lands of the globe where liberty and independence are prized, the free and the thoughtful mourn the tough old warrior who had fought their fight with rare purpose, skill and dedication."

These stories of real people say that you *can* get there from here— here, where you are now in education, in maturity, in work habits, in responsibilities. However, they emphasize the fact that you aren't there yet.

Educationally, you are not "there." Actually, we would hope that, as with these at whose case histories we have looked, your drive to learn never stops.

Dr. Lionel Crocker, professor of speech at Denison University, speaks to a high school graduating class—

Today you are a personality on its way to a full blossoming. We might call our schools personality laboratories. Your parents and friends may think they know who is sitting here tonight, but it will take another fifteen or twenty years to discover who you are really.

For example, a few years ago there graduated from Ironton, Ohio, a young man destined to be President of my alma mater, the University of Michigan, Harlan Hatcher; a few years ago at Spencerville, Ohio, there sat, as you are sitting here tonight at graduation, a young man by the name of Grayson Kirk who developed into the President of Columbia University. In the village of Fredericktown, Ohio, there grew up a young man who flowered into the great Methodist preacher, Ralph Sockman. Who could guess at their graduation their eventful unfolding? I repeat: who knows who is sitting on this platform tonight? Really?

Did any of the teachers in Abilene or Denton single out Milton Eisenhower as the potential president of Manhattan State, Pennsylvania State, and Johns Hopkins University? Did one teacher whisper to another that she had the leader of the Crusade in Europe . . . the one to be chosen to be president of Columbia University, the one to be elected to two terms in the White House? So I say tonight who knows, the potential of this class?

Dr. Crocker gave another interesting illustration in the same address—

Straight from the shoulder, may I say that getting along with others is a problem you must solve. I hope you have learned in these twelve years to make yourself agreeable. I hope you have developed your manners so that people like to be with you. If your environment is not all you want it to be, start working on yourself. How about your relationships with those in your immediate family? The other day one of my students said he was not going home this summer because he and his father did not get along together. What a pity! Out of his home should come the love that will help him bear the slings and arrows of outrageous fortune. It has been said that greater than any other gift Henry Clay possessed was his talent for companionship. People liked to be with him.

Straight from the shoulder, have you found out who you are? Do you have any dreams? Do you have any ideals? One of my students told me it was the example of her grandmother that kept spurring her on. Has there been a person, a book, an event that has stirred you deeply? When you call on yourself is there anybody home? I like the title of Althea Gibson's book, *I Wanted To Be Somebody*. That would make a fitting motto for every member of this class. We all need the pull of an ideal. As you study history, I am sure you have been impressed by the compassion of an Abraham Lincoln, the energy of a Theodore Roosevelt, the intelligence of a Woodrow Wilson, the integrity of a Robert Taft, and the devotion of a John Foster Dulles.

Ambition, determination, responsibility, follow through—these can not be measured and no one can give them to you. Mental tests often are deceptive. Your grades in the principal's office may and may not be a true index of your capacity. You may not have awakened yet. Some young men and women get into college without maturing. There is no greater joy for a teacher than to sit along side a student who has finally awakened to his possibilities, one who finds he has a mind capable of great things. Be firm but patient with yourself. Make yourself count!

John Foster Dulles at the age of seven dreamed of being Secretary of State. Daniel Webster's father took home with him from a country fair a silk handkerchief with the constitution printed on it. What an omen! Daniel Webster earned the title of "defender of the constitution."

No man has a greater battle than the conquest of himself: to liberate his God given talents.

Marion Harper, Jr., chairman of the board and president of McCann Erickson, Inc., illustrates an address with figures on hours of work—

You know, as I do, that leisure was once a symbol of aristocracy. What made a noble man noble was his exemption from productive work. His exertions were dedicated to the honorable profession of arms and to the high-born excitement of the chase. For the rest of the population working was absolutely and clearly and utterly synonymous with living.

Just to take you back a little bit into history, when Thomas Jefferson was President, the average work week was eighty-five hours. By the end of the Civil War we had become humane, and we had moved that to seventy. At the turn of the century it had dropped to sixty. At the end of 1929 it dropped to fifty, and thirty years later had moved to forty.

Today's manufacturing employes work a little less than 2,000 hours a year, and that's in contrast to 3,000 hours at the turn of the century.

You have got to realize, too, that those 2,000 hours include paid holidays that were unknown to workers just as far back as when most of us were in school.

What have been these pressures for less working time? Well, I guess it's fair to say that hours were first taken out of the work week for health and humanitarian reasons. During the depression hours were taken out of the work week to spread work, and in time of prosperity the work week has been reduced further in order that we may enjoy the benefit of what many of our philosophers call the good life.

Dr. Richard C. Bates, a heart specialist, speaking on the subject, "How to Have a Heart Attack"—

Now the usual medical speaker always begins by getting your instant attention with some grim and startling fact. For example, if we are going to talk about cancer, I would begin by saying, "One person in eight in this room is going to die of cancer"—which is true! On our subject today, I could be far more alarming by stating that half the people in this room are going to die of heart disease, which is also true, but then, these other speakers never go on and point out that the rest of you are going to die of something else, and this, of course, makes all the difference. As a matter of fact, if you escape dying of heart disease, you enormously increase your chances of dying of cancer. And, if you are so unfortunate as to escape both heart disease and cancer, you run great risk of dying of the most lingering malady of all, the one that takes 90 years to kill, senility. Everyone agrees that a heart attack is the best way to die. If you doubt that statement, recall how many times you have heard a conversation that goes like this:

Two people meet on the street and one says to the other, "Say, did you hear about poor old Bill?"

The other fellow says, "Yeah, the poor devil dropped dead of a heart attack last night."

Then you can just wait and one or the other, or both of them in unison, will say, "Still, if I have to die, that's the way I want to go." They never say, "When I die," they always say, "If I *have* to die."

The Honorable Howard Beale, Australian Ambassador to the United States—

Australia is now a nation of ten million people, living in a country about the same size as the continental United States. I do not apologize for our population because when you were 172 years old you only had about 4 million people! We have increased our population about 25 per cent since the war, including 1½ million migrants from Britain and Europe—a remarkably high figure by comparison with any other migration flow in the history of the world. . . .

We are still more than 90 per cent British stock, and this gives us great social homogeneity and political stability; at the same time the influence of European migrants has been wonderfully beneficial to us in adding color and diversity to our life and culture, just as it has been in this country. . . .

We are the largest industrial nation in the Southern Hemisphere. Though we are small in numbers, we grow most of the world's wool, most of the world's fine wool. We grow a great deal of the world's wheat and a good deal of its sugar, meat and things of that sort. . . .

We produce the majority of the world's mined lead; we are one of the world's biggest copper producers and will be, some day, I think, the biggest, especially in connection with new discoveries which have just been made. We produce great quantities of bauxite, uranium and many other minerals. We are, in our own right, an important contributor to the world's goods or rather to the world's raw materials. . . .

We are also a great trade nation. Australia lives or dies by trade. Trade is 20 per cent of our national income, it is 6 per cent of your national income and, therefore, what happens in the field of trade is important to us. Per capita we are the third largest trading nation in the world and the seventh or eighth largest over-all. This gives Australians an international point of view which we might not perhaps otherwise possess. We have the fourth highest standard of living of any country in the world.

We regard ourselves as we would hope you would regard us also, as the bastion of the free world in the South Pacific and given peace and security, no Australian has anything but the highest confidence about his destiny, his country's destiny in the world.

III. *If the audience is to be convinced of some proposition, begin with subject matter with which there is agreement.*

This is the old principle of proceeding from the known, and agreed upon, to the unknown. There must be agreement between the speaker and the audience at the beginning. Read and reread the speech Shakespeare gave Mark Antony as his oration over the dead body of Caesar. Mark Antony began, "For Brutus is an honorable man. So are they all honorable men." Thus he called the conspirators honorable men. But gradually as he presented the facts, he turned the mob on Brutus and his conspirators. Before that address had been completed those Roman citizens were crying, "We'll burn the house of Brutus. Away, then! Come, seek the conspirators." Antony began by agreement with the hostile listeners, but finally he led them to his viewpoint.

IV. *Do not argue, but explain.*

No audience likes the speaker who states at the outset that he is going to convince them of his viewpoint or change their ideas. The immediate reaction is "I don't believe it," or skeptically, "Well, let's hear what you have to say." Again, give the audience facts, information and figures. Explain your story. Let the facts change the viewpoint of the audience. The proper attitude is one of "Come, let us reason together." The object of public speaking is to present truth convincingly.

A business executive who recently spoke on "Tests of Management" did not argue on the general merit of accurate cost accounting. He told a simple story to his audience, many of whom were retailers. "In a little middle western town," he said, "there is a very successful hardware retailer. Several years ago he determined to know more about the turnover of each class of goods in his store. He found over one hundred classes of goods—paint, stoves, cutlery, nails and many others. He discovered that some goods sold much less readily than other merchandise. In fact, some articles stayed in the store four, ten and sixteen times as long as other goods. Consequently, the capital invested and the space in the store were used four, ten, and sixteen times longer for these slower-moving items. Therefore, the interest cost and the rent were much higher on these items. Then he started to reduce his inventory on the slower-moving less profitable items. An example of what this merchant accomplished after he knew the turnover and cost of each class of goods is enlightening. On one counter he reduced the space occupied by slow-moving goods 66 per cent. In the vacant space he placed faster-moving items with the result that in one year his sales on that one counter increased $7,000. He followed the same policy over his entire store, reducing the inventory of slow-moving items and increasing his sales and net profits."

No amount of argument could have been as influential as that one illustration of what another retailer had done with problems identical to those of the men in the audience.

Frederick L. Schuman, noted author and educator, broadcasting an address, "And There Is No Peace," over the Columbia Network one year before World War II began, described the confusion in Europe and Asia. In pointing out the need, as he saw it, for action by the

Western powers, he explained his viewpoint by a simple reference to Shakespeare's *Hamlet*.

I would suggest to you that the source of this confusion is quite simple. It is as simple and as bitter in its implications as Shakespeare's tragedy of *Hamlet*. In that drama you will recall that the Gloomy Prince of Denmark asks himself whether " 'tis nobler in the mind to suffer the slings and arrows of outrageous fortune or to take up arms against a sea of troubles, and by opposing end them." He is hesitant and irresolute and confesses that his "native hue of resolution is all sicklied o'er with the pale casts of thought." He shrinks from action and prefers empty words. He does nothing and thus plunges himself and his family and his people into disaster.

Hamlet's question is the question which for seven long years has faced those peoples and governments of the world which are committed to peace and are fearful of war.

V. *State briefly and clearly either at the beginning of the body of the speech or better, one by one, as the main part of the address unfolds, the two, three, or four points to be discussed.*

Illustrations

Former Under Secretary of Labor James T. O'Connell outlines three points he proposes to discuss—

Now let's consider the facts. What's ahead in the nation's manpower picture?

To begin with, there are three major points which will have an important impact upon all of us. They are:

(1) A substantial, a significantly larger increase in the number of people seeking work in the American labor market,

(2) A continuation, probably an acceleration, of the trend toward white-collar occupations,

(3) A rise in the training and educational level of all jobs across the board.

I would like to break those three statements down into the facts from which they originate and to give you some idea of the human resources available to us, and the type and kind they are.

Dean Ernest C. Arbuckle of the Graduate School of Business, Stanford University, stated concisely the subjects he wished to discuss—

I would like to ask, then try and answer four questions:

(1) What are the important trends that have been professionalizing the

practice of business and are likely to become more important in terms of managerial qualifications in the next decade or two?

(2) What are the qualifications that make for managerial competence?

(3) How are these qualifications developed?

(4) How are they recognized—or how do you know a well-managed company when you see one?

Writing the Conclusion

The ability to prepare an address so that it gradually becomes more intensified in its thoughts from the beginning to the end is one of the highest achievements in public speaking. It enables the speaker to hold an audience increasingly in suspense as he proceeds with his speech. The audience is aware that the speech is becoming stronger and stronger in its argument and in its eloquence. Whenever a speech begins with a climax and descends in its interest, it is certain to be a failure. After an introduction which obtains the attention of the audience, the first point in the body of the speech should be good, but each succeeding one should be better until the speech reaches a grand climax.

Almost every American adult is familiar with the great climax of the address that won for William Jennings Bryan the nomination for the Presidency of the United States when he said:

Having behind us the producing masses of this nation and the world, supported by the commercial interests, the laboring interests, and the toilers everywhere, we will answer their demand for a gold standard by saying to them: You shall not press down upon the brow of labor this crown of thorns; you shall not crucify mankind upon a cross of gold.

Abraham Lincoln's Second Inaugural Address had one of the most magnificent endings of any speeech in history.

Fondly do we hope, fervently do we pray, that this mighty scourge of war may speedily pass away. Yet if God wills that it continue until all the wealth piled by the bondman's two hundred and fifty years of unrequited toil shall be sunk, and until every drop of blood drawn with the lash shall be paid by another drawn with the sword, as was said three thousand years ago, so still it must be said that "the judgments of the Lord are true and righteous altogether."

With malice toward none; with charity for all; with firmness in the right, as God gives us to see the right, let us strive on to finish the work we are in; to bind up the nation's wounds; to care for him who shall have borne the battle, and for his widow and his orphan—to do all which may achieve and cherish a just and lasting peace among ourselves, and with all nations.

The closing sentence of Webster's first Bunker Hill Monument Oration is also majestic in its sweep.

And let the sacred obligations which have devolved on this generation, and on us, sink deep into our hearts. Those who established our liberty and our government are daily dropping from among us. The great trust now descends to new hands. Let us apply ourselves to that which is presented to us, as our appropriate object. We can win no laurels in a war for independence. Earlier and worthier hands have gathered them all. Nor are there places for us by the side of Solon, and Alfred, and other founders of states. Our fathers have filled them. But there remains to us a great duty of defense and preservation; and there is opened to us, also, a noble pursuit, to which the spirit of the times strongly invites us. Our proper business is improvement. Let our age be the age of improvement. In a day of peace, let us advance the arts of peace and the works of peace. Let us develop the resources of our land, call forth its powers, build up its institutions, promote all its great interests, and see whether we also, in our day and generation, may not perform something worthy to be remembered. Let us cultivate a true spirit of union and harmony. In pursuing the great objects which our condition points out to us, let us act under a settled conviction, and an habitual feeling, that these twenty-four States are one country. Let our conceptions be enlarged to the circle of our duties. Let us extend our ideas over the whole of the vast field in which we are called to act. Let our object be, *our country, our whole country, and nothing but our country.* And, by the blessing of God, may that country itself become a vast and splendid monument, not of oppression and terror, but of wisdom, of peace, and of liberty, upon which the world may gaze with admiration forever!

No speech should be left "hanging in the air" without a conclusion. The words at the end of the speech are generally remembered the longest by the audience. Therefore, the speaker must take the greatest possible advantage of the opportunity the conclusion affords to re-emphasize his message. The following methods for closing a speech are practical, and they are helpful to most speakers; it is suggested that you choose the method which is best suited for each of your speeches:

I. *Outline concisely the major points you have made in the body of the speech.*

This is the method which will be most helpful on most occasions, as it serves to place special emphasis upon the points which the speaker has tried to establish. It summarizes the entire speech in a few words.

Robert L. Garner, former president of the International Finance Corporation, Washington, D. C., gave the following summary of an address—

> To sum up.
> We in private enterprise are under deadly attack. The communists are determined to destroy us.
> If we are destroyed, so likewise will be the modern civilizations, both of West and East.
> We have the best, the most productive economic system in history. Its benefits are more widely distributed among more people. We concentrate on our own job, to produce, to sell, to make profits. All desirable, but unless we convince the people of the world that our system is best, they may well be won over by our more articulate enemies.
> The question is—will private enterprise pay the price and make the fight necessary to survive?

A banker addressing a convocation at Allegheny College on the subject, "The Banker's Stewardship," had discussed in the body of the address four essential requirements of that stewardship. In his conclusion, he summarized and repeated slowly and with emphasis the four points of that address as follows:

> These are but meager and insufficient outlines of the banker's stewardship, but they indicate four major requirements of his stewardship:
> (1) A knowledge of the development of the American banking system;
> (2) A knowledge of his bank;
> (3) A knowledge of the operation of the American economic order and of the importance of thrift in our economy; and finally
> (4) A knowledge of the world banking and financial problems.

Herbert V. Prochnow, president of the First National Bank of Chicago, closed an address with a summary of the major points, historical material, and a question—

> These then are three of the most far-reaching developments of our time:
> *First*—The rise of communism with its threat to the foundations of our society;
> *Second*—The rise of a vast world of one billion hungry men and women in the new nations who are struggling to create political stability out of chaos and economic growth out of poverty; and
> *Third*—The rise of Western Europe to a position of potential power so

great that it may with the United States now decisively influence the course of world events.

Sometimes it is good to look back over the years and bring the difficult problems of our time into perspective. As I prepared these remarks, my mind turned back one by one the pages of American history. I saw in retrospect again two world wars and a depression with all their hardships and heartaches. I saw the fabulous half century from 1870 to 1920, when despite the crises of 1873 and 1893, our people were taking gigantic economic strides, spanning a continent with covered wagons and railroads, as they conquered the forests and rich prairies with their dreams. I saw Robert E. Lee struggling with those heartbreaking decisions in Virginia, and Lincoln at his second inaugural spreading the wings of his generous spirit over a great tragedy, urging malice toward none and charity for all.

Turning back the pages of history still further, I saw Washington in the bitter winter of 1778 at Valley Forge with only eleven thousand ragged men, one-fourth of them unfit for duty, and I heard him say, "We have no money, no powder, and no arms." I saw also a small group of dedicated men prepare a written Constitution and set up a new nation with Washington as President and Jefferson as Secretary of State.

At last, I turned back over three hundred years to 1620 and saw a small group of courageous men and women, after five weary months on the Atlantic, bring a little boat to anchor in a driving snow storm in Plymouth Harbor. They cleared away snow and built log cabins. This was December.

By the end of the first winter, half of that immortal company had died. The first summer was one of relative plenty, but the second summer brought drought and an early frost. With starvation and winter confronting them, a day of fasting and prayer was set aside. Before the day arrived, through good fortune a ship from home came into the harbor bringing food, medicine and seed. Filled with gratitude at this manifestation of the goodness of Providence, they changed the day of fasting to one of Thanksgiving.

Thus was launched the conquest of a wilderness. Thus began a new venture in faith and ideals to determine whether any nation so conceived and so dedicated could long endure. The foundations of this nation were laid by men who were willing to endure hardship because of their convictions. They did not subscribe to the philosophy that power is the goal of government and pleasure the goal of the people. They never thought that the conditions of life ought to be anything but a challenge.

They did not believe that the reward of life could be possessed except through valiant effort. They went their individual ways without dismay and with a definiteness of purpose and high aspiration. All the comforts of life had to be created. Work was honored as a virtue. With every man on his own, there grew up a feeling of equality and of the right to self-government. The march to empire was on its way, manned by people generally poor in the goods of this world, but rich in the qualities that make men and nations great.

The United States has now come to the pinnacle of world power largely because her people have had the opportunity to develop this nation with its vast resources under a government and a Constitution that encourage initiative, enterprise, industry, thrift and inventive genius. They have cherished and held secure the blessings of liberty, and they have recognized the dignity of man.

Two thousand years ago a question was asked which has challenged men down through the centuries. That question was, "For what will it profit a man if he shall gain the whole world and lose his own soul?" We may well ask today, "For what will it profit a nation to become the greatest economic power in history, if its people lose the qualities of their greatness—self-discipline, self-reliance, industry, thrift, courage, character, faith?" This is not a crisis of economic power. We have the potential power. This is not even a crisis of defense. We have the potential strength. This is a crisis of the inward spirit of man. The question is, "Have we as a people the spirit of greatness?"

II. *Use a quotation from the Bible or literature.*

An appropriate quotation is one of the most effective means of concluding a speech. It tends to lift the conclusion to a particularly high level because it adds style, dignity and beauty. Chapter X with almost 300 quotations from the Bible and Chapter XI with almost 1,200 quotations from the world's great literature and from various other sources will be distinctly helpful to you.

Illustrations

Howell Appling, Jr., Oregon Secretary of State, closed an address with these words—

Poets, of course, have a strong bent for contemplation, and so often get to the very heart of the matter. What I have said today has been put more aptly in these lines:

>   We reap today the fruit we have not sown;
>   We thoughtlessly inhale the breath of life,
>   Free flowing all about us without stint;
>   We pay scant heed to thickening sky.
>   The ground-swell rumble of the coming storm
>   Attracts our sidelong glance a moment,
>   And then, absorbed with momentary cares,
>   We bind our soul about with weeds and tares

> Until we are enmeshed, enchained,
> By all the trivia of our lives.
> God set our spirit free.

Herbert V. Prochnow, president of the First National Bank of Chicago, concludes a commencement address at the University of Wisconsin—

This, then, is the decision, and the one single and great objective in life: to take whatever occupation or profession one may be in—doctor, business man, farmer, dentist, banker, attorney, school teacher, housewife—and to live life greatly, nobly—to live for those ideals that will outlast your own life.

As a good citizen earnestly trying to live a good life, you have certain responsibilities if you are to live your best.

For example, if you demand wise and honest government in your city, your state and your country, you must recognize that wise and honest government is the product of wise and honest citizens, and nothing else.

If you demand that crime is punished, you must support honest law enforcement in your community without any personal privileges or exceptions for yourself.

If you demand unfair advantages, government bonuses, and special privileges for your business, your union, your city, or your state, remember that the price of such selfishness is the destruction of a nation's character.

If you demand balanced budgets of your government, you must not advocate expenditures, which, when demanded by all citizens, bring unbalanced budgets. Every dollar which a government spends comes from the toil and sweat of its citizens.

If you demand freedom of worship for yourself, you must respect the rights of other creeds.

If you demand free speech, you must not suppress it in others, or use it to destroy the government from which that privilege flows.

If you demand that the government give you complete economic security, you must not forget that a nation's strength comes from each person standing on his own feet.

If you would like to live in a community in which you may have pride, then dedicate yourself in a spirit of humility to your own responsibilities in that community. These are practical ways in which to live the good life as a citizen.

You may remember the play *Green Pastures*. In that play, Noah said to the Lord, "I ain't very much, but I'm all I got."

Well, *you're* all *you've* got. The question is, "What are *you* going to do with what you've got? Will you press for the goal of a great and good life? Will you use yourself to make life richer, better, nobler?

Someone may say that this is the counsel of perfection. This is the good life. And so it is. The person who lives it will be able to say with joy, "I have fought the good fight, I have finished my course, I have kept the faith."

Attorney-General Robert F. Kennedy uses a quotation from another address—

All the high rhetoric on Law Day about the noble mansions of the law; all the high-sounding speeches about liberty and justice, are meaningless unless people—you and I—breathe meaning and force into it. For our liberties depend upon our respect for the law.

On December 13, 1889, Henry W. Grady of Georgia said these words to an audience in my home state of Massachusetts:

"This hour little needs the loyalty that is loyal to one section and yet holds the other in enduring suspicion and estrangement. Give us the broad and perfect loyalty that loves and trusts Georgia alike with Massachusetts—that knows no South, no North, no East, no West, but endears with equal and patriotic love every foot of our soil, every State of our Union.

"A mighty duty, sir, and a mighty inspiration impels everyone of us tonight to lose in patriotic consecration whatever estranges, whatever divides. We, sir, are Americans—and we stand for human liberty!"

Ten days later Mr. Grady was dead but his words live today. We stand for human liberty.

The road ahead is full of difficulties and discomforts. But as for me, I welcome the challenge, I welcome the opportunity and I pledge my best effort—all I have in material things and physical strength and spirit to see that freedom shall advance and that our children will grow old under the rule of law.

Dr. Edgar De Witt Jones, talking on great Americans of the past—Washington, Jefferson, Webster, Clay, Lincoln, Cleveland, and Bryan—

And as for these great characters that I have presented tonight, and the still larger company of which there is a glorious galaxy, let me say in the noble words of Tennyson:

> "They are gone who seem'd so great.—
> Gone; but nothing can bereave them
> Of the force they made their own
> Being here, and we believe them

> Something far advanced in State,
> And that they wear a truer crown
> Than any wreath that man can weave them.
>
> "Speak no more of their renown,
> Lay your earthly fancies down,
> And in the vast cathedral leave them,
> God accept them, Christ receive them."

Newton N. Minow, former chairman of the Federal Communications Commission—

Let us recall what Henry David Thoreau wrote more than 100 years ago. Thoreau said:

"We are in great haste to construct a magnetic telegraph from Maine to Texas; but Maine and Texas, it may be, have nothing important to communicate. Either is in such a predicament as the man who was anxious to be introduced to a distinguished deaf woman, but when he was presented, and one end of her trumpet was put into his hand, had nothing to say. As if the main object were to talk fast and not talk sensibly. We are eager to tunnel under the Atlantic and bring the Old World some weeks nearer to the new; but perchance the first news that will leak through into the broad, flapping American ear will be that the Princess Adelaide has the whooping cough."

We live in an hour of testing the nerves of man and of his suicidal weapons. It is a complex time, not a simple time. It is a time of trouble, not a time of ease. Yesterday's slogans and yesterday's answers have little meaning. . . .

What can save us? It has been wisely observed that mankind's saving grace may be just this—our technical capacity for mass communication has kept pace with our mastery of the means of mass destruction.

To survive, we can and we must talk to each other. And we must talk not only of Princess Adelaide's whooping cough.

III. *Bring the speech to a grand climax.*

The difficulty of bringing a speech to a grand climax has already been discussed. However, after experience and practice a speaker may use this form of conclusion.

Illustrations

Franklin D. Roosevelt, speaking on "International Affairs" at Chautauqua, New York—

We seek to dominate no other nation. We ask no territorial expansion. We oppose imperialism. We desire reduction in world armaments.

We believe in democracy; we believe in freedom; we believe in peace. We offer to every nation of the world the handclasp of the good neighbor. Let those who wish our friendship look us in the eye and take our hand.

Former Vice-President Richard Nixon, speaking on "The Meaning of Communism"—

If mankind is to survive at a level of dignity worthy of its great past, we must help the world recapture some sense of the teachings of the great thinkers of former ages. It must come again to see that sound legal and political institutions not only express man's highest ideal of what he may become, but that they are indispensable instruments for enabling him to realize that ideal. It would be comforting to believe that the forces of history are working inevitably toward this realization and that we too are cooperating with the inevitable. We can only hope that this is so. But we can know that the forces of human life, struggling to realize itself on its highest plane, are working with us and that those forces need our help desperately.

John Davis Lodge, former United States Ambassador to Spain, closes a Lincoln Day address—

And so, my Spanish and American friends of the American Club of Madrid, it is in a spirit of reverence and love for Lincoln, a hero, and, like most heroes, a martyr, that we gather here today. We Americans are happy to share this precious commemoration with our Spanish friends, for we truly believe that the real meaning of Lincoln is not simply American but that it is universal. We believe that, while for us Americans Lincoln is still a beacon light of hope and faith in a dark and distracted world, he symbolizes to all men everywhere the higher aspirations of man. His life and works remind us that our constant objective must be the brotherhood of man under the fatherhood of God. Abraham Lincoln does indeed belong to the ages and he belongs also to all mankind.

IV. *Compliment the audience or leave a note of encouragement or optimism.*

A sincere compliment or expression of hope for the future pleases an audience.

Illustrations

Henry J. Kaiser, Jr., of Kaiser Industries, closes with a note of encouragement—

In closing I would like to leave you with these few lines which have become a favorite of us Kaisers:

"What do we plant, when we plant a tree:
We plant a ship, that will cross the sea,
We plant the mast to carry the sails,
We plant the planks to withstand the gales,
The keel and keelson, beam and knee,
We plant a ship, when we plant a tree."

We have it in our power, friends, to plant such a tree, which, instead of a single ship, may provide an endless fleet of vessels, bringing a flourishing trade and with it, the possibility of an enduring peace to all of humanity. With God's help, and with work and faith, I know we will do these things. Thank you, friends, for this opportunity. May God bless each and everyone of you.

Arthur J. Goldberg closes an address with a message of encouragement—

This ambition—to create a world without fear, without hunger, a world where justice rules supreme and where a man can stand erect—can be realized if we are firm in our support of peace in freedom. This aspiration can be achieved if we maintain the faith of the founders of this nation, if we believe, as the President does, that liberty is winning and will win because mankind, enriched by the divine spirit, was not made for slavery. That is the message we are bringing and must continue to bring to the world.

V. *Describe a dramatic scene, a great moment in history, science or business, or give a brief biographical story.*

Illustrations

Lieutenant General Ira C. Eaker concludes an address on "Leadership"—

One of my favorite quotations in this vein comes from a message General Foch sent to General Joffre during the first battle of the Marne—"My right has been rolled up, my left has been driven back; my center has been crushed. I shall attack."

There have been great leaders who were blind, more who were deaf, but there have been none who were dumb. All have had the wit, the timing and the courage to influence their followers to action at the critical time by a few well chosen words or by example, or both.

The day may not be far away when we shall need urgently the greatest leader we have ever had. It is my hope that he will have the stature for the occasion. May he be well trained for his task. I pray that he have the audacity to assume the task, and the courage to make the fateful de-

cision in time to save us. May we have the good luck to find him, and the
good sense to follow him.

Herbert V. Prochnow, president of the First National Bank of
Chicago, closed an address on "A Time for Critical Decisions" with
an illustration—

Our decisions on these critical problems will play a significant role in
determining how we meet the economic challenges now confronting us.
Although we must be strong in military defense, it seems certain that the
struggle for world leadership will be determined to a significant degree by
economic power.

Modern capitalism in this country has given us the highest standards of
living in the world. It has made this nation the greatest economic power in
the history of the human race.

If Russia with its bleak and barren materialism becomes in history a
blind Samson who pushes down the economic temple of the capitalistic
world, it will be because weaknesses had developed in the temple before
the shoulders of communism were brought against its pillars. It will not
be because of the spiritual and secular strength of communism. It will not
be because communism has subordinated man and made him the serf
of the state. It will be because you and I have failed. It will be because
our ideals, our vision, our character and our minds were not equal to the
challenge of democracy, freedom, and modern capitalism with its sense
of social responsibility.

Perhaps I may close with a brief story of the first time I met John Foster
Dulles. It was an experience I shall never forget.

The Secretary and I had discussed travel over the world. I commented
that my major interest in visits abroad was in the economic and financial
problems of foreign nations. As the discussion turned to other nations,
the Secretary became deeply reflective. When he spoke, his words came
with great feeling. "When I travel in various parts of the world," he said,
"I seem to see different things than many other persons. For example,"
he explained, "many persons who visit Egypt marvel at the pyramids as
great monuments of earlier civilizations. But the pyramids do not appeal
to me primarily as great monuments of earlier civilizations. When I see
the pyramids, I see tens of thousands of poor, under-nourished Egyptians
carrying heavy physical burdens as they painfully struggle to build the
pyramids. I see these poverty-stricken people carrying for years the op-
pressive burden of the great costs of the pyramids. Thousands toiled,
suffered and died to build them. That is what I see when I look at the
pyramids."

After a moment the Secretary continued, "And when I look at the
world today, I see hundreds of millions of men and women carrying on

their backs the crushing burden of the costs of government and the costs of war. We must remove from the backs of the common people some of the great burdens of the mounting costs of government and armament so that men and women over the world may enjoy the fruits of their labor. We must find the way to lasting peace for all mankind. This is what I see when I look at the world."

The Secretary was speaking with a profound conviction. He was pouring out thoughts that were deep in his heart. This was his great challenge and his great goal.

Later, as we walked to the door, the Secretary said, "Every man needs to make the decision to dedicate at least a part of his life to his country and to the attainment of these objectives."

We may also say that today our people need to make great decisions. We are heirs to a priceless and costly legacy. In our hearts you and I know that there are no easy devices by which men or nations attain distinction and greatness. We know that sound economic and fiscal policies require principles to which men hold fast. We know that hard work and thrift require character and self-denial. We know that balanced budgets rest on financial integrity.

If we have the courage to make the right decisions in these times, and if we have an abiding faith that only the right will ultimately survive, we shall meet the difficult problems of our time with a deep inner serenity and a calm confidence. We shall know that we are helping to build a nation and a world in which the finer values of man's spirit may flower.

Dr. Charles H. Malik, former president of the General Assembly of the United Nations, makes a call to an heroic mission—

The basic truth today is that there is an inescapable confrontation between Communism and the rest of the world calling for historic decision, and I am not sure the effective forces of freedom are sufficiently aware of what is at stake, nor whether they are adequately prepared, *on every level of human existence,* to meet the challenge. Perhaps the Berlin crisis or the Middle East crisis or the Tibet crisis will awaken them; but I am not sure. A vision of something great and tremendous, a call to an heroic mission, the challenge of a truly universal message—this is what is required today and this is alas what is lacking. The immediate situation then presents the aspect of a final and total judgment: everything is being weighed—one's life, one's values, one's culture, the vitality of the whole civilization to which one belongs.

It is very much then like the last day. And those who believe will tell you that God is there and that most certainly He watches over His own, even if He should sorely chasten them still.

T. Keith Glennan of the Aeronautics and Space Administration speaks of the great challenge of space—

Speaking more prosaically—as I wrote these words I was reminded of a story told about Mark Twain. In a discussion with the pilot of a river boat at the time in our history when steam was beginning to replace sail, Twain answered the protests of the pilot against the new fangled invention by saying to him—"When it's steamboat time, you steam."

This is the time for space research and space travel. It is a time of challenge and change. Let us remind ourselves of the words of Brutus spoken in Shakespeare's *Julius Caesar*—

> "There is a tide in the affairs of men
> Which, taken at the flood, leads on to fortune;
> Omitted, all the voyage of their life
> Is bound in shallows and in miseries.
> On such a full sea are we now afloat;
> And we must take the current when it serves
> Or lose our venture."

Ladies and gentlemen of Worcester, it has been a privilege for me to be here with you and to discuss this great adventure into the unknown.

Bob Trout, C.B.S. news commentator, broadcasting a speech on "Cardinal of Charity" at the time of the death of Patrick Cardinal Hayes, Archbishop of New York—

In the dim soft light, George Cardinal Mundelein stood high above the body of the seventy-one-year-old Cardinal and sang the solemn Mass. With holy water and incense, the final blessing was given, while outside in the sunshine, listening through loudspeakers, men knelt in the streets, and women wept and forgot to dry their tears.

Sabers flashed, and white gloves snapped to salute when a bugle sounded taps, and the flags were dipped one last time. And the words of the prayer were all around, louder than the muffled drums, louder than the tolling bells:

> "Eternal rest grant unto him, Oh Lord,
> And let perpetual light shine upon him."

Thus, in shadowy cathedral and in city streets, did New York say farewell to a dear and great friend, His Eminence, Patrick Cardinal Hayes, Prince of the Church, Cardinal of Charity.

Jean Monnet, distinguished French statesman, closes a commencement address at Dartmouth College—

In this connection, I would like to leave you by telling the story of a statesman who was once asked the secret of his success. He replied that in his youth, he had met God in the desert and that God had revealed to him the attitude that was essential to any great achievement. What God had said was this: "For me all things are means to my end—even the obstacles."

VI. *Ask the audience to take some form of action or to adopt a certain viewpoint on some matter.*

Illustrations

T. Keith Glennan, administrator of the National Aeronautics and Space Administration, Washington, D. C., speaking on "Space Exploration"—

Over-all, I want to leave with you two basic facts to be considered and weighed by both yourselves and the now more educationally-sophisticated parents of your students.
   (1) There will be a constantly rising demand for skilled workers in the years ahead.
   (2) The unskilled worker with a low level of education is likely to share very little in the economic fruits of our expanding business and industrial machine.
On the strength of these two points alone, I would implore every parent, teacher, and student to unite in following the logical course:— job career preparation at as early an age as possible.
   Thank you.

Dr. Preston Bradley closed one of his addresses with a challenge to the audience to adopt the viewpoint of sacrifice, and not greed, if America is to stand as a great example to the world.

Let us, ladies and gentlemen, settle down to the task of making this thing called democracy work, and when we make it work in America, and in our hearts, God will see to it that it finally works in all the world. And this world will become the kingdom of our God and the brotherhood of man, a reality, because of the Fatherhood of God.
   And the challenge to you, and the challenge to me, is that before we are Democrats, or Republicans, before we are any of the things that separate us, let us, above all, and in all, and through all, let us upon the altar of our country place a sacrifice and stop treating that altar as a crib out of which to feed.

The author of this book closed an address before the Oregon Bankers Association with the following appeal:

If we could read the human story back of every savings and commercial passbook; if we could see the home, the work, the business trials, and the hopes each passbook represents; if we could clearly visualize the problems of each depositor, the education of his children, the care of dependents, the hope, after years of work, for a competence in old age; if we could really evaluate the significant role the banker plays in the economic advancement of a nation; I believe we would approach our daily work tomorrow with a new sense of its great importance. No other responsibility in our business life transcends it. Let us bring to it thorough knowledge, broad experience, and outstanding management ability.

VII. *Tell a humorous story or give a suitable witty comment.*

Humor that definitely relates itself to the speech makes a splendid conclusion. Chapter IV with more than 1,000 carefully chosen humorous stories, Chapter V with over 500 epigrams and witty comments, and Chapter VI with 200 humorous definitions will provide an almost inexhaustible source of materials for this purpose.

Illustrations

Professor C. Northcote Parkinson, the author of a number of books, concluded an address as follows:

And at this point I will end my talk in order to leave time for any questions, if there are any questions, from any members who should happen by any chance to be awake.

Professor Parkinson then answered questions and closed his questions with a comment on socialized medicine and the general practitioner in medicine—

Another result, and I think this is one common to Britain and the United States and perhaps not directly the result of socialized medicine, is the disappearance of that creature known as the G.P. or general practitioner, a rare form now on the zoological landscape and his place is being taken by the medical clerk, the new character of lower level medicine who simply sorts out the patients by a quick glance as they say, "I have got a cough," and the medi-clerk says, "Down that corridor, the first door on the left for coughs."

Another patient says, "I have got a tummy ache," and he says, "Down that corridor, third door to the left," and that goes for tummy pains and so forth.

In other words, the basic function of the general practitioner is to sort people out and put them in an appropriate medical slot. As it happens, I live in one of the few places of the world where the general practitioner still flourishes. That is, in the Channel Islands between England and France, and there is a sort of preserve of wild life and the general practitioner is still to be observed in his natural habitat. He is to be detected by his drab plumage, his plaintive cry and his long bill.

II

How to Make Your Speech Sparkle

After the first written draft or outline of a speech is prepared, it should be painstakingly revised and refined. Each sentence must be written and rewritten until every unnecessary word is eliminated. However, great care must be exercised that the revisions and polishing do not remove the freshness, naturalness, and vigor that may have been in the first draft.

In seeking to give style and effectiveness to the wording and phrasing of a speech, one must never forget that clearness of expression is the first imperative. Everything in style must yield to clarity.

The effort that eloquent speakers make to obtain style and effectiveness of expression is well illustrated by the comment of Phyllis Moir writing of Winston Churchill in *I Was Winston Churchill's Private Secretary*.

I can see him now, pacing slowly up and down the room, his hands clasped behind his back, his shoulders hunched, his head sunk forward in deep thought, slowly and haltingly dictating the beginning of a speech or an article. I wait, my pencil poised in midair, as he whispers phrases to himself, carefully weighing each word and striving to make his thoughts balance. Nothing may be put down until it has been tested aloud and found satisfactory. A happy choice brings a glint of triumph to his eye; a poor one is instantly discarded. He will continue the search until every detail—of sound, rhythm and harmony—is to his liking. Sometimes there are long halts, during which he patiently sounds out a phrase a dozen times, this way and that, making the cigar in his hand serve as a baton to punctuate the rhythm of his words.*

From this statement it is evident that Winston Churchill's eloquence did not just happen. It was not accidental. It was the most carefully studied effort of a great mind that had struggled word by word and phrase by phrase for the brilliant expression of ideas that would move nations.

There are a number of tools of effective speech which enable one to refine and perfect expression. They enable even the most inexperienced speaker to give a speech a sparkling quality. The order in which they are presented is not one of their relative importance, because these speech tools may be used on different occasions and for different purposes. Keep these effective speech tools definitely in mind as you revise your speeches to make them sparkle.

I. *Insert suitable humorous stories, epigrams, and amusing definitions.*

Study the written draft or outline of your speech thoughtfully to determine exactly where a humorous comment would be appropriate, if the speech permits humor. Chapter IV contains over one thousand humorous stories suitable for introducing a speaker, beginning an address, making statistical or other dry material interesting, lightening a speech that has necessarily been long or has dwelt on many subjects, expressing appreciation for attention, and generally assisting a speaker to give just the right touch of humor needed to make a speech successful. Speeches on particularly serious occasions may not permit of humor. However, for the great majority of addresses, and also in daily conversation, no tool of speech is more generally helpful than good humor. Abraham Lincoln's political speeches and conversation with their generous use of humor are excellent illustrations.

The humorous stories in Chapter IV have been chosen from many thousands. Each story may be successfully adapted to a large number of different types of situations. For example, consider the following story: A professor in a western university taught mathematics and statistics. One day he was standing, dressed in his bathing suit, at the edge of a swimming pool on the university campus when a beautiful coed accidentally dropped her camera into the deep end of the pool. She called to the elderly professor for help. He said he would be glad

* Phyllis Moir, *I Was Winston Churchill's Private Secretary* (New York: Wilfred Funk, Inc., 1941), pp. 154-155.

to dive after the camera, but first wanted to know why she happened to choose him when there were so many young men within easy reach to do the job. She answered, "Professor, you have apparently forgotten me, but I am in your large statistics class. I have found that you can *go down deeper, stay down longer, and come up drier* than anyone I know."

The speaker can use this story in almost any address containing statistics or facts which may be essential to the address, but a bit dry. He may add that in explaining his statistics he does not propose to go down too deep, stay down too long, or come up too dry. The story may also be used in connection with the relationships of professors and students, and with topics dealing with education.

The speaker should generally select those humorous stories which are definitely appropriate to the subject matter and which illustrate points he wishes to emphasize. The humor should not all come at one point, but should be spaced at intervals through the speech. However, never use a humorous story which is entirely irrelevant and is merely inserted to wake up a drowsy audience in the hope that its members will listen to a dull speech. The way to wake up a drowsy audience is to wake up the speaker. The humor must always relate itself directly to the discussion.

Sometimes another tool—an epigram or witty comment—is more effective than a humorous story. Subtly introduced, the epigram may serve fully as well as a comparatively long humorous story. Moreover, it conserves time. A speaker talking about the shortage of labor in some fields might say, "A woman doesn't hire domestic help now; she marries it." The change from a serious statement to a witty comment is so rapid it surprises the listeners, and as they catch the full significance of the humor, they enjoy it. It takes but a moment to give a witty comment, and the speaker goes on immediately. The humor provides "the pause that refreshes" for the audience.

Dr. Will Durant, the distinguished philosopher, was giving an address before the Rotary Club of Chicago in which he was discussing for a few minutes the philosophy of Friedrich Nietzsche. Remember that Dr. Durant had for many years been a university professor. Commenting on Nietzsche, Dr. Durant said—

in 1870 . . . Friedrich Nietzsche walked out of a hospital. He had been rejected from military service. He had weak ribs. He had poor eyes. He was flat-footed. He was a professor.

The last sentence caught the audience by surprise, but in a moment the laughter spread over that large audience. It was a terse, un-expected, humorous comment, and it was on the speaker, which made it twice as good.

A businessman was speaking of the necessity for work and thrift in any economic order, whether it be capitalistic or socialistic. "Of course," he added, "I know there are some men who would say that my philosophy is one of 'Work hard and save your money, and when you are old, you can have the things that only the young can enjoy.' " The audience liked that bit of humor which the speaker credited to his critics. Then he went on to prove his case.

A speaker on international problems might say, "You may ask why the nations of the world cannot live as one big family. The answer is they do." A brief humorous comment of this kind often provides a stimulating pause in an address.

Over 500 epigrammatic comments from many sources and on many subjects are included in Chapter V. These short and pointed state-ments will be of great assistance in creating effective speeches. They also assist in making ordinary conversation sparkle. Almost every address has a place for one or two pertinent quotable epigrams.

Occasionally also a speaker may find an opportunity to use an amusing definition and more than 200 such definitions will be found in Chapter VI. With a little practice anyone can create such defini-tions out of humorous stories and jokes. They provide a different type of humor combining some of the qualities of jokes and epigrams. Dr. Joseph Jastrow, famous professor of psychology at the University of Wisconsin, began one of his addresses with this amusing defini-tion: "The psychologist has been slanderously defined as a man who tells you what everybody knows in language nobody can understand." That definition made an attention-winning introduction.

Fred Allen's definition of a conference as "a gathering of impor-tant people who singly can do nothing, but together can decide that nothing can be done" is a typical amusing definition which tells a good story in one sentence.

II. *Use illustrations from biography, from plays, or from literature.*

If the speech is one of inspiration, perhaps to a body of students, a college graduating class, a church congregation, or an after-dinner audience, stories of achievement, persistence, courage, tact and patience from the lives of statesmen, scientists, industrialists, writers, musicians, artists, and others whose lives have been of widespread interest, will help to illustrate the speech and make it entertaining and instructive. Few things in the world are more inspiring to an audience than the stories of lives lived significantly. Chapter VII includes a number of short stories of the character suggested.

Illustrations

The author closed an address with illustrations and with a quotation from a book—

With a massive political, economic and social revolution over the world, we need to be certain our own house is in order. It is a time to be strong. One evening at the height of a Presidential campaign some of us visited on a university campus with one of the most respected and experienced members of the Senate of the United States. He said regretfully that it was no longer possible to be elected and to ask anything of the American people. One could only promise them benefits without sacrifices. This was not the comment of a cynic. It was the thoughtful judgment of a public servant who has served his country for many years with distinction. If a nation ultimately is only as strong, and only as great, as the character, integrity, ideals, and vision of its people, then this statement constitutes a tragic indictment. But is it true? Is there a widespread intellectual and social disintegration of our people, or is it a failure to understand clearly that continued sacrifices are essential if a nation is to remain free? Have we offered this alternative, or have we offered the people merely the deceptive lure of benefits without sacrifices? We may well be at a critical turning point in our history when a courageous decision to put our affairs in order would meet the overwhelming approval of the American people.

Recently a few of us were at luncheon with a leading statesman of West Germany. One American asked this question, "How do you explain the remarkable economic growth, or so-called economic miracle, of West Germany since the end of World War II?" The German statesman replied, "This was not a miracle. When a people lack bread, four walls for a room, and a bed in which to sleep, they will work hard for long hours and save. The economic rewards have been great for our people. But some of us are fearful that wealth and comforts are beginning now to bring ease and complacency."

We may ask ourselves, "Is it necessary for the people of any nation continually to face hardships in order to live greatly?"

In a recent book, *The Agony and the Ecstasy*, the teacher of Michelangelo, the great artist, says, "Sculpture is hard, brutal labor. . . . Talent is cheap; dedication is expensive. It will cost you your life." Michelangelo replies, "What else is life for?"

May I ask, "What else is life for in a nation if it is not for a dedication by the people to freedom and to greatness? But a dedication to freedom and to greatness carries with it responsibilities and strict disciplines. It carries with it the challenge to individual men to strive to make the most of their abilities and talents. It carries with it the responsibility of hard work, so that the economic well-being of all our people may be improved. It carries with it the responsibility of living within the nation's income. It demands self-reliance and self-discipline. To paraphrase John Adams, freedom requires that each individual conduct himself so that his life demonstrates the dignity of man and the noble rank man holds among the works of Providence. This is the meaning of freedom and these are its responsibilities in our time.

Dr. Glenn Frank, speaking on "If the Young Can but See," used a dramatic illustration from a play.

I was a guest at the Chicago opening of Shaw's *Saint Joan* as her triumphant spirit sang through the lips of Katharine Cornell. . . . For me the high moment of the play came in the much abused Epilogue.

Here was the scene.

It was twenty-five years after the burning of the maid. The curtain rose on the bed-chamber of King Charles the Seventh of France, who, at the opening of the play, was the none-too-bright Dauphin. The spirits of those who played a part in the trial and burning at the stake of Joan were entering the King's chamber. Among them was an old rector, formerly a chaplain to the Cardinal of Winchester, a little deaf and a little daft. He had gone somewhat crazy from brooding over the burning of Joan, but insisted that the sight of that burning had saved him.

"Well you see," he said, "I did a very cruel thing once because I did not know what cruelty was like. I had not seen it, you know. That is the great thing: You must see it. And then you are redeemed and saved."

"Were not the sufferings of our Lord Christ enough for you?" asked the Bishop of Beauvais.

"No," said the old rector. "Oh no, not at all. I had seen them in pictures, and read of them in books, and been greatly moved by them, as I thought. But it was no use. It was not our Lord that redeemed me, but a young woman whom I saw actually burnt to death. It was dreadful. But it saved me. I have been a different man ever since."

Poor old priest, driven astray in his wits by the haunting memory of his youthful inability to see what cruelty is like without watching a maid burn slowly to death at the hands of her executioners, a man who had to wait for events to educate his judgments!

The Bishop of Beauvais looked at him pityingly and, with infinite pathos in his voice, cried out, "Must then a Christ perish in torment in every age to save those that have no imagination?"

I covet for you who are about to be graduated . . . the godlike gifts of insight and understanding. You will need them in the days ahead.

There are many stories in literature. Wide reading in the field of biography is strongly recommended. Interesting facts and interesting incidents from interesting lives may make the difference between a dull and a worthwhile and colorful speech. Searching until one finds this material pays rich rewards.

An official of the American Bankers Association addressed a convention of the American Institute of Banking which has as its members many thousands of young people in the banking business. He spoke of some of the practical aspects of bank operation, and then for the last half of his address, which was on the subject of, "The Challenge for Banking Leadership," he discussed the five qualities essential to leadership in banking. This part of his address is presented because it applies to leadership in every field. Note also the clarity with which the five points are developed and the use of biography at the end of the discussion.

Having presented some of the problems confronting us, let us consider the five qualities that are essential to leadership in the banking business today. How can the banker train himself to sound judgment and to decisive, courageous, and persistent action in line with his findings; how can he inspire that confidence and loyalty throughout his organization which makes his business a team instead of a rabble?

First of all, the banker of today and of the future must know—he must have knowledge. There are countless people who are crammed with information, but totally lacking in knowledge. In place of guesses, conjectures, and prejudices, we must substitute knowledge. The difference between knowledge and information, as I am thinking of it, is that knowledge is a clean-cut grasp of all the facts you need in order to solve your problem; while information is ill-assorted, encyclopedic, but not necessarily complete and pertinent.

We come then to the second essential of a successful banker—imagination. Perhaps something of the difference between knowledge and information depends upon the constructive imagination that is brought to bear upon the facts, for facts in themselves are not important except as their influence is projected and their destiny foretold.

The banking business, frankly, was for many years transacted between four stone walls. It is within the present generation that banking has very largely broken away from behind the four walls, and without sacrificing its ability to pass upon credits with cool judgment, it has given some rein to contructive imagination.

I believe that there are going to be further fundamental changes in our financial and economic life, before which tradition and prejudice will prove to be blind leadership. The banking leaders of the future must think, imagine, dream—and then work out the substance of their dreams. The characteristic of the great thinkers in any field has always been their freedom from tradition and their ability to give their imagination free rein. Originality always follows imagination. On imagination is dependent most of the great inventions and forward movements in our history. Imagination takes facts or materials and from countless unrelated parts combines a unit that produces or accomplishes something new in the world. Of course any of us can cite examples where imagination which has gone headlong in the pursuit of new ideas has suffered severe losses. But how much greater, immeasurably, have been the losses inflicted by frozen adherence to outworn methods.

All the elements that make up television were in existence before television was invented. These elements were combined by the imagination in a new way to develop something as new and as important in its day as the invention of printing. The basic essentials of our Federal Reserve System were in existence before the act was passed under which these forces were interrelated and placed in operation.

Imagination is the intangible, the spirit, the flame, the breath of life that animates common clay. Nothing is more essential to leadership than imagination; yet it must be controlled, constructive, balanced. The leader must tread the high ground that lies between iron-bound tradition and unbridled dreaming.

And so we arrive at the third essential quality of the young bank executive—sound thinking. The balancing quality that must be linked with imagination is sound thinking. The dreamer dreams himself a castle in the air. The man with imagination and ability to think consecutively dreams a castle and delves into the earth, plans a foundation able to bear the crushing weights above it, actually erects his beams and arches, and builds up solidly to the very pinnacle of the structure.

Cultivate the thinking habit and the ability to think. We should not be carried away by the idea that in this day of rush and hurry there is something sacred about the snap judgment of the go-getter. Emerson once said that the hardest job in the world is to think. How many bankers are there who daily sit down alone, with the door shut against the deadly routine of detail, to think through independently some major problem in bank operation that confronts them? How many banks are there whose policies have been determined by the directors and officers through logical thinking based upon all the factors involved?

Some may feel that imagination and thinking are synonymous. I believe, however, that we have here three separate and distinct essentials of leadership—knowledge, imagination, thinking. Too many bankers have looked at the problem of increasing profits as a hopeless one. They lacked the imagination to dream of a better day. Some have set up wrong standards and thus brought their institutions to grief. They lacked knowledge. Others have misinterpreted the figures and have arrived at conclusions that involved them in trouble. They lacked the ability to think straight.

The fourth essential of leadership is initiative. There are a surprising number of people who know how their business should be organized and operated, but who do nothing about it. There are intelligent thinkers who lack the impulse, the ambition, the initiative to put their ideas and convictions and dreams into practice.

Banking needs more self-starters. It needs more leaders who are convinced they are right and who are determined to see the matter through. There are plenty of bankers who have thought of plans for leveling up the bank's profits, but they have failed to act. While some hesitate and question whether their conclusions are correct, while others procrastinate and wait for someone else to take the lead, while still others claim the time is not yet ripe, the true leader rallies his organization and carries the matter through.

Even when a person has all the essential qualifications for success, it may take great courage and initiative to shoulder responsibility and step to the head of the column. The greatest losses in history have been in the lives of the millions whose powers remained dormant all through their lives.

One other essential—hard work—sheer application, resolute, persevering, tough-fibered.

There has never been an army in which the rank and file did not picture the leaders as enjoying ease and luxury. But the great military leaders— Caesar, Napoleon, Grant, Pershing, Eisenhower—were indefatigable workers. They had almost unbreakable health. They had bulldog tenaciousness. Early and late they were at their problems. They outdid other men in leadership, just as an engine that runs longer and faster will outdo the motor that slows down, that runs intermittently, that never produces in any twenty-four hours all the power that maximum operation would derive from it.

Business is full of the romance of youngsters whose chief characteristic was working hard and keeping at it.

There was a green farmer boy who decided he would rather stand behind a counter than follow a plow. He seemed so obviously lacking in sales ability that for a time no merchant would hire him. He failed in his first position, and in his second his salary was reduced. He even agreed that he was a misfit—but he stuck. Out of his first five stores, I believe, three failed. But he persisted and worked hard. And that boy, Frank W. Woolworth, became one of the greatest retail merchants in the world with a store in every city of 8,000 or more population in this country.

There was a young man named Cyrus McCormick who worked and

waited eight harvest times for a chance to sell a queer new contraption.

Finally he sold a reaper—and the revolution of the agricultural industry began.

Leadership is not play. Leadership in the banking of the future, as I have tried to vizualize it, offers countless positions of varying opportunity, of which the highest pinnacles will carry almost unbearable responsibility in the new era that may lie just over the next hill. There will be men with the fire and iron to qualify even for these places. Such men must have had the very finest preparation and the most grueling tests which the banking profession knows. Their reward will be the attainment of these highest pinnacles of achievement, and the rendering of an immeasurable service to their times.

III. *Repeat some words or phrases to stamp them indelibly upon the minds of the listeners.*

Illustrations

A classic example of reiteration is found in one of the greatest addresses of all time, the Sermon on the Mount. In that address, as it is recorded in Chapter 7 of St. Matthew, verses 24 to 27, the Master says, "Therefore whosoever heareth these sayings of mine, and doeth them, I will liken him unto a wise man, which built his house upon a rock: And the rain descended, and the floods came, and the winds blew, and beat upon that house; and it fell not: for it was founded upon a rock. And everyone that heareth these sayings of mine, and doeth them not, shall be likened unto a foolish man, which built his house upon the sand: And the rain descended, and the floods came, and the winds blew, and beat upon that house; and it fell: and great was the fall of it."

Again in St. Matthew, Chapter 5, verses 29 and 30, we find the Master saying, "And if thy right eye offend thee, pluck it out, and cast it from thee: for it is profitable for thee that one of thy members should perish, and not that thy whole body should be cast into hell. And if thy right hand offend thee, cut it off, and cast it from thee: for it is profitable for thee that one of thy members should perish, and not that thy whole body should be cast into hell."

The late Dr. Glenn Frank speaking on "The Statesmanship of Business and the Business of Statesmanship," uses repetition at the beginning only of three sentences to re-emphasize the fact that the nation has changed.

So I suggest that sooner or later, as a nation, we shall have to face the political implications of the following obvious facts:

We are no longer a small nation; we are a large nation.

We are no longer a simple civilization; we are an increasingly complex and technical civilization.

We are no longer an agricultural nation alone; we are an industrial nation as well.

In an address before the Mortgage Bankers Association of America, the author used repetition to emphasize the seriousness of our international problems as follows—

In 1945, after six weary years of war, the economic and social order of the world lay half in ruins. Less than two decades later the healing ministry of work and thrift has brought to millions of men and women in a number of nations economic achievements unparalleled in history.

And yet, thoughtful men are today asking whether all that mankind has painstakingly built over the long centuries is to come to a decisive and disastrous end as nations engage in the grim enterprise of nuclear destruction. Where once we were certain that human genius could wisely guide our society, there is now a cynical distrust of the course of world events. Where once there was a buoyant confidence that mankind was equal to the challenge of peace, there now is a disturbing fear which haunts the minds of free men as they face crisis after crisis in a mounting cold war. Where once such phrases as democracy and dictatorship, freedom and regimentation, individualism, and collectivism were only abstract ideas for college debate, they now are the center of a vast and bitter world struggle for the minds of men.

We are in a period of grave confusion. We seem sometimes to be in the grip of a paralyzing fatalism. We thrust great satellites far into the skies as if to defy the very heavens, while we talk of shelters on earth where each man will run like a frightened animal for his little cave to save himself, if he can, from the terrible fury of the last wrath. But must the outlook for humanity be so dismal? must it be one of despair? Are the cards of destiny stacked against us? Are the skies of freedom darkening hopelessly across the earth? Is mankind prepared to accept complete subserviency to the state as its way of life, sheer materialism as its goal and self-destruction as its inevitable end? Can this nation ride through the storms of these years without political liberty and private enterprise being ultimately brought to their ruin? To gain some insight into the answers to these questions, let us consider what may be the major world developments of our time, their challenges to American foreign policy and their possible impact upon the future of our people.

One of the best known and most striking illustrations of repetition is to be found in the following quotation from an address by Robert Ingersoll:

A little while ago, I stood by the grave of the old Napoleon—a magnificent tomb of gilt and gold, almost fit for a dead deity—and gazed upon
the sarcophagus of black Egyptian marble, where rest the ashes of that
restless man. I leaned over the balustrade and thought about the career
of the greatest soldier of the modern world.

I saw him walking upon the banks of the Seine contemplating suicide.
I saw him at Toulon; I saw him putting down the mob in the streets of
Paris; I saw him at the head of the army in Italy; I saw him crossing
the bridge of Lodi with the tricolor in his hand; I saw him in Egypt in
the shadow of the Pyramids; I saw him conquer the Alps and mingle the
eagles of France with the eagles of the crags; I saw him at Marengo, at
Ulm, and Austerlitz; I saw him in Russia where the infantry of the snow
and the cavalry of the wild blast scattered his legions like winter's withered
leaves; I saw him at Leipzig in defeat and disaster—driven by a million
bayonets back upon Paris—clutched like a wild beast—banished to Elba.
I saw him escape and retake an empire by the force of his genius. I saw
him upon the frightful field of Waterloo, where Chance and Fortune
combined to wreck the fortunes of their former king, and I saw him at St.
Helena, with his hands crossed behind him, gazing out upon the sad and
solemn sea.

I thought of the orphans and widows he had made, of the tears that had
been shed for his glory, and of the only woman he ever loved, pushed
from his heart by the cold hand of ambition; and I said I would rather
have been a French peasant and worn wooden shoes; I would rather have
lived in a hut with a vine growing over the door and the grapes growing
purple in the rays of the autumn sun; I would rather have been that poor
peasant with my loving wife by my side, knitting as the day died out of the
sky, with my children about my knee and their arms about me, I would
rather have been that man and gone down to the tongueless silence of
the dreamless dust than have been that imperial personification of force
and murder.

Note also in the following short passage from Edmund Burke's
address, "The Age of Chivalry Is Gone," how repetition aids the
emphasis: "But the age of chivalry is gone. That of sophisters, econo-
mists, and calculators, has succeeded; and the glory of Europe is
extinguished forever. Never, never more, shall we behold that generous loyalty to rank and sex, that proud submission, that dignified
obedience, that subordination of the heart, which kept alive, even in
servitude itself the spirit of an exalted freedom. The unbought grace
of life, the cheap defence of nations, the nurse of manly sentiment
and heroic enterprise, is gone. It is gone, that sensibility of principle,
that chastity of honour, which felt a stain like a wound, which inspired courage . . . which ennobled whatever it touched."

A simple but slightly different use of repetition in which a question is first asked, and is then followed by variations in the question, is illustrated in the following quotation from an address on the subject of a liberal education by Thomas Henry Huxley: "Let us ask ourselves, what is education? Above all things, what is our ideal of a thoroughly liberal education?—of that education which, if we could begin life again, we would give ourselves—of that education which, if we could mould the fates to our own will, we would give our children."

In a speech on "The Romance of Life," Dr. Preston Bradley, well-known Chicago minister, lecturer, and author, said, "First, there must be within our democracy a revival, a renaissance, a new birth—call it what you will—there must be a new realization of the value of human personality. We must have a new birth of value as to human personality." Note in this quotation also the mastery of the art of repetition.

IV. *Intersperse short sentences with long ones.*

In baseball, this might be called changing the pace. It makes it easier for the listener to understand the speech, because he does not have continually to follow tedious, long sentences. It relieves the monotony that would accompany the repeated use of nothing but long sentences or the recurrent use of the staccato-like short sentence.

Illustrations

The late Dr. Glenn Frank, giving a baccalaureate address at The University of Wisconsin—

I am not so old as to have lost my memory of what must be surging through the minds of you who are about to step from the sheltered life of the student into active participation in the life of your time. And unless I have forgotten the emotions that swept my mind, some twenty-five years ago, when I completed my university training and stood poised, as you are poised, for a plunge into the outer world, I know that all sorts of anxieties haunt your minds, anxieties about the first and further steps in your careers. And these normal anxieties that you would feel even if all skies were cloudless, have, I know, been trebled by the political and economic distraction through which your nation has been passing as you have pursued your training.

What shall you do with these anxieties?

I want to be honest with you. I do not want to minimize one whit the uncertainties that infest the economic affairs of your time. I do not want to raise in your minds a single hope that will be doomed to die unfulfilled. But I do want to stir in you, if I can, every hope that can be fulfilled.

What, then, shall I say?

With a full sense of my responsibility to be realistic with you, I beg you not to let anxiety rest too heavily upon your minds.

Life is still conquerable for your generation both in the field of public policy and in the field of personal achievement.

The author of this book used this technique in a commencement address—

You will remember the story of the two sons. The younger son said to his father, "Give me the share of goods now that I am to inherit later." The father gave it to him and the young man left for a far country, where he wasted his entire estate. A depression came in that country, and the young man was in great need. He was hungry. He had no friends. He was destitute. As this young man meditated, he might have thought: "Well, my father was too indulgent. He was mature. I was a boy. He should not have been so foolish as to give me my estate." But this young man learned a hard lesson from this sobering and bitter experience. He said to himself, "Many servants in my father's house have bread enough and to spare, and I perish with hunger!" And then came his great decision. He said, "I will go to my father, and will say to him, 'Father I was wrong . . . and am no more worthy to be called your son; make me one of your hired servants.' " Of course, his father accepted him, and with that courageous decision, the young man found the life that he had lost.

Dr. Will Durant speaking on "What Are the Lessons of History?":

Now we come to another lesson of history, which is a little more dangerous: That the concentration of wealth in the hands of a minority of the population is inevitable in any society. Why? Because men are naturally unequal. Some are clever; some are virtuous; some are strong; some are weak; some are healthy; some are sickly; some are brave; some are timid; and out of small natural differences that give you a headstart come the tremendous differences in the development of society such as you see growing rapidly in America from 1750 to 1940.

V. *Use a series of short, crisp sentences.*

The experienced speaker may not only intersperse occasional short sentences with longer ones, but he may also insert in his address one or two paragraphs of short, sharp, and clean-cut sentences that introduce a certain briskness.

Illustrations

In one of his addresses, Arthur M. Hyde said, "Justice is not social, economic or political. It is all of them, Justice is Justice, plain and unqualified. It cannot be qualified. If limited to a class, it is no

longer justice. Every citizen, not merely a class, is entitled to justice."
The author used this idea in an address to university students—

As Walt Whitman said, "I was simmering, simmering, simmering:
Emerson brought me to a boil." Many of us in life succeed to where we
almost reach the boiling point. Nearly, you see, almost, but not quite.

It takes struggles in life to make strength. It takes fight for principles
to make fortitude. It takes crises to give courage. Suffering to make sympathy. Pain to make patience. It takes singleness of purpose to reach an
objective.

The late Knute Rockne, famous football coach of Notre Dame, in
talking on "Athletics and Leadership," gave an excellent example of
the use of a series of terse comments. He said:

Some of you may say, this will to win is a bad thing. In what way is it
a bad thing? Education is supposed to prepare a young man for life. Life
is competition. Success in life goes only to the man who competes successfully. A successful lawyer is the man who goes out and wins—wins
law cases. A successful physician is a man who goes out and wins—saves
lives and restores men to health. A successful sales manager is a man
who goes out and wins—sells the goods. The successful executive is the
man who can make money and stay out of the bankruptcy court. There
is no reward for the loser. There is nothing wrong with the will to win.
The only penalty should be that the man who wins unfairly should be set
down.

All of these illustrations indicate how the short, crisp sentence may
be used to give a speech "punch."

VI. *Use similes occasionally.*

Webster's *New Collegiate Dictionary* states that a simile is "a figure
of speech by which one thing, action, or relation is likened or explic-
itly compared, often with *as* or *like*, to something of different kind or
quality." The simile is one of the oldest forms of speech. The 300
examples of similes in Chapter VIII are included to indicate their
exact nature. These similes do not at all exhaust the field, for there
are thousands of illustrations in speeches, literature, and newspaper
and magazine articles. New similes are being created daily. The
similes given are not to be memorized unless one wishes to learn
them. With a little patience and practice each of us can create similes
for his own use—similes fully as sparkling and fascinating. How
much more interesting it is to say "the man went through things like
a customs inspector" instead of "he examined everything." How much
more colorful to state "the village was as desolate as a cemetery,"

instead of "the village was desolate." Make it a practice to use similes both in speeches and in conversation.

VII. *Avoid boring repetition by the use of appropriate synonyms.*

The dictionary and a book of synonyms are necessary additions to your library if you wish to speak, write, or converse well. They will enable you to find exactly the right word for a particular use.

A synonym is a word having the same or nearly the same meaning as another word. Synonyms enable the speaker to have some variation in his language when otherwise he might use the same word repeatedly. A well-known American executive repeats the word "tremendous" twenty-five or more times in one speech. In fact, he uses the word a *tremendous* number of times.

There are few perfect synonyms, that is, words with exactly the same meaning as other words, so the speaker must choose his synonyms with judgment. The word *weak*, for example, may suggest as possible synonyms—feeble, infirm, faint, sickly, exhausted, groggy, spent, wasted, powerless, helpless, impotent, spineless, frail, fragile, flimsy, enervated, languishing, and debilitated. Examine a speech carefully, sentence by sentence, to see whether suitable synonyms may be chosen for words which have been used so often they have become monotonous.

VIII. *Use appropriate antonyms to create contrasts.*

An antonym is a word whose meaning is opposite that of another word. The choice of good antonyms is necessary to create strong contrasts. A possible choice, for example, of antonyms for *weak* or *weakness* might be strength, power, potency, energy, vigor, force, stamina, virility, vitality, and puissance. Examine a speech critically to see whether words that are used to bring out contrasts do so with the greatest effectiveness; if not, replace them with words which do.

IX. *Use questions.*

A question often serves to challenge the attention of an audience and to give emphasis to a point. In Chapter I we called attention to the possibility of using questions in the introduction. However, questions are equally valuable in the body of the address.

Illustrations

John Sergeant, speaking on "Militarism and Progress," said, "I would ask: What did Cromwell, with all his military genius, do for England? He overthrew the monarchy, and he established dictatorial power in his own person. And what happened next? Another soldier overthrew the dictatorship, and restored the monarchy. The sword effected both. Cromwell made one revolution, and Monk another. And what did the people of England gain by it? Nothing. Absolutely nothing."

Chief Justice Marshall, speaking on the "Federal Constitution"—

What are the favorite maxims of democracy? A strict observance of justice and public faith and a steady adherence to virtue. These, sir, are the principles of a good government. No mischief, no misfortune, ought to deter us from a strict observance of justice and public faith. Would to heaven that these principles had been observed under the present government! Had this been the case the friends of liberty would not be so willing now to part with it. Can we boast that our government is founded on these maxims? Can we pretend to the enjoyment of political freedom or security when we are told that a man has been, by an act of Assembly, struck out of existence without a trial by jury, without examination, without being confronted with his accusers and witnesses, without the benefits of the law of the land? Where is our safety when we are told that this act was justifiable because the person was not a Socrates? What has become of the worthy member's maxims? Is this one of them? Shall it be a maxim that a man shall be deprived of his life without the benefit of law? Shall such a deprivation of life be justified by answering that a man's life was not taken *secundum artem*, because he was a bad man? Shall it be a maxim that government ought not to be empowered to protect virtue?

These questions are vital ones. They go directly to the heart of Marshall's discussion.

The author discussed the emergence of the new nations out of the former colonial empires and then asked these questions—

What course will the new nations follow? Will they regiment their people, as communism does, force long hours of work, make saving compulsory and restrict consumer goods in order to build basic industry and achieve economic growth more rapidly? Will they sacrifice present generations for the future as Red China does, or will they seek economic growth within the framework of freedom? The peace and security of the world may well be involved in the answers to these questions.

X. *Place ideas in contrast to each other.*

Placing ideas in contrast to one another is sometimes called antithesis. Occasionally one even finds antithesis within single sentences as in Burke's speech on "The Age of Chivalry" when he speaks of "All the pleasing allusions which made power gentle and obedience liberal." Note the contrast between power and gentle, obedience and liberal. In another place he says: "Never, never more shall we behold . . . that proud submission, that dignified obedience. . . ." Again note the contrast, particularly of proud and submission.

Illustrations

Demosthenes often used contrasts in his addresses, as illustrated in his speech "On the Crown."

Contrast now the circumstances of your life and mine, gently and with temper, Aeschines; and then ask these people whose fortune they would each of them prefer. You taught reading, I went to school: you performed initiations, I received them: you danced in the chorus, I furnished it: you were assembly-clerk, I was a speaker: you acted third parts, I heard you: you broke down, and I hissed: you have worked as a statesman for the enemy, I for my country. I pass by the rest; but this very day I am on my probation for a crown, and am acknowledged to be innocent of all offense; while you are already judged to be a pettifogger, and the question is, whether you shall continue that trade, or at once be silenced by not getting a fifth part of the votes. A happy fortune, do you see, you have enjoyed, that you should denounce mine as miserable!

The author used contrast in repeated paragraphs of the commencement address quoted earlier—

As a good citizen earnestly trying to live a good life, you have certain responsibilities if you are to live your best.

For example, if you demand wise and honest government in your city, your state and your country, you must recognize that wise and honest government is the product of wise and honest citizens, and nothing else.

If you demand that crime be punished, you must support honest law enforcement in your community without any personal privileges or exceptions for yourself.

If you demand unfair advantages, government bonuses, and special privileges for your business, your union, your city or your state, remember that the price of such selfishness is the destruction of a nation's character.

If you demand balanced budgets of your government, you must not advocate expenditures, which, when demanded by all citizens, bring unbalanced budgets. Every dollar which a government spends comes from the toil and sweat of its citizens.

If you demand freedom of worship for yourself, you must respect the rights of other creeds.

If you demand free speech, you must not suppress it in others, or use it to destroy the government from which that privilege flows.

If you demand that the government give you complete economic security, you must not forget that a nation's strength comes from each person standing on his own feet.

If you would like to live in a community in which you may have pride, then dedicate yourself in a spirit of humility to your own responsibilities in that community. These are practical ways in which to live the good life as a citizen.

The element of contrast is present also in these sentences of Dr. Glenn Frank's: (1) "A stage-coach citizenship may prove the undoing of an express-train world." (2) "And whether it be noble or ignoble, religious or irreligious, the able young man of today is not interested in the exclusive task of 'labeling men and women for transportation to a realm unknown' and sedulously avoiding straightforward consideration of that reconstruction of human society which Jesus of Nazareth had in mind when he talked of the Kingdom of God coming on earth."

XI. *Use colorful phrases and figures of speech.*

Chapter IX contains 175 phrases and figures of speech which may be employed to give an address character and style. "Barkis is willin'," "Greeks bearing gifts," "a Jason's quest" are typical expressions which assist the speaker and writer to give more color to his ideas. A speaker who was describing the slow evolution of great ideas in industry, and in all fields of life, mentioned the gradual development of the automobile from the earliest models three decades ago to the streamlined cars of the present day. "It is apparent," he said, "that this great industry did not develop overnight. It did not spring Minerva-like from the head of Jove."

Dr. Will Durant, speaking on "What are the Lessons of History?," said, "So I should say that civilizations begin with religion and stoicism; they end with skepticism and unbelief, and the undisciplined pursuit of individual pleasure. A civilization is born stoic and dies epicurean." In that one last short sentence of only eight words, using two colorful words, "stoic" and "epicurean," Dr. Durant made a splendid summary of his viewpoint.

Comprehensive reading will be helpful in adding many figures of speech to your vocabulary. Those chosen for Chapter IX will make an excellent start.

Biblical quotations may be used not only in the introduction and in the conclusion of many speeches, but they may also be used vividly to express ideas in the body of speeches. It is not possible to use a Biblical quotation in every speech, but where it can be done to emphasize a point, it makes a distinctly worthwhile addition. The Bible is the richest source book of quotations in the world. The Presidents of the United States have often quoted from the Old and New Testaments to convey their messages to the people. A frequent study of the almost 300 Biblical quotations in Chapter X will bring gratifying returns in the ability to express your ideas well.

Illustrations

Dr. Glenn Frank, delivering a baccalaureate address on the subject, "If the Young Can But See"—

The dullard must wait for events to overtake him. He lacks the sensitive imagination and disciplined powers of analysis to enable him to anticipate and to discount events. He never knows that a policy is bad until it has worked havoc in his life or in the life of his time. He never knows that a policy is good until it has dropped the ripe fruits of its goodness in his lap. Thus he must go through life victimized by the tragic results of bad policies that wiser men would have forestalled and robbed of the benefits of good policies that more farseeing men would have brought into being. With all this, he may be technically a learned man, but, lacking insight and understanding, his learning becomes so much waste lumber.

Down the ages the capacity to anticipate and to discount bad ideas and the capacity to sense in advance and to appropriate good ideas, without waiting for events to indicate their badness or their goodness, has been considered the supreme achievement of man as a thinking animal.

When the Lord of Ancient Israel was searching for the most withering rebuke and the most devastating penalty he could lay upon a recreant people, he asked that they be robbed of the capacity to see and to understand.

"Make the heart of his people fat," he cried, "and make their ears heavy, and shut their eyes; lest they see with their eyes, and hear with their ears and understand with their heart, and be healed."

And from Isaiah to Bernard Shaw this belief that insight and understanding are the godlike gifts has held.

President John F. Kennedy used a Biblical quotation as follows in an address—

But neither can two great and powerful groups of nations take comfort from our present course—both sides overburdened by the cost of modern weapons, both rightly alarmed by the steady spread of the deadly atom, yet both racing to alter that uncertain balance of terror that stays the hand of mankind's final war.

So let us begin anew—remembering on both sides that civility is not a sign of weakness, and sincerity is always subject to proof. Let us never negotiate out of fear. But let us never fear to negotiate.

Let both sides explore what problems unite us instead of belaboring those problems which divide us.

Let both sides, for the first time, formulate serious and precise proposals for the inspection and control of arms—and bring the absolute power to destroy other nations under the absolute control of all nations.

Let both sides seek to invoke the wonders of science instead of its terrors. Together let us explore the stars, conquer the deserts, eradicate disease, tap the ocean depths and encourage the arts and commerce.

Let both sides unite to heed in all corners of the earth the command of Isaiah—to "undo the heavy burdens . . . [and] let the oppressed go free."

President Daniel L. Marsh of Boston University, addressing the National Council of Education—

I do not know of any finer expression of values, any better cataloguing of ideas to which our emotions might properly be attached, or any more adequate ideal as a stimulus to the will, than St. Paul gives in his letter to the Philippians: "Whatsoever things are true, whatsoever things are honorable, whatsoever things are just, whatsoever things are pure, whatsoever things are lovely, whatsoever things are of good report: if there be any virtue, and if there be any praise, think on these things."

That ideal is the touchstone of freedom. Examine your life and see if what I say is not true. "The unexamined life is not worthy of being lived by one who calls himself a man," said Socrates. "*Think* on these things," said Paul; take an inventory of these things, keep your mind upon them, set a value upon them; for thought precedes accomplishment. We grow like the things we think about. The good is positive, not negative.

XIII. *Use appropriate quotations from literature.*

Other than the Bible, perhaps the most frequently quoted sources are the writings of Shakespeare. Among the more than 1,100 quotations in Chapter XI, there are many from Shakespeare. The 1,100 quotations have been carefully selected from the world's great literature, from addresses and from other sources. In almost every speech you will be able to use one or more quotations. Choose them carefully and they are certain to give style to your address.

Illustrations

An educator addressing a Wisconsin High School commencement class on the great significance of decision in life said:

On the importance of decision we may say with James Russell Lowell:
. . . Once to every man and nation comes the moment to decide,
In the strife of Truth with Falsehood, for the good or evil side. . . .

John Haynes Holmes, speaking at Lehigh University on "Are We in the Hands of Fate?"—

There is no such thing as security any more. There is as little permanency in values as stability in institutions. For years, the preachers of religion have proclaimed "the deceitfulness of riches," and the emptiness of all merely material possession. Well, here they are—the prophecies come true! Now we know that the things of the spirit alone endure. In our time, as in times before, there has come the moment described by Prospero, in Shakespeare's play, *The Tempest*, when

> ". . . all which [we] inherit shall dissolve,
> And, like this insubstantial pageant faded,
> Leave not a rack behind."

XIV. *Use words, phrases, clauses, and sentences in groups of two or three occasionally.*

The use of words, phrases and sentences in groups of two or three gives rhythm and force to a speech. No attempt should be made to arrange these groups in every sentence or paragraph as it would lead to monotony. But most of us will not be guilty of the excessive use of this tool of speech.

Illustrations

In just three famous words, "Veni, vidi, vici," or, "I came, I saw, I conquered," Julius Caesar described his triumph over King Pharnaces of the Bosporus in 47 B.C. Those words, "having all the same cadence," said Plutarch, "carry with them a very suitable air of brevity" which brevity conforms to the swiftness and completeness of Caesar's victory. Cadence runs thought a close second in evoking the applause of an audience.

"Give me liberty, or give me death" was the expression of a great conviction. But it was even more. It was the brilliant expression of that conviction. Consider the sentence carefully. Two ideas are balanced on each side of the word "or." The ideas of liberty or death also are in contrast. Both clauses begin with the same words "give me," so that there is alliteration.

The eulogy delivered by General (Light Horse Harry) Henry Lee on the death of George Washington contains a famous phrase illustrating the grouping of three phrases. Lee said upon that historic occasion, "To the memory of the man, first in war, first in peace, and first in the hearts of his countrymen."

Franklin D. Roosevelt concluded an address with this climactic sentence:

And with that inner strength that comes to a free people conscious of their duty, conscious of the righteousness of what they do, they will— with divine help and guidance—stand their ground against this latest assault upon their democracy, their sovereignty and their freedom.

Observe the rhythm and the power in the last eight words.

The author used two or three words of phrases several times in the following remarks. Note particularly the quotation from Winston Churchill with the three ideas in Churchill's second sentence.

One night in August 1914, the members of the British Cabinet waited, hour after hour, as the deadline approached for the German reply to the British ultimatum. At last there fell upon their ears the deep boom of Big Ben, the great clock above the Parliament buildings, as it sounded the midnight hour. Then Lloyd George, his voice heavy with emotion, uttered the fateful words, "It's war."

Lloyd George said in his autobiography that the heavy boom of Big Ben sounded like doom to him through the stillness of that August night. Lloyd George was right. It was the doom of the world as we then knew it. By the end of the First World War, great empires began to totter. Communist revolutions erupted. Dictatorships sprang up. Currencies collapsed. Economic depression overtook the world. Then, unbelievably, came the second World War with its disastrous consequences, engulfing almost all of mankind. War recruits emotional energies as it seeks to justify its motives with subtle hypocrisies and flaming phrases promising a brave new world in the future. Then it proceeds ruthlessly to destroy what mankind has achieved in a slow and painful struggle upward through the centuries. Winston Churchill could say at the end of World War II, "What is Europe now? It is a rubbleheap, a charnel house, a breeding ground of pestilence and hate."

Those were dark and disillusioning days as men awakened from their war-time dreams and surveyed the dismal wreckage. There were few grounds for courage. And yet, as we now know, the raw materials of economic and social renewal were present in Western Europe, waiting only to be given the leadership which was in less than two decades to make this one of the great areas of strength in the world.

At the outset of World War II in 1939, Soviet Russia was the only country in the world controlled by communists. Then a relentless drift to socialism and communism began. Ten years later communism had swept over one-third of the world's population, one-fourth of the earth's surface and a number of nations.

A banker speaking before a state bankers' association said: "It would be gratifying if it were possible to suggest here a program of the banker's responsibility, so comprehensive in its plan, so complete in its parts, and so convincing in its presentation that it would challenge the thinking of this intelligent audience." This sentence not only illustrates the grouping of three phrases, but also the use of alliteration which follows in Point XV.

XV. *Alliteration.*

Webster's *New Collegiate Dictionary* defines alliteration as the "repetition of the same sound at the beginning of two or more consecutive words or of words near one another; specifically, recurrence of the same consonant sound or of vowel sounds initially in accented syllables of verse, as in 'In a somer seson when soft was the sonne.' (*Piers Plowman.*)"

Alliteration gives a speech sparkle because it adds harmony, swing and rhythm. It would become distinctly tiresome if used in every sentence, but employed occasionally in a speech it thrills an audience. The speaker who may hope that at least parts of his speeches will be quoted, or will live, will find (1) the arrangement of words, phrases, clauses, and sentences in groups of two or three, and (2) the use of alliteration to be two of the most effective speech tools to assist him.

Winston Churchill knew that alliteration fascinates an audience and makes speeches moving and forceful. He said, "We cannot *fail* or *falter.*" He commented of a certain person that he was "a man of *light* and *learning*"; in a great emergency he declared, "Let us to the task, to the battle and the toil."

Claude G. Bowers, distinguished American diplomat, talking to the Phi Beta Kappa chapter at Yale, said, "The American Democracy is mobilized today to wage a war of extermination against privilege and pillage. We prime our guns against bureaucracy and plutocracy." "Privilege and pillage," "bureaucracy and plutocracy" are ringing phrases because of the alliteration.

The late Dr. Glenn Frank was one of the greatest masters of alliteration America has ever known, as indicated by the following examples chosen at random from his speeches and writings:

"They say that when the acid test was applied, the prophet turned politician, and the realist was lost in the rhetorician."

"We are convicted of plain bankruptcy of political intelligence."

"It is better that we frankly take our latitude and longitude in relation to our war-time ideals than that we attempt the perilous practice of self-delusion."

"The mind and the mood of the masses is the soil of the policy."

"We place our foreign affairs in the hands . . . of men who bring to the politics of a planet the vision of a parish."

"The most perilous disease in the world is not leprosy, but lop-sidedness."

"The West may face ruin instead of renaissance."

"Shall we give our loyalty to leaders who will clarify our needs or to leaders who will cater to our desires."

"Facts are not concerned with flattery."

"He became the partisan and pamphleteer of Christianity."

"It is not the analyses of the classroom, but the actualities of the market-place."

"A nation's army is only the clenched fist of its factories and farms."

Alliteration enables one to give to a speech what Lynn Harold Hough called "the gracious loveliness of finely wrought phrases."

The Requirements of Public Speaking

How to Prepare Your Speech

I. Determine the exact subject so that it is entirely clear in your mind. If you have a hazy conception of the precise limitations of your topic, the audience naturally will be confused.

II. Think through the whole subject and formulate your own ideas and conclusions.

III. Read exhaustively all important speeches, pamphlets, and books on the subject with which you are not familiar. Take notes on significant points.

IV. Outline the subject as follows:
   A. Introduction.
   B. Body of the speech, subdivided generally into two, three, or four parts.
   C. Conclusion.

V. Write out the speech fully. Experienced speakers may find it possible simply to outline an address and speak from the outline, but writing a speech eliminates wordiness and gives exactness to expression.
   A. The introduction must be short. It may be developed in one of the following seven ways:
      1. Announce the subject directly in the first sentence or paragraph.

2. Tell a story of human interest, "paint a picture," or give an illustration.
3. Use a statement that excites attention, arouses curiosity, surprises the audience, or is particularly informative.
4. Tell a humorous story that is definitely related to the subject or to the situation under which you are addressing the audience.
5. Ask a challenging question.
6. State facts which show the importance of the subject to the welfare of the audience.
7. Begin by a significant quotation or idea from some other person.

B. The body is the substance of the speech. Fill it with facts and concrete illustrations, and not simply with generalities. The following ideas will be of assistance in writing this part of your speech.
1. Know the subject thoroughly.
2. Use facts, figures, and illustrations.
3. If the audience is to be convinced of some proposition, begin with subject matter with which there is agreement.
4. Do not argue, but explain.
5. State briefly and clearly either at the beginning of the body of the speech or one by one, as the main part of the address unfolds, the two, three, or four points to be discussed. To provide suspense, it is generally better to give the points, one by one, as the speech progresses.

C. The conclusion must ordinarily be short, and it is generally advisable to use it to re-emphasize the points developed in the body of a speech. The following seven methods may be used to conclude a speech:
1. Outline concisely the major points you have made in the body of the speech.
2. Use a quotation from the Bible or literature.
3. Bring the speech to a grand climax.
4. Compliment the audience or leave a note of encouragement or optimism.
5. Describe a dramatic scene, a great moment in his-

tory, science or business, or give a brief biographical story.

6. Ask the audience to take some form of action or to adopt a certain viewpoint on some matter.
7. Tell a humorous story or give a suitable witty comment.

How to Make Your Speech Sparkle

Rewrite and refine the speech until every unnecessary word is eliminated. The following fifteen effective speech tools will greatly assist you in the revision of your speech and will help to make it sparkle:

I. Insert suitable humorous stories, epigrams, and amusing definitions.
II. Use illustrations from biography, from plays, or from literature.
III. Repeat some words or phrases to stamp them indelibly upon the minds of the listeners.
IV. Intersperse short sentences with long ones.
V. Use a series of short, crisp sentences.
VI. Use similes occasionally.
VII. Avoid boresome repetition by the use of appropriate synonyms.
VIII. Use appropriate antonyms to create contrasts.
IX. Use questions.
X. Place ideas in contrast to each other.
XI. Use colorful phrases and figures of speech.
XII. Use suitable Biblical quotations.
XIII. Use appropriate quotations from literature.
XIV. Use words, phrases, clauses, and sentences in groups of two or three occasionally.
XV. Use alliteration.

When You Are Before the Audience

I. Open your mouth and speak distinctly and loudly enough to be heard by every person in the audience.
II. Don't worry about nervousness as you start speaking. It's a good sign. Almost every able speaker is nervous at the outset. It indicates he is "on edge" and ready. The time to worry is when you are not "keyed up" with nervous energy. If you have thoroughly prepared, you are the master of the situation.

III. Give your speech in one of the following ways:
   1. Read it if you must, but read it so well it sounds as if you were speaking without a manuscript.
   2. You may have your manuscript before you, but refer to it only occasionally. This requires reading the manuscript over and over until you are thoroughly familiar with it.
   3. Write out the address or outline it in detail. Then go over it repeatedly until you are entirely familiar with it. Speak only from notes.
   4. Write out the speech or outline it in detail. Then go over it repeatedly until you are completely familiar with it. Speak without notes.
   5. Write out the speech and memorize it. Be sure you speak naturally. Follow whichever method is best for you. Try gradually to eliminate reading as much as you can. Whatever you do read, must be read well, or you will lose your audience at once. All important state addresses necessarily must be read to avoid even the slightest misstatement.

IV. Should you gesture? You may, but your gestures must come naturally. You never learn gestures solely from a book of rules. The following simple suggestions may help you:
   1. Merely permit your hands to fall loosely to your sides. You may place your hands behind your back and even occasionally in your pockets if you wish.
   2. If you must twiddle your fingers, do it behind your back.
   3. Stand in one place, and do not pace up and down the platform like a caged lion. These nervous movements distract an audience.
   4. Do not point your forefinger at the audience as if you were scolding the neighbor's children.
   5. Generally avoid: repeated wide swings of the arms; numerous lightning-like movements of the forearms; and constant pounding on the table. Any frequently repeated gesture is tiresome.
   6. It is better to err on the side of too few gestures than too many.
   7. Above all, be natural.

V. Keep your speech within the limits of the time allotted to you.

What Public Speaking Requires

I. Sincere convictions earnestly expressed. You cannot convince others of what you do not believe.

II. Unquestioned knowledge of your subject. You cannot explain to others what you do not understand.

III. Painstaking preparation of every speech. You are deeply indebted to the audience for the privilege they have given you. A good speech is the best expression of your gratitude.

IV. Practice at home, but never before an audience.

SINCERITY, KNOWLEDGE, PREPARATION, and PRACTICE —these are the four great requirements of public speaking.

Humorous Stories*

1   *Just Any Time*

Hotels and motels were jammed in Newport, R. I., during the America's Cup yacht races, and the overcrowding bred confusion. Two White House reporters sharing a motel room left separate wakeup calls one night for 8 and 9 A.M. the next morning. This puzzled a greenhorn desk clerk. At 7 A.M. he rang the reporters' room and asked: "Which time do you want to be called—8 or 9?"

2   *A New One Each Year?*

Doctor: "Why do you have A-5906 tattooed on your back?"
Patient: "That's not tattooed. That's where my wife ran into me while I was opening the garage door."

3   *Practice*

A lady was entertaining the small son of a friend.
"Are you sure you can cut your own meat, Tommy?" she inquired.
"Oh, yes, thanks," answered the child politely. "I've often had it as tough as this at home."

* The numbers which appear in consecutive order at the left-hand margin beginning with Chapter IV refer to the index. The use of the index will make it possible to refer instantly to related ideas and source material throughout the book.

4 *And Then?*

The retiring usher was instructing his youthful successor in the details of his office. "And remember, my boy, that we have nothing but good, kind Christians in this church—until you try to put someone else in their pew."

5 *Progress*

"Good news, Jackson, starting next month your take-home pay will exceed your deductions!"

6 *There Are Times*

It's nice to see people with plenty of get-up-and-go, especially if some of them are visiting you.

7 *Cramped in His Style*

A speaker said that as he surveyed the breadth of his subject, he could not help but think of Bishop Jones who was invited to speak before a great convention. A telegram he received from the program committee read as follows: "We should like to have you address our convention on the subject, 'THE WORLD, THE WAR, AND THE CHURCH.' " He gave the matter some consideration and felt he would like to address the convention, but the magnitude of the subject bothered him considerably. So he wired them as follows: "Gentlemen, I should like to address your great convention. However, I should not like to be cramped in my style or restricted in my remarks by any such narrow subject as 'THE WORLD, THE WAR, AND THE CHURCH.' I should be glad to come if you will add to it, 'THE SUN, THE MOON, AND THE STARS.' " (A story when one is given a very broad subject to discuss.)

8 *Out the Window He Must Go*

There are audiences and audiences. Some rank high in the scale of intelligence (like this one), and have a peculiar ability to disconcert a speaker. Even those low in the scale of intelligence provide their embarrassing moments. Henry Brown had a great desire to become a public speaker and accepted every invitation that came his way. One day the superintendent of the state insane asylum asked him to speak to an assembly of the inmates. The day came for the speech; Brown had hardly begun when a fellow in the back of the room said, "Rotten." Brown was nervous, but continued. The inmate yelled "Rotten" still louder. Brown considered the nature of his audience and decided to give his speech one more whirl. He began all over, but the fellow yelled "Rotten" again so loudly that the whole audience was disturbed. Brown finally turned to the superintendent and said, "Steve, shall I go on, or shall I stop?" The superintendent said, "Henry, you go right ahead. We've had that fellow in here ten years, and this is the first time he ever showed any intelligence." (A speaker might add, "When a speaker can get in that position with an unintelligent audience, it is obvious that he faces real hazards in talking to an intelligent audience.")

9   *Worth Remembering*

We knew a man who thought he was overloaded in the "trouble department" until he found this memo on his desk: "Be thankful for the problems, for if they were less difficult, someone with less ability would have your job."

10   *Seldom Dines Well*

Husband: "I have no bad habits."
Friend: "Don't you even smoke?"
Husband: "Only in moderation. I like a cigar after a good dinner, but I don't suppose I smoke two cigars a month."

11   *Do It Over Right*

Farmer (to new hired hand): "Where's that mule I told you to take out and have shod?"
New Hand: "Did you say 'shod'? I thought you said 'shot.' I've just been buryin' her."

12   *Start Over*

Customer: "I haven't come to any ham in this sandwich yet."
Waiter: "Try another bite."
Customer (taking huge mouthful): "Nope, not yet."
Waiter: "Doggone it! You must have gone right past it."

13   *What?*

Teacher: "Now, Robert, what are you doing—learning something?"
Robert: "No sir; I'm listening to you."

14   *We All Work for Him*

Sign on Farmer's barn: "The Jones Farm. Uncle Sam, Operator."

15   *It Shrinks in the Heat*

"Is a ton of coal very much, Papa?"
"That depends, my son, on whether you are shoveling or buying it."

16   *This Is Discipline*

Mrs. Shopalot: "Can you alter this dress to fit me?"
Salesman: "Certainly not. That isn't done any more. You will have to be altered to fit the dress."

17   *A Wee Bit Too Pious*

A Scottish lady invited a gentleman to dinner on a particular day and he accepted with the reservation, "If I am spared."
"Weel, weel," replied she, "if ye're deid I'll no' expect ye."

18   *A Statistics Story*

I never listen to a speaker launch out on one of those long discussions, filled with statistics of all kinds, or commit the same error myself, but that I think of the professor in a western university who taught mathematics and statistics. One day he was standing, dressed in his bathing suit, at the edge of a swimming pool on the university campus when a beautiful coed accidentally dropped her camera into the deep end of the pool. She called to the elderly professor for help. He said he would be glad to dive down after the camera, but first wanted to know why she happened to choose him when there were so many young men within easy reach to do the job. She answered, "Professor, you have apparently forgotten me, but I am in your large statistics class. I have found that you can *go down deeper, stay down longer, and come up drier* than anyone I know."—I do not propose to go down too deep, stay down too long, or come up too dry with these statistics.

19   *Sometimes We All Do*

Said a frustrated young mother as she heard her children crying, and looked over her dirty house, "I sometimes wish I'd loved and lost."

20   *It Made a Difference*

Visitor: If your mother gave you two apples and told you to give one to your brother, would you give him the little one or the big one?
Johnny: Do you mean my little brother or my big one?

21   *Getting Out of a Bad Fix*

A businessman who had been through several years of depression decided he needed a vacation. When he discussed the matter with his wife, she said that she wanted to go along with him on a trip which he was planning to take around the world. He agreed, and then she added that she would like to take her mother along. He was not certain that he wished to take his mother-in-law along with him on a trip around the world for his health. They argued about it for a while; the argument finally was compromised—and the three of them went on the trip. One day when they were in Central Africa, halfway around the world, camping out in the open, they arose in the morning, and lo and behold! the mother-in-law was missing. They looked for her for several hours and finally found her standing in a cleared spot in a dense forest with a mountain lion ten feet away, roaring.

The wife cried: "John, John, what shall we do for mother?"

He looked the situation over carefully, meditated for a moment and said, "Mary, it looks to me as if the lion got himself into that fix. Let him get himself out the best way that he can." (A speaker might say, "Considering the controversial nature of this subject, I presume I ought to get myself out of this situation as quickly and with as little embarrassment as possible.")

22   You Put Him to Sleep

A man fell asleep in an audience. The speaker stopped and asked a young boy sitting beside the man to wake him up. The boy said, "Wake him up yourself—you put him to sleep." (Suitable if a speech is long.)

23   Seems Fair

The phone rang and the young mother answered. Came her mother's voice saying: "I phoned, dear, to find out if Dad and I could leave your children with Tom and you tonight. We are invited out for the evening."

24   Concise

A waitress came to the tired traveler who had just seated himself in a small-town restaurant. The menu was a very short one. The waitress said, "Will you have roast beef for dinner?" He said, "No." She said, "In that case dinner's over." (A good illustration of conciseness.)

25   Proud Father

Two parsons were having lunch at a farm during the progress of certain anniversary celebrations. The farmer's wife cooked a couple of chickens, saying that the family could dine on the remains after the visitors had gone. But the hungry parsons wolfed the chickens bare.

Later the farmer was conducting his guests round the farm, when an old rooster commenced to crow *ad lib.* "Seems mighty proud of himself," said one of the guests.

"No wonder," growled the farmer, "he's got two sons in the ministry."

26   *Visiting Card*

Sandy joined a golf club and was told by the professional that if his name was on his golf balls and they were lost, they would be returned to him when found.

"Good," said the Scot. "Put my name on this ball."

The pro did so.

"Would you also put M.D. after it?" said the new member. "I'm a doctor." The pro obeyed.

"There's just one more thing," went on the Scot. "Can ye squeeze 'Hours 10 to 3' on it as well?"

27   *Spelling*

"How is Hennery gettin' along with school, Eph?"

"Not so well, Garge. They're learnin' him to spell taters with a 'p'."

28   *Fair Enough*

An exasperated candidate was being heckled.

"There seem to be a great many fools here tonight," he exclaimed. "I wonder if it would be advisable to hear one at a time."

"That's fair enough," shouted a man in the audience. "Finish your speech."

29   *Who Wouldn't!*

A candidate for the police force was being verbally examined. "If you were by yourself in a police car and were pursued by a desperate gang of criminals in another car doing forty miles an hour along a lonely road, what would you do?" The candidate looked puzzled for a moment. Then he replied: "Fifty."

30   *No Leisure*

A farmer who went to a large city to see the sights engaged a room at a hotel and before retiring asked the clerk about the hours for meals.

"We have breakfast 7 to 11, dinner from 12 to 3, and supper from 6 to 8," explained the clerk.

"Look here," inquired the farmer in surprise, "What time am I going to see the town?"

31   *From Missouri*

"Aren't people funny?"

"Yes. If you tell a man that there are 270,678,934,341 stars in the universe, he'll believe you—but if a sign says 'Fresh Paint,' that same man has to make a personal investigation."

32   A Friend in Need

The midday whistle had blown when Murphy shouted, "Has anyone seen me vest?"

"Sure, Murphy," said Pat, "And ye've got it on."

"Right and I have," replied Murphy, gazing solemnly at his bosom, "and it's a good thing ye seen it or I'd have gone home without it."

33   Stumbling Block

Prisoner: "Judge, I don't know what to do."

Judge: "Why, how's that?"

Prisoner: "I swore to tell the truth, but every time I try some lawyer objects."

34   Good Aim

The big-game hunter took his wife on his newest safari. After several weeks they returned. The sportsman had bagged a few minor trophies, but the great prize was the head of a huge lion, killed by his wife.

"What did she hit it with?" asked a friend admiringly. "That fine rifle you gave her?"

"No," answered her husband, dryly. "With the station wagon we hired!"

35   Might Be Worse

"What do you think of our two candidates for mayor?"

"Well, I'm glad only one can be elected."

36   He Learned

A Chicago teacher received the following from one of her pupils:

Dear Miss Gorman:

I've ingoid having you for a teacher. Insted of forsing lerning, you inspiare it. You do not yell, you have pachines, and thats the way a teacher shood be. I think you are the best teacher in the hole school. I've lerned more in your room than in the hole school.

Your pupal,

Robert

37   Not Over-Demanding

Rexford: "I suppose you think I'm a perfect idiot?"

Roberts: "Oh, none of us is perfect."

38   No Laughing Matter

Draper: "These are especially strong shirts, madam. They simply laugh at the laundry."

Customer: "I know that kind; I had some which came back with their sides split."

39　Too Busy for Current Events

A traveler was marooned in a town because of a landslide caused by heavy rain, which was still falling in torrents after three days. Looking out of the window of the restaurant, he remarked to the waitress:

"This is like the flood."

"The what?"

"The flood. Surely you have heard about the great flood and Noah and the Ark."

"Mister," she replied, "I haven't seen a paper for four days."

40　Success

"How is your doctor son getting on in his practice?"

"Excellently—he has made enough money so he can occasionally tell a patient that there is nothing wrong with him."

41　Plenty

"What would I get," inquired the man who had just insured his property against fire, "if this building should burn down tonight?" "I would say," replied the insurance agent, "about ten years."

42　About Complete

"So you are building a new house, eh? How are you getting along with it?"

"Fine. I've got the roof and the mortgage on it, and I expect to have the furnace and the sheriff in before fall."

43　No Regrets

"I'm sorry—I quite forgot your party the other evening!"

"Oh, weren't you there?"

44　Familiar

Guide: "This castle has stood for six hundred years. Not a stone has been touched, nothing altered, nothing replaced."

Visitor: "Um, they must have the same landlord we have."

45　Chit-Chat

Officer (to driver who has been whipping his horse pulling a tourist surrey): "Don't whip him, man—talk to him."

Driver (to horse, by way of opening the conversation): "Ah comes from N'Awleans. Where does you-all come from?"

46 Diagnosis

The middle-aged man shuffled along, bent over at the waist, as his wife helped him into the doctor's waiting room. The doctor's nurse viewed the scene in sympathy. "Arthritis with complications?" she asked.

The wife shook her head. "Do-it-yourself," she explained, "with concrete blocks."

47 With a Speedy Recovery

Hewitt: "You don't seem to think much of him."

Jewell: "If he had his conscience taken out, it would be a minor operation."

48 On the Spot

Office Boy (nervously): "Please, sir, I think you're wanted on the 'phone."

Employer: "You think! What's the good of thinking?"

Office Boy: "Well, sir, the voice at the other end said, 'Hello, is that you, you old idiot?' "

49 A System

"Are you saving any money since you started your budget system?"

"Sure. By the time we have balanced it up every evening, it's too late to go anywhere."

50 He Made Sure

Many are the stories told about the care General Smedley D. Butler always took in looking after the welfare of the men in his command—especially as regarded their food. One relates that when he was in command of Camp Pontenazen, France, he met two soldiers carrying a large soup kettle from the kitchen.

"Here you," he ordered, "let me taste that."

"But, Gen——"

"Don't give me any buts—get a spoon!"

"Yes, sir!" the soldier replied, and running back in the kitchen, brought a spoon.

The General took the desired taste, and gingerly spat it out. "You don't call that stuff soup, do you?" he shouted. "No, sir!" replied the soldier. "That's what I was trying to tell you—it's dishwater, sir!"

51 Be Careful

Mikhail: "You look positively beautiful tonight."

Elsie: "Oh, you flatterer!"

Mikhail: "No, it's true. I had to look twice before I recognized you."

52   Educational

A young mother was looking at a toy for her small child. "Isn't this awfully complicated for him?" she asked the salesman.

"That, madam," replied the salesman, "is an educational toy, designed to prepare the child for life in today's world. Any way he puts it together is wrong."

53   Enthusiastic

Husband (after the theater): "But, dear, what did you object to?"

Wife: "Why, the idea of your bellowing 'Author! Author!' at a Shakespearean drama."

54   Slow Motion

A cameraman, working for the educational department of a film company, met an old farmer in town and said:

"I've just been taking some moving pictures of life out on your farm."

"Did you catch any of my men in motion?" asked the old farmer curiously.

"Sure I did."

The farmer shook his head reflectively, then commented: "Science is a wonderful thing."

55   He Will Fix It

"Waiter, I find that I have just enough money to pay for the dinner, but I have nothing in the way of a tip for yourself."

"Let me add up that bill again, sir."

56   Advantages of a Small Town

A traveling salesman visited a small town, and sold the proprietor of its general store an order of jewelry.

When the jewelry arrived it was not as represented, and the merchant returned it. But the wholesale house, nevertheless, attempted to collect the bill, and drew a sight draft on the merchant through the local bank, which returned the draft unhonored.

The wholesalers then wrote to the postmaster inquiring about the financial standing of the merchant, and the postmaster replied laconically that it was "O.K."

By return mail the wholesalers requested him to "hand the enclosed account to the leading lawyer of the place for collection."

This is the reply they received.

"The undersigned is the merchant on whom you attempted to palm off your worthless goods.

"The undersigned is the president and owner of the bank to which you sent your sight draft.

"The undersigned is the postmaster to whom you wrote, and the undersigned is the lawyer whose service you sought to obtain for your nefarious business.

"If the undersigned were not also pastor of the church at this place, he would tell you to go jump in the lake."

57   That's Too Vague

Heard in the subway: "How old should you say she is?"

"Oh, somewhere in the middle flirties!"

58   Handy

"Can you serve company?" asked the housewife when she was hiring the servant.

"Yes, mum; both ways."

"What do you mean?" asked the puzzled one.

"So's they'll come again, or stay away."

59   Heard at the Zoo

A huge elephant and a tiny mouse were in the same cage at the zoo. The elephant was in a particularly ugly and truculent mood. Looking down at the mouse with disgust he trumpeted, "You're the puniest, the weakest, the most insignificant thing I've ever seen!" "Well," piped the mouse in a plaintive squeak, "don't forget, I've been sick."

60   Exclusive

"Yes," said the boastful young man, "my family can trace its ancestry back to William the Conqueror."

"I suppose," remarked his friend, "you'll be telling us that your ancestors were in the Ark with Noah?"

"Certainly not," said the other. "My people had a boat of their own."

61   He Should Know

Professor (much annoyed by his students' interruptions): "The minute I get up to speak some fool begins to talk."

62   Still Green

Boss: "You are twenty minutes late again. Don't you know what time we start work at this factory?"

New employee: "No sir, they're always at it when I get here."

63 Staying Safe

In a small hotel in Kingston, Ontario, so a returning traveler reports, there is a yellowing sign tacked to the dingy wall behind the desk on which the proprietor proclaims his fixed inbred skepticism of all humanity. It reads: "No checks cashed. Not even good ones."

64 Preferred

"Your fiancé is a charming man. He has a certain something."
"Yes, but I would rather he had something certain."

65 Music

Daughter: "Did you ever hear anything so wonderful?" (as the radio ground out the latest music).
Father: "Can't say I have, although I once heard a collision between a truckload of milk cans and a car filled with ducks."

66 Insulted

"What do you mean," roared the politician, "by publicly insulting me in your old rag of a paper? I will not stand for it, and I demand an immediate apology."

"Just a moment," answered the editor. "Didn't the news item appear exactly as you gave it to us, namely, that you had resigned as city treasurer?"

"It did, but where did you put it?—in the column under the heading 'Public Improvements.'"

67 Hole-in-One

Then there was the sweet young thing who was being initiated into the mysteries of golf by her boy friend. "And now tell me," she said coyly, "which club do I use to make a hole-in-one?"

68 Still Advertising

A traveler seeking advertisements for a local paper called at the village grocer's. Upon presenting his card, he was surprised when the gray-haired proprietor said: "Nothing doing. Been established eighty years, and never advertised."

"Excuse me, sir, but what is that building on the hill?" asked the traveler.

"The village church," said the grocer.

"Been there long?" asked the other.

"About three hundred years."

"Well," was the reply, "they still ring the bell."

69 Statistics

Chief Instructor: "Now remember, men, statistics don't lie. Now, for an example, if twelve men could build a house in one day, one man could build the same house in twelve days. Do you understand what I mean? Jeep, give me an example."

Jeep: "You mean that if one boat could cross the ocean in six days, six boats could cross the ocean in one day."

70 It Is, Dear

"You know, dear, John doesn't seem to be as well dressed as he was when you married him."

"That's funny. I'm sure it's the same suit."

71 Believe in Signs

Teacher (to tardy student): "Why are you late?"
Bobby: "Well, a sign down here—"
Teacher: "Well, what has a sign got to do with it?"
Bobby: "The sign said: 'School ahead; go slow.'"

72 Was That Nice?

An author, in referring to his books, said: "They will be read long after Milton and Homer have been forgotten—" "And not till then," replied a listener.

73 A Dry Speaker

Everything that could be done to make the great unemployed meeting a success had been accomplished. A large hall and a good speaker had been engaged. When the latter arrived, he seemed to be in a crabby frame of mind. Looking around, he beckoned the chairman.

"I would like to have a glass of water on my table, if you please," he said.

"To drink?" was the chairman's idiotic question.

"Oh, no," was the sarcastic retort, "when I've been speaking a half-hour, I do a high dive."

74 From the Inside

"Look at that one—the one staring at us through the bars. Doesn't he look intelligent?"

"Yes. There is something uncanny about it."

"He looks as if he understood every word we're saying."

"Walks on his hind legs, too, and swings his arms."

"There! He's got a peanut. Let's see what he does with it."

"Well, what do you think about that! He knows enough to take the shell off before he eats it just like we do."

"That's a female alongside of him. Listen to her chatter at him. He doesn't seem to be paying much attention to her, though."

"She must be his mate."

"They look kind of sad, don't they?"

"Yes. I guess they wish they were in here with us monkeys."

75 Finished His Speech but Hasn't Stopped Talking

A man walked out of a hall where a speaker was addressing a meeting. Some one in the corridor asked him if the speaker had finished his speech. He said, "Yes, he finished his speech shortly after he started, but he hasn't stopped talking." (Suitable if a speech is long.)

76 If You Are Discouraged

If you are discouraged, compare your problems with those of the father who wrote this letter. Note particularly the last paragraph. The daughter wrote that she was coming home with her husband to live with father. Father wrote as follows:

"Dear Daughter:

I note from your letter that you are coming home with Wilfred and the children to live with us because Wilfred received an 'adjustment' in his salary, which was an insult to him. Wilfred, I assume, feels he cannot endure the insult.

As you know, your brother Frank came home with his wife about a month ago after his salary had been 'reconsidered.' Your sister Elsie, who had been a secretary to an officer of a corporation recently had to take a position as a stenographer. She resigned because she refused to be reduced to the level of a plain stenographer, so we are expecting her any day.

You ask about my own business. It is coming along fine. It was sold on the court house steps last Friday, but there were no bidders, so the sheriff let me keep it. That makes the best month I have had in recent years.

Your loving father"

77 Adaptation

In a physiology class the teacher said, "Johnnie, can you give a familiar example of the human body as it adapts itself to changed conditions?"

"Yes, ma'am," said Johnnie, "my aunt gained 50 pounds in a year, and her skin never cracked."

78 *Over the Line*

Wifey: "Don't you think, dear, that a man has more sense after he is married?"

Hubby: "Yes, but it's too late then."

79 *Subtle, Indeed*

Little Georgie received a new drum for Christmas, and shortly thereafter, when father came home from work one evening, mother said: "I don't think that man upstairs likes to hear Georgie play his drum, but he's certainly subtle about it."

Father: "Why?"

Mother: "Well, this afternoon he gave Georgie a knife, and asked him if he knew what was inside the drum."

80 *Good Hunting*

1st Hunter: "Hey, Bill."

2nd Hunter: "Yeah."

1st Hunter: "Are you all right?"

2nd Hunter: "Yeah."

1st Hunter: "Then I've shot a bear."

81 *Self-Made Man*

A youngster stood gazing intently at his father's visitor, a homely man of large proportions. At length the portly one becoming a bit embarrassed, said: "Well, my boy, what are you looking at me for?"

"Why," replied the boy, "Daddy told Mother that you were a self-made man, and I want to see what you look like."

"Quite right," said the gratified guest. "I am a self-made man."

"But what did you make yourself like that for?" asked the boy, with considerable surprise.

82 *The Good Old Way*

Judge: "Couldn't this case have been settled out of court?"

Defendant: "Yer honor, shure an' that is exactly what we wuz thryin' to do whin a couple av police butted in."

83 *When Uncertain*

The kind of alertness that makes wit possible is shown in Lincoln's case, who, as a captain in the Mexican War, led his company to a fence but did not know what order to give to get them over.

"Halt," said he, "the company will disband and meet on the other side of the fence."

84   Full Information

He: "If you'll give me your telephone number, I'll call you up some time."

She: "It's in the book."

He: "Fine! And what's your name?"

She: "That's in the book, too!"

85   Putting on the Ritz

The newly rich woman was trying to make an impression: "I clean my diamonds with ammonia, my rubies with wine, my emeralds with brandy, and my sapphires with fresh milk."

"I don't clean mine," said the quiet woman sitting next to her. "When mine get dirty, I just throw them away."

86   Daddy

Officer (to man pacing sidewalk at three o'clock in the morning): "What are you doing here?"

Gentleman: "I forgot my key, officer, and I'm waiting for my children to come home and let me in."

87   Likely

Mother (to son wandering around the room): "What are you looking for?"

Son: "Nothing."

Mother: "You'll find it in the box where the candy was."

88   Queer Names

Englishman: "Odd names your towns have. Hoboken, Weehawken, Oshkosh, Poughkeepsie."

American: "I suppose they do sound queer to English ears. Do you live in London all of the time?"

Englishman: "No indeed. I spend part of my time at Chipping Norton, and divide the rest between Bigglewade and Leighton Buzzard."

89   Full Stop

The genius of a local man had carried him to big success in business without much aid of education.

He was asked to distribute the prizes at a school, and made the usual speech of good counsel.

"Now, boys," he said, "Always remember that education is a great thing. There's nothing like education. Take arithmetic. Through education we learn that twice two make four, that twice six makes twelve, that seven sevens make—and then there's geography."

90   A Letter to Teacher

Dear Teacher: Kindly excuse Joe's absence yesterday, as he fell into the mud on his way to school. By doing the same you will oblige

Mrs. Henry Jones

91   Practically None

Albert: "What's the difference between a drama and a melodrama?"
Bernard: "Well in a drama the heroine merely throws the villain over. In a melodrama, she throws him over the cliff!"

92   Model?

Wife: "My husband has no bad habits whatsoever. He never drinks, and he spends all his evenings at home. Why he doesn't even belong to a club."
Friend: "Does he smoke?"
Wife: "Not very often. He likes a cigar after he has had a good dinner, but I can't recall the last time he smoked."

93   Misunderstanding

Salesman: "Sonny, is your mother at home?"
Small Boy: "Yes, sir."
Salesman (after knocking in vain): "I thought you said she was at home?"
Small Boy: "Yes, sir, but I don't live here."

94   His Example

Teacher: "Can you give me a good example of how heat expands things and cold contracts them?"
Pupil: "Well the days are much longer in the summer."

95   Difficulties

Joe: "What's become of the Hikers' Club?"
Jim: "Oh, it disbanded. It was getting too hard to persuade passing motorists to pick us up and give us a lift."

96   Repartee

Edward Everett and Judge Story were at a public dinner, during which Story proposed this sentiment: "Genius is sure to be recognized where Everett goes."
Everett promptly responded with the sentiment: "Equity and jurisprudence—no efforts can raise them beyond one Story."

97   Point Scored

Waiters, of course, are not in a position to snap back at ill-bred guests; but one English head waiter once made the perfect retort to an uncouth customer:

"My position, sir," he said, "does not allow me to argue with you; but if it ever came to a choice of weapons, I would choose grammar."

98   Appeal to Reason

Answer received by the credit department of a Chicago firm:

"I don't expect to beat you out of any money. But I am going to say one thing I am not working so I don't make anything and until I go to work I can't pay you anything so keep your shirt on and as soon as I start to work I will send some money. But if you don't keep it on, well just take it off and hold it until after Christmas."

99   Pilot

Smith: "My wife asked me to take our old cat off somewhere and lose it. So I put it in a basket and tramped out into the country for about eight miles."

Jones: "Did you lose the cat?"

Smith: "Lose it! If I hadn't followed it, I'd never have got back home."

100   Enterprise

"Almost every man can find work if he uses his brains," asserted the man who had traveled a good deal. "That is, if he has the ability to adapt himself like the piano-tuner I once met in the Far West.

"We were in a wild, unsettled country, and I said to him, 'Surely piano-tuning can't be very lucrative here. I should not imagine that pianos were very plentiful in this region.'

'No, they're not,' said the piano-tuner, 'but I make a pretty fair income by tightening up barbed-wire fences.' "

101   Understandable

"What is your kitty's name, Jimmy?" asked the woman.

"Ben Hur," answered Jimmy.

"That's a funny name for a cat. Why did you name it that?"

"Well, we just called him Ben until he had kittens."

102   Problem

Father: "Isn't it wonderful how little chicks get out of their shells?"
Son: "What get's me is how they get in."

103   Too Big to Cry

When Douglas defeated Lincoln in the Illinois senatorial contest, some asked him how he felt. Said he: "I feel like the boy who stubbed his toe, he was too big to cry and it hurt too darned much to laugh."

104   Hm-m

"Weak eyes have you? Well how many lines can you read on that chart?"
"What chart?"

105   Naturally

Usher: "How far down do you wish to sit, sir?"
Patron: "All the way, of course."

106   No Mystery

Jones: "How do you spend your income?"
Smith: "About 30 per cent for shelter, 30 per cent for clothing, 40 per cent for food, and 20 per cent for amusement."
Jones: "But that adds up to 120 per cent."
Smith: "That's right."

107   Futile

Teacher Tourist: "This seems to be a very dangerous precipice. It's a wonder they don't put up a warning sign."
Native: "Yes, it is dangerous, but they kept a warning sign up for two years and no one fell over, so it was taken down."

108   Match

Mike: "That's a queer pair of stockings you have on, Pat—one red and the other green."
Pat: "Yes, and I've got another pair like it at home."

109   Called

The teacher was testing the knowledge of the kindergarten class. Slapping a half-dollar on the desk, she asked sharply, "What is that?" Instantly a voice from the back row said, "Tails!"

110   A Good Reason

A youngster was being chided for his low grades. As an alibi he said, "Well all of the boys at school got C's and D's, too."

"All of them?" he was cross-questioned. "How about little Johnny Jones, who lives down the street?"

"Oh, he got high grades," the youngster admitted. "But you see, he's different. He has two bright parents."

111   Predicament

Q. "My lawn is full of weeds. I have tried weed-killer and digging them up, but they return. What should I do?"

A. "You must just learn to love them."

112   Alibi

This repartee took place between two rabid Californians during a heavy rainstorm in Los Angeles. Both watched the downpour with embarrassed expressions. . . . Finally, after a deep silence, one said to the other: "Boy, some terrible weather certainly blows in from Nevada, doesn't it?"

113   Whiskers

Ernie: "My uncle can play the piano by ear."

Gurney: "That's nothing. My uncle fiddles with his whiskers."

114   Polite

A New York traffic expert says that the London drivers and chauffeurs enliven many occasions by their wit and sarcasm. One London driver drew up when he saw a pedestrian directly in his way, leaned over, and very politely inquired:

"I say, sir, may I ask what are your plans?"

115   Strategy

Officer: "Now tell me, what is your idea of strategy?"

Rookie: "It's when you're out of ammunition, but keep right on firing."

116   Rest in Peace

A party of sailors were being shown over the cathedral by a guide.

"Behind the altar," he told them, "lies Richard the Second. In the churchyard outside lies Mary Queen of Scots; also Henry the Eighth. And who," he demanded, halting above an unmarked flagstone, "who do you think is a-lying 'ere?"

"Well," answered a salt, "I don't know for sure, but I have my suspicions."

117   Sunday

Of all the days that's in the week,
I dearly love but one day,

> And that's the day that comes betwixt
> A Saturday and Monday.—*Henry Carey*

118 *Acid Tongue*

Chemistry Professor: "Jones, what does HNO_3 signify?"

Cadet Jones: "Well, ah, er'r—I've got it right on the tip of my tongue, sir."

Chemistry Professor: "Well, you'd better spit it out. It's nitric acid."

119 *Too Restless*

Angler: "You've been watching me for three hours. Why don't you try fishing yourself?"

Onlooker: "I ain't got the patience."

120 *That's Different*

"You didn't take a vacation this year, did you?"

"No, I thought I needed a rest."

121 *Delay*

"A nice sort of welcome!" said the father visiting his son at a boarding school. "I am hardly out of the train when you ask me for money."

"Well, Dad, you must admit the train was twenty minutes late."

122 *Doctor's Prescription*

"Your doctor's out here with a flat tire."

"Diagnose the case as flatulency of the perimeter and charge him accordingly," ordered the garage man. "That's the way he does."

123 *Salesmanship*

A fruit dealer in Georgia has a sign above his wares that reads:

Watermelons

Our choice .... 25 cents

Your choice .... 35 cents

124 *Was That Nice?*

The family had overslept, and the lady of the house awoke with a start to the clanking of cans down the street. She remembered that the garbage had not been put out, so she raced down to the front door, struggled into her robe, hair in curlers, and looking sleepy-eyed, yelled, "Yoo-hoo! Am I too late for the garbage?"

Replied the accommodating collector, "No, ma'am, jump right in."

125 Ambition

I want to be an author,
My hand up to my face;
A thought upon my forehead,
An air of studied grace!
I want to be an author,
With genius on my brow;
I want to be an author,
And I want to be it now!—*Ella Hutchison Ellwanger*

126 Hard Question

Visitor: "How old are you, sonny?"

Boston Boy: "That's hard to say, sir. According to my latest school tests, I have a psychological age of 11 and a moral age of 10. Anatomically, I'm 7; mentally I'm 9. But I suppose you refer to my chronological age. That's 8—but nobody pays any attention to that nowadays."

127 Not Wholly Dumb

"Don't they teach you to salute in your company?" roared the major to Patrick Malone, who had passed him without raising his hand.

"Yes, sir," replied Pat.

"Then why didn't you salute?"

"Well, sir," was the candid reply, "I didn't want to attract more attention than I had to, 'cause I ain't supposed to be out here without a pass."

128 Generosity

Marine: "Say, pal, will you loan me a dime. I want to call a friend."

Sailor: "Here's a quarter, call all your friends."

129 Lucky

"Mr. Chairman," complained the speaker, "I have been on my feet for nearly ten minutes, but there is so much interruption I can hardly hear myself speak."

"Cheer up, my friend," came a voice from the rear, "you are not missin' much."

130 Experienced Party Goer

"Your friend Joe seemed to be the life of the party."

"Yes, he was the only one who could talk louder than the TV."

131 Bigoted

"How do you like your new boss, Mayme?"

"Oh, he ain't so bad, Lil, only he's kinda bigoted."

"Whadda y'mean, bigoted?"
"Well, he thinks words can only be spelled one way."

132   Silencer

Betty: "Your new overcoat is pretty loud, isn't it?"
Billy: "Yeah, but I'm gonna buy a muffler to go with it."

133   Snobbery

Snobbery is the pride of those who are not sure of their position.

134   His Turn

A club of eccentric young men had for one of their rules that on Tuesday evenings any man who asked in the clubroom a question which he was unable to answer himself should pay a fine of one dollar. One evening Tomkinson asked: "Why doesn't a ground squirrel leave any dirt around the top of his hole when he digs it?"

After some deliberation he was called upon to answer his own question.

"That's easy," he said. "The squirrel starts at the bottom and digs up."

"All very nice," suggested a member, "but how does it get to the bottom?"

"That's your question," answered Tomkinson.

135   Stretching the Point

A railroad agent in Africa had been "bawled out" for doing things without orders from headquarters. One day his boss received the following startling telegram:

"Tiger on platform eating conductor. Wire instructions."

136   Efficiency

A retailer, on receiving the first delivery of a large order, was annoyed to find the goods not up to sample. "Cancel my order immediately," he wired the manufacturer.

They replied: "Regret cannot cancel immediately. You must take your turn."

137   One That Was Too Fast for Him

A Frenchman was relating his experience in studying the English language. He said: "When I first discovered that if I was quick, I was fast; that if I was tied, I was fast; if I spent too freely, I was fast; and that not to eat was to fast, I was discouraged. But when I came across the sentence, 'The first one won one dollar prize,' I gave up trying."

138   *Variety*

"What are you raising in your garden this year?"

"Johnson's Plymouth Rocks, Brown's Leghorns, and Smith's Wyandottes."

139   *Viewpoint*

> Well, whiles I am a beggar I will rail
> And say, there is no sin but to be rich;
> And being rich, my virtue then shall be
> To say, there is no vice but beggary.—*Shakespeare*

140   *Only When Necessary*

Preacher: "Do you say your prayers at night, little boy?"

Jimmy: "Yes, sir."

Preacher: "And do you always say them in the morning, too?"

Jimmy: "No, sir. I ain't scared in the daytime."

141   *Accounting*

A man doing a hauling job was told that he couldn't get his money until he submitted a statement. After much meditation he evolved the following bill:

"Three comes and three goes, at four bits a went, $3."

142   *Smart Youngster*

A young school teacher was telling a small boy about a lamb that had strayed from the flock and had been eaten by a wolf.

"You see, Billy," she said, "had the lamb been obedient and stayed in the flock, it would not have been eaten by the wolf, would it?"

"No," the youngster answered quickly. "It would have been eaten by us."

143   *Welcome Relief*

Little Mary: "Mother, they are going to teach us domestic silence at school now."

Mother: "Don't you mean domestic science?"

Father: "There is a bare hope our little girl means what she is saying."

144   *Strange*

Little Bobby was sitting with his mother in church during the wedding of her eldest daughter. Halfway through the service, he observed his mother crying.

"Why are you crying, Mama?" he asked. "It's not your wedding."

145   Nature Story

A tourist traveling through the Texas Panhandle got into conversation with an old settler and his son at a filling station.

"Looks as though we might have rain," said the tourist.

"Well, I hope so," replied the native, "not so much for myself as for my boy here. I've seen it rain."

146   Was He?

"Father," said a little boy, "had Solomon seven hundred wives?"

"I believe so, my son," said the father.

"Well, Father, was he the man who said, 'Give me liberty or give me death?' "

147   Legitimate Objection

The teacher was trying to impress upon her class the advantages of peace and disarmament. "How many of you boys object to war?" she asked. Up went several hands.

"Jimmy, will you tell the class why you object to war?"

" 'Cause wars make history," replied Jimmy soberly.

148   Willing to Reciprocate

Professor: "Er—my dear, what's the meaning of this vase of flowers on the table today?"

Wife: "Meaning? Why, today is your wedding anniversary."

Professor: "Indeed! Well, well, do let me know when yours is so I may do the same for you."

149   The Egotist

Him: "I dreamed I was married to the most beautiful girl in the world."

Her: "Were we happy?"

150   Appropriate

John D. Rockefeller, Jr., once asked a clergyman to give him an appropriate Bible verse on which to base an address he was to make at the latter's church.

"I was thinking," said Rockefeller, "that I would take the verse from the Twenty-third Psalm: 'The Lord is my shepherd.' Would that seem appropriate?"

"Quite," said the clergyman. "But do you really want an appropriate verse?"

"I certainly do," was the reply.

"Well, then," said the clergyman, with a twinkle in his eye, "I would select the verse in the same Psalm: 'Thou anointest my head with oil; my cup runneth over.' "

151   Correct

Teacher: "Johnny, can you tell me the name of an animal that travels great distances?"

Johnny: "Yes, a goldfish. It travels around the globe."

152   In Reverse

Little Dickie, aged six, seized with hiccoughs, ran to his mother and said, "Oh, Mother, I believe I'm coughing backwards."

153   Flavor for Bath

The little grandson, who had been using toilet water in his bath, called to his mother, saying, "Mother, where is the bath flavoring?"

154   A Vote of Thanks

An elderly maiden aunt received this note from her ten-year-old niece: "Dear Aunt: Thank you for your nice present. I have always wanted a pin cushion, but not very much."

155   Harder Than a Diamond

Dorothy (admiring her engagement ring): "There's nothing in the world harder than a diamond, is there?"

Howard: "Yes, sweetheart—keeping up the installment payments on it."

156   Why He Couldn't Do It

My five-year-old son and I made an agreement. He was to make his little bed while I made the large bed. After I had finished straightening my bedroom I went into his room to see how he was getting along. He was struggling violently to get a clean pillow slip over a large feather pillow.

"Here, son, this is the way to do that," I said, and taking one end of the pillow firmly in my teeth, slipped the cover on.

"Oh! Mother," he cried, "I know! I was biting on the wrong end!"

157   Success

Customer: "To what do you owe your extraordinary success as a house-to-house salesman?"

Salesman: "To the first five words I utter when a woman opens the door—'Miss, is your mother in?' "

158   *Man's Wants*

"Man wants but little here below
Nor wants that little long,"
'Tis not with me exactly so;
But 'tis so in the song.
My wants are many, and, if told,
Would muster many a score;
And were each wish a mint of gold,
I still should long for more.—*John Quincy Adams*

159   *Passing Fancy*

The Boss: "On your way to Smith and Sons you will pass a football ground."
Office Boy (hopefully): "Yes, sir!"
The Boss: "Well, pass it!"

160   *Embarrassing for Train*

Junior was visiting his grandmother who lived near the railroad yards in a small town. Noticing a train switching back and forth, he exclaimed, "Mother, the train can't find anywhere to park."

161   *A Warning*

Teacher: "Yes, Johnny, what is it?"
Johnny: "I don't want to scare you, but Papa said if I didn't get better grades someone is due for a licking."

162   *It Certainly Does*

One senator to another: "You spend a billion here, a billion there, and the first thing you know it all adds up."

163   *A Martyr to Her Faith*

"Marie," observed Muriel, "has suffered much for her belief."
"Indeed?" asked Millicent, lifting her eyebrows in polite curiosity. "What is her belief?"
"That she can wear a number four shoe on a number six foot."

164   *Modern Marriage*

Mr. Newlywed: "Darling, did you sew the button on my coat?"
Mrs. Newlywed: "No, sweetheart, I couldn't find a button, but it's all right now. I sewed up the buttonhole."

165　Silence

Ball: "What is silence?"

Hall: "The college yell of the school of experience."

166　One Year Later

"Oh, George, do you realize it's almost a year since our honeymoon, and that glorious day we spent on the sands? I wonder how we'll spend this one?"

"On the rocks."

167　Not Yet Out of Danger

"How's your wife coming along with her driving?"

"She took a turn for the worse last week."

168　A Shining Face

"The new patient in Ward B is very good looking," said the nurse.

"Yes," agreed the matron, "but don't wash his face. He's had that done by four nurses this morning."

169　Reason for Being Present

Teacher: "How is it you cannot answer any of my questions?"

Pupil: "Well, if I could, what would be the use of my coming here?"

170　A Long Way to Go

Weary Willie's financial position was very shaky, and when he met a kind old lady in the park he decided to tell her his story.

"Yes, Ma'am," he said, "I've asked for money, and begged for money, and cried for money."

"Have you ever thought of working for it, my man?" she asked.

"No, not yet, ma'am," said Willie. "You see, it's like this, I'm going through the alphabet, and I ain't got to 'W' yet."

171　He Should Know

Prospective Bridegroom (gaily): "Will it take much to feather a nest?"

Furniture Dealer: "Oh, no; only a little down."

172　Is This Routine

First Doctor: "I operated on him for appendicitis."

Second Doctor: "What was the matter with him?"

173　Safety First

A woman motorist was driving along a country road when she noticed a couple of repairmen climbing telephone poles.

"Fools!" she exclaimed to her companion, "they must think I never drove a car before."

174   Night Life

"My isn't a night club a great place on a rainy night?"
"You said it! Stay outside and get wet and come in and get soaked."

175   Dry Country

The mayor of a tough border town was about to engage a preacher for the new church.
"Parson, you aren't by any chance a Baptist, are you?"
"No. Why?"
"Well, I was just going to say that we have to haul our water twelve miles."

176   Cold

Arctic Explorer: "It was so cold where we were that the candle froze and we couldn't blow it out."
Second Explorer: "That's nothing. Where we were the words came out of our mouths in pieces of ice, and we had to fry them to see what we were talking about."

177   Wasted Effort

Professor (finishing long algebra problem): "And so we find X equals zero."
Sophomore: "All that work for nothing."

178   Blended Coffee

"What kind of coffee do you serve here?" asked the diner. "It's terrible."
"That's good blended coffee," defended the waiter, "last week's and this week's."

179   'Tain't Fair

Life isn't fair to us men. When we are born, our mothers get the compliments and the flowers. When we are married, our brides get the presents and the publicity. When we die, our widows get the life insurance and the winters in Florida.

180   Cold

"The cold in the Arctic was so intense that we couldn't pat our dogs."
"Why not?"
"Their tails were frozen so stiff that they broke off if they wagged them."

181   Jujitsu

"Did I ever tell you how I tried my jujitsu on a burglar?"
"No."
"Well, I got hold of his leg and twisted it over his shoulder. Then I got hold of his arm and twisted it round his neck, and before he knew where he was I was flat on my back."

182   Wrong Number

Irate subscriber to operator: "Am I crazy or are you?"
Operator: "I am sorry, but we do not have that information."

183   Independence

Wifey: "Oh, Bill, baby can walk."
Hubby: "That's fine. Now he can walk up and down at night by himself."

184   Squall or Squeal

Young Father: "In your sermon this morning you spoke about a baby being a new wave on the ocean of life."
Minister: "That's right. Do you think a fresh squall would have been nearer the truth?"

185   Make it Snappy

A fellow rushed into a barbershop.
"Cut everything short," he said. "Hair, whiskers, and conversation."

186   Etiquette

The district engineer and his wife were entertaining at dinner. Suddenly a child's voice was heard from the floor above. "Mother." "What is it Archie?" she asked. "There's only clean towels in the bathroom. Shall I start one?"

187   Spendthrift

Tramp: "Lady, I'm almost famished."
Housewife: "Here's a nickel. But how did you fall so low?"
Tramp: "I had your fault. I was too extravagant."

188   Commence

A coach was teaching some cowboys how to play football. He explained the rules and ended as follows:
"Remember, fellows, if you can't kick the ball, kick a man on the other side. Now let's get busy. Where's the ball?"

One of the cowboys shouted: "T'heck with the ball! Let's start the game!"

189 Pretty Fix

Woman Driver: "Can you fix this fender so my husband will never know I bent it?"

Garage Mechanic: "No, but I can fix it so that you can ask him in a few days how he bent it."

190 Matrimonially Inclined

Doris: "When is your sister thinking of getting married?"
Tom: "Constantly."

191 Cramped

"That fellow must live in a very small flat."
"How can you tell?"
"Why, haven't you noticed that his dog wags his tail up and down, instead of sideways?"

192 Epitaph

"Here Lies an Atheist; All Dressed Up and No Place to Go."

193 Coincidence

"So he is a reckless driver?"
"Say, when the road turns the same way as he does, it's just a coincidence."

194 Thoughtful

Freshman: "Say, what's the idea of wearing my raincoat?"
Roommate: "Well you wouldn't want your new suit to get wet, would you?"

195 Substitute

"Tommy, what is a synonym?" the teacher asked.
"A synonym," said Tommy, wisely, "is a word you use when you can't spell the other one."

196 Living on Their Income

Householder (to prospective maid): "Why did you leave your last place?"
Maid: "Oh, it was so dull. They were trying to live on their income."

197   Wasted Effort

"Ah," sighed the serious-faced passenger, "how little we know of the future and what it has in store for us."

"That's true," responded the other.

"Little did I think when some thirty years ago I carved my initials on the desk in the old country school that I would some day grow up and fail to become famous."

198   His Saving Grace

Doctor (after examining patient): "I don't like the looks of your husband, Mrs. Brown."

Mrs. Brown: "Neither do I, Doctor, but he's good to our children."

199   Sez You

"The piano is hard hit by the radio," says a dealer. And by the little girl next door.

200   Tsch! Tsch!

Mrs. Knicker: "We are told one-third of the nation is ill-housed, ill-nourished, and ill-clad."

Mr. Knicker: "I didn't realize so many go away for the summer."

201   Slightly Scrambled

Another audition in the family of Mr. and Mrs. Jed Draper occurred Friday night, this time a bouncing boy.—*Martinez (Cal.) Citizen*

The bride is a member of Coulton's social set, a member of the Junior League, and a skillet musician.—*Coulton (Ore.) Advocate*

202   In Hunting Season

"Sorry, sir, but I'm all out of wild ducks. I could let you have a fine end of ham."

"Don't kid me. How could I go home and say I shot an end of ham?"

203   Correct

Here's to the man who is wisest and best.
Here's to the man who with judgment is blest.
Here's to the man who's as smart as can be—
I mean the man who agrees with me.

204   Two of a Kind

Mr. Nagg: "Those newlyweds are pretty well matched, aren't they?"
Mrs. Nagg: "Yeah, she's a grass widow and he's a vegetarian."

205   A Howling Success

Oletimer: "Is your married life one grand sweet song?"

Newlywed: "Well, since our baby's been born it's more like an opera, full of grand marches, with loud calls for the author every night."

206   Transport Has Changed

"If witches came back they'd flourish in some parts of the country as much as they ever did," says a writer. "But they'd find it a little awkward getting about on a vacuum cleaner, wouldn't they?"

207   Trees

I think that I shall never see along the road an unscraped tree, with bark intact, and painted white, that no car ever hit at night. For every tree that's near the road has caused some auto to be towed.

Sideswiping trees is done a lot by drivers who are plumb half shot. God gave them eyes so they might see, yet any fool can hit a tree.

208   Considerate

Soph: "But I don't think I deserve a zero."

Prof: "Neither do I, but it's the lowest mark I'm allowed to give."

209   Can't Fire the Cook

Woman: "Does your husband kick about the meals?"

Other Bridge Player (smiling): "No, what he kicks about is having to get them."

210   Stepping on It

Employer: "Do you believe in love at first sight, Miss Vamper?"

Stenographer: "Well, I think it saves a lot of time."

211   Try a Sextant

Golfer (far off in the rough): "Say, caddy, who do you keep looking at your watch?"

Caddy: "It isn't a watch, sir; it's a compass."

212   Permanent Guest

A little Logan Heights girl said there was a new baby at her house. "Has the baby come to stay?" she was asked.

"I think so," she said, "he's taken all his things off."

213 Both Ends Against the Middle

Two men who had been bachelor cronies met for the first time in five years.

"Tell me, Tom," said one, "did you marry that girl, or do you still darn your own socks and do your cooking?"

"Yes," was Tom's reply.

214 She Knew Her Menfolk

A recent speaker before a woman's organization, talking on Iran, was telling about how careless the men over there are with their wives, and said it was no uncommon sight to see a woman and a donkey hitched up together. Then he laughed, and said when he made that statement in a speech at Detroit one of the ladies in the audience piped up:

"That's not so unusual—you often see it over here, too."

215 One on the Button

Mr. Grouch: "Woman is nothing but a rag, a bone, and a hank of hair."

Mrs. Grouch: "Man is nothing but a brag, a groan, and a tank of air."

216 A Diplomat

Judge O'Flaherty: "Haven't you been before me before?"

Prisoner: "No, yer honor. Oi never saw but one face that looked loike yours and that was a photygraf of an Irish king."

Judge O'Flaherty: "Discharged! Call the next case!"

217 This Modern Age

"Why, what are you crying so for, sonny?" asked Dad of his four-year-old heir.

"I heard you say you were going to get a new baby and I suppose that means you'll trade me in on it," he sobbed.

218 Like a Cricket in a Cabbage

"When a man is asleep, he's a mere vegetable," says a scientific writer. "He is, however, not edible—only audible."

219 Cashing in on a Correspondence Course

My friend laughed when I spoke to the waiter in French, but the laugh was on him. I told the waiter to give him the check.

220 That Silver Lining

Jean: "So you mortgaged our little home."

Joe: "Just temporarily, honey, until the mortgage is foreclosed."

221 Costly Delusion

"My wife had a dream last night and thought she was married to a millionaire."

"You're lucky! My wife thinks that in the daytime."

222 Safety First

Diner: "Waiter, this soup is cold. Bring me some that's hot."

Waiter: "What do you want me to do? Burn my thumb?"

223 Alger Heroes Are Extinct

Gruff father to son: "Why don't you get out and find a job? When I was your age I was working for $3 a week in a store, and at the end of five years I owned the store."

Son: "You can't do that nowadays. They have cash registers."

224 Minus a Mind

Wife: "I can't decide whether to go to a palmist or to a mind-reader."

Husband: "Go to a palmist. It's obvious that you have a palm."

225 Couldn't Miss Him

"Waiter, have you forgotten me?"

"Oh, no, sir, you are the ham."

226 Call a Plumber

City Boy: "Say, Dad, how many kinds of milk are there?"

Father: "Well, there's evaporated milk, buttermilk, malted milk, and—but why do you wish to know?"

City Boy: "Oh, I'm drawing a picture of a cow and I want to know how many spigots to put on her."

227 Just in Time

A German shoe repairman left the gas turned on in his little shop one night and upon arriving in the morning struck a match to light it.

There was a terrific explosion, and the German was blown out through the door.

A passer-by rushed to his assistance, and inquired if he was injured.

The little German gazed at his place of business, which was now burning quite briskly, and said:

"No, I ain't hurt. But I got out shust in time, eh?"

228 Or Try Head Cheese

"Yes, I know fish is brain food, but I don't care so much for fish. H'ain't there some other brain food?"

"Well, there's noodle soup."

229 Hometown Custom

Boy: "Do you know, Dad, that in some parts of Africa a man doesn't know his wife until he marries her?"
Dad: "Why single out Africa?"

230 Boom in Agriculture

"How's your farm work coming?"
"Oh fine! Got the billboard and hotdog stand painted and the filling station full of gas."

231 Ready for the Worst

Dorothy: "How long is it to my birthday?"
Mother: "Not very long dear."
Dorothy: "Well, is it time for me to begin to be a good girl?"

232 Game to the Last

"So you are undertaking to keep bees?"
"Yes," answered Farmer Corntossel. "I don't want to miss anything, and I've been stung every other way there is."

233 Immobilizing Bossy

The little city boy stood and watched the farmer milk the only cow he had. The next morning the farmer was much excited, as the cow had been stolen during the night.
Farmer: "Drat the thief that stole that cow. He's miles away from here by now."
Little Boy: "I wouldn't worry 'bout it, mister; they can't get so far away with it, 'cause you drained her crankcase last night."

234 Cutting In

Margery had been watching a fashionable wedding from outside the church. Returning home she reported: "Well, I can't make out who she married. She went in with quite an old man and when she came out she was with a different one altogether."

235 Solid!

"Do you guarantee this hair-restorer?"
"Better than that, sir. We give a comb with every bottle."

236 Well, It Helps

"Murphy got rich quick, didn't he?"
"He got rich so quick that he can't swing a golf club without spitting on his hands."

237 Something Nice

Hubby: "The bank has returned that check."
Wife: "Isn't that splendid! What can we buy with it this time?"

238 He'll Catch Up

Neighbor: "Where is your brother, Freddie?"
Freddie: "He's in the house playing a duet. I finished first."

239 That's One Way of Putting It

Vicar: "I was grieved to hear your husband has gone at last."
Mrs. Black: "Yas, 'e 'as, sir, and I only hope 'e's gone where I know 'e ain't."

240 Good Description

Johnny, who had been to the circus, was telling his teacher about the wonderful things he had seen.

"An' teacher," he cried, "they had one big animal they called the hip—hip—

"Hippopotamus, dear," prompted the teacher.

"I can't just say its name," exclaimed Johnny, "but it looks just like 9,000 pounds of liver."

241 A Little Less of Something

He: "You are always wishing for what you haven't got."
She: "Well, what else can one wish for?"

242 He'll Get Along

Small Bobby had been to a birthday party, and, knowing his weakness, his mother looked him straight in the eye and said, "I hope you didn't ask for a second piece of cake?"

"No," replied Bobby. "I only asked Mrs. Smith for the recipe so you could make some like it and she gave me two more pieces just of her own accord."

243 And Like It

"I never clash with my boss."
"No?"
"No; he goes his way and I go his."

244 Independent

Arthur: "So your new job makes you independent?"
Albert: "Absolutely. I get here any time I want before eight, and leave just when I please after five."

245 Two Seasons

It happened in New York's lower East Side.
"How many seasons are there?" asked the teacher.
"Just two," answered Rachel.
"What are they?" inquired the puzzled instructor.
"Slack and busy," replied Rachel.

246 Ask Dad

Young Husband (in early morning): "It must be time to get up."
Wife: "Why?"
Young Husband: "Baby's fallen asleep."

247 Better Ask the Driver

"Are you quite sure this bus is going to Shepherd's Bush?"
"If it isn't, lady," said the conductor, "I'm in a worse mess than you are!"

248 That's Prevarication

Employer (to newly hired typist): "Now I hope you thoroughly understand the importance of punctuation?"
Stenographer: "Oh, yes, indeed. I always get to work on time."

249 It's an Expensive Way

"Has your son's college education been of any value?"
"Oh, yes; it cured his mother of bragging about him."

250 Take That

"It's going to be a real battle of wits, I tell you," said the sophomore member of the debating team.
"How brave of you," said his roommate, "to go unarmed."

251 Not at All Exclusive

Diner: "Do you serve crabs here?"
Waiter: "We serve anyone; sit down."

252 Nosey People

The teacher was explaining to the class the meaning of the word "recuperate." "Now, Tommy," she said to a small boy. "When your father has worked hard all day, he is tired and worn out, isn't he?"
"Yes, ma'am."
"Then, when night comes, and his work is over for the day, what does he do?"
"That's what mother wants to know," Tommy explained.

253 *Methuselah*

Methuselah ate what he found on his plate, and never, as people do now, did he note the amount of the calorie count; he ate because it was chow.

He wasn't disturbed as at dinner he sat, devouring a roast or a pie, to think it was lacking in granular fat, or a couple of vitamins shy. He cheerfully chewed each species of food, unmindful of troubles or fears lest his health might be hurt by some fancy dessert—and he lived over nine hundred years!

254 *Forgive and Forget*

A man was arrested and brought before a commissioner for having a still on his premises. He was asked by the commissioner, "How do you plead?"

The man said: "I plead guilty and waive the hearing."

"What do you mean, 'Waive the hearing'?" asked the commissioner.

"I mean I don't want to hear no more about it."

255 *Milquetoast in Africa*

Angry Guide: "Why didn't you shoot that tiger?"

The Timid Hunter: "He didn't have the right kind of expression on his face for a rug."

256 *Pity the Moth*

"A moth leads an awful life."

"How come?"

"He spends the summer in a fur coat and the winter in a bathing suit."

257 *There's Money in It*

"Did you know that I had taken up story-writing as a career?"

"No. Sold anything yet?"

"Yes; my watch, my saxophone, and my overcoat."

258 *Surprise*

He was at the fountain pen counter making a purchase. "You see," he said, "I'm buying this for my wife."

"A surprise, eh?"

"I'll say so. You see, she's expecting a mink coat."

259 *Happy Combination*

The boys of the Fairmont (W. Va.) American Legion Post were discussing the impending marriage of a buddy.

"That's an accomplished girl Ben is going to marry," observed one of the men. "She can swim, ride, dance, drive a car, and pilot a plane; a real all-around girl."

"They should get along fine," replied another. "You know Ben is a good cook."

260   Takes Experience

A boyish-looking minister, serving his first church, noticed that one of his flock had been absent from services several Sundays in a row, so he decided to see her and ask the reason.

The woman shook her head and looked at him pityingly. "Son," she said, "you're not old enough to have sinned enough to have repented enough to be able to preach about it."

261   Nerve

"I envy the man who sang the tenor solo."

"Really? I thought he had a very poor voice."

"So did I, but just think of his nerve."

262   Bankruptcy

First Businessman: "Old Sharklee is going to retire from business."

Second Businessman: "I heard him say that before."

First Businessman: "I know, but the judge said it this time."

263   Conceit

"I hope you don't think I'm conceited," he said, after he had finished telling her all about himself.

"Oh, no," she replied, "but I'm just wondering how you keep from giving three hearty cheers whenever you look at yourself in the glass."

264   That's Different

Stranger in town: "Did you see a pedestrian go by here awhile ago?"

Villager: "No, sir. I've been here for an hour, and there hasn't been a thing go by except one man, and he was walking."

265   Are They Strict?

Frosh: "Are they very strict at Cornell?"

Soph: "Are they? Why, when a man dies during a lecture, they prop him up in the seat until the end of the hour."

266 How to Succeed

"My boy," said the businessman to his son, "there are two things that are vitally necessary if you are to succeed in business."

"What are they, dad?"

"Honesty and sagacity."

"What is honesty?"

"Always—no matter what happens, no matter how adversely it may affect you—always keep your word once you have given it."

"And sagacity?"

"Never give your word."

267 Unexpectedly

Two freshmen were trying to define the word, "collision." "Collision," said one freshman, "is when two things come together unexpectedly."

"I know," brightly replied the other freshie. "Twins."

268 Boasting

The young wife was boasting to a friend what a big man her hubby was. "Why, he's bigger than Ford," bragged the wifey. "He's even bigger than Rockefeller." The friend asked, "Is he bigger than God?" "Well. I wouldn't say that," replied the wife, "but he's young yet.'

269 A Tough Order

The meek little gent in the restaurant finally sighed and decided to give up his steak. It was tougher than sole leather. He called the waiter and pleaded that it be taken back to the kitchen. The waiter dolefully shook his head and said: "Sorry, pal, I can't take it back now. You've bent it!"

270 Seein' Stars

A high school girl, seated next to a famous astronomer at a dinner party, struck up a conversation with him by asking, "What do you do in life?"

He replied, "I study astronomy."

"Dear me," said the girl. "I finished astronomy last year."

271 Honestly?

A candidate came home in the small hours and gave his wife the glorious news:

"Darling, I have been elected."

She was delighted. "Honestly?" she said.

He laughed in an embarrassed way.

"Oh, why bring that up?"

272   *How Many Learn It?*

Young Mother: "Nurse, what is the most difficult thing for a young mother to learn?"

Nurse: "That other people have perfect children too."

273   *Suitability*

"Aren't some of the hats women wear absurd?"

"Yes," replied Miss Cayenne, "and yet when some people put them on they *do* look *so appropriate.*"

274   *Opportunity Knocks*

A new pulpit having been erected, the minister and the verger tested the acoustics.

"Stand you well to the back and see how this sounds," said the minister, repeating the text.

"Fine, Minister, fine!"

"Now you go up into the pulpit and say anything you like."

The verger went up. "I have not had a raise in pay for three years. How does that sound?"

275   *Angler Logic*

"What for did ye tell him there was plenty of fishin' when there aren't two fish in the stream?"

"Well, an' the less fishes there is, the more fishin' to get 'em, ain't there?"

276   *Take the Bad with the Good*

Wife (heatedly): "You're lazy, you're worthless, you're bad-tempered, you're shiftless, you're a liar."

Husband (reasonably): "Well, my dear, no man is perfect."

277   *It Certainly Is*

The way of the transgressor is well written up.

278   *Last Stand*

The father was reading the school report which had just been handed to him by his hopeful son. His brow was wrathful as he read: "English, poor; French, weak; mathematics, fair"; and he gave a glance of disgust at the quaking lad. "Well, Dad," said the son, "it is not as good as it might be, but have you seen that?" And he pointed to the next line, which read: "Health, excellent."

279   Sign Reading

A denizen of the hills of East Tennessee, who was appearing as a witness in a lawsuit, was being questioned as to his educational qualifications by the plaintiff's lawyer.

"Can you write?" asked the lawyer.

"Nope."

"Can you read?"

"Wa'al, I kin read figgers pretty well, but I don't do so good with writin'."

"How is that?"

"Wa'al take these here signs along the road when I want to go sommers; I kin read how fur, but not whurto."

280   Salesmanship

Customer: "Are those eggs strictly fresh?"

Grocer (to his clerk): "Feel of those eggs, George, and see if they're cool enough to sell yet."

281   Why Not

At a meeting of senior citizens, the speaker reached the climax of his talk and declared: "The time has come when we must get rid of socialism and communism and anarchism, and . . ."

At that point, a little old lady at the rear of the room arose feebly but with enthusiasm and shouted: "Let's throw out rheumatism, too!"

282   Say That Again

Husband: "But you must admit that men have better judgment than women."

Wife: "Oh, yes—you married me, and I you."—Life

283   Paid Up

Sam: "Listen hear, boy, just what kind of life you been livin'?"

Bill: "Oh, ordinary, just ordinary."

Sam: "Well, if you pull any more aces out of your shoe, your ordinary lift is going to mature."

284   Eternity Case

The doctor's five-year-old answered the call at the door. "Is the doctor in?" inquired the caller.

"No, sir."

"Have you any idea when he will be back?"

"I don't know, sir—he went out on an eternity case."

285   *Slow Service*

A kindergarten tot described the painting, "Whistler's Mother" as: "It shows a nice old lady waiting for the repairman to bring back her TV set."

286   *Romeo Miz'n*

> Sam held her hand and she held hiz'n
> And then they hugged and went to kiz'n.
> They did not know her dad had riz'n.
> Madder than hops and simply siz'n;
> And really 'tiz'n right to liz'n,
> But Sam got hiz'n and went out whiz'n.

287   *Young Webster*

School Teacher: "Johnny, can you tell me the difference between perseverance and obstinacy?"

Johnny: "One is a strong will, and the other is a strong won't."

288   *Yes!*

> "Mr. Brown, these are very small oysters you are selling me."
> "Yes, ma'am."
> "They don't appear to be very fresh, either."
> "Then it's lucky they're small, ain't it?"

289   *Ho, Hum*

An English tourist was on his first visit to Niagara Falls, and the guide was trying to impress him with its magnificence.

"Grand," suggested the guide.

The visitor did not seem much impressed.

"Millions of gallons a minute," explained the guide.

"How many in a day?" asked the tourist.

"Oh, billions and billions," answered the guide.

The visitor looked across, and down and up, as if gauging the flow. Then he turned away with a shrug, apparently unaffected.

"Runs all night, too, I suppose," he remarked.

290   *A Riddle to End All Riddles*

A train operated by a Norwegian engineer starts to New York from Albany just as a train with a drunken engineer leaves New York for Albany. There's only one track, no switches or sidings, yet the trains do not collide. Why? Because Norse is Norse and Souse is Souse and never the twain shall meet.

291 Economics

"It's tough to pay sixty cents a pound for meat."
"Mmm. But it's tougher when you pay only forty."

292 It's Perfect

"Is that hair tonic any good?"
"Say, I spilled some of it on my comb last week and now it's a brush."

293 In a Big Way

A tourist was enjoying the wonders of California as pointed out by a native.
"What beautiful grapefruit," he said, as they passed through a grove of citrus trees.
"Oh, those lemons are a bit small owing to a comparatively bad season," explained the Californian.
"What are those enormous blossoms?" questioned the tourist a little bit farther on.
"Just a patch of dandelions," answered the guide.
Presently they reached the Sacramento River.
"Ah," said the tourist, "some one's radiator is leaking."

294 Far-Sighted

A father was taking his blonde toddler on a tour of the zoo and they had stopped outside the lion's cage.
"Daddy," the little tyke asked, "if the lion gets out and eats you up, what bus do I take to get home?"

295 Doubting Thomas

The one-ring circus was visiting a town in the hills. The folks there recognized all the instruments of the band except the slide trombone.
One old settler watched the player for quite some time, then said:
"There's a trick to it; he ain't really swallerin' it."

296 Ghosts

Two boys were having an argument about ghosts. One of them claimed to have seen a ghost the night before.
"What was this ghost doing when you last saw him?" asked the doubting one.
"Just falling behind, falling behind rapid."

297   *Librarians*

A newspaper in the county seat printed the following announcement: "The Public Library will close for two weeks, beginning August 3, for the annual cleaning and vacation of the librarians."

298   *Recognition*

A recruit failed to salute a captain. The captain followed him inside and demanded: "Don't you recognize the uniform?"

"Yes, sir," replied the recruit, feeling of the captain's coat. "Pretty nice uniform; look at this thing they issued me."

299   *An Old Saying at Dinner in India*

More was prepared than was served.
More was served than was eaten.
More was eaten than was necessary.

300   *Simpler*

"Give me a glass of milk and a muttered buffin."
"You mean a buffered muttin."
"No, I mean a muffered buttin."
"Why not take doughnuts and milk?"

301   *Viewpoint*

She: "Doesn't the bride look stunning?"
He: "Yeah, and doesn't the groom look stunned?"

302   *Happy Ending*

Three Britons, each hard of hearing:
First Limey: "Is this Wembley?"
Second Pelter: "No, it's Thursday."
Third Limey: "So am I. Let's have a Scotch and soda."

303   *Current Case*

A chap was arraigned for assault and brought before the judge.

Judge: "What is your name, occupation, and what are you charged with?"

Prisoner: "My name is Sparks; I am an electrician, and I'm charged with battery."

Judge (after recovering his equilibrium): "Officer, put this guy in a dry cell."

304 Grammar

"Are your father and mother in?" asked the visitor of the small boy who opened the door.

"They was in," said the child, "but they is out."

"They was in. They is out. Where's your grammar?"

"She's gone upstairs," said the boy, "for a lay-down."

305 Right Answer

An old man had the habit of always prophesying great calamities to his friends. One day he was predicting to a disgusted listener that a great famine was coming soon, and dolefully asked, "And what would you say, my friend, if in a short time the rivers in our country would all dry up?"

"I'd say," was the tired answer, "go thou and do likewise."

306 Addition

Rich Man: "There's no sense in teaching the boy to count over 100. He can hire accountants to do his bookkeeping."

Tutor: "Yes, sir, but he'll want to play his own game of golf, won't he?"

307 Washing Up

Smith: "I wear the trousers in my home."

Friend: "Yeah, but right after supper I notice you wear an apron over them."

308 Collective

Teacher: "Name three collective nouns."

Tommy: "Flypaper, wastebasket, and vacuum cleaner."

309 Second Attack

Diner: "Waiter, I was here yesterday and had a steak."

Waiter: "Yes, sir; will you have the same today."

Diner: "Well, I might as well, if no one else is using it."

310 Edited

An English cub reporter, frequently reprimanded for relating too many details and warned to be brief, turned in the following:

"A shooting affair occurred last night. Sir Dwight Hopeless, a guest at Lady Panmore's ball, complained of feeling ill, took a highball, his hat, his coat, his departure, no notice to his friends, a taxi, a pistol from his pocket and finally his life. Nice chap. Regrets and all that sort of thing."

311   *Cautious*

Father was standing at the edge of a cliff admiring the sea below, the sandwiches clutched in his hand. His son approached him and tugged at his coat.

"Mother says it isn't safe here," said the boy, "and you're either to come away or else give me the sandwiches."

312   *Challenge*

A hard-driving taxi driver ignored a red signal, threatened a policeman's knees, missed the street island by a hair, and grazed a bus, all in one dash.

The policeman hailed him, then strolled over to the taxi, pulling a big handkerchief from his pocket en route.

"Listen, cowboy," he growled. "On the way back I'll drop this and see if you can pick it up with yer teeth."

313   *Slight Error*

Auctioneer: "What am I offered for this beautiful bust of Robert Burns?"

Man in Crowd: "That ain't Burns . . . that's Shakespeare."

Auctioneer: "Well, folks, the joke's on me. That shows what I know about the Bible."

314   *Open-Handed*

First Caddie: "What's your man like, Skeeter?"

Second Caddie: "Left-handed, and keeps his change in his right-hand pocket."

315   *Another Necktie*

Lady Customer: "I want a birthday present for my husband."

Floorwalker: "How long have you been married, madam?"

Lady Customer: "Twelve years."

Floorwalker: "Bargain basement is on the left."

316   *Efficient Nagging*

"My husband is an efficiency expert in a large office."

"What does an efficiency expert do?"

"Well, if we women did it, they'd call it nagging."

317   *Practically Bald*

Customer: "Does a man with as little hair as I've got have to pay full price to have it cut?"

Barber: "Yes, and sometimes more. We usually charge double when we have to hunt for the hair."

318   Of Course

Professor: "I forgot my umbrella this morning."
King Arthur: "How did you remember you forgot it?"
Professor: "Well, I missed it when I raised my hand to close it, after it had stopped raining."

319   Correct Spelling

A teacher was taking her first golf lesson. "Is the word spelled 'put' or 'putt'?" she asked the instructor.

" 'Putt' is correct, he replied. " 'Put' means to place a thing where you want it. 'Putt' means a vain attempt to do the same thing."

320   Bovine

Artist: "That, sir, is a cow grazing."
Visitor: "Where is the grass?"
Artist: "The cow has eaten it."
Visitor: "But where is the cow?"
Artist: "You don't suppose she'd be fool enough to stay there after she'd eaten all the grass, do you?"

321   She Knows

A man who had been keeping company with a girl for a number of years took her out one night to a Chinese restaurant. They began studying the menu and he asked, "How would you like your rice—fried or boiled?"

She looked at him and said, very distinctly, "Thrown."

322   He Almost Got Angry

A bricklayer working on top of a high building carelessly dropped a brick, which landed on the head of his helper below.

"You better be careful up there, boss," said the helper, dusting his hat off. "You made me bite my tongue!"

323   Story-Telling Dad

Six-year-old Mary woke up about two in the morning. "Tell me a story, mamma," she pleaded.

"Hush, darling," said mother. "Daddy will be in soon and tell us both one."

324 A Burned Offering

She (on the 'phone): "I'm afraid your dinner will be burned a little tonight, darling."

He: "What's the matter? Did they have a fire at the delicatessen?"

325 What Mother Calls Father

Teacher (pointing to a deer at the zoo): "Johnny, what is that?"

Johnny: "I don't know."

Teacher: "What does your mother call your father?"

Johnny: "Don't tell me that's a louse!"

326 Cure for Nervousness

Phyllis: "Were you nervous when George proposed?"

Mabel: "No, dear, that's when I stopped being nervous."

327 The Difference

A nut and a joke are alike in that they can both be cracked, and different in that the joke can be cracked again.—*William J. Burtscher*

328 Speaking from Experience

Wally: "Gee, Pop, there's a man in the circus who jumps on a horse's back, slips underneath, catches hold of its tail, and finishes up on the horse's neck."

Father: "That's nothing. I did all that, and more, the first time I ever rode a horse."

329 Why Worry About It?

Teacher: "Take 13½ from 29¼ and what's the difference?"

Class Dunce: "Yeah, that's what I say, who cares anyhow?"

330 Difficult Days

A person has to be a contortionist to get along these days. First of all, he's got to keep his back to the wall, and his ear to the ground. He's expected to put his shoulder to the wheel, his nose to the grindstone, keep a level head, and both feet on the ground. And, at the same time have his head in the clouds, so he can look for the silver lining.

331 Modest

Goodsby: "Did anyone in your family ever make a brilliant marriage?"

Harefoot: "Only my wife."

332 The Inevitable End

Man wants but little here below,
He's ready to admit it,
And if Uncle Sam keeps taxing him
He's pretty sure to get it.

333 Remiss

Vicar (benevolently): "And what is your name, my little man?"
Small boy: "Well, if that ain't the limit. Why, it was you that christened me."

334 Having Wonderful Time

Says a postcard from a truth-telling vacationist at an expensive mountain resort: "Having a wonderful time; wish I could afford it."

335 The Let-Down

For months he had been her devoted admirer. Now, at long last, he had collected up sufficient courage to ask her the most momentous of all questions.

"There are quite a lot of advantages in being a bachelor," he began, "but there comes a time when one longs for the companionship of another being—a being who will regard one as perfect, as an idol; whom one can treat as one's absolute property; who will be kind and faithful when times are hard; who will share one's joys and sorrows—"

To his delight he saw a sympathetic gleam in her eyes. Then she nodded in agreement.

"So you're thinking of buying a dog?" she said. "I think it's a fine idea. Do let me help you choose one!"

336 Modern Youth

"Is your daughter home from school for the holidays?"
"I think so. One of her sisters said she saw her day before yesterday."

337 He Knew

Three boys about four years of age were displaying a new toy. One boy said, "Let's see your gun."
The other said, "It's not a gun, it's a pistol!"
Our four-year-old daughter added, "I know what a pistol is! Our minister talks about one every Sunday."—*Christian Parent*

338 Unpredictable

"I turned the way I signaled," said the lady, indignantly, after the crash.

"I know it," retorted the man. "That's what fooled me."

339 Live on His Income

"Do you love me?"

"Yes, handsome."

"Can you live on my income?"

"Yes, but what will you live on?"

340 Knew It All the Time

Jim: "When you proposed to her, I suppose she said 'This is so sudden'?"

George: "No, she was honest about it and said: 'The suspense has been terrible.' "

341 Doubtful Character

Customer: "Remember that cheese you sold me yesterday?"

Grocer: "Yes, madam."

Customer: "Did you say it was imported or deported from Switzerland?"

342 Two of a Kind

Mrs. John: "Wake up, John, there's a burglar going through your pants pockets."

John (turning over): "Oh, you two just fight it out between yourselves."

343 Too Coarse

Mr. Newlywed: "What's wrong with this cake, dear? It tastes kind of gritty."

Mrs. Newlywed: "Don't be silly, darling. The recipe calls for three whole eggs and I guess I didn't get the shells beaten up fine enough."

344 Sponged Cake

Hubby: "What are we having for dessert tonight, dear?"

Wife: "Sponge cake. I sponged the eggs from Mrs. Brown, the flour from Mrs. Smith, and the milk from Mrs. Jones."

345 Too Long to Wait

"What inspired the old-time pioneers to set forth in their covered wagons?"

"Well, maybe they didn't want to wait about thirty years for a train."

346 *She Was Listening*

A child who went to Sunday school came home and told her father she learned the train song—"Lead Us Not into Penn Station." Later her father learned that the children had sung a hymn, "Lead Us Not into Temptation."

347 *Commercial*

British Guide (showing places of historical interest): "And it was in this room that Lord Wellington received his first commission."

Insurance Man: "How many renewals?"

348 *Go Easy*

The girl had just said "Yes."

"Do your people know that I write poetry?" he asked.

"Not yet, dear," she said. "I've told them about your drinking and gambling, but I couldn't tell them everything at once."

349 *Or Jump Up*

The excited sportsman heaved a mighty heave, then reeled madly till the poor troutling was nine feet aloft, with its head against the tip of the rod, flapping feebly there.

"Now what'll I do?" he demanded.

"So fur ez I can see," said the puzzled lumberjack, "there ain't nuthin' fur you to do except climb the pole."

350 *In Training*

The vicar was paying a visit to the houses of his poorer parishioners, and in one of the houses he asked a good many questions about the family. A very grubby but very cheerful little boy attracted the kindly cleric's attention, and he asked him his name.

"Reginald d'Arcy Smif, sir," replied the boy with a grin.

The vicar turned to the boy's father.

"What made you give the boy a name like that?" he asked.

" 'Cause I want 'im to be a professional boxer," returned the parent, "an' wiv a name like that he'll get plenty o'practice at school."

351 *He Must Be an Economist*

"I'm glad you're so impressed, dear, by all these explanations I have been giving you about banking and economics," remarked the young husband.

"Yes, darling. It seems wonderful that anybody could know as much as you do about money without having any."

352   Criticism

A woman who had been in modest circumstances before she came into a large inheritance attended a baseball game. She was wearing a smart tweed outfit with a diamond brooch about the size of a large English walnut.

"My dear," cooed a woman friend in the box with her, "you shouldn't wear such a large piece of jewelry with tweeds."

"I know," snapped the wealthy woman. "That's what I always said . . . before I owned one!"

353   Or Minnie the Moocher

"Now boys," said the teacher, "tell me the signs of the zodiac. You first, Thomas."

"Taurus, the Bull."

"Right! Now, you, Harold, another one."

"Cancer, the Crab."

"Right again. And now it's your turn, Albert."

The boy looked puzzled, hesitated a moment, and then blurted out, "Mickey, the Mouse."

354   Hard Problem

A father had taken his small son to church. The boy listened attentively without saying a word until the clergyman announced, "We will now sing hymn two hundred and twenty-two: 'Ten Thousand Times Ten Thousand,' two hundred and twenty-two."

The puzzled boy nudged his father. "Daddy, we don't have to work this out, do we?"

355   Injustice

Tenant: "This roof is so bad that it rains on our heads. How long is this going to continue?"

Owner: "What do you think I am, a weather prophet?"

356   Cure

Voice over 'phone: "I can't sleep, Doctor. Can you do anything for me?"

Doctor: "Hold the 'phone and I'll sing you a lullaby."

357   Witness

The men were swapping stories.

"When I was logging up in Oregon," said one of them, "I saw a wildcat come right up to the skidder one day. It was a fierce beast, but with great presence of mind, I threw a bucket of water in its face and it slunk away."

"Boys," said a man sitting in the corner, "I can vouch for the truth of that story. A few minutes after that happened, I was coming down the side of the hill. I met this wildcat and, as is my habit, stopped to stroke its whiskers. Boys, those whiskers were wet!"

358   Worried

A visitor at the Capitol was accompanied by his small son. The little boy watched from the gallery when the House came to order.

"Why did the minister pray for all those men, Pop?"

"He didn't. He looked them over and prayed for the country."

359   Truth

Teacher (brightly): "As we walk out-of-doors on a cold winter's morning, and look about us, what do we see on every hand?"

Class (as a man): "Gloves!"

360   We Wonder Too

Husband: "Have you ever wondered what you would do if you had Rockefeller's income?"

Wife: "No, but I have often wondered what he would do if he had mine!"

361   Service

The motorist had just bought a tankful of gasoline, and the station attendant was going through his little ritual.

Attendant: "Check your oil, sir?"

Motorist: "No, it's O.K."

Attendant: "Got enough water in your radiator?"

Motorist: "Yes, filled up."

Attendant: "Anything else, sir?"

Motorist: "Yes, would you please stick out your tongue so I can seal this letter?"

362   7,000 Jingling Noises

Along a country road came a $9,000 limousine. As it caught up with the compact car, the owner of the big car could not resist the temptation to slow down and jolly the other driver a bit.

"Heavens, man," he said, "what is it about your car that makes such a dreadful rattling sound?"

"That? Oh, that's the $7,000 jingling around in my pocket," said the compact car driver.

363   Definition

Sometimes you run across a farmer who wants to know just what the Russians mean by a "kulak." Well, there may be exact definitions, but an example can be given of the "gentleman farmer," whose daughter was asked if their hens laid eggs.

"They can, of course," she replied haughtily, "but in our position, you understand, they don't have to."

364   Darn!

"Does your husband talk in his sleep?"

"No, and it's terribly exasperating. He just grins."

365   Epithet

"Yes, the smallest things seem to upset my wife. The other day she was doing a crossword puzzle and she asked me, 'What is a female sheep?' I said, 'Ewe,' and she burst into tears."

366   Compensation

Man (to small son of workman who has met with an accident): "When will dad be fit to work again?"

Boy: "Can't say for certain, but it will be a long time."

Man: "What makes you think that?"

Boy: " 'Cause compensation's set in."

367   Toasts

To woman: the only loved autocrat who governs without law; and decides without appeal.

Here's to the light that lies in women's eyes,
And lies, and lies and lies.

368   Generous

The young bride was extolling the virtues of her husband to a friend.

"George is just the most generous man in the world," she declared. "He gives me everything credit can buy."

369   Eye for Eye

A small boy leading a donkey passed by an army camp. A couple of soldiers wanted to have some fun with the lad.

"What are you holding onto your brother so tight for, sonny?" said one of them.

"So he won't join the army," the youngster replied without blinking an eye.

370 Too Easy

During a review one Sunday the teacher asked if the class knew who the twin boys were in the Bible.

"That's easy," said Charles. "First and Second Samuel."

371 Good Formula

When the late Mr. and Mrs. Henry Ford celebrated their golden wedding anniversary, a reporter asked them, "To what do you attribute your fifty years of successful married life?"

"The formula," said Ford, "is the same formula I have always used in making cars—just stick to one model."

372 Still Circulating

An old gentleman approached a nattily attired man at an elaborate wedding.

"Pardon me, suh," said the old man, "are you de bridegroom?"

The young man shook his head dolefully. "No, suh," he replied, "Ah wuz eliminated in de semi-finals!"

373 Two Years Should Do It

Her Suitor: "Sir, I came to—er—ask you whether you would object—er—to my marrying your daughter."

Her Father: "My boy, you're only twenty-one and my daughter is twenty-seven. Why not wait a few years till you're both about the same age?"

374 Highly Competent

A man of six feet eight inches applied for a job as a life guard.

"Can you swim?" said the official.

"No, but I can wade pretty far out."

375 Diplomacy

A young man proved himself a past master of flattery when he entered an elevator and forgot to take off his hat. There was only one other passenger in the elevator, but she was a rather fussy, middle-aged woman, and she asked: "Don't you take off your hat to ladies?"

"Only to old ones, madam," he replied with a little bow.

376　Slow Motion

Patient: "What do you charge for extracting a tooth?"
Dentist: "Five dollars."
Patient: "Five dollars for only two seconds' work?"
Dentist: "Well, if you wish, I can extract it very slowly."

377　Working Late at the Office

"I don't see Charlie half as much as I used to."
"You should have married him when you had the chance."
"I did."

378　Imports

Gibbs: "Did you see much poverty in Europe?"
Biggs: "A great deal. In fact, I brought some home with me."

379　Not That Bold

Ma: "That new couple next door seem to be very devoted. He kisses her every time they meet. Why don't you do that?"
Pa: "I don't know her well enough."

380　Credit

A man mortgaged his home to buy an automobile. Then he went around and tried to mortgage the car to get money to build a garage.

"How are you going to buy gas?" curiously inquired the man of whom the loan was asked.

"Well," replied the other slowly, "if I own a house, a car, and a garage, I should think any dealer would be willing to trust me for gas."

381　Correct

New Teacher: "Where is the elephant found?"
Jane: "It's so big, it's hardly ever lost."

382　Too Inquisitive

Professor: "And whatever on earth made you write a paragraph like that?"
Student: "I quoted it, sir, from Dickens."
Professor: "Beautiful lines, aren't they?"

383　Short on Collateral

Two men were discussing the financial condition of the country. They didn't agree.

"You are wrong," one vociferated. "Dey ain't no money sh'tage. Ah asked mah bankuh is he out o' money and he tuk me in de vault and showed me piles an' piles o'money. And Ah says could he let me have a little. And he says he sho' could. Has Ah any collat'rul? Ah hasn't. Now, dat's what's de mattuh wid dis country. Dey's plenty o'money, but we's jest runnin' sho't on collat'rul."

384 Power

"What is the greatest water power known to man?"
"Woman's tears."

385 Wrong Number

"I called on Mabel last night, and I was hardly inside the door before her mother asked me about my intentions."
"That must have been embarrassing."
"Yes. But the worst of it was Mabel called from upstairs and said: 'That isn't the one, mother!' "

386 Slightly Scrambled

A newspaper account of a disastrous shipwreck stated: "The vessel sank with all aboard except one lady passenger. She was insured for a large sum and loaded with pig iron."

387 Sad Mistake

Mr. Brown: "So your son had to leave college on account of poor eyesight?"
Mr. White: "Yes, he mistook the dean of women for a coed."

388 O Wonderful Horse!

O horse, you are a wonderful thing;
No buttons to push, no horn to honk;
You start yourself, no clutch to slip;
No spark to miss, no gears to strip;
No license buying every year,
With plates to screw on front and rear;
No gas bills climbing up each day,
Stealing the joy of life away;
No speed cops chugging in your rear.
Yelling summons in your ear.
Your inner tubes are all O.K.
And thank the Lord, they stay that way;
Your spark plugs never miss and fuss;
Your motor never makes us cuss.
Your frame is good for many a mile;

> Your body never changes style.
> Your wants are few and easy met;
> You've something on the auto yet.
> —*Northwestern Banker*

389   *Following Orders*

Bill: "You look all out of sorts. What's the matter?"

Jack: "Plenty. On account of my rheumatism the doctor told me to avoid all dampness—and you've no idea how silly I feel sitting in an empty bathtub and going over myself with a vacuum cleaner."

390   *Schemer*

Billy (who has eaten his apple): "Let's play Adam and Eve."

Small Sister: "How do you play that, Billy?"

Billy: "Well, you tempt me to eat your apple and I'll give in."

391   *Knowledge*

A junior high school student wrote about the "writ of hideous corpus" in an examination.

Another junior high student quoted thus from the Declaration of Independence: ". . . Every man should be divided equal."—*NEA Journal*

392   *Taking No Chances*

Passer-by: "Kinda cold sitting on your front porch this weather, isn't it, Mr. Davis?"

Mr. Davis: "Well, yes, a little, but you see my wife is taking her singing lesson, and I don't want the neighbors to think I'm beating her up."

393   *'Twas Ever Thus*

"Has your wife changed very much since you married her?"

"Yes, she's changed my friends, my habits, and my hours."

394   *The Way It Sounded*

Waiter: "May I help you with that soup, sir?"

Diner: "What do you mean, help me? I don't need any help."

Waiter: "Sorry, sir. From the sound, I thought you might want to be dragged ashore."

395   *Reason Enough*

"Just tell me one good reason why you can't buy a new car now," said the persistent automobile salesman.

"Well, I'll tell you, man," replied the farmer. "I'm still paying installments on the car I swapped for the car I traded in as part payment on the car I own now."

396 Slight Transposition

The visitor paid his bill at the fashionable hotel, and as he went out, he noticed a sign near the door, "Have you left anything?"

So he went back and spoke to the manager. "That sign's wrong," he said. "It should read 'Have you anything left?'"

397 Spoiled His Wish

Sonny: "Kin I have the wishbone, mother?"
Mother: "Not until you've eaten your spinach."
Sonny: "Yes, but I wanted to wish I didn't have to eat it."

398 His Oversight

Waiter: "How did you order your steak, sir?"
Diner (impatiently): "Orally, but I realize now I should have ordered it by mail in advance."

399 Candid Answer

Boy Friend: "You're dancing with me tonight, and I suppose tomorrow you'll be making a date with some other man."
Girl Friend: "Yes, with my chiropodist."

400 Spelling

Teacher: "Why did you spell pneumatic 'neumatic'?"
Pupil: "The 'k' on my typewriter isn't working."

401 Staying Home

"Boy, if I had a wife like yours, I'd stay home every night in the week."
"I'll say you would, or get your neck broken."

402 Quite Important

A Chinese was worried by a vicious-looking dog.

"Don't be afraid of him," the owner reassured. "You know the old proverb, 'A barking dog never bites.'"

"Yes," replied the Chinese, "you know ploverb, me know ploverb, but do dog know ploverb?"

403 The World Moves Too Fast

"Nothing to read around this place," stormed the man of the house who had settled down for an evening, "but some old next month's magazines!"

404 The Parrot

Orville Wright was reproached by a friend for not taking up the challenge of some that it was Professor Langley, and not the Wright brothers, who flew first.

"Your trouble," said the friend, "is that you're too taciturn. You don't assert yourself enough. You should talk more."

"My friend," replied Mr. Wright, "the best talker and the worst flier among the birds is the parrot!"

405 Evolution of a Man's Ambition

"Two old timers were discussing the evolution of their ambitions.

"When I was twenty I made up my mind to get rich," one of them said.

"But you never got rich."

"No. By the time I was twenty-five I decided it was easier to change my mind than to make a million dollars. Once I wanted to be a circus clown, then a football star and then I wanted fame. Now I want to make ends meet and get an old age pension."

406 So Unselfish

Teacher: "Unselfishness means going without something you need, voluntarily. Can you give me an example of that Bobby?"

Bobby: "Yessum. Sometimes I go without a bath when I need one."

407 A Reminder

I rose and gave her my seat—
I could not let her stand.
She made me think of Mother,
With that strap held in her hand.

408 Logical Request

Three-year-old Bobby didn't like the routine of being scrubbed, especially when soap was applied.

"Bobby, don't you want to be nice and clean?" his mother asked.

"Sure," replied Bobby, "but can't you just dust me?"

409 *Secondhand*

Daughter of first film star: "How do you like your new father?"
Daughter of second film star: "Oh, he's very nice."
Daughter of first film star: "Yes, isn't he? We had him last year."

410 *Genesis*

A surgeon, an architect, and a politician were arguing as to whose profession was the oldest.

Said the surgeon: "Eve was made from Adam's rib, and that surely was a surgical operation."

"Maybe," said the architect, "but prior to that, order was created out of chaos, and that was an architectural job."

"But," interrupted the politician, "somebody created the chaos first!"

411 *No Place for Him*

A young lawyer from the North sought to locate in the South. He wrote to a friend in Alabama, asking him what the prospects seemed to be in the city for "an honest young lawyer and Republican."

In reply the friend wrote: "If you are an honest lawyer, you will have absolutely no competition. If you are a Republican, the game laws will protect you."

412 *A Little Slow*

New typist (following rapid-fire dictation): "Now, Mr. Jones—what did you say between 'Dear Sir' and 'Sincerely yours'?"

413 *Peace*

Grandmother decided to send a playpen to her daughter on the arrival of her fourth child.

"Thank you so much for the pen," she wrote. "It is wonderful—I sit in it every afternoon and read. The children can't get near me."

414 *The Way of Fame*

Author: "Well, sir, the upshot of it was that it took me ten years to discover that I had absolutely no talent for writing literature."
Friend: "You gave up?"
Author: "Oh, no; by that time I was too famous."

415 *Makes a Difference*

Passenger: "Have I time to say good-bye to my wife?"
Porter: "I don't know, sir; how long have you been married?"

416   Gradual Progress

Victim: "Hey, that wasn't the tooth I wanted pulled."
Dentist: "Calm yourself, I'm coming to it!"

417   Voyageur

Visitor: "How far is it to Washington?"
Native: "Wa'al, I don't rightly know, but I'll call Eph. Eph'll know. He's traveled all over. He's got shoes."

418   Substitute Your Party

The Southern father was introducing his family of boys to a visiting governor.

"Seventeen boys," exclaimed the Governor. "And all Democrats, I suppose."

"All but one," said the father proudly. "They're all Democrats but John, the little rascal. He got to readin'.'"

419   Tactful

First Clerk: "Have you and your boss ever had any differences of opinion?"
Second Ditto: "Yes, but he doesn't know it!"

420   Definition

The identity of the young lady is withheld, but the memory of her answer lingers with the instructor conducting a science course at a local high school. One of the requirements in the written quiz was: "Define a bolt and nut and explain the difference, if any." The girl wrote:

"A bolt is a thing like a stick of hard metal such as iron with a bunch on one end and a lot of scratching wound around the other end. A nut is similar to the bolt only just the opposite being a hole in a little chunk of iron sawed off short with wrinkles around the inside of the hole."

The startled professor marked that one with a large "A."

421   Obliging

Fat Man (in a movie to little boy sitting behind him): "Can't you see, little fellow?"
Little Fellow: "Not a thing."
Fat Man: "Then keep your eye on me and laugh when I do."

422   A Long Way

The fine symphony orchestra from the big city had played in a small New England town, the first experience of the kind for many of the inhabitants. Next day some of the oldtimers gathered in the general store and expressed their opinions. The comment of one of the oldest inhabitants was: "All I got to say is—it was an awful long way to bring that big bass drum only to bang it once."

423   *Difference*

"That means fight where I come from!"

"Well, why don't you fight then?"

" 'Cause I ain't where I come from."

424   *Hint*

The Vicar: "I want to speak to you, Fishner, about the milk you've been delivering lately. We don't require it for christenings."

425   *Enough*

The telephone rang in the clergyman's office of the Washington church which President Franklin Roosevelt attended. An eager voice inquired, "Do you expect the President to be in church Sunday?"

"That," answered the clergyman, "I cannot promise. But we expect God to be there and we fancy that should be incentive enough for a reasonably large attendance."—*Together*

426   *Ameliorating Circumstances*

An old farmer was moodily regarding the ravages of the flood.

"Hiram," yelled a neighbor, "your pigs were all washed down the creek."

"How about Flaherty's pigs?" asked the farmer.

"They're gone, too."

"And Larsen's?"

"Yes."

"Humph!" ejaculated the farmer, cheering up. " 'Tain't as bad as I thought."

427   *Intricacies of Finance*

Sam borrowed $35 from his friend Amos and gave a note for the amount. The note became long past due. One day Amos called on Sam and demanded: "When you-all gwine pay dat note?"

"Ah ain't got no money now, but Ah gwine pay just as soon as Ah kin."

"Dat don't git me nothin'," retorted Amos. "If you-all don't pay me here an' now, Ah gwine burn up your old note; den where you-all gwine be at?"

"You better not! You better not!" shouted Sam. "You just burn dat note of mine, and Ah'll burn you up wid a lawsuit."

428   Getting Right Along

"A telegram from George, dear."
"Well, did he pass the examination this time?"
"No, but he is almost at the top of the list of those who failed."

429   A New Angle

As he was drilling a batch of recruits, the sergeant saw that one of them was marching out of step. Going to the man as they marched, he said sarcastically:
"Do you know they are all out of step except you?"
"What?" asked the recruit innocently.
"I said they are all out of step except you," repeated the sergeant.
"Well," was the retort, "you tell 'em. You're in charge."

430   What a Life!

Husband (reading): "The tusks of 4,700 elephants were used last year to make billiard balls."
Wife: "Isn't it wonderful that such big beasts can be taught to do such delicate work!"

431   Following Orders

Mr. Wimpus: "You sure made a poor job of painting this door."
Mrs. Wimpus: "Well, you declared this morning that it needed painting badly."

432   Conscience on the Installment

A man who had his purse stolen some years previously, received the following letter:
"Sur, sum years ago I stole your muny. Remorse is gnawin' me, so I send sum back. When it gnaws me again I will send sum more."

433   It's a Clean Life!

Mother: "Junior, go wash your hands and face."
Junior: "Aw, I just took a bath this morning."
Mother: "Then go wash the bathtub."

434   Food Jargon

She balanced herself daintily on a stool at the hamburger counter, looked over the pastries and, after a few minutes of indecision, addressed the counter man: "I would like to have two hamburgers well done; no pickle, but you may put a little mustard on them, if you don't mind."

Without turning his head the counter man shouted to the short-order cook: "Elmers, on two; hobnailed; hold the pucker and make 'em dirty."

435   Wrong Impression

Junior: "That man wasn't a painless dentist like he advertised."

Senior: "Why? Did he hurt you?"

Junior: "No, but he yelled when I bit his thumb, just like any other dentist."

436   Correct

Teacher: "Now, which boy can name five things that contain milk?"

Jimmie: "Butter, cheese, ice cream, and two cows."

437   Payment

An editor once received a letter accompanying a number of would-be jokes in which the writer asked: "What will you give me for these?"

"Ten yards start," was the editor's offer.

438   Wrong Recipe

Groom: "How did you make this cake, dear?"

Bride: "Here's the recipe. I clipped it from a magazine."

Groom: "Are you sure you read the right side? The other side tells how to make a rock garden."

439   His Error

The owner of a cheap watch brought the timepiece into the jeweler's shop to see what could be done for it. "The mistake I made, of course," he admitted, "was in dropping this watch."

"Well, I don't suppose you could help that," the jeweler remarked. "The mistake you made was picking it up."

440   Good Question

The optimist said, "A year from now we will all be begging."

The pessimist asked, "From whom?"

441   His Good Deed!

A naval officer fell overboard. He was rescued by a deck hand. The officer asked how he could reward him.

"The best way, sir," said the gob, "is to say nothing about it. If the other fellows knew I'd pulled you out, they'd chuck me in."

442 Hopes Realized

Bill: "Have you ever realized any of your childhood hopes?"
Pete: "Yes; when mother used to comb my hair, I often wished I didn't have any."

443 A "Tense" Situation

A schoolteacher was correcting a boy who said, "I ain't gwine."
Teacher: "You have not studied your lesson. Listen: 'We are not going. You are not going. They are not going.' Now do you understand?"
Boy: "Yes, teacher. Nobody ain't gwine."

444 Identified

Sentry: "Halt; who's there?"
Voice: "American."
Sentry: "Advance and recite the second verse of 'The Star Spangled Banner.' "
Voice: "I don't know it."
Sentry: "Proceed, American."

445 Possibly

"What a boy you are for asking questions," said the father. "I'd like to know what would have happened if I'd asked as many questions when I was a boy."
"Perhaps," suggested the young hopeful, "you'd have been able to answer some of mine."

446 The Majority

"I won't defend a man whom I believe to be guilty."
"My boy, you mustn't set your judgment up against that of the majority. I have defended plenty of men whom I believed to be guilty, but the jury decided otherwise."

447 Question

"Did youse git anything." whispered the burglar on guard as his pal emerged from the window.
"Naw, de bloke wot lives here is a lawyer," replied the other in disgust.
"Dat's hard luck," said the first. "Did youse lose anyt'ing?"

448 Head of the Firm

"Is this Peabody, Finchley, Longworth, and Fitzgerald?"
"Yes, this is Peabody, Finchley, Longworth, and Fitzgerald."
"I want to speak to Mr. Smith."

449 People Are Too Suspicious

Judge: "How could you swindle people who trusted in you?"

Prisoner: "But, Judge, people who don't trust you cannot be swindled."

450 Sunk

Two old settlers, confirmed bachelors, sat in the backwoods. The conversation drifted from politics and finally got around to cooking.

"I got one o' them cookery books once, but couldn't do nothing with it."

"Too much fancy work in it, eh?"

"You've said it! Every one o' them recipes began the same way: 'Take a clean dish'—and that settled me."

451 Domestic Corporation

"So your wife takes in washing?" the Montgomery County judge asked a man who was up for vagrancy. "What do you do?"

"Well, Judge," explained the accused, "I takes in the washin', the old woman does the washin', I takes the washin' back, the old woman collects the money, and I talks her out of most of it."

452 New Twist

Householder: "Well, I see you brought your tools with you."

Plumber: "Yeah, I'm getting more absent-minded every day."

453 Rapid

A golf professional, hired by a big department store to give golf lessons, was approached by two women.

"Do you wish to learn to play golf, madam?" he asked one.

"Oh, no," she said, "it's my friend who wants to learn. I learned yesterday."

454 How're You Betting?

"The people in our part of town are watching the result of a very interesting conflict."

"What is it?"

"An irresistible blonde has just met an immovable bachelor."

455 Poser

"Why does a woman say she's been shopping when she hasn't bought a thing?"

"Why does a man say he's been fishing when he hasn't caught anything?"

456 Don't Like the Type

Mrs. Brown: "Do you know, dear, I was reading the other day that an ostrich can see very little, and can digest anything."

Mrs. Smith: "What an ideal husband!"

457 More Next Week

Dora had returned from Sunday school where she had been for the first time.

"What did my little daughter learn this morning?" asked her father.

"That I am a child of Satan," was the beaming reply.

458 Public Speaking

Someone has said that the writer of Psalm 91 must have been speaking at a luncheon club when he wrote about "The Destruction that wasteth at noon day." Perhaps he referred to banquets when he spoke of "The Pestilence that walketh in darkness."—*Charles F. Banning, in Church Management*

459 Nothing to Worry About

Overheard on the beach: "Mummy, may I go in for a swim?"

"Certainly not, my dear, it's far too deep."

"But daddy is swimming."

"Yes, dear, but he's insured."

460 On the Fairways

Golfer: "Listen, kid, I'll swat you with a club if you don't stop wisecracking me about my game!"

Caddie: "Yeah, but you wouldn't know which club to use!"

461 That's It

Woman learning to drive: "But I don't know what to do!"

Husband: "Just imagine that I'm driving."

462 Here We Go

Lady: "So you are on a submarine. What do you do?"

Sailor: "Oh, I run forward, ma'am, and hold her nose when we want to take a dive."

463 Bad Company

An elderly man of convivial habits, but also bookish, was hailed before the bar of justice in a small country town.

"Ye're charged with bein' drunk and disorderly," snapped the magistrate. "Have ye anything to say why sentence should not be pronounced?"

"Man's inhumanity to man makes countless thousands mourn," began the prisoner, in a flight of oratory. "I am not so debased as Poe, so profligate as Byron, so ungrateful as Keats, so intemperate as Burns, so timid as Tennyson, so vulgar as Shakespeare, so——"

"That'll do, that'll do," interrupted the magistrate. "Seven days. And, officer, take down that list of names he mentioned and round 'em up. I think they're as bad as he is."

464 Depends Upon the Viewpoint

A London doctor touring in the provinces had difficulty in obtaining suitable lodgings in a small town.

One landlady, showing him a dingy bedroom, remarked persuasively, "As a whole, this is quite a nice room, isn't it?"

"Yes, madam," he agreed, "but as a bedroom it's no good."

465 Justified

Johnnie was gazing at his one-day-old brother, who lay squealing and wailing in his cot.

"Has he come from Heaven?" inquired Johnnie.

"Yes, dear."

"No wonder they put him out."

466 Call the Manager

"Look here, waiter, is this peach or apple pie?"

"Can't you tell from the taste?"

"No, I can't."

"Well, then, what difference does it make?"

467 And Collect Your Commission

"Doctor, I want you to look after my office, while I'm on my vacation."

"But I've just graduated, Doctor. I've had no experience."

"That's all right, my boy. My practice is strictly fashionable. Tell the men to play golf and send the lady patients abroad."

468 Let's Go!

Sonny: "Mother, we're going to play elephants at the zoo and we want you to help us."

Mother: "What on earth can I do?"

Sonny: "You can be the lady who gives them peanuts and candy."

469   There's a Time

> There's a time to part and a time to meet,
> There's a time to sleep and a time to eat,
> There's a time to work and a time to play,
> There's a time to sing and a time to pray,
> There's a time that's glad and a time that's blue,
> There's a time to plan and a time to do,
> There's a time to grin and to show your grit,
> But there never was a time to quit.

470   Tragic

"I understand," said a young woman to another, "that at your church you are having very small congregations. Is that so?"

"Yes," answered the other girl, "so small that every time the rector says 'Dearly Beloved' you feel as if you had received a proposal."

471   Budget

"What is a budget?"

"Well, it is a method of worrying before you spend instead of afterward."

472   Gentlemen of the Jury

The prosecuting counsel was having a little trouble with a rather difficult witness. Exasperated by the man's evasive answers, he asked him if he was acquainted with any of the jury.

"Yes, sir, more than half of them," replied the man in the box.

"Are you willing to swear that you know more than half of them?" asked the counsel.

"If it comes to that, I'm willing to swear that I know more than all of 'em put together," said the witness.

473   The Good Old Joke

> Here's to the joke, the good old joke,
> The joke that our fathers told;
> It is ready tonight and is jolly and bright
> As it was in the days of old.
>
> When Adam was young it was on his tongue,
> And Noah got in the swim

By telling the jest as the brightest and best
That ever happened to him.

So here's to the joke, the good old joke—
We'll hear it again tonight.
It's health we will quaff; that will help us to laugh,
And to treat it in manner polite.—*Lew Dockstader*

474 *Who's Driving This Car?*

Timid Wife (to husband who has fallen asleep at the wheel): "I don't mean to dictate to you, George, but isn't that billboard coming at us awfully fast?"

475 *And a Dollar*

Teacher: "Tommy, if your father could save a dollar a week for three weeks what would he have?"
Tommy: "A radio, a new suit, and a set of furniture."

476 *Where It Belonged*

Judge (to amateur yegg): "So they caught you with this bundle of silverware. Whom did you plunder?"
Yegg: "Two fraternity houses, your honor."
Judge (to Sergeant): "Call up the downtown hotels and distribute the stuff."

477 *Reverse English*

Teacher: "Correct the sentence, 'Before any damage could be done the fire was put out by the volunteer fire brigade.'"
Boy: "The fire was put out before any damage could be done by the volunteer fire brigade."

478 *Sensitive*

Two men were seated together in a crowded bus. One of them noticed that the other had his eyes closed.
"What's the matter, Bill," he asked, "feeling ill?"
"I'm all right," answered Bill, "but I hate to see ladies standing."

479 *Don't Wait*

A mistress engaging a new maid said: "Mary, we have breakfast promptly at 8 A.M."
New Maid: "All right, mum. If I ain't down, don't you wait!"

480   *Too Good*

A newspaper man named Fling
Could make "copy" from any old thing.
But the copy he wrote
Of a five dollar note
Was so good he is now in Sing Sing.—*Columbia Jester*

481   *Acquainted*

Judge: "Have you ever seen the prisoner at the bar?"
Witness: "Yes, that's where I met him."

482   *City and Country*

Amos: "Did you find much difference between the city and the country, Hiram?"
Hiram: "They h'ain't much difference. In the country you go to bed feeling all in, and you get up feeling fine. In the city you go to bed feeling fine, and you get up feeling all in."

483   *No Objection*

Suitor: "I am seeking your daughter's hand, sir. Have you any objection?"
Father: "None at all. Take the one that's always in my pocket."

484   *Not So Dumb*

Jack: "Why is your car painted blue on one side and red on the other?"
Mac: "It's a great scheme. You should hear the witnesses contradicting each other."

485   *Foolin' Himself*

A boy was taking a stroll through a cemetery and reading the inscriptions on tombstones. He came to one which declared: "Not dead, but sleeping."
After contemplating the phrase for a moment, and scratching his head, he exclaimed: "He sure ain't foolin' nobody but himself."

486   *Repartee*

The audience in the college auditorium was impatiently awaiting the appearance of the out-of-town entertainer, who was already an hour late. The chairman of the evening, fearing the people would leave, scribbled a frantic appeal for help and had it passed down the aisle to Professor B., who was a ready and witty speaker. To break up the stony atmosphere,

Professor B. began: "I've just received a message asking me to come up here and say something funny."

A young student at the back of the room called loudly: "You'll tell us when you say it, won't you?"

To which the grave professor made instant reply: "I'll tell *you*; the rest will know!"

487　Wrong Diagnosis

Doctor: "Did you tell that young man I think he is no good?"

Daughter: "Yes, I did, Dad, but he did not seem at all upset. He said it wasn't the first wrong diagnosis you have made."

488　Puzzling

Henry James once reviewed a new novel by Gertrude Atherton. After reading the review, Mrs. Atherton wrote to Mr. James as follows:

"Dear Mr. James: I have read with much pleasure your review of my novel. Will you kindly let me know whether you liked it or not? Sincerely,
Gertrude Atherton"

489　Lost Cause

"They say your daughter has made up her mind to marry a struggling young doctor."

"Well, if she's made up her mind, he might as well stop struggling."

490　That's Different

"What is the matter, my little man?" asked a sympathetic stranger to a small boy whom he saw crying.

"Please, sir, my dog's dead," sobbed the boy.

"Well," said the man, "You mustn't make such a trouble of it. My grandmother died last week, and I'm not crying."

"No," said the boy, "but you didn't bring her up from a pup."

491　X Marks the Spot

Gus and Ole, at a Northern fishing resort, rented a hotel boat and found great fishing at a certain spot in a nearby lake, so great that they decided to mark the place and come back for more sport the next day. At the dock Gus said, "Ole did you mark the spot?"

"Yah," replied Ole. "Ay put a chalk mark on this side of the boat."

"Boy, are you dumb!" exclaimed Gus. "Maybe ve von't get the same boat."

492 We've Heard Them

Richmond: "That fellow can speak three languages?"
Kingston: "Yes! Manhattan, Brooklyn, and Bronx!"

493 Her Responsibility

There was a terrible crash as the train struck the car. A few seconds later, Mr. and Mrs. crawled out of the wreckage. Mrs. opened her mouth to speak, but her husband stopped her. "Don't say a word," he snapped. "I got my end of the car across. You were driving in the back seat, and if you let it get hit it's no fault of mine."

494 The Cad at Eve

Husband: "If a man steals, no matter what, he will live to regret it."
Wife (coyly): "You used to steal kisses from me before we were married."
Husband: "Well, you heard what I said."

495 Why Worry?

Father: "Ned, why are you always at the bottom of your class?"
Ned: "It doesn't really matter, Dad. We get the same instruction at both ends of the class."

496 Frank

He: "You know, you are not a bad looking sort of girl."
She: "Oh, you'd say so even if you didn't think so."
He: "Well, we're squared then. You'd think so even if I didn't say so."

497 Throw Out Antiques?

Husband: "One more payment and the furniture's ours."
Wife: "Good! Then we can throw it out and get some new stuff."

498 Taking No Chances

Old Lady to Old Tar: "Excuse me. Do those tattoo marks wash off?"
Old Tar: "I can't say, lady."

499 Looking Backward

"George comes from a very poor family."
"Why, they sent him through medical school, didn't they?"
"Yes, that's how they got so poor."

500   Let's Forget the Whole Thing

Employer: "There's $10 gone from my cash drawer, Johnny; you and I were the only people who had keys to that drawer."

Office Boy: "Well, s'pose we each pay $5 and say no more about it."

501   The Whole Story

Johnny had been the guest of honor at a party the day before, and his friend was regarding him enviously.

"How was it? Have a good time?" he asked.

"Did I?" was the emphatic reply. "I ain't hungry yet!"

502   Tact

That a certain young man is wise beyond his years was proved when he paused before answering a widow who had asked him to guess her age.

"You must have some idea," she said.

"I have several ideas," said the young man, with a smile. "The only trouble is that I hesitate whether to make you ten years younger on account of your looks, or ten years older on account of your intelligence."

503   Polished

He: "She certainly is polished, don't you think so?"

She: "Yeah. Everything she says casts a reflection on someone."

504   Did He Get the Job?

Employer: "Personal appearance is a helpful factor in business success."

Employee: "Yes, and business success is a helpful factor in personal appearance."

505   Add Golf Woe

"When I put the ball where I can reach it," said the stout golfer, on being asked how he liked the game, "I can't see it, and when I put it where I can see it I can't reach it."

506   Can't Complain, Sir

"Are you the waiter who took my order?"

"Yes, sir."

"H'm, still looking well, I see. How are your grandchildren?"

507   Presto!

Teacher was giving a lesson on the weather idiosyncrasies of March. "What is it," she asked, "that comes in like a lion and goes out like a lamb?"

And little Julia, in the back row, replied: "Father."

508   We're Still Friends

Mrs. Jones: "I understand you've got your divorce, Sally. Did you get any alimony from your husband?"

Laundress: "No, Mrs. Jones but he gave me a first-class reference."

509   Day of Doom

Flo: "I don't intend to be married until I'm thirty."

Rea: "I don't intend to be thirty until I'm married!"

510   She'd No Mechanical Taste

Betty (who has been served with a wing of chicken): "Mother, can't I have another bit? This is nothing but hinges."

511   Modern Model

Wife (reading): "It says here they have found sheep in the Himalaya mountains that can run forty miles an hour."

Her Hubby: "Well, it would take a lamb like that to follow Mary nowadays."

512   Mistakes

A certain fraternal society sent out announcements that the annual "instillation" would be held. It caused a great deal of amusement. They meant, of course, "Installation." One letter makes a big difference, as, for example, when a man wrote a letter addressed, "Dear Fiends," having omitted the "r", and the newspaper that spoke of the "bottle-scarred veterans" who marched in the parade. This was almost as bad as the other paper which spoke of the "battle-scared veterans."

513   Sh-h!

A Union Pacific shopman had been drawn on a federal grand jury and didn't want to serve. When his name was called he asked Judge Pollock to excuse him. "We are very busy at the shops," said he, "and I ought to be there."

"So you are one of those men who think the Union Pacific couldn't get along without you," remarked the judge.

"No, your honor," said the shopman. "I know it could get along without me, but I don't want it to find out."

"Excused," said the judge.

514 Sit Down

Teacher: "Johnny, can you define nonsense?"

Johnny: "Yes, teacher—an elephant hanging over a cliff with his tail tied to a daisy."

515 The Restless Age

Teacher: "Willie, give the definition of home."

Willie: "Home is where part of the family waits until the others are through with the car."

516 Smart Boy

A schoolteacher from the city was questioning her small farm nephew to see how his country school education was progressing. "If a farmer had 5,000 bushels of corn," she asked, "and corn is worth 40 cents a bushel, what will he get?"

"A government loan!" promptly replied the nephew.

517 One Kind

Teacher: "What is capital punishment?"

Pupil (whose father was a big businessman): "It's when the government sets up business in competition with you, and then takes all your profits with taxes in order to make up its loss."

518 Bossy's Epitaph

A farmer was trying hard to fill out a railway company claim sheet for a cow that had been killed on the track. He came down to the last item: "Disposition of the carcass." After puzzling over the question for some time, he wrote: "Kind and gentle."

519 Stand It on Its Head

"Have you any alarm clocks?" inquired the customer. "What I want is one that will rouse father without waking the whole family."

"I don't know of any such alarm clock as that, madam," said the shopkeeper. "We keep just the ordinary kind that will wake the whole family without disturbing father."

520   Tit for Tat

She: "You certainly do keep your car nice and clean."
He: "It's an even deal—my car keeps me clean, too."

521   Solomon Said It First

"Anything new in the paper today, George?"
"No, my dear—just the same old things, only happening to different people."

522   Correct Analysis

A suburbanite put on a last-minute spurt of speed to catch his train—but missed it. A by-stander remarked, "If you had just run a little faster you would have made it."
"No," the suburbanite replied, "it wasn't a case of running faster, but of starting sooner."

523   Growls of Recognition

While on the bench one day Judge Daniel called a case for trial, and two lawyers appeared as attorneys for the litigants.
"You're a dirty shyster," snarled one of the lawyers to the other, "and before this case is through I'll show you up for the crooked ape that you are."
"Sez you," snapped the other. "You are a cheat and a liar."
"Come, come," broke in the judge. "Let the case proceed now that the learned counsel have identified each other."

524   Call an Ambulance

"Cup o' tea, weak," said a customer at a London coffee stall. When the decoction was brought to him, he eyed it critically.
"Well, what's wrong with it? You said weak, didn't you?"
"Weak, yes," was the reply, "but not helpless."

525   Typographical Error

Describing a young bride, the editor wrote: "Her dainty feet were encased in shoes that might be taken for fairy boots." It appeared in print, "Her dirty feet were encased in shoes that might have been taken for ferry boats."

526   Finally

Diogenes met a World War veteran.
"What were you in the war?" he asked.
"A private," the soldier answered.
And Diogenes blew out his lamp and went home.

527 Fashions

A man who had been waiting patiently in the post office could not attract the attention of either of the girls behind the counter.

"The evening cloak," explained one of the girls to her companion, "was a redingote design in gorgeous lamé brocade with fox fur and wide pagoda sleeves."

At this point the long-suffering customer broke in with, "I wonder if you could provide me with a neat purple stamp with a dinky perforated hem. The tout ensemble deliberately treated on the reverse side with mucilage. Something at about five cents."

528 School

"Were you copying his paper?"

"No, sir, I was only looking to see if he had mine right."

529 Skating

1st Frosh: "My, what a skating rink!"

2nd Frosh: "Yes. It has a seating capacity of 5,000."

530 Amazing

Professor: "What happens when the human body is immersed in water?"

Student: "The telephone rings."

531 Lesser of Two Evils

During a recent flood in the Kentucky lowlands, one family sent its little boy to stay with an uncle in another part of the state, accompanied by a letter explaining the reason for the nephew's sudden and unexpected visit. Two days later the parents received a telegram: "Am returning boy. Send the flood."

532 Another Version

Prof: "Mr. Smith, will you tell me why you look at your timepiece so often?"

Smith (suavely): "Yes, sir! I was afraid that you wouldn't have time to finish your interesting lecture, sir."

533 Quickly Explained

In speaking of the song, "The Bonnie Banks o' Loch Lomond," a country teacher asked his pupils for an explanation of the line, "Yu'll tak' the high road and I'll tak' the low road."

"One was going by air and the other by bus," answered a boy.

534   New Recruit

"Does the Sergeant know about this?" inquired the Colonel as he surveyed a barricade of sandbags which had just collapsed.

"He ought to," replied a private. "He's underneath!"

535   Disappointment!

"John, dear," said Mrs. Brown, "such an odd thing happened today. The clock fell off the wall, and if it had fallen a moment sooner, it would have hit mother."

"I always said that clock was slow."

536   Prepared

Little Tommy had been forbidden to swim in the river, owing to the danger. One day he came home with signs of having been in the water. His mother scolded him.

"But I was tempted, Mother," said Tommy.

"That's all very well. But how did you come to have your bathing suit with you?" Tommy paused and said: "Well, Mother, I took my bathing suit with me, thinking I might be tempted."

537   Breaking It Gently

"Mrs. Upton's pet dog has been run over; she'll be heartbroken."

"Don't tell her abruptly."

"No, I'll begin by saying it's her husband."

538   Debtor or Creditor

"What is a debtor, Pa?"

"A man who owes money"

"And what is a creditor?"

"The man who thinks he's going to get it."

539   All Set for Thrift Week

An insurance man walked into a lunchroom and taking his place on one of the vacant stools, ordered bread and milk. The fellow sitting on the next stool asked:

"On a diet?"

"No. Commission."

540   Ancestry

A modest gentleman, in speaking of his family, said: "The Hardson family is a very, very old family. The line runs away back into antiquity.

We do not know how far back it runs, but it's a long, long way back, and the history of the Hardson family is recorded in five volumes. In about the middle of the third volume, in a marginal note, we read, 'About this time the world was created.' "

541   Usual

A lady was entertaining her friend's small son.

"Are you sure you can cut your meat?" she asked, after watching his struggles.

"Oh, yes," he replied, without looking up from his plate. "We often have it as tough as this at home."

542   Modern

Grandma: "Would you like to go to the fair and ride in the merry-go-round, dear?"

Modern Child: "I don't really mind, if it will amuse you."

543   Naturally Fitted

"What profession is your boy going to select?"

"I'm going to educate him to be a lawyer," replied Jones. "He's naturally argumentative and bent on mixing into other people's troubles and he might just as well get paid for his time."

544   Suspense

Old Lady (to parachutist): "I really don't know how you can hang from that silk thing. The suspense must be terrible."

Parachutist: "No, mum; it's when the suspense ain't there that it's terrible."

545   Touchy

Barry Winton remarks that a college boy's definition of a male parent is, "The kin you love to touch."

546   Courteous

And then there was the customer who told the elevator operator she'd like to get off at the sixth floor, "if it isn't out of your way."

547   Strategy

"Talk about Napoleon! That fellow Johnson is something of a strategist himself."

"As to how?"

"Got his salary raised six months ago, and his wife hasn't found it out yet."

548 Dual Purposes

A husband and wife came to a bank to open a joint account. Being in a hurry, the man made out his signature card and left.

"Let me see," an official of the bank said to the wife. "This is to be a joint account, it is not?"

"That's right," smiled the wife. "Deposit for him—checking for me."

549 Such Gallantry

"Dearest Annabelle," wrote a lovesick swain, "I could swim the mighty ocean for one glance from your lovely eyes. I could walk through a wall of flame for one touch of your little hand. I would leap the widest stream for a word from your warm lips.—As always, your own Oscar."

"P.S.—I'll be over to see you Sunday night, if it doesn't rain."

550 Salesmanship

She was a new sales clerk. She had a slow mind and a quick tongue and thought herself awfully smart.

A timid-looking man entered the studio. "Do you keep fountain pens?" asked he.

"No, we sell them," snapped she.

"Well," said he, "You'll keep the ones you might have sold me. Good morning."

551 His Political Opponent

Eng'ish political speeches, at their best, have long been noted for their pungent humor. A rejoinder of John Morley, given in the heat of battle, is a typical example.

Morley had just finished a campaign address by requesting his listeners to vote for him, when a man jumped angrily to his feet and shouted, "I'd rather vote for the devil!"

"Quite so," rejoined Morley with a smile, "but in case your friend declines to run, may I count on your support?"

552 Memories

"Dear Clara," wrote the young man, "pardon me, but I'm getting so forgetful. I proposed to you last night, but really forgot whether you said yes or no."

"Dear Will," she replied by note, "so glad to hear from you. I knew that I had said no to somebody last night, but had forgotten who it was."

553 Just a Difference

"Oh, what a strange looking cow," exclaimed the sweet young thing from Chicago. "But why hasn't she any horns?"

"Well, you see," exclaimed the farmer, "some cows are born without horns and never had any, and others shed theirs, and some we dehorn, and some breeds aren't supposed to have horns at all. There are a lot of reasons why some cows haven't got horns, but the reason why that cow hasn't got horns is because she isn't a cow—she's a horse."

554 Likewise

Conductor: "Next station is Long Wait Junction. Change cars for Mauch Chunk, Squeedunk, Quakake, and Podunk, Hokendaqua, Catasaqua, Mecanaqua, and Tamaqua."

Green Brakeman (at other end of car): "Same at this end."

555 Mistake

They were twins. It was bathing time and from the twins' bedroom came sounds of hearty laughter and loud crying. Their father went up to find the cause.

"What's the matter up here?" he inquired.

The laughing twin pointed to his weeping brother.

"Nothing," he giggled, "only nurse has given Alexander two baths and hasn't given me any at all."

556 Raw Recruit

Rifle Instructor: "Do you know where you are aiming?"

New Recruit: "No, sir. I'm a stranger in this district."

557 Corpse

Mathematics Teacher: "Robert, can you tell me what is meant by a polygon?"

Robert (a freshman): "I guess it means a parrot that's died, doesn't it?"

558 Easily Pleased

Father: "Remember, son, beauty is only skin deep."

Son: " 'S'deep enough for me. I'm no cannibal."

559 Do As I Say, etc.

Student (to Prof): "What's that you wrote on my paper?"

Prof: "I told you to write plainer."

560   *One Advantage of Irrigation*

Customer: "Say, this hair restorer you sold me didn't grow one hair on my head."

Barber: "Mebbe not, but it has a nice cooling effect when it runs down around your ears, hasn't it?"

561   *Statistics*

Office Boy: "I et six pancakes for breakfast this morning."

Bookkeeper: "You mean ate, don't you?"

Office Boy: "Well maybe it was eight I et."

562   *Biting*

Game Warden: "Are the fish biting today?"

Weary Angler: "I don't know. If they are, they're biting each other."

563   *Ignorant*

Lecturer: "Of course you all know what the inside of a corpuscle is like."

Chairman (interrupting): "Most of us do, but you had better explain for the benefit of them that have never been inside one."

564   *Seeking a Pastor*

> When a church seeks a pastor,
> They often want
> The strength of an eagle,
> The grace of a swan,
> The gentleness of a dove,
> The friendliness of a sparrow,
> And the night hours of an owl;
> And when they catch that bird
> They expect him to live
> On the food of a canary.

565   *Information, Please*

An example of youthful pessimism was provided by a little boy who was about to start on a railway journey. It was the first time he had ever traveled alone, and his mother told him to write his name and address on a card and keep it in his pocket. He wrote: "In case of accident, this was Johnny Jones."

566 Dumb Trees

Sonny sat on the lower steps, his face resting in his two chubby hands.

"What's the matter, Sonny?"

"Nothin'—just thinkin'."

"What about?"

"Thinkin' how dumb trees are to take off their clothes in winter and put 'em on in summer."

567 Two to One

Some few years ago, just after Jimmy Foxx had broken into the regular lineup with the Philadelphia Athletics, the Boston Red Sox came to Philly to play a series. George Moriarty was umpiring behind the plate.

Foxx took two terrific cuts at the first two pitches, and let the third one float by.

"Strike three, you're out," said Moriarty.

Foxx turned indignantly, "You missed that one, George."

"Well, you missed the other two," Moriarty replied. "You're still one up on me."

568 Earning His Bit

The plumber was working and his new assistant was looking on. The latter was learning the trade and this was his first day.

"Say," he inquired, "do you charge for my time?"

"Certainly," was the reply.

"But I haven't done anything."

The plumber had been inspecting the finished job with a lighted candle, which he handed to his helper. "Here," he said, "if you've got to be so conscientious, blow that out!"

569 Too Bad

> Mary had a little lamb
> 'Twas awful dumb and so
> It couldn't tell the red from green
> Nor which was stop or go.
> It followed her to school one day
> A silly thing to do
> Was caught between the red and green
> And now it's mutton stew.

570 Sometimes It Sounds That Way

As the soprano began to sing, little Johnnie became greatly excited over the gesticulations of the orchestra conductor.

"What's that man shaking his stick at her for?" he demanded.
"Sh-h! He's not shaking his stick at her."
But Johnnie was not convinced.
"Then what is she hollering for?"

571   Sinister Connotation

"I wish you boys wouldn't call me Big Bill."
"Why not?"
"Those college names stick—and I'm going to be a doctor."

572   Two-Thirty Plenty

Chinese patient (on telephone): "Doctor what time you fixee teeth for me?"
Doctor: "Two-thirty—all right?"
Chinese: "Yes, tooth hurty, all right, but what time you fixee?"

573   Ministerial Tact

A minister was known by a few of his parishioners to be fond of cherry brandy and one of them in a mischievous frame of mind offered to present him with a bottle on condition that it was fully acknowledged in the next issue of the church magazine. The offer was promptly accepted and in due course the notice appeared in the magazine: "The Vicar thanks Mr. McTavish for his gift of fruit and the spirit in which it was given."

574   One Drawback

Tom: "How do you like your new job selling on the road?"
Harry: "Oh, it's dandy. You meet some fine fellows at the hotels and have lots of fun in the evenings, but what I don't like is calling on those jobbers every day."

575   Revenge

A wholesaler wrote a threatening letter. This is the reply he received:
"Dear Sir: What do you mean by sending me a letter like that?
"Every month I place all my bills in a basket and then figure out how much money I have to pay them. Next, I draw as many bills out of the basket as I have money to pay.
"If you don't like my way of doing business, I won't even put your bill in the basket next month."

576 Observant

"Mother, I'm the best-looking boy in Sunday school."

"Why, Tommy! Who told you that?"

"Nobody, Mother. Nobody told me. I saw all the rest of them."

577 Left in Doubt

Policeman (after the collision): "You saw this lady driving toward you. Why didn't you give her the road?"

Motorist: "I was going to, as soon as I could discover which half she wanted."

578 A Break for the Birds

After a day's shooting in India, a young Englishman who was a poor shot said to his Indian attendant: "I did not do so well today."

"Oh, the young sahib shot very well, very well indeed," said the diplomatic Hindu, "but God was very merciful to the birds."

579 What Goes Up

It seems that one of the boys on army maneuvers in Texas came floating into camp near the Davis Mountains. When he was brought to the officer's tent, slightly bruised, he was told, "You've got real nerve to come down in a parachute with this 100-mile wind blowing. That's dangerous!"

"I didn't come down in a parachute," said the private. "I went up in a tent."

580 Calvin Coolidge

Speaking of the Coolidge reserve, a reporter attempted an interview: "Do you wish to say anything about the strike?" was the first question.

"No."

"About the farm bloc?"

"No."

"About the World Court?"

"No."

The reporter turned to go. "By the way," added Coolidge, unexpectedly calling him back, "don't quote me."

581 Wise Girl

Student: "To whom was Minerva married?"

Professor: "My boy, when will you learn that Minerva was the Goddess of Wisdom? She wasn't married."

582   Nutshell

Student: "Yes, sir, I always carry my notes in my hat."
Prof: "I see—knowledge in a nutshell."

583   Direct Hit

The squad of recruits had been out to the rifle range for their first try at marksmanship. They knelt at 250 yards and fired. Not a hit. They moved up to 200 yards. Not a hit. They tried at 100 yards. Not a hit.

"'Tenshun!" the sergeant barked. "Fix bayonets! Charge! It's your only chance."

584   He's Safe

"You know the old saying, what you don't know won't hurt you."
"So what?"
"You lucky dog, you're invulnerable."

585   Golf Club Lunch Menu

Scotch Broth

Club Sandwich   Sliced Tomatoes

Link Sausage

Dandelion Green   Puttatoes

Parsnips
Cup Custard
Rolls   Nuts
Tea

586   Sometimes Too Long Also

The American public dinner has been described by a popular after-dinner speaker as "an affair where a speaker first eats a lot of food he doesn't want and then proceeds to talk about something he doesn't understand to a lot of people who don't want to hear him."

587   Considerable Difference

"Give me a chicken salad," said the man in a suburban restaurant.
"Do you want the 40-cent one or the 50-cent one?" asked the waitress.
"What's the difference?"
"The 40-cent ones are made of veal and pork and the 50-cent ones are made of tuna."

588   Mountain Guide

Be careful not to fall here. It's dangerous. But if you do fall, remember to look to the left. You get a wonderful view on that side.

589   It Helps

"I drink about fifty cups of coffee a day."
"Doesn't that keep you awake?"
"It helps."

590   Not a Total Loss

There was a young man of Devises,
Whose ears were of different sizes;
The one that was small
Was of no use at all
But the other won several prizes.

591   Number, Please

A gentleman visiting in Washington wanted to phone someone in Baltimore. It proved annoying when the operator said: "Deposit seventy-five cents, please."
"What!" he cried. "Seventy-five cents to call Baltimore? Why, at home we can phone to Hades and back for a dime."
"Oh, yes," she replied, "but that's a local call."

592   College Exams

Prof (gazing over the room during an examination): "Will some kind gentleman who isn't using his textbook be so kind as to permit me to have it for a few minutes?"

593   Capital and Labor

Willie: "What is the difference between capital and labor, Dad?"
Dad: "Well, son, the money you lend represents capital—and getting it back represents labor."

594   Cross-Examination

State's Attorney: "Are you sure this is the man who stole your car last Thursday?"
Much-Befuddled Plaintiff: "Well, I was. Now after the cross-examination, I'm not sure I ever owned a car."

595   Modest Fellow

Her: "I suppose all geniuses are conceited."
Him: "Some of them—but I'm not."

596   Never Mind the Details

A somewhat inebriated gentleman was walking down State Street and did not know his location. He turned to a passer-by and said, "Mister, where am I?" The passer-by answered, "You are at the corner of State and Madison streets." The inebriated gentleman said, "Never mind the details, what city?"

597   Conspicuous

An American advertising man told an Englishman that an electric sign being constructed had 30,000 white lights, 40,000 green lights, 60,000 pink lights, and, in addition, it would have a great sunburst of 100,000 orange lights. The Englishman looked at it a moment and said, "Yes, that's a marvelous sign, but don't you think it is going to be a little bit conspicuous?"

598   Trouble

Two little boys were playing in a train. The conductor said the children must behave or he would make trouble. The boys' father said. "You don't know what trouble is. My wife's in the hospital. I am on my way to see my sick mother-in-law; my daughter has had triplets; one of the boys has just smashed his finger, and the other has chewed up our tickets. To top it all off, we are on the wrong train."

599   A Difficult Golf Course

A guest on a golf course placed the ball in position, missed three times, hit it the fourth time, and then turned to his host and said, "This is a difficult course, isn't it?"

600   Fast Driving

Two fraternity brothers headed toward Philadelphia. They were zipping along the highway at some eighty or ninety miles an hour, when a policeman appeared from nowhere and forced them over to the side of the road.

"What's the matter, officer?" they asked. "Were we driving too fast?"

"No," he answered sarcastically. "You were flying too low."

601   The Way to Do It

"What's the best way to appeal to audiences?"

"First find out what they think about something," answered the orator, "and then tell 'em they're perfectly right."

602   *Farsighted*

Doctor: "I'd like to have a quart of blood for a transfusion. Can you give it?"
Stude: "I can only give you a pint. I gotta shave tomorrow."

603   *Tin You*

> I bought a wooden whistle,
> But it wooden whistle,
> So I bought a steel whistle,
> But steel it wooden whistle,
> So I bought a lead whistle,
> Still they wooden lead me whistle,
> So I bought a tin whistle,
> And now I tin whistle.

604   *The Old Gent Should Know*

"Now," said the lad to his father, at the college football game, "you'll see more excitement for two dollars than you ever saw before."
"I don't know," replied the old gent. "That's what my marriage license cost me."

605   *That's All*

"Say, pal, how much money does your wife demand every pay day?"
"Don't ask foolish questions. You know my salary is one hundred dollars a week."

606   *Expensive*

"Can you tell if the defendant was expensively garbed?"
"Indeed she was. Ah knows expensive garbage when Ah sees it."

607   *A Good Question*

When the family returned from Sunday morning service father criticized the sermon, daughter thought the choir's singing was atrocious, and mother found fault with the organist's playing. The small boy of the family piped up, "But it was a good show for a quarter, don't you think, Dad?"

608   *Invoice*

Hubby: "You never tell me what you buy! Don't I get any voice in the buying?"
Wifey: "Certainly, darling! You get the invoice."

609 *Clever, These Chinese*

A sailor, after placing some flowers on a grave in a cemetery, noticed an old Chinese man placing a bowl of rice on a nearby grave, and asked: "What time do you expect your friend to come up and eat the rice?"

The old Chinese man replied with a smile: "Same time your friend come up to smell flowers."

610 *Court Scene*

Judge to Prisoner: "Say, when were you born?"

(No reply.)

Judge: "I say, when was your birthday?"

Prisoner (sullenly): "Wot do you care? You ain't gonner give me nothin'!"

611 *Explanation*

Doctor: "Now you see what comes of eating green apples when your mother told you not to."

Boy: "I didn't eat 'em because I liked 'em. I ate 'em to find out why she told me not to."

612 *Back in the Good Old Days*

"Crop failures?" asked the old timer.

"Yep, I've seen a few of 'em in my days. Now in 1910 the corn crop was purt' nigh nothing. We cooked some for dinner one day, and Dad ate fourteen acres of corn at one meal!"

613 *Near By*

He: "Meet me at the Waldorf-Astoria at eight."

She: "The Waldorf? . . . Say, that's a nice place."

He: "Yeah, and it's close to where we're going, too."

614 *Ambition*

An ambitious Chinese sent the following letter of application in answer to an advertisement for a stenographer:

"Sir.—I am Chang. . . . I can drive a typewriter with good noise and my English is great. My last job left itself from me for the good reason that the large man has dead. It was on account of no fault of mine. So, honorable sir, what about it? If I can be of big use to you, I will arrive on some date that you should guess."

615 *Behind His Ears*

In a church, at the font, her small brother was being christened.

Little Girl—*"Behind his ears, too, Reverend Smyth!"*

616   *In Demand*

> An epicure, dining at Crewe,
> Found quite a large mouse in his stew.
> Said the waiter, "Don't shout,
> And wave it about,
> Or the rest will be wanting one, too!"

617   *Play Ball*

In a small town in Louisiana on a hot dusty day two baseball teams, surrounded by their devotees, were engaged in a very important baseball game.

The preacher of the community had been approved by both teams for the position of umpire in this contest—because, as the home team pointed out, a parson couldn't do wrong.

The visiting team's clean-up man stood in the batter's box. The bases were loaded.

"Ball one, high!" the voice of authority boomed.

"Ball two, low!"

"Ball three, inside!"

"Ball fo', low and wide—you is out!"

"How does you talk, Mister Ump? Ah gets a base fo' dat!" screamed the mutinous batsman.

"Brother, you is right—but de bases am loaded, an' Ah ain't got no place to put you. You is out!"

618   *Not Ashamed of Dad!*

"My boy," said the millionaire, "when I was your age, I carried water for a gang of bricklayers."

"I'm mighty proud of you, Father. If it hadn't been for your pluck and perseverance, I might have had to do something like that myself."

619   *Not So Big*

"He's not as big a fool as he used to be."

"Getting wiser?"

"No, thinner."

620   *Regular Once a Year*

"Does your wife attend church regularly?"

"Very. She hasn't missed an Easter Sunday since we were married."

621   *To the Point*

Chairman: "Congratulations, my boy, congratulations on your typical married man's speech!"

Timid Speaker: "But I said only a couple of words."
Chairman: "Precisely!"

622   That Suffocating Feeling

Have you ever had that cooped-up feeling as if you were in a very small cell? Have you ever felt that closed-in suffocating feeling? Have you ever found yourself talking when there was actually no one present for you to talk to? Were you ever worried by this condition? Then, why don't you get out of the telephone booth?

623   Architectural Triumph

Two ladies were attending a concert at the Civic Auditorium.
"Nice building," said one lady. "What style of architecture is it?"
"I'm not quite sure," said the other lady, "but I think it's Reminiscence."

624   And Lady Uncles Are O.K.

A schoolteacher asked the pupils to write a short essay and to choose their own subjects.
A little girl sent in the following paper:—
"My subjek is 'Ants.' Ants is of two kinds, insects and lady uncles.
"Sometimes they live in holes and sometimes they crawl into the sugar bole, and sometimes they live with their married sisters.
"That is all I know about ants."

625   Grandpappy Knew

A Yankee motorist, driving through Georgia, lost his way. Coming to a stop alongside an elderly native, he asked, "Which way's Atlanta?"
The old man surveyed the car's license plate, then said, "Your grandpappy didn't have any trouble finding it!"

626   Looking Ahead

They had just become engaged.
"I shall love," she cooed, "to share all your troubles."
"But darling," he murmured, "I have none."
"No," she agreed, "but I mean when we are married."

627   Stolen Sweets

The rector had invited the village boys to the rectory for strawberries. After they had finished he, seeking to point the moral said: "Now, boys, wasn't that nicer than breaking into my garden and helping yourselves?"

"Oh, yes," chorused the boys.

"And why was it nicer?" he asked a chubby-faced boy.

"Because, sir," was the reply, "we shouldn't have had any sugar and cream with them."

628 Bird of Paradise

Customer: "That chicken I bought yesterday had no wishbone."

Butcher (smoothly): "It was a happy and contented chicken, madam, and had nothing to wish for."

629 A Positive Situation

Jack: "My wife talks to me positively awful."

Ed: "That's nothing. Mine talks to me awfully positive."

630 He Will Start Now

A colonel got a case of cold feet before the battle. Calling his command together, he said: "Boys, we're going to get licked, but you must fight as you never fought before. If worse comes to worst, run for it; as for me, I'm a little lame, so I'll start now."

631 Not Near Enough

"Mr. Jones," asked the instructor, "how far were you from the correct answer?"

"Only three seats, sir."

632 Experienced

Henry: "My dear, I really don't believe you can ever teach that dog to obey you."

Mrs. Peck: "Nonsense, darling. Just remember how obstinate you were when we were first married."

633 Heard on the Links

At the club golf tournament the club secretary caught one of the entrants driving off about a foot in front of the teeing mark.

"Here!" he cried indignantly. "You can't do that. You're disqualified!"

"What for?" demanded the golfer.

"Why, you're driving off in front of the mark."

The player looked at the secretary with pity. "G'wan back to the clubhouse," he said tersely. "I'm playing my third stroke!"

634 A Good Start

The first morning after the honeymoon, the husband got up early, went down to the kitchen, and brought his wife her breakfast in bed. Naturally, she was delighted. Then her husband spoke:

"Have you noticed just what I have done?"

"Of course, dear; every single detail."

"Good. That's how I want my breakfast served every morning after this."

635 Wins Her Diploma

An inspector, examining a class in religious knowledge, asked the following question of a little girl intending it for a catch:

"What was the difference between Noah's Ark and Joan of Arc?" He was not a little surprised when the child, answering, said: "Noah's Ark was made of wood and Joan of Arc was maid of Orleans."

636 Annoying

Nothing is quite so annoying as to have someone go right on talking when you're interrupting.

637 Not to Pitch

Vernon "Lefty" Gomez, famed pitcher of the New York Yankees during the thirties was separated for a time from his actress wife, but effected a reconciliation just before the World Series started. In the lobby of the Yankees' hotel, Gomez was accosted for an interview by a female reporter.

Gomez greeted her and then introduced Mrs. Gomez. "Oh, dear," blurted the lady reporter. "Am I to construe this as a reconciliation?"

Without batting an eye, Gomez retorted, "Well, I didn't bring her along to pitch."—Donald McGraw, in True

638 Veteran Speaks

Young Harry: "Father, what's the difference between a gun and a machine gun?"

Dad: "There is a big difference. It is just as if I spoke, and then your mother spoke."

639 Double Jointed

Fifer: "What sort of fellow is Groot?"

Zimpir: "Oh, he's one of those people who will pat you on the back before your face and hit you in the face behind your back."

640   Blackout

A mother noticed the other night that her high school son who was getting ready to go to a dance got dressed in record time.

"Did you take a bath?" she asked him accusingly.

"No," came the reply.

"Now listen, son," she remonstrated, "you wouldn't go to a dance without taking a bath, would you?"

"Sure I would, Mom," came the reply. "It's not formal."

641   You're Fired

The foreman, a tough, conceited individual, was boasting of his strength.

"I can lick any man working for me!" he declared.

"You can't lick me," said a new employee.

The foreman looked over the young man's muscular frame very carefully, then spoke.

"You're fired," he said.

642   Knows His Neptune

A young naval student was being put through the paces by an old sea captain.

"What would you do if a storm sprang up on the starboard?"

"Throw out an anchor, sir." "What would you do if another storm sprang up aft?" "Throw out another anchor, sir." "And if another terrific storm sprang up forward, what would you do?" "Throw out another anchor." "Hold on," said the Captain, "Where are you getting all your anchors from?" "From the same place you're getting your storms, sir."

643   Domestic Business College

Momma (singing): "By low, my baby."

Poppa: "That's right; you tell him to buy low and I'll teach him to sell high."

644   Triumph of Comfort

"I'm not sure I quite understand those flexible-action wheels."

"Why, it's like this—the wheels give. So if you run over a pedestrian you hardly feel it."

645   Shouldn't Be Tight

He: "What part of the car causes the most accidents?"

She: "The nut that holds the wheel."

646   A Happy Family

P.T. Barnum, the great showman, used to exhibit a happy family. This family consisted of a lion, a tiger, a wolf, a bear, and a lamb, all in one cage.

"Remarkable," a visitor said one day to Mr. Barnum. "Remarkable, impressive. How long have these animals dwelt together in this way?"

"Eight months," Barnum replied. "But the lamb has to be renewed occasionally."

647   Stop, Thief!

Niece (in the picture gallery): "Aunt Sarah, this is the famous 'Angelus' by Millet."

Aunt Sarah: "Well, I never! That man had the nerve to copy the calendar that has hung in our kitchen for a dozen years or more."

648   Rattling the Skeleton

Pupil (after lesson on creation): "But, teacher, daddy says we are descended from monkeys."

Teacher: "We can't discuss your private family affairs in class."

649   Try Bran Mash

Neighbor: "How is that incubator doing that you bought?"

Mrs. Newbride: "I suppose it's all right, but I'm a little worried about it. It hasn't laid a single egg yet."

650   Gets 'em Going and Coming

Schultz: "Your opening sale has closed. What now?"
Schwartz: "Our closing sale opens."

651   Impromptu Howler

Teacher: "William, construct a sentence using the word 'archaic.' "
William: "We can't have archaic and eat it too."

652   Politically Inclined

A farmer had a razorback hog that was a great runner. One day he set out to find her, and after hours in following the tracks, over the creek and back, he came home and said: "I can't find that hog, but after studying her tracks, I believe she's on both sides of the creek."

653   Cover Charge

Waiter: "Would you mind settling your bill, sir? We're closing now."
Irate Patron: "But, hang it all, I haven't been served yet."
Waiter: "Well, in that case, there'll only be the cover charge."

654   Travel Note

"What is the difference between valor and discretion?"
"Well, to travel on an ocean liner without tipping would be valor."
"I see."
"And to come back on a different boat would be discretion."

655   She Knew Her Neck

The barber had used his electric clippers in cutting small Betty's hair.
"I guess my neck wasn't clean," she told her mother on coming home,
" 'cause that man used his vacuum cleaner on it."

656   Plenty Back-Seat Driving

Sunday School Teacher: "Why was Solomon the wisest man in the world?"
Sarkis: "Because he had so many wives to advise him."

657   And Was His Face Red!

In the congregation of an Oak Park church during Sunday morning service was a young bride whose husband was an usher. Becoming terribly worried about having left the roast in the oven, she wrote a note to her husband, sending it to him by another usher.
The latter, thinking it was a note for the pastor, hurried down the aisle and laid it on the pulpit. Stopping abruptly in the middle of his sermon to read the note, the astonished pastor was met with the written injunction:
"Please go home and turn off the gas."

658   But Did She Fall for It?

Wife: "Mrs. Jones has another new hat."
Hubby: "Well, if she were as attractive as you are, my dear, she wouldn't have to depend so much upon the milliner."

659   Just a Smart Dreamer

A spinster was stopped on the street by a ragged man.
"Could you spare a dime for something to eat, ma'am?"

"Why are you begging—a big, strong man like you? I should think you'd be ashamed."

"Mademoiselle," he said, removing his hat and bowing courteously. "I am a disappointed romanticist. I have woven dreams of cobweb stuff and the wind has swept them away. And so I have turned to this profession—the only one I know in which a gentleman can address a beautiful girl without the formality of an introduction."

Yes, he got a dollar.

660 *"Atchoo!"*

"Who invented the hole in the doughnut?"
"Oh, some fresh air fiend, I suppose."

661 *Noblesse Oblige*

Professor: "This exam will be conducted on the honor system. Please take seats three seats apart and in alternate rows."

662 *Cure for Extravagance*

"Are you saving any money?"
"Sure. We have a budget. By the time we balance it every evening, all the places we could spend money are closed."

663 *Staying Power*

"Your wife seems a garrulous woman."
"Garrulous? Why, if I suddenly went dumb it would take her a week to find it out."

664 *Cramping His Style*

Golfer: "Hi, caddy! Isn't Major Pepper out of that bunker yet? How many strokes has he had?"
Caddy: "Seventeen ordinary, sir, and one apoplectic!"

665 *Just Lucky*

"I've got an idea," said the freshman.
"Beginner's luck," said the sophomore.

666 *Perfect Alibi*

Hubby: "What became of that unpaid bill Dunn and Company sent to us?"
Wife: "Oh, that? I sent it back marked insufficient funds."

667 Giving It the Works

Maud: "So Jack said that I had a skin one loves to touch."
Marie: "Not exactly, dear; he said you had a skin you love to retouch."

668 Long-Winded Toastmaster

"What is the hardest part of your work as a lecturer?" asked the toast-master.

"As a rule," replied the speaker, "the hardest part of my work is waking the audience up after the man who introduces me has concluded his remarks."

669 Rock of Ages

"What is the mortarboard I hear mentioned so often?" asked the little girl.

"I'll try to explain," said Miss Cayenne, "although it is a slightly complicated matter. A mortarboard carried by a builder often has cement on top and worn by a college professor often has concrete under it."

670 All Sewed Up

"John, I found this letter in your coat pocket this morning. I gave it to you a month ago to mail."

"Yes, dear, I remember. I took that coat off for you to sew a button on and I'm still waiting."

671 Dead Letter Baritone

"I've learned to sing."
"Where did you learn to sing?"
"I graduated from a correspondence school."
"Boy, you sure lost lots of your mail."

672 What Is So Funny?

"Did you ever hear that joke about the museum in Philadelphia that had a skull of Benjamin Franklin when he was twelve in one room, and a skull when he was fifty in another?"

"No," said the Englishman. "What was it?"

673 Success

Bride: "I cooked my first meal last night—it was a grand success."
Visitor: "How nice!"
Bride: "Yes, he's going to get me a cook right away."

674   *When Words Fail*

The golfer stepped up to the tee and drove off. The ball sailed straight down the fairway, leaped onto the green and rolled into the hole. The golfer threw his club in the air with excitement.

"What have you suddenly gone crazy about?" asked his wife, who was trying to learn something about the game.

"Why, I just did a hole-in-one," yelled the golfer, a wild gleam of delight in his eyes.

"Did you?" asked his wife placidly. "Do it again, dear, I didn't see you."

675   *Executive Ability*

"What is executive ability, Father?" asked a serious lad.

"Executive ability, my son, is the art of getting the credit for all the hard work that somebody else does."

676   *Out of Tune*

Two elderly men at a club were discussing the table manners of a new member.

"Well, what do you think of him?" asked one.

"Very remarkable," replied the other, thoughtfully, "I've heard soup gargled and siphoned, but that's the first time I've ever heard it yodeled."

677   *Slight Error*

Joan: "John, dear, your office is on Broad Street, isn't it?"

John: "Yes, why?"

Joan: "That's funny. I told that to Daddy and he said he'd been looking you up in Bradstreet."

678   *Chronic Knocker*

"Anything the matter with the car?"

"Well, there's only one part of it that doesn't make a noise and that's the horn."

679   *Principles Are Principal*

When William died suddenly the neighbors were shocked, and a kindly woman proceeded to comfort William's wife by describing his good points.

"He was such a man of principle," said the neighbor.

"And am I not the one to know it?" said the bereaved woman. "Every Saturday night didn't he come home and place his pay envelope in front of me as regular as clockwork? Not a night did he miss all the time we were married."

"Of course, the envelope was always empty, but look at the principle of the thing!"

680 *He Done Fine*

"Well, Albert, how did you get along in the examination in English grammar today?"

"Oh, I done fine, Pop. I only made one mistake and I seen that as soon as I done it."

681 *Irresistible*

Customer: "I've come back to buy that car you showed me yesterday."

Salesman: "That's fine, I thought you'd be back. Now tell we what was the dominant feature that made you decide to buy this car?"

Customer: "My wife, sir."

682 *Unanimous*

Warden: "Boys, I've had charge of this prison for ten years and we ought to celebrate the occasion. What kind of party would you suggest?"

Prisoners (in unison): "Open house."

683 *Attributed Sometimes to Lincoln*

A business firm considering the employment of a young attorney wrote to Lincoln about him.

Lincoln wrote: "He's a bright young fellow, hasn't had much practice yet, but is ambitious. He has an office in the Blackstone block, small library, worth $50, a table and two chairs, $5 will cover them, and in the southeast corner of the room is a rat hole that will bear looking into."

684 *What They Think*

What they think when little Oswald starts to school for the first time.

His mother: "Just think, my little darling is almost grown up."

His father: "I hope he makes a fullback."

His older sister: "That means I've got to walk to school with him and can't go to school with the kids."

His teacher: "I hope he's smarter than he looks."

His neighbors: "Thank heaven! Now we can have peace for a few hours a day."

His dog: "Yo-o-o-ow-l-l-l."

685 *He Knows*

Teacher: "Johnny! Can you tell me what a waffle is?"

Johnny: "Yes'm; it's a pancake with a non-skid tread."

686   An Omission

A London welfare club gives an annual bathing outing to newsboys.
Said one: "I say, Bill, ain't you dirty!"
Bill: "Yes, I missed the train last year."

687   "Socialized" Medicine

Janice: "So Lillie threw over that young doctor she was going with!"
Clarice: "Yes, and what do you think? He not only requested her to
return his presents but sent her a bill for forty-seven visits."

688   Couldn't Fool Him

John Smith happened to witness a minor holdup. In due time the police
arrived, and one officer asked the witness his name.
"John Smith," said Smith.
"Cut the comedy," snapped the cop. "What's your real name?"
"All right," said Smith, "put me down as Winston Churchill."
"That's more like it," said the officer. "You can't fool me with that
John Smith stuff.'

689   Quiz

"Are you a good student?"
"Yes and no."
"What do you mean?"
"Yes, I am no good."

690   As Usual?

Policeman (calling up station): "A man has been robbed down here,
and I've got one of them."
Chief: "Which one have you?"
Policeman: "The man that was robbed."

691   Ladies Note

Quiggle: "Why is it that you women always insist on having the last
word!"
Mrs. Quiggle: "We don't. The only reason we get it is that we always
have a dozen arguments left when you stupid men are all run out."

692   A Nag, a Bone, and a Hunk of Hay

He: "How do you feel after your ride on that horse?"
She: "Gosh! I never thought anything filled with hay could be so
hard!"

693 Boston

A motorist driving through Boston, drew up to the curb and asked one of the natives:

"My good man, could you tell me where I might stop at?"

"I would advise," said the native coldly, "stopping just before the 'at.'"

694 Diplomacy

Customer: "Have you anything for gray hair?"

Conscientious Druggist: "Nothing, madam, but the greatest respect."

695 Baffling

She had spent a full hour instructing her third grade class in some of the wonders of nature, and just by way of a clincher she said: "Isn't it wonderful how little chickens got out of their shells?" One little eight-year-old lad, quite practical, quizzed back, "What gets me is how they got in!"

696 Careful

The *Shelby* (Ala.) *Democrat* reports the case of a man who was defeated ignominiously when he ran for the office of sheriff.

He got 55 votes out of a total of 3,500, and the next day he walked down Main Street with two guns hanging from his belt.

"You were not elected, and you have no right to carry guns," fellow-citizens told him.

"Listen, folks," he replied, "a man with no more friends than I've got in this county needs to carry guns."

697 One Stubborn

The jury foreman was asked by the sheriff if he should send in twelve dinners as usual? "No," said the foreman, "make it eleven dinners and a bale of hay."

698 Results Dubious

"Did Mr. Borer sing a popular song at the concert?"

"Well, it had been popular before he sang it."

699 No Bluffing Necessary

"Now that you're a success as a character actor and are going to be married, will you build your house on a bluff?"

"I should say not—her father's paying for it."

700 With One Exception

"Why, he's the loudest-mouthed man I ever heard."
"Shush, dear, you forget yourself."

701 It's Easy

Hunter: "How do you detect an elephant?"
Guide: "You smell a faint odor of peanuts on his breath."

702 The Old Thief

"The new washerwoman has stolen two of our towels."
"The thief! Which ones, dear?"
"The ones we got from the hotel in Miami."

703 Hopeful

Boss: "Henry, you're a liar. You took a day off to bury your mother-in-law, and I met her in the park this morning."
Henry: "Oh, I didn't say she was dead, sir. I just said I would like to go to her funeral."

704 Modern Art

Critic: "Ah! And what is this? It is superb! What soul! What expression!"
Artist: "That's where I clean the paint off my brushes."

705 Clipped Wings

At a fancy dress dance for children a policeman stationed at the door was instructed not to admit any adults.

An excited woman came running up to the door and demanded admission.

"I'm sorry, ma'am," replied the policeman, "but I can't let anyone in but children."

"But my child is in there as a butterfly," exclaimed the woman, "and has forgotten her wings!"

"Can't help it," replied the policeman, "orders is orders. You'll have to let her represent a caterpillar!"

706 Sister's Viewpoint

Coed: "What position does your brother play on the team?"
Sister: "A sort of crouched, bent position."

707 Wonderful World

The young couple were finding out about the joys of a joint bank account.

"The bank has returned your last check," said the husband grimly. "Goody," said the bride. "What should I buy with it next?"

708 *A Gracious Rival*

Modern political campaigners might take a lesson in graciousness and kindness from Edward Campbell, the great British statesman.

Once when Campbell was opposing Thackeray for a seat in Parliament, the two contenders, in the course of their campaigning, met and engaged in friendly conversation.

On taking leave of his rival Thackeray remarked, "May the best man win!"

"Oh, no," replied Campbell, "I hope not, I want to win!"

709 *Really Remarkable*

"If Shakespeare were here today, he would be looked on as a remarkable man."

"Yes, he'd be more than 350 years old."

710 *Highland Playboys*

MacGregor and MacPherson decided to become teetotalers, but MacGregor thought it would be best if they had one bottle of whiskey to put in the cupboard in case of illness.

After three days MacPherson could bear it no longer and said: "MacGregor, Ah'm not verra weel."

"Too late, MacPherson, Ah was verra sick m'sel' all day yesterday."

711 *Wanted a Lesson*

Gentleman (at police station): "Could I see the man who was arrested for robbing our house last night?"

Desk Sergeant: "This is very irregular. Why do you want to see him?"

Gentleman: "I don't mind telling you. I only want to ask how he got in the house without awakening my wife."

712 *Correct Answer*

"When Lot's wife looked back," said the Sunday school teacher, "what happened to her?"

"She was transmuted into chloride of sodium," answered the boy with the high I.Q.

713 *No Driver*

An inebriate boarded a two-deck bus and sat near the driver. He talked so much that the driver suggested he go to the top deck and enjoy the fresh air. In a few minutes he was back.

"Didn't you like it upstairs?" said the driver.

"Yes, nice view," answered the drunk, "but it ain't safe—no driver!"

714   Leave It Out

Mrs. Newbride: "I took the recipe for this cake out of the cook book."
Hubby: "You did perfectly right, dear. It never should have been put in."

715   Good Swimmer

Sally Anne (aged six): "Granddad, were you in the ark?"
Granddad: "Why no, honey."
Sally Anne: "Then why weren't you drowned?"

716   Short Cut

"Officer, what's the quickest way to the hospital?"
"Close your eyes, cross this street, and you'll be there in fifteen minutes."

717   Another Hardship

The Pilgrim mothers stood all the trials the Pilgrim fathers stood, but, in addition, stood the Pilgrim fathers.

718   Safety First

Singer: "Now that you've heard my voice, what would you suggest to accompany me?"
Impresario: "A bodyguard."

719   The Average Motorist

Service Station Man: "How much gasoline does the tank in your car hold?"
Autoist: "I don't know. I've never had enough money to get it filled yet."

720   Some Rest

Sergeant: "Did you sleep well on your cot? I'm afraid it was a little hard and uneven, but—"
Conscript: "It was all right, sir. I got up now and then during the night and rested a little, you know."

721   Flattered

The new traffic cop had been told by his inspector to overtake and stop a speeding car. Ten minutes later he called to report: "Car was being driven by an actress. I stops her, pulls out my notebook. She snatches it, writes her autograph, and leaves me standing."

722 Arctic Style Hints

Teacher: "Now, Freddy, why does a polar bear wear a fur coat?"
Freddy: "Oh—er, well, I suppose he would look funny in a tweed one."

723 Same Bread

The officer received a complaint about the issue of bread.
"Soldiers should not make a fuss about trivialities, my man," he said. "If Napoleon had had that bread when he was crossing the Alps, he'd have eaten it with delight."
"Yes, sir," said the corporal, "but it was fresh then."

724 Sphere of Influence

Frederick S. Isham, the novelist, has offered this story to refute the belief that the Chinese are not a humorous people.
Two Chinese many years ago were discussing a visit William Howard Taft had just made to Shanghai.
"Taft is a big man," one of them exclaimed, making a gesture to outline a big circle.
"Big man," the other repeated. "We have certainly had large sphere of American influence in our midst recently."

725 Perfect Fit

Salesman: "See there, mister, that hat fits perfectly. How does it feel?"
Buyer: "Okay, unless my ears get tired."

726 Unexpected

Editor: "Did you write this poem yourself?"
Contributor: "Yes, every line of it."
Editor: "Then I'm glad to meet you, Edgar Allan Poe, I thought you were dead long ago."

727 Standing Room

Patient: "Doctor, is my mouth opened wide enough?"
Doctor: "Yes. You see, I always stand on the outside while pulling a tooth."

728 Safety Zone

Cop: "Hey, what are you doing there?"
Driver: "Parking my car. It seemed such a good place. The sign said 'Safety Zone'."

729 *Of Course Not*

Interviewer: "What have you to say about anonymous letters?"
Professor: "They're stupid; I read them, but I never answer them."

730 *Just a Pawn*

"He is the secretary of a chess club."
"But what does he do?"
"He reads the hours of the last meeting."

731 *A Simple Answer*

Two main things have kept us all back—man's love of wet goods and woman's love of dry goods.

732 *Correct*

"What is the chief end of man?" said the teacher to the class.
"The end with the head on," said the small boy.

733 *Always Faithful*

"Is he the sort of fellow who forgets you when you have no money?"
"No, he's an installment collector."

734 *Generous*

Sue: "My husband is the most generous man in the world."
Lou: "How's that?"
Sue: "Well, I gave him a dozen of the loveliest neckties for Christmas, and he took them right down and gave them to the Salvation Army."

735 *The Power of Education*

The new minister in a Georgia church was delivering his first sermon. The janitor was a critical listener from a back corner of the church. The minister's sermon was eloquent and his prayers seemed to cover the whole category of human wants.

After the service one of the deacons asked the old janitor what he thought of the new minister. "Don't you think he offers up a good prayer, Joe?"

"I most certainly do. Why, that man asked the good Lord for things the other preacher didn't even know He had!"

736 *Fitting Comparison*

She: "You remind me of the ocean."
He: "Wild, restless, and romantic?"
She: "No; you just make me sick."

737 The Proof Was There

"It says the man was shot by his wife at close range."
"Then there must have been powder marks on the body."
"Yes, that's why she shot him."

738 Fame

A hundred autograph collectors after one man who will soon be forgotten.

739 Just Curious

Boss: "Now what do you want? I thought I fired you two weeks ago."
Ex-Office Boy: "Oh, I just came back to see if you were still in business."

740 Forewarned

Mistress: "Marie, when you wait on the table tonight for my guests, please don t spill anything."
Maid: "Don't you worry, ma'am, I never talk much."

741 A Happy Home

Where a wife asks her husband's opinion and accepts it.

742 Classroom Candor

The president of the school board, being of a conscientious nature, made it a point to visit all the schoolrooms frequently. In each room he would make a little talk in an effort to interest the children in the everyday things of life.

On one such occasion, he was telling them of the carpenter. "And what kind of arm has the carpenter?" he asked.

"Big!" shouted the children.

"And why is the carpenter's arm bigger than mine?"

"He works!" came the chorused reply.

743 Broad-Minded Traveler

Mr. Newrich (touring in his new car): "Where are we now?"
Chauffeur: "Halfway between Paris and Marseilles, sir."
Mr. Newrich: "Don't bother me with little details. What country are we in?"

744 Mug Drill

Sergeant: "Did you shave this morning, Jones?"
Recruit: "Yes, sergeant."
Sergeant: "Well, next time stand a bit closer to the razor."

745   Streamlined

"Say," said the woman customer over the phone, "the next time I order chicken don't send me any more airplane fowls."

"What do you mean—airplane fowls?" asked the butcher.

"You know what I mean: all wings and machinery and no body."

746   Cheerful Deadhead

Filling-station Attendant: "Here comes another I.W.W. customer."

Patron: "What's that?"

Attendant: "A motorist who wants only Information, Wind, and Water."

747   Fresh Eggs

A bachelor was breakfasting in a restaurant when he saw an inscription on an egg: "Should this meet the eye of some young man who desires to marry a farmer's daughter, age 20, write . . ."

The bachelor wrote and in a few days received the following note:

"Your letter came too late. I am now married and have four children."

748   Never Wrong

A gentleman, quite backward about proposing to the lady of his choice, finally popped the question by saying:

"I was chatting with Mr. Smith the other day and I asked him if he thought you would say yes if I asked you to marry me. He thought you would."

"Mr. Smith is never wrong," was her tactful answer.

749   Another Scotch Story

"How much are your peaches?"

"Penny each, lady."

"I'll have one, please."

"Givin' a party?"

750   Alpine Journey

"Does the giraffe get a sore throat if he gets wet feet?"

"Yes, but not until the next week."

751   Canine Erudition

"Lay down, pup; lay down," ordered the man. "Good doggie—lay down, I say."

"You'll have to say, 'Lie down,' mister," declared a small bystander. "That's a Boston terrier."

752 Sign on Back of Truck

Crime doesn't pay. Neither does trucking.

753 Unscrambling Hes and Shes

The vicar, awarding prizes at the local dog show, was scandalized at the costumes worn by some members of the younger fair sex.

"Look at that youngster," said he; "the one with cropped hair, the cigarette and breeches, holding two pups. Is it a boy or a girl?"

"A girl," said his companion. "She's my daughter."

"My dear sir!" The vicar was flustered. "Do forgive me. I would never have been so outspoken had I know you were her father."

"I'm not," said the other. "I'm her mother."

754 Primitive Cellophane

Teacher: "Robert, explain what are the functions of the skin."

Bobby: "The chief function of the skin is to keep us from looking raw."

755 Hush! The Walls Have Ears

Willie: "Paw, does bigamy mean that a man has one wife too many?"

Paw: "Not necessarily, my son. A man can have one wife too many and still not be a bigamist."

756 Time to Duck

"I see you advertised your saxophone for sale," said the friend.

"Yes," he sighed. "I saw my neighbor in the hardware store yesterday buying a gun."

757 Rushed

Joe: "Are you doing much in your business now?"

Harry: "I should say so! Why, we are so busy that we employ a man to insult new customers."

758 Nowadays One Specifies

"Get my broker, Miss Jones."

"Yes, sir, stock or pawn?"

759 Chicago or New York

A bookseller wrote to a publisher in Chicago asking that a dozen copies of *Seekers after God* be shipped to him at once.

Within two days he received this reply by wire:

"No seekers after God in Chicago or New York. Try Philadelphia."

760 Up the Other Alley

The Congressman's wife sat up in bed, a startled look on her face. "Jim," she whispered. "There's a robber in the house."

"Impossible," was her husband's sleepy reply. "In the Senate, yes, but in the House, never."

761 Modern Child

Photographer: "Watch and see the dicky bird."

Child: "Just pay attention to your exposure so that you do not ruin the plate."

762 On the Safe Side

Sam was in trouble again, and the judge asked him if he were guilty or not guilty.

"Guilty, suh, Ah thinks, but Ah'd rather be tried 'n make sure of it."

763 Contrast

"I'll bet if I was married I'd be boss and tell my wife where to head in," declared the bachelor.

"Yes," retorted the old married man, "and I suppose when you get to a railroad crossing you honk your horn to warn the oncoming train to get out of your way, don't you?"

764 Frank Prospect

Life Insurance Agent: "Do you want a straight life?"

Prospect: "Well, I like to step out once in a while."

765 Grammar

The question before the class was whether "trousers" was singular or plural.

The point was settled by declaring them singular at the top and plural at the other extremity.

766 Lost Opportunity

Wife (to husband inquiring what she thought of his speech): "You didn't make the most of your opportunities."

Husband: "What opportunities?"

Wife: "Why, the opportunities you had of sitting down."

767 While There's Life There's Hope

Husband: "I've got to get rid of my chauffeur. He's nearly killed me four times."

Wife: "Oh, give him another chance."

768   *Not a Bad Wish*

Mother was telling stories of the time she was a little girl. Little Harold listened thoughtfully as she told of riding a pony, sliding down the haystack, and wading in the brook on the farm.

Finally he said with a sigh, "I wish I had met you earlier, Mother."

769   *Perfect Specimen*

"And at her request you gave up drinking?"

"Yes."

"And you stopped smoking, for the same reason?"

"I did."

"And it was for her that you gave up dancing, card parties, and billiards?"

"Absolutely."

"Then why didn't you marry her?"

"Well, after all this reforming I realized I could do better."

770   *One at a Time*

A very stout man was walking on the promenade of a seaside town when he noticed a weighing machine with the notice: "I speak your weight."

He put a penny in the slot and stood on the platform. A voice answered: "One at a time, please!"

771   *Gr-r-r*

Noticing that little Joan was struggling with an ear of corn, her mother offered to cut off the kernels. However, she was quickly rebuffed when Joan replied:

"No, I like it on the bone!"

772   *Comparisons*

She: "The Brownes must be awfully rich, judging from the clothes they wear."

He: "Oh, one can never tell. Some of the most gorgeous flowers haven't got a scent."

773   *Wise Boy*

Teacher: "Jimmy, name a great time saver."

Jimmy: "Love at first sight."

774   *Back on the Pay Roll*

"Did that star football player graduate last year?"

"No, he renewed his contract for another year."

775   Old-Timer

"What model is your car?"
"This car ain't no model—it's a horrible example."

776   Bragging

"I started in life without a penny in my pocket," said Smith.
"And I," put in Jones, "started in life without a pocket."

777   Couldn't Fool Him

A sheriff was taking a prisoner to jail. A gust of wind came around the corner and blew off the prisoner's hat. The prisoner made a sudden lunge forward to get it.

"No, you don't, wise guy," said the sheriff. "You stand where you are. I'll run and get it."

778   His Error

Him: "Well, I suppose you're plenty angry because I came home with this black eye last night."

Her (sweetly): "Not at all, dear. You may not remember it, but when you came home you didn't have that black eye."

779   Surely Feminine

Visitor: "And what will you do, little girl, when you get as big as your mother?"

Little Girl: "Diet!"

780   A Problem Over the World

A fellow was walking along the street one day with two small boys, each wailing loudly. A neighbor yelled to him, asking what was the matter. "The problem that's wrong with the whole world," replied the man. "I've got three pieces of candy and each boy wants two."

781   Perfectly Gentle

Insurance Agent: "Now that you're married and have the responsibility of a wife, you will want to take out some insurance."

Mr. Newlywed: "Insurance? Shucks, no. Why she's not the least bit dangerous."

782   Government Planning

Some time a politician with courage will come right out and run for office on a program of planned extravagance.

783   Well Charged

Two women were discussing a mutual acquaintance.

"She has a very magnetic personality," said one woman.

"She ought to have," replied the other woman, "every stitch she has on is charged."

784   High-Hat Pooch

Customer: "Has this dog a good pedigree?"

Salesman: "Has he? Say, if that dog could talk, he wouldn't speak to either of us."

785   On the Way

Actor (to manager): "Poor house, tonight!"

Manager: "You're wrong. It's the poorhouse tomorrow."

786   Tried Them All

"Do we have to wait very much longer for mummy, Daddy?"

"No, not now. They've just taken the last pair of shoes from the shelf."

787   Courteous Retort

Operator: "Pardon me, madam, but your girl seems more than twelve."

Her Mother: "Operator, would you take me to be the mother of a girl that age?"

Operator: "Lady, don't tell me you're her grandmother!"

788   Common Failing

Mother: "Do you know what happens to little girls who tell lies?"

Small Betty: "Yes, they grow up and tell their little girls they'll get curly hair if they eat their spinach."

789   Pretty Smart

After a speech a famous lecturer and wit was approached by a little white-haired woman who told him how much she had enjoyed his talk. "I take the liberty to speak to you," she admitted, "because you said you loved old ladies."

"I do, I do," was the gallant reply, "and I also like them your age, my dear."

790   Worth Any Price?

A husband took his wife to the doctor. The doctor put a thermometer in her mouth.

"Now don't open your mouth for fifteen minutes," he instructed.
"Doc," said the husband, "what will you take for that thing?"

791   Compliment

Stout Lady (at a street crossing): "Officer, could you see me across the street?"
Officer (inclined to flattery): "Why, Ma'm, I could see you a mile off."

792   Government Spending

An exasperated matron, being questioned by an Internal Revenue Service agent about her deductions, was heard to say: "I wish the Government were half as fussy about how it spends money as it is about how I spend it!"

793   Hm-m

It was during the impaneling of a jury that the following colloquy occurred:
"You are a property holder?"
"Yes, your honor."
"Married or single?"
"I have been married five years, your honor."
"Have you formed or expressed an opinion?"
"Not in five years, your honor."

794   Right

"So you want to try that proofreader job, eh?"
"Yes, sir."
"And do you understand all the responsibility attached to it?"
"Yes, sir, when you make a mistake, I take all the blame."

795   Psychiatrists

Two psychiatrists passed each other. One said, "You're feeling fine, how am I doing?"

796   Unnatural History

Teacher: "Can anyone tell me what causes trees to become petrified?"
Bright Student: "The wind makes them rock."

797   Not Taking a Chance

Two caterpillars were crawling across the grass when a butterfly flew over them. They looked up, and one nudged the other and said: "You couldn't get me up in one of those things for a million dollars!"

798 *House Detective*

"Mummy, I want to whisper something."

"Darling, big girls who are nearly five never whisper before company."

"All right then, but that gentleman over there took another cake when you weren't looking."

799 *New Crop*

"What do you think is the trouble with farming?"

"Well," replied Farmer Bentover, "in my day when we talked about what we could raise on 60 acres, we meant corn—not government loans."

800 *No Hurry*

A doctor had an urgent phone call from a gentleman saying his small son had swallowed his fountain pen.

"All right! I'll come at once," replied the doctor, "but what are you doing in the meantime?"

Whereto came the unexpected answer, "Using a pencil."

801 *Soviet Russia*

In contrast to the United States the position of woman in Soviet Russia is only equal to that of man.

802 *Nothing to It*

"We don't need any of them new-fangled scales in Ireland," said O'Hara. "There's an aisy way to weigh a pig without scales. You get a plank and put it across a stool. Then you get a big stone. Put the pig on one end of the plank and the stone on the other end of the plank, and shift the plank until they balance. Then you guess the weight of the stone and you have the weight of the pig."

803 *Evolution*

Teacher: "Yes, go on, Tommy. After the horse comes the motor car, and (prompting) after the motor car comes the—"

Tommy (whose father has a car): "Installment man, miss."

804 *He Meant Well*

An expectant father was pacing up and down the hospital corridor.

"I hope it's a girl! I hope it's a girl!" he kept repeating.

"What do you mean, you hope it's a girl?" asked a nurse.

"Then she'll never have to go through what I'm going through."

805   More Than Was Expected

Johnny, 10 years old, applied for a job as grocery boy for the summer. The grocer wanted a serious-minded youth, so he put Johnny to a little test. "Well, my boy, what would you do with a million dollars?" he asked.

"Oh, I don't know—I wasn't expecting so much at the start," said Johnny.

806   Pressing

"I must pay my tailor's bill first."
"Why so?"
"Well, it's the most pressing one."

807   House-Broken

"Does your husband expect you to obey him?"
"Oh, dear, no. You see he's been married before."

808   To Have Lived

> 'Tis better to have lived and loved
> Than never to have lived at all.—*Judge*

809   All Explained

Johnnie: "Why does the whistle blow for a fire?"
Billy: "It doesn't blow for the fire, it blows for water. They've got the fire."

810   Wasted Alarm

"Pat," said the manager of the factory, "I want you to report to me at six o'clock tomorrow morning. Here's an alarm clock."

The next morning arrived. Pat was met by a frowning manager.

"Well, what was the matter? Didn't the alarm clock go off?"

"Oh, yes, sorr, it went off all right, but the trouble was that it went off while I was asleep."

811   Theological Mainspring

Two ministers were driving in a cab to the station, and were in some anxiety lest they should miss their train. One of them pulled out his watch and discovered it had stopped.

"How annoying!" he exclaimed. "And I always put such faith in that watch!"

"In a case like this," answered the other, "good works would evidently have answered the purpose better."

812 *Still Cackling*

Customer: "Are these eggs fresh?"
Grocer: "Fresh! Why, the hens haven't missed them yet."

813 *Lucid Intervals*

An American film actress was applying for a passport.
"Unmarried?" asked the clerk.
"Occasionally," answered the actress.

814 *Proof*

Orator: "I thought your paper was friendly to me?"
Editor: "So it is. What's the matter?"
Orator: "I made a speech at the dinner last night, and you didn't print a line of it."
Editor: "Well, what further proof do you want?"

815 *Alibi Ike*

Bobby: "Mamma, what is a 'Second-Story Man'?"
Mamma: "Your father's one. If I don't believe his first story, he always has another one ready."

816 *Long, Long Trail*

The chief objection to the school of experience is that you never finish the post-graduate courses, says an exchange.
When you graduate from that school, brother, your diploma is a tombstone.

817 *Fleas and Elephants*

Teacher (to bring out the idea of size): "Mention a difference between an elephant and a flea."
Tommy: "Well, an elephant can have fleas, but a flea can't have elephants."

818 *Strictly Original Blundering*

Teacher: "Did your father help you with the problem?"
Willie: "No, I got it wrong myself."

819 *Penalty of Being Adored*

First Guy: "She treats her husband like a Grecian god."
Second Guy: "How's that?"
First Guy: "She places a burnt offering before him at every meal."

820 Prosperity

May bad fortune follow you all your days
And never catch up with you.

821 Down and Out

The aviation instructor, having delivered a lecture on parachute work, concluded:

"And if it doesn't open—well, gentlemen, that's what is known as 'jumping to a conclusion.' "

822 Bossie's Little Weakness

A city girl visiting her uncle on the farm was watching a cow chewing her cud.

"Pretty fine cow, that," said her uncle as he came by.

"Yes," said the girl, "but doesn't it cost a lot to keep her in chewing gum?"

823 When Maude Gets Left

"Doesn't that mule ever kick you?"

"No, sah, he ain't yet, but he frequently kicks de place where Ah recently was."

824 Chapter and Verse

"My wife has the worst memory I ever heard of."

"Forgets everything, eh?"

"No; remembers everything."

825 Out for the Long Shots

"Where's the cashier?"

"Gone to the races."

"Gone to the races in business hours?"

"Yes, sir, it's his last chance of making the books balance."

826 No Lagging Veteran

Betty on a visit to her aunt, being offered some left-over fragments, politely declined them.

"Why, dear, don't you like turkey?" inquired her aunt.

"Only when it's new," said Betty.

827 Out of the Frying Pan

Teacher: "Really, Johnny, your handwriting is terrible. You must learn to write better."

Johnny: "Well, if I did, you'd be finding fault with my spelling."

828   *Patient Research*

A party of tourists were enjoying the wonders of the Grand Canyon. A native passing by was asked by the driver of the car:

"I say, neighbor, can you tell us what caused this terrible gorge?"

"Well, they say a Scotchman once owned a ranch near here, and one day he lost a golf ball down a gopher hole."

829   *Emulating a Master*

"You say your son plays the piano like Paderewski?"

"Yes. He uses both hands."

830   *One-Way Argument*

Telephone Operator: "It costs seventy-five cents to talk to Bloomfield."

Caller: "Can't you make a special rate for just listening? I want to call my wife."

831   *Educational Limitations*

"How soon shall I know anything after I come out of the anesthetic?"

"Well, that's expecting a lot from an anesthetic."

832   *Blessed Are the Humble*

Editor: "Do you know how to run a newspaper?"

Applicant: "No, sir."

Editor: "Well, I'll try you. You talk like you've had experience."

833   *Shocking Politeness*

Policeman: "How did you knock him down?"

Motorist: "I didn't! I pulled up to let him go across—and he fainted."

834   *Salvation*

Jim: "Some rich persons seem to think they can buy their way into heaven by leaving a million dollars to a church when they die."

John: "I don't know but that they stand as much chance as some of these other persons who are trying to get in on the instalment plan of 25 cents a Sunday while they're living."

835   *Too Much Competition*

Not long ago a jury went out early in the day on a simple case, and when it came near the time for court to adjourn, his honor sent for the jury, and asked the foreman if they required any further instruction. "We need no instruction, your honor," replied the foreman, "but here are eleven prejudiced and unreasonable men who won't agree to anything."

836   *In a Conference*

A little boy was saying his go-to-bed prayers in a very low voice.
"I can't hear you, dear," his mother whispered.
"Wasn't talking to you," said the small one firmly.

837   *Pedagogy*

At a recent "panel discussion" in one of our great universities several speakers aired their views on "creative education," solemnly or otherwise. One speaker got up to remark: "I have discovered that if you have pupils of greater ability, you will get better results"; and the wall of that university (it is averred) rocked with this momentous announcement. Someone suggested that the speaker would have been much better advised had he said something like this: "If the correlation of intrinsic competency to actual numerical representation is definitely high, then the thoroughly objective conclusion may inexpugnably be reached that the scholastic derivations and outgrowths will attain a pattern of unified superiority." No one would have known what he was talking about, and he would thereafter have been regarded with awe as a pedagogical pundit.—*Henry Grattan Doyle*

838   *Cheers for Willie!*

"Who gave the bride away?"
"Her little brother, Willie. He stood right up in the middle of the ceremony and yelled, 'Hurray, Louise, you've got him at last!' "

839   *No Reference*

Would-be Employer: "Young man, do you have references from your last place of employment?"
Applicant: "Yes, sir. Here's their letter. It reads:
'To whom it may concern. We had Sam Jones working for us for three weeks and we can truthfully say we are satisfied!' "

840   *Frigid Air*

An electrician was examining an electric refrigerator that was using too much electricity and could not find the reason.
He idly asked the cook, "How do you like the refrigerator?"
"I like it fine," she said. "I open the door and it cools off the whole kitchen."

841   *Fashion Notes*

"Anna Mae," said the mistress of the house, finally giving way to curiosity. "I notice you have been taking our empty grapefruit hulls home with you. Do you mind telling me what you do with them?"

"Yes'm," the maid admitted, "I been takin' 'em 'cause I think they make my garbage look so stylish."

842 Call an Ambulance

"Waiter, are you sure this ham was cured?"

"Yes, sir."

"Well, it's had a relapse."

843 A Challenge

A certain young pastor in his first charge announced nervously:

"I will take for my text the words, 'And they fed five men with five thousand loaves of bread and two thousand fishes.' "

At this misquotation an old parishioner said audibly:

"That's no miracle—I could do it myself."

The young preacher said nothing, but the next Sunday he announced the same text again. This time he got it right:

"And they fed five thousand men on five loaves of bread and two fishes."

He waited a moment, and then, leaning over the pulpit and looking at the parishioner, he said:

"And could you do that, too, Mr. Smith?"

"Of course I could," Mr. Smith replied.

"And how would you do it?" said the preacher.

"With what was left over from last Sunday," said Mr. Smith.

844 Inn Luck or Inn Dutch

"Why don't you give your new bungalow a name? Something appropriate. Other people do. There's 'Seldom Inn,' 'Walk Inn,' 'Cosy Inn,' and a lot of others."

"That's an idea. As I've just finished paying for it, I'll name it 'All Inn.' "

845 Mom Was No Prophet

When supper was served, Helen refused a second helping of ice cream with a polite but wistful, "No, thank you!"

"Do have some more, dear!" her hostess urged.

"Mother told me to say, 'No, thank you,' " Helen explained naively, "but I don't think she could have known how small that first helping was going to be!"

846 Super Service

Speaking of banks, there was an Irishman who opened an account, his first. At the end of the month he got a statement, which meant absolutely nothing to him, but he was delighted to receive his checks.

"Sure, An' it's a smart bank I'm after dealin' with," he told a pal.

"Is it that now?" was the rejoinder.

"Faith, and it is. Them fellers was smart enough to get every one av me checks back for me."

847 Southpaw

"Does it make any difference on which side of you I sit?" she asked.

"Not a bit," he replied. "I'm ambidextrous."

848 Alive and Fresh

Fish Dealer: "Lobsters, madam; nice lobsters? Look, they're all alive."

Lady: "Yes, but are they fresh?"

849 Mrs. Beaver: Mr. Mud-Turtle

Mistress: "So your married life was very unhappy? What was the trouble? December wedded to May?"

Chloe Johnson: "Lan' sake, no, mum! It was Labor Day wedded to de Day of Rest!"

850 Short Circuit

An electrician returned home from work one night to find his small son waiting for him with his right hand swathed in a bandage.

"Hello, sonny!" he exclaimed. "Cut your hand?"

"No, Dad," was the reply. "I picked up a pretty little fly and one end wasn't insulated."

851 Annual Stew

"Do you summer in the country?"

"No, I simmer in the city."

852 A Common Experience

"The first day out was perfectly lovely," said the young lady just back from abroad. "The water was as smooth as glass, and it was simply gorgeous. But the second day was rough and—er—decidedly disgorgeous."

853 Thumbs Down Slightly

Children have their own peculiar way of expressing themselves.

"Well, Peggy," said the neighbor, "and how do you like your new governess?"

Peggy thought a moment and then said: "I half like her and I half don't like her, but I think I half don't like her the most."

854 Job for the Iceman

Bride: "I made this pudding all by myself."
Hubby: "Splendid! But who helped you lift it out of the oven?"

855 Early Bird Variety

"Is your husband a bookworm?"
"No, just an ordinary one."

856 Always a Night Owl

The young bride was asked what she thought of married life.
"Oh, there's not much difference." she replied. "I used to wait up half the night for George to go, and now I wait up half the night for him to come home."

857 The Worst Boom

When the president of the Los Angeles Chamber of Commerce was asked recently how the depression had hit Los Angeles, he replied, "Depression? We have no depression in Los Angeles, but I will admit that we are having the worst boom in many, many years."

858 Cheering Innovation

Real Estate Agent: "Well, what do you think of our little city?"
Prospect: "I'll tell you, brother. This is the first cemetery I ever saw with lights."

859 When Dads Disappoint

Tommy: "That problem you helped me with last night was all wrong, Daddy."
Father: "All wrong, was it? Well, I'm sorry."
Tommy: "Well, you needn't exactly worry about it, because none of the other daddies got it right, either."

860 Call for Progress

Little Joan: "What do the angels do in Heaven, Mummy?"
Mother: "They sing and play harps."
Little Joan: "Haven't they any radios?"

861 Where Whoppers Breed

"Can any of you," the teacher asked, "tell me what 'amphibious' means and give a sentence to illustrate?"
A bright little boy held up his hand. "I know. It's fibbing. John's fish stories am fibious!"

862   *Domestic Treasure*

Wife: "How do you like the potato salad, dear?"
Hub: "Delicious! Did you buy it yourself?"

863   *Ducking Destiny*

"Pop, will I look like you when I grow up?"
"Everybody seems to think so, son."
"Well, I won't have to grow up for a long time, will I, Pop?"

864   *Accredited Delegate*

"Who will help a man to correct personality defects if not his wife?"
asks a heart-throb editor.
Well, sister, there is his wife's mother.

865   *Full Explanation*

A man who was invited to a house party he didn't wish to attend,
telegraphed to the hostess: "Regret I can't come. Complete lie follows by
letter."

866   *Let Him Do His Stuff*

"What! Another new dress? How ever do you think I can find the
money to pay for it?"
"Darling, you know I'm not inquisitive."

867   *Financial Genius*

"Father," said Junior, "what is a financial genius?"
"A financial genius, my son," answered his harassed pater, "is a man
who can earn money faster than his family can spend it."

868   *When Nerves Are Raw*

His Wife: "It's about time to think about where we shall spend the
summer."
Husband: "I wish you'd say 'pass' the summer, Helen; 'spend' is so
confoundedly suggestive."

869   *Human Nature*

"Bill," groaned the managing editor of the tabloid, "nothing scandalous
has happened in twenty-four hours. What'll we do for the front page?"
"Aw, don't get discouraged, Steve," the city editor comforted. "Something'll happen. I've still got faith in human nature."

870   *House-Broken*

We congratulated a lady on her silver wedding anniversary for living twenty-five years with the same man.

"But he is not the same man he was when I first got hold of him," she replied.

871   *Figs of Thistles*

"Your methods of cultivation are hopelessly out of date," said the youthful agricultural college graduate to the old farmer. "Why, I'd be astonished if you even got ten pounds of apples from that tree."

"So would I," replied the farmer. "It's a pear tree."

872   *Balancing the Budget*

Teacher: "We borrowed our numerals from the Arabs, our calendar from the Romans, and our banking from the Italians. Can any one think of other examples?"

Charlie: "Our lawn-mower from the Smiths, and our ladder from the Browns."

873   *On the Frontier*

A backwoodswoman, the soles of whose feet had been toughened by a lifetime of shoelessness, was standing in front of her cabin fireplace one day when her husband addressed her:

"You'd better move your foot a mite, Maw, you're standin' on a live coal."

Said she, nonchalantly: "Which foot, Paw?"

874   *Pawnshop*

"What do the three balls in front of a pawnshop mean?"

"Two to one you don't get it back."

875   *Must Have Been a Close Shave*

Barber: "What's the matter? Isn't the razor taking hold?"

Victim: "Yeah, it's taking holt all right, but it ain't lettin' go again."

876   *Wanted to Help on the Treasure Hunt*

A burglar, who had entered a poor minister's house at midnight, was disturbed by the awakening of the occupant of the room he was in. Drawing his weapon, he said:

"If you stir, you are a dead man. I'm hunting for your money."

"Let me get up and strike a light," said the minister, "and I'll hunt with you."

877   Maybe She Was Tired

"When you asked her to dance did she accept quickly?"
"Did she? Why, she was on my feet in an instant."

878   Conclusions

The young bachelor was asked which he thought were happier, people who were married or people who were not.
"Well, I don't know," he replied, "sometimes I think there is as many as is that aren't, as aren't that is."

879   A Perfect Example

The lecturer waxed eloquent as he warmed up to his subject. He wound up in this manner:
"Man, as we have seen, is a progressive being, but many other creatures are stationary. Take the ass, for example. Always and everywhere the ass is the same creature. You never have seen, and never will see, a more perfect ass than you see at the present moment!" A fellow in the back row: "Brother, you said it."

880   Experienced

"I can take a hundred words a minute," said the stenographer.
"I often take more than that," said the prospective employer. "But then I have to, I'm married."

881   Read the Directions That Come with Each One

The city girl watching the farmer milk a cow: "That looks easy, but how do you turn it off?"

882   When Greek Meets Greek

Greek Tailor (looking at men's trousers just brought in): "Euripides?"
Greek Customer: "Yah; Eumenides."

883   Boys Who Tell Lies

Mother: "Do you know what happens to little boys who tell lies?"
Johnny: "Yes, Mother; they travel for half-fare."

884   Philosophy

Philosophy is finding out how many things there are in the world which you can't have if you want them, and don't want if you can have them.—Puck

885 Center Aisle

A woman who had approached the office of a Broadway theater, was making great fuss over the seat they gave her.

"Are you quite positive," she asked for the third time, "that this seat is near enough to the stage?"

"Madam," said the box office man, "if it was much nearer, you'd have to act in the play."

886 Calling All Cost Accountants

"Why does cream cost more than milk?"

"Because it's harder for the cows to sit on the small bottles."

887 English

A Frenchman learning English said to his British tutor: "English is a queer language. What does this sentence mean: 'Should Mr. Noble, who sits for this constituency, consent to stand again, he will in all probability have a walk-over'?"

888 Page the Government Weather Bureau

A Swedish farmer who wanted to make his permanent home in this country appeared for his naturalization papers.

"Are you satisfied with the general conditions of this country?" he was asked.

"Yah, sure," answered the hopeful one.

"And does this government of ours suit you?"

"Well, yah, mostly," stammered the man, "only I lak see more rain."

889 Almost Missed

A big Indian had just ordered a ham sandwich at a drug store and was peering between the slices of bread when he turned and said to the waiter: "Ugh, you slice 'em ham?"

The waiter replied: "Yes, I sliced the ham."

"Ugh," grunted the Indian. "You almost missed 'em."

890 The Rewards of Authorship

The critic started to leave in the middle of the second act of the play.

"Don't go now," said the manager. "I promise there's a terrific kick in the next act."

"Fine," was the retort. "Give it to the author."

891   *Indecisive*

Politician to aide: "About their charge that I'm indecisive—do you think I should answer it, or let it go, or answer it in part, or what?"

892   *Good Reason*

"But this officer says that while you were in a drunken state you tried to climb a lamp-post."

"Yes, I did, your worship, but three crocodiles have been following me about all night, and they were getting on my nerves."

893   *It's All Clear Now*

A Cockney telephoned to inquire the rate to Ealing, a suburb of London. The man at the other end of the line couldn't catch the name of the station, so in desperation he asked the Cockney to spell it. Quickly came the reply: "E—for 'Erbert, A—wot the 'orses heat, L—w'ere yer goes w'en yer dies, I—wot yer sees wiv, N—wot lays a hegg, G—Gowd bless me. Get me?"—*Wall Street Journal*

894   *Not Sure*

"You've been out with worse-looking fellows than I am, haven't you?"
She did not reply.
"I said, you've been out with worse-looking fellows than I am, haven't you?"
"I heard you the first time. I was trying to think."

895   *How to Paraphrase*

The pupil was asked to paraphrase the sentence: "He was bent on seeing her."
He wrote: "The sight of her doubled him up."

896   *Never Over Thirty*

Friend: "You can't cheat old father time."
Man: "No, but some of the women drive a mighty close bargain with him."

897   *Silence*

Sir Lewis Morris was complaining to Oscar Wilde about the neglect of his poems by the press. "It is a complete conspiracy of silence against me, a conspiracy of silence. What ought I to do, Oscar?" "Join it," replied Wilde.

898   *Not Brave but Generous*

"Did he take his misfortunes like a man?"
"Precisely. He laid the blame on his wife."

899   *Stew Bad*

Diner: "Waiter! This stew is terrible. What kind is it?"
Waiter: "The chef calls this his enthusiastic stew."
Diner: "Why?"
Waiter: "He puts everything he has into it."

900   *One Time They Don't Change Their Minds*

A little girl, sitting in church watching a wedding, suddenly exclaimed:
"Mummy, has the lady changed her mind?"
"What do you mean?" the mother asked.
"Why," replied the child, "she went up the aisle with one man and came back with another."

901   *Slightly Sarcastic*

"How is it that you are late this morning?" the clerk was asked by his manager.
"I overslept," was the reply.
"What? Do you sleep at home as well?" inquired the manager.

902   *So That's Where They Go After Graduation*

Tourist (in Yellowstone Park): "Those Indians have a blood-curdling yell."
Guide: "Yes, ma'am; every one of 'em was a college cheerleader."

903   *The Enemy*

"Sir, the enemy are before us as thick as peas!"
"All right, shell them!"

904   *Why Stay Longer*

Mother (to small son who is going to a party): "Now, dear, what are you going to do when you've had enough to eat?"
Little Tommy: "Come home."

905   *Three Beans*

A teacher called for sentences using the word "beans."
"My father grows beans," said the bright boy of the class.
"My mother cooks beans," said another pupil.
Then a third popped up: "We are all human beans."

906 No, Thanks

Mother: "Marilyn, were you a good little girl at church today?"
Marilyn: "Yes, mother. A man offered me a big plate of money, and I said, 'No, thank you.' "

907 Using His Head

Sergeant: "Why is it important not to lose your head in an attack?"
Recruit: "Because that would leave no place to put the helmet."

908 Higher Mathematics

Judge: "What's the charge against this man, officer?"
Officer: "Bigotry, yer honor. He's got three wives."
Judge: "I'm surprised at your ignorance, officer. That's trigonometry, not bigotry."

909 The Frog Are a Wonderful Bird

This short essay on frogs, by a young immigrant from Norway, was reported by the Chicago Board of Education: "What a wonderful bird the frog are. When he stand, he sit almost. When he hop, he fly almost. He ain't got no sense hardly. He ain't got no tail hardly, either, when he sit on what he ain't got almost."—*Houston Chronicle*

910 Hash

"Bring me a plate of hash," said the diner.
The waiter walked over to the kitchen elevator. "Gent wants to take a chance," he called down the speaking tube.
"I'll have some hash too," said a second customer.
The waiter picked up the tube again. "Another sport," he yelled.

911 Her Address

Jane was always glad to say her prayers, but she wanted to be sure she was heard in heaven.
One night after the usual "Amen," she dropped her head upon her pillow and closed her eyes. After a moment she said, "Lord! this prayer comes from 203 Selden Avenue."

912 Of One Mind

"You say you never have a quarrel with your wife?"
"Never. She goes her way and I go hers."

913 Smart Worms

Earth flew in all directions as the crimson-faced would-be golfer attempted to strike the ball. "My word," he blurted out to his caddie, "the worms will think there's been an earthquake."

"I don't know," replied the caddie, "the worms 'round here are smart. I'll bet most of them are hiding underneath the ball for safety."

914 That Makes Them Even

Matron (at the counter): "I suspect that you're giving me awfully short weight for my money!"

Grocer: "Well I'm positive you're giving me an awfully long wait for mine."

915 The Last Word

Wife: "Must I persuade you to have some more alphabet soup?"
Hubby: "No, thanks, not another word."

916 Definitely

"My wife doesn't know what she wants."
"Hah, you're lucky. Mine does!"

917 It Southernly Was

He: "Honey, will yo'all marry me?"
She: "Oh, this is so southern!"

918 Aquatic Engineer

"My brother's an aquatic engineer."
"What's that?"
"He's in charge of the dish-washing!"

919 Make Mine Well

An old cowpuncher entered a restaurant and ordered a steak. The waiter brought it to him, and it was rare, very rare. The cowpuncher demanded that it be taken back and cooked.

"It's already cooked," the waiter snapped.

"Cooked," roared the cowpuncher. "I've seen cows hurt worse than that and they got well."

920 Weighty Evidence

The portly man was trying to get to his seat at the circus. "Pardon me," he said to a woman, "did I step on your foot?"

"Possibly so," she said, after glancing at the ring. "All the elephants are still out there. You must have."

921 How Many Rabbits Make a Mink Coat?

Glad: "Wonder why the magician wanted to borrow my mink coat."
Puss: "He probably wanted to pull rabbits out of it."

922 A Sound Sleeper

"I slept like a log."
"Yes, I heard the sawmill."

923 One Is Enough

"There are ten reasons why I won't marry Joe."
"What are they?"
"Well, the first is he hasn't any money and the other nine are things I want."

924 A Shin-Bruising Game

"Is your wife a bridge fiend?"
"Yes, only a fiend could kick as hard as she does."

925 Sweet Young Thing

Virginia Military Institute, the pride of the South, is sometimes referred to as "The West Point of the South." A sweet young thing from Lexington, Va., had been invited to one of the dances at West Point, and after a busy day of sightseeing over the grounds, she was asked by her escort how it had impressed her.

"Oh, it's wonderful," she answered admiringly. "Why, this must be the V.M.I. of the North."

926 Too Thin

"Bring me another sandwich, please."
"Will there be anything else?"
"Yes, a paper weight. The last sandwich blew away."

927 Soon or Late

There swims no goose so gray, but soon or late
She finds some honest gander for her mate.—*Pope*

928 Poor Memory

Scientist (to Pharmacist): "Give me some prepared monaceticacidester of salicylic acid."
Pharmacist: "Do you mean aspirin?"
Scientist: "That's right! I can never think of that name."

929 A Sizzler

A man in Chicago was grumbling about the heat. Said another, who had just returned from a trip through the South.

"Hot! Boy, you don't know what hot is. One day this week in Mississippi I saw a dog chasing a cat and they were both walking."

930 Disillusioned

Every year college deans pop the routine question to their undergraduates: "Why did you come to college?" Traditionally the answers match the question in triteness. But last year one University of Arizona coed unexpectedly confided: "I came to be went with—but I ain't yet!"

931 Fowl Talk

"Gosh, this is a tough chicken."

"Yeah, must have been a bad egg in its youth."

932 How to Reduce in One Lesson

"What's the best exercise for reducing?"

"Just move the head slowly from right to left when asked to have a second helping."

933 Too Personal

Judge: "Are you guilty or not guilty?"

Prisoner: "It seems to me that is a mighty personal question."

934 Well Laid Out

"Isn't this town laid out prettily?"

"It's laid out all right. How long has it been dead?"

935 Two Sides to Every Question

"There are two sides to every question," proclaimed the wise man.

"Yes," said the fool, "and there are two sides to a sheet of flypaper, but it makes a difference to the fly which side he chooses."

936 One Stranger Present

The preacher was at ease after service Sunday night.

"Many folks in church?" asked his wife.

"Yes, good attendance—and a stranger was present, but I did not see him."

"But how do you know?"

"There was a dollar bill in the contribution box."

937 Coward

"How'd you get along with that fight with your wife, the other night?"
"Aw, she came crawling to me on her knees."
"Yeah, what did she say?"
" 'Come out from under that bed, you coward.' "

938 The American Tourist

"Yes, there is something smaller still than an atom," said the patriotic citizen to his friend.
"What is it?"
"The American tourist in Europe who curries favor by knocking his own country."

939 Holding Out

Mr. Meek: "Darling, haven't I always given you my salary check the first of every month?"
Mrs. Meek: "Yes, but you never told me you got paid twice a month— you low-down, unprincipled embezzler."

940 Are You Ill

Consider the member of the Chamber of Deputies who had been a veterinary before he became a politician. One day, during a bitter debate, an aristocratic opponent who was being worsted in the argument descended to personal remarks.
"Is it true, my good man," he inquired sneeringly, "that you are actually a veterinary?"
"It is, sir. Are you ill?"

941 Too Fresh

Mrs. Newlywed: "Aren't these eggs rather small today?"
Grocer: "Yes'm but the farmer who sells me my eggs had to start to town early this morning and took them out of the nest too soon."

942 Ghost Stories

"I'm a great lover of ghost stories."
"So'm I, pal. Let's shake."

943 There Is a Difference

Teacher: "What is the difference between results and consequences?"
Bright Pupil: "Results are what you expect; consequences are what you get."

944 *College*

"Do you think your son will forget everything he learned in college?"
"I hope so. He can't make a living just making love to the girls."

945 *Courtesy*

"What would be the proper thing to say if, in carving the duck, it should skid off the platter and into your neighbor's lap?"
"Be very courteous. Say, 'May I trouble you for that duck?' "

946 *In the Dumps*

"Whenever I'm in the dumps I just get myself another hat."
"I wondered where you get them."

947 *Poor Management*

Ole, the night porter, was testifying before the jury after the big bank robbery.
"You say," thundered the attorney, "that at midnight you were cleaning the office, and eight masked men brushed past you and went on into the vault room with revolvers drawn?"
"Yah," said Ole.
"And a moment later a terrific explosion blew the vault door off, and the same men went out past you carrying currency and bonds."
"Yah," said Ole.
"Well, what did you do then?"
"Aye put down my mop."
"Yes, but what did you do after that?"
"Vel, Aye say to myself, 'Dis bane terrible way to run a bank.' "

948 *The Effect of Radio*

The Man: "I want a loaf of Mumsie's Bread, a package of Krunchies, some Goody Sanny Spread, Ole Mammy's Lasses, Orange Pulley, a pound of Aunt Annie's sugar candy, Bitsey-bite size."
The Clerk: "Sorry. No Krunchies. How about Krinkly Krisps, Oatsie-Toasties, Malty-Wheaties, Riceltes, or Eatum-Wheatums?"
The Man: "The Wheatums, then."
The Clerk: "Anything else? Tootsies, Tatery Chips, Cheesie Weesies, Gingile Bits, Itsey Cakes, Sweetzie Toofums, or Dramma's Doughnies?"
The Man (toddling toward the meat department): "Dot to det some meat."

949 *Weighed and Found Wanting*

"So you met Marian today?"
"Yes. I hadn't seen her for ten years."

"Has she kept her girlish figure?"

"Kept it? She's doubled it."

950　Definite Proof

Counsel (to police witness): "But if a man is on his hands and knees in the middle of the road, that does not prove he is drunk."

Policeman: "No, sir, it does not. But this one was trying to roll up the white line!"

951　Special Service

Owner of Midget Car: "I want a pint of gasoline and a cup of oil, please."

Garage Hand: "And shall I cough into the tires, sir?"

952　A Raise Was Necessary

Bookkeeper: "I'll have to have a raise, sir; there are three other companies after me."

Employer: "Is that so? What companies?"

Bookkeeper: "Light, phone, and gas."

953　Colorful Writing

The native student, writing a letter to the superintendent of the mission, desired to end with the words: "May Heaven preserve you."

Not being quite confident of the meaning of "preserve," he looked it up in a dictionary. When the letter reached the superintendent, it ended with the words: "And may Heaven pickle you."

954　The Wrong Time

One night, as a messenger from the office of an evening paper was passing along the ways on the banks of the river, he heard the sound of someone struggling in the water.

"Are you drowning?" he shouted.

"I am," replied a feeble voice from the water.

"What a pity!" said the lad consolingly. "You are just too late for the last edition tonight. But cheer up; you'll have a nice little paragraph all to yourself in the morning."

955　Obstinate

The clergyman was walking through the village when he met one of his parishioners.

"How's your cold, Donald?" he asked.

"Verra obstinate," replied the parishioner.

"And how is your wife?"
"About the same."

956 Wild Oats and Rye

Mother: "After all, he's only a boy, and boys will sow their wild oats."
Father: "Yes, but I wouldn't mind if he didn't mix so much rye with it."

957 He May Be Right

"How many students are there in the university?"
"About one in every five."

958 Hypnotism and Marriage

"I was hypnotized last week."
"What's 'hypnotized' mean?"
"Why, to hypnotize is to get a man in your power, and make him do whatever you want."
"That's not hypnotism, that's marriage."

959 No Mind Reader

First New Year's Eve Celebrator: "What are you doing?"
Second Celebrator: "Writing a letter to myself."
First: "What does it say?"
Second: "I don't know. I won't get it until tomorrow."

960 Spelling

School Visitor: "What's the matter my boy?"
Pupil: "Palpitation and insomnia."
School Visitor: "But you can't be suffering from these things."
Pupil: "It isn't suffering, sir. It's spelling."

961 He Looked Familiar

An enthusiastic golfer came home to dinner. During the meal his wife said:
"Willie tells me he caddied for you this afternoon."
"Well, do you know," said Willie's father, "I thought I'd seen that boy before."

962 Teaching by Illustration

Prof: "How much does a twelve-pound shot weigh?"
Frosh: "Don't know, sir."
Prof: "Well, then, what time does the ten o'clock train leave?"
Frosh: "Ten o'clock."

Prof: "Then what is the weight of the twelve-pound shot?"
Frosh: "Ten pounds, sir."

963 Giving the Password

The young recruit was the victim of so many practical jokes that he doubted all men and their motives. One night while he was on guard, the figure of one of the officers loomed up in the darkness.

"Who goes there?" he challenged.

"Major Moses," replied the officer.

The young recruit scented a joke.

"Glad to meet you, Moses," he said cheerfully. "Advance and give the Ten Commandments."

964 Impossible

Visiting Delegate (to hotel clerk): "Why didn't you call me at seven-thirty this morning?"

Clerk (politely): "Because you didn't go to bed till eight."

965 Punctual

"Well, son," wrote the fond mother to her soldier son, "I hope you have been punctual in rising every morning so that you haven't kept the regiment waiting breakfast for you."

966 False Arrest

"What were you arrested for?" asked the friend.

"I found an automobile."

"Found? Nonsense! They wouldn't arrest you for finding an automobile."

"Well, you see I found it before the owner lost it."

967 The Tied and the Untied

Inquiring Schoolboy: "Dad, what effect does the moon have on the tide?"

Dad (from the depths of his newspaper): "Not any, son. Only on the untied."

968 Five Men on a Horse

Beta (at riding academy): "I wish to rent a horse."
Groom: "How long?"
Beta: "The longest you've got, there will be five of us going."

969 Without Asking Questions

A doctor was called in to see a very testy aristocrat. "Well, sir, what's the matter?" he asked cheerfully.

"That, sir," snapped the patient, "is for you to find out."

"I see," said the doctor thoughtfully. "Well, if you'll excuse me for an hour or so, I'll go along and fetch a friend of mine—a veterinarian. He's the only chap I know who can make a diagnosis without asking questions."

970 Trees to a Golfer Poet

"I think that I shall never see a hazard rougher than a tree—a tree o'er which my ball must fly if on the green it is to lie; a tree which stands that green to guard, and makes the shots extremely hard; a tree whose leafy arms extend, to kill the mashie shot I send; a tree that stands in silence there, while angry golfers rave and swear. Niblicks were made for fools like me, who cannot ever miss a tree."

971 He Knew the Answers

A member of a psych class on tour asked an inmate his name.

"George Washington," was the reply.

"But," said the perplexed lad, "last time we were here you were Abraham Lincoln."

"That," said the inmate sadly, "was by my first wife."

972 Keep on Going

Keep on going and the chances are you will stumble on something, perhaps when you are least expecting it. I have never heard of anyone stumbling on something sitting down.—C. F. Kettering

973 The Sergeant and the Rookie

"Com-pa-nee atten-shun," bawled the drill sergeant to the awkward squad. "Com-pa-nee, lift your left leg and hold it straight in front of you."

By mistake one member held up his right leg, which brought it out side by side with his neighbor's left leg.

"And who is the galoot over there holding up both legs?" shouted the hard-boiled sergeant.

974 Counsel for the Defense Rests

A case was being heard in court in which a farmer was claiming indemnity for a cow killed by a railway train. Counsel for the defense put many tedious and superfluous questions.

"Was the cow on the track?" he asked the engineer.

The engineer had had about enough. He replied: "No, of course not. She was in a field half a mile away. But when it saw her, the engine left the rails, jumped the fence, and chased her across the field and up a tree. There it strangled her to death."

975 Hopeless

"You've read my last book, haven't you?" asked the author.
"I hope so," groaned the critic.

976 Straight to the Point

During the progress of a lawsuit a witness was on the stand for cross-examination regarding the character and habits of the defendant. "I believe you testified a little while ago," began the counsel for the plaintiff, "that Mr. Smith, defendant in this case, has a reputation for being very lazy and personally incompetent."

"No, sir; no, sir," protested the witness. "I didn't say that. What I said was he changed jobs pretty often; that he seemed to get tired of work very quickly."

"Has he or has he not a reputation in the community for being lazy?" persisted the lawyer.

"Well, sir, I don't want to do the gentleman any injustice, and I don't go so far as to say he is lazy; but it's the general impression around the community that if it required any voluntary and sustained exertion on his part to digest his food, he would have died years ago from lack of nourishment."

977 Worried About His Future

Joe: "You look down-hearted, old man. What are you worried about?"
Bill: "My future."
Joe: "What makes your future seem so hopeless?"
Bill: "My past."

978 The Poor Animal

When Mrs. Berg's expensive new fur coat was delivered to her home, she fondled it ecstatically for a time, and then looked sad for a moment.

"What's the matter, aren't you satisfied with it?" inquired her husband.

"Yes," she answered, "but I feel so sorry for the poor thing that was skinned."

"Thanks," said Mr. Berg.

979 Information, Please

Mother: "Stop asking so many questions. Don't you know that curiosity killed the cat?"

Small Daughter: "Is that so? What did the cat want to know?"

980 The Strategy of Handling People

A girl was driving in her new car when something went wrong with the engine. The traffic light changed from green to red and back to green and still she could not get the car to budge. The traffic cop came up.

"What's the matter, miss?" he inquired. "Ain't we got colors you like?"

981 Curious

"These rock formations," explained the guide, "were piled up here by the glaciers."

"But where are the glaciers?" asked a curious old lady.

"They've gone back, madam, to get more rocks," said the guide.

982 Politeness

Father: "Well, Willie, what did you learn at school today?"

Willie (proudly): "I learned to say 'Yes, sir' and 'No, sir' and 'Yes, ma'am' and 'No, ma'am'."

Father: "You did?"

Willie: "Yeah."

983 Showers for the Groom

"Daddy," said Bobby, "don't they ever give any showers for the groom?"

"No, son," replied his dad, "there will be plenty of storms for him after the bride begins to reign."

984 Middle Class

William: "Dad, what is the middle class?"

Dad: "The middle class consists of people who are not poor enough to accept charity and not rich enough to donate anything."

985 All Prepared

"I want to grow some trees in my garden. Can you sell me a few seeds?" inquired Mrs. Newlywed.

"Certainly, madam," replied the clerk. He fetched her a packet.

"Can you guarantee these?" she asked.

"Yes, madam, we can."

"Will the trees be tall and thick in the trunk?"

"They should be, madam."

"And quite strong at the roots, I suppose?"

"Oh yes, madam."

"Very well, I'll take a hammock at the same time."

986 A Poor Substitute

There is a church that holds annual strawberry festivals. Each year they put out the same large sign in front of the church. A stranger was driving through the town. He saw the big sign in front of the church reading: "Everybody come to the annual strawberry festival. All the delicious strawberry shortcake you can eat for 50¢. Everybody welcome at the strawberry festival." Then at the bottom, they had tacked on this small notice: "P.S. This year, because of the drought, we are serving prunes." (This story can be used when one is called upon to substitute for another speaker. To illustrate, the substitute speaker might say after telling the story, "I rather fear that tonight what you will get will be prunes compared to the strawberry shortcake you would have received if the distinguished speaker who is absent could have addressed you.")

987 The Reason They Hurry

Recently I told a fireman that I could understand why they hurried to the fires, but I never could understand why they hurried back from them so rapidly. He said they had to hurry back, because if they didn't they would forget what was trump.

988 All of One Mind

It is sometimes dangerous to have only one idea. In this case, there were three men who had taken a few too many drinks. They had one idea in mind, which was to catch the 11:05 P.M. train. A moment before train time they rushed into the depot and got to the train just as it was pulling out. One of them managed to get aboard; the second one caught hold of the hand-rail on the coach and finally pulled himself up; the third fellow missed the train altogether. As he sat on the platform, he began laughing, and one of the spectators said, "I don't see what you have to laugh about, when you missed the train." He said, "Well, the joke is on the other fellows who caught the train, because they just came down to see me off."

989 Credit Only

Mr. Smith, a southern merchant, had sold a cotton planter on credit during the period before the cotton was ready to be picked and sold. When the planter sold his cotton, he went to Smith's competitor across the street and bought for cash. The next time Smith met the planter he said, "I sold you on credit for months and now the first time you get cash you go across the street and buy, instead of coming to me. What's the idea?" The planter said, "Boss, I'm sorry, but I didn't even know you-all sold for cash."

990 Professor

> I once had a classmate named Guesser
> Whose knowledge got lesser and lesser.
> It at last grew so small
> He knew nothing at all—
> And now he's a college professor.—Arizona Kitty Kat

991   A Good Simile

As successful as a traffic cop selling tickets for the policeman's ball.

992   The Golfer

> "Who's that stranger, mother dear—
> Look, he knows us, ain't he queer?"
> "Hush, my own, don't talk so wild;
> "That's your father, dearest child."
> "That's my father? No such thing!
> Father died away last spring."
> "Father didn't die, you dub;
> Father joined a golfing club.
> Now the club is closed, so he
> Has no place to go, you see.
> No place left for him to roam,
> That is why he's coming home.
> Kiss him, he won't bite you, child;
> All them golfing guys look wild."
> —Boardwalk Illustrated News

993   Same Fellow

The guide was showing the tourist the sights of Italy. He said, "Now here is the Leaning Tower of Pisa." The tourist said, "I didn't get the name." The guide repeated, "This is the Leaning Tower of Pisa." The tourist answered, "I still don't recognize the name, but it looks like the work of the contractor who built my garage."

994   It Has to Be Heard

A musical critic wrote: "Here is Tchaikovsky at his best. Music so beautiful it has to be heard to be appreciated."

A lot of music is like that.

995   Help, Your Honor

To swear to tell the truth in a courtroom and then have some lawyer constantly object.

996   A Fresh Start

The famous Colonel Page of Civil War days, having been given the command of a company of raw recruits, put them through a preparatory drill, and then led them down a street in Philadelphia.

Suddenly from out of the ranks, came the command, "Halt!"

Involuntarily the men came to a stop.

"Who gave that command?" yelled the enraged Colonel.

"Potts, sir, Potts," answered a dozen voices.

"What do you mean, sir, by giving that command?" the Colonel inquired.

"Well, sir," replied Private Potts, "I've been trying for two blocks to get the company to keep step with me, and they wouldn't do it. So I had to stop them so they could get started all over again."

997   Up on His Hybrids

Little Jimmy, age four, was looking at a picture book. When he came to a picture of a zebra, mother asked him what animal that was.

Jimmy thought a moment, then replied, "That's a cow that ate hybrid corn."

998   Troubled Him Just Once

Doctor: "Have you ever had trouble with dyspepsia?"
Patient: "Only once."
Doctor: "And when was that?"
Patient: "When I tried to spell it."

999   Paid in Full

A country doctor called upon a widow, soon after the death of her husband, and announced his intentions of cutting his bill, for services rendered, in half. With tears in her eyes, the old lady reached out and clasped the doctor's hand and in a trembling voice said, "God bless you, my good friend. I'll be as good as you and knock off the other half."

1000   Comedian's Lament

> I cannot repeat the good old gags,
> Which always stop the show,
> Because you hear them nightly
> On TV and radio.

1001   Give 'em More Time

"Have you any children, Mr. Smith?"
"Yes—three."
"Do they live at home with you?"
"Not one of them—they are not married, yet."

1002   Why It Can't Be Done

Boy: "But they say, dear, that two can live as cheaply as one."
Girl: "That may be so, darling, but it'll take something for mother."

1003   Good Philosophy

One day, on my asking him why he took such long steps in walking, a Scottish friend of mine replied: "Whin I was a wee lad me mither used to say to me, 'Laddie, whin ye're a walkin' ye should take longer steps an' wear yer brogs the less the mile.' "

1004   Magic

A little girl went into a large business establishment, and had her first ride in an elevator. "How did you like it?" asked her father.

"Why, it was so funny," answered the child. "We went into a little house, and the upstairs came down."

1005   Orders

Joe: "I traveled as a salesman the entire summer, and only received two orders."

Sympathetic One: "Too bad; who gave you those?"

Joe: "Every one—Get out, and stay out!"

1006   Completely Outfitted

Visitor (speaking of little boy): "He has his mother's eyes."

Mother: "And his father's mouth."

Child: "And his brother's trousers."

1007   Just a Small Error

Three piano-movers knocked on the door of a house. A meek-looking man with an inferiority complex opened the door.

"Did you order a piano from the Flatnote Music Store?" asked the first piano-mover.

The tenant shook his head.

"Not a piano," he corrected. "I ordered a flute."

"Accordin' to this bill of ladin'," he grumbled, "you ordered a piano."

The gentleman with the inferiority complex studied the three husky piano-movers.

"Very well," he said nervously, "move it in. But if your firm makes any more errors like that, I'll have to deal somewhere else!"

1008   Correct

Teacher: "Johnny, can you tell me the name of a city in Alaska?"

Johnny: "Nome."

1009   Competition

Guests of an eastern night club were held up. The management took it calmly, realizing that these are days of keen competition.

1010 *Wasting Gas*

Little George was visiting his aunt. He found the cat in a sunny window purring cheerfully.

"Oh, Auntie, come quick," said Little George, "the cat has gone to sleep and left his engine running."

1011 *The Reason*

A servant asked her mistress if she would be good enough to advance her a few dollars out of her next month's wages, and gave the reason as follows:

"You see our minister is leaving and we are collecting money so that we can give him a little 'momentum.'"

1012 *American?*

"Is he a typical American?"

"Yes, he likes baseball, has a fast car, owes a mortgage, pays alimony, and thinks moving pictures have grand opera beaten a mile."

1013 *Confused*

"What parable in the Bible do you like best?" was the question asked of a little boy. And the answer was, "The one about the fellow that loafs and fishes."

1014 *Traffic Cop*

Traffic Cop (producing notebook): "Name, please."

Motorist: "Aloysius Alastair Cyprian."

Traffic Cop (putting book away): "Well, don't let me catch you again."

1015 *Empty Head*

"I have a cold or something in my head."

"A cold, undoubtedly."

1016 *Tact*

Young Husband: "Last night when I got home, my wife had my chair drawn up before the fire, my slippers ready for me to put on, my pipe all filled, and—"

Old Friend: "How did you like her new hat?"

1017 *Free*

"How long are you in jail for?"

"Two weeks."

"What is the charge?"

"No charge; everything is free."

1018 Ancestors

"Speaking of old families," said the aristocrat of the party, "one of my ancestors was present at the signing of the Magna Charta."

"And one of mine," said Abe, "was present at the signing of the Ten Commandments."

1019 D.D. or M.D.

The temporary member of a golf club wished to fix up a game. The secretary introduced him to one Doctor Clark.

"Now, Doctor," said the stranger with a twinkle of the eye, "it is important for me to know whether you are a doctor who preaches or one who practices."

1020 A Little Hoarse

Aunt Prudence: "Keep away from the loudspeaker, Denny. The announcer sounds as if he had a cold."

1021 The Other Half-Pound

"I sent my little boy for two pounds of plums and you only sent a pound and a half. Are your scales correct?"

"My scales are all right, madam. Have you weighed your little boy?"

1022 Efficiency

The department store engaged an efficiency expert, whose obsession was to move the departments to different parts of the store every day. One day a section would be on the top floor, the next it would be in the basement, and on the third it would be placed where the restaurant had been.

After three weeks of this an old lady approached a harassed floor-walker and asked him if he could tell her where the draperies department was.

"No, madam," he said wearily; "but if you'll stand here for a few minutes I'm sure you'll see it go by!"

1023 Reincarnation

She (thoughtfully): "Did you ever think much about reincarnation, dear?"

He (otherwise): "Think about it? I eat it nearly every day, only we call it hash."

1024 I Don't Know

Prof: "What three words are used most among college men?"
Frosh: "I don't know."
Prof: "Correct."

1025 *Should Know Better*

Mother: "Willie, why did you kick your little brother in the stomach?"
Willie: "It was his own fault. He turned around."

1026 *Last Chance*

Flying over the Bay of Naples, an air pilot turned to his passenger and
said: "Have you ever heard that phrase, 'See Naples and Die'?"
"Yes," said the passenger.
"Well," said the pilot, "take a good look—two engines are dead."

1027 *Football*

No football team is so good that it satisfies the alumni or the Monday
morning quarterbacks.

1028 *Usually the Case*

Smith: "So your son is in college? How is he making it?"
Smithers: "He isn't. I'm making it and he's spending it."

1029 *It Makes a Difference*

A bride asked the butcher the price of his hamburger meat.
"Fifty cents a pound," he replied.
She complained and said she could get it down the street for forty cents
a pound, and he asked why she didn't get some there.
"They're out of it today," she said.
"When I'm out of it," the butcher replied, "I sell it for twenty cents a
pound!"

1030 *He Was First*

Oliver was careless about his personal effects. When his mother saw
clothing scattered about on the chair and floor, she inquired: "Who
didn't hang up his clothes when he went to bed?"
A muffled voice from under the covers murmured, "Adam."

1031 *Half-Educated*

Over in a corner near the fireplace, Uncle Ezry had been working in-
dustriously with a stub pencil and a piece of paper. Suddenly he looked
up and smiled. "Wow!" he exclaimed. "If I ain't learned to write."
Maw got up and looked over his shoulder at the lines scrawled across
the paper. "What do it say?" she asked.
"I don't know," said Uncle Ezry, puzzled. "I ain't learned to read yet."

1032 *Afraid*

Mother: "Has William come in yet?"
Sister: "I think so. I haven't seen him, but the cat is hiding."

1033 *Rural Free Delivery*

A Kansas farmer stopped at a bank to see if he could get a loan on his farm.
"It might be arranged," said the banker. "I'll drive out with you and appraise it."
"You don't need to bother," said the farmer, noticing a huge cloud of dust rolling up the road. "Here it comes now."

1034 *My Mistake*

She: "Sorry, darling, I'm afraid I'm late."
He: "Humph! Only half an hour."
She: "Oh, I thought I was late."

1035 *Drastic Change*

"Father," said the minister's son, "my teacher says that 'collect' and 'congregate' mean the same thing. Do they?"
"Perhaps, my son; perhaps they do," said the clergyman. "But there is a vast difference between a 'congregation' and a 'collection.'"

1036 *Ancient Egypt*

The main thing that the ruins of Ancient Egypt prove is that Ancient Egyptian wives insisted on having a shot at backing the chariot into the garage.

1037 *Subtraction*

The schoolteacher was endeavoring to drum into her small pupils the fundamentals of arithmetic.
"Now, listen," she said rather desperately, "in order to subtract, things have to be the same denomination. This is what I mean. Now, you couldn't take three apples from four bananas, or six plums from eight peaches. It must be three apples from four apples, six plums from eight plums, and so on. Do you understand now?"
The majority of the children seemed to grasp the idea. One chubby-faced youngster very near the bottom of the class, however, raised a timid hand.
"Please, teacher," he said rather timidly, "you can take three quarts of milk from two cows."

1038 He Knew

Hotel Guest: "Is there an Encyclopaedia Britannica in the hotel?"
Clerk (with polite attention and regret): "There is not, sir; but what is it you wish to know?"

1039 Style Note

"I see where a Chicago man proposed that a badge be given every person who pays all of his taxes promptly."
"Huh! A barrel would be more appropriate."

1040 Fair Offer

Suitor: "I would like to marry your daughter."
Businessman: "Well, sir, you can leave your name and address, and if nothing better turns up, we can notify you."

1041 Budget

Most of us find some of our ambitions are nipped in the budget.

1042 Qualified to Talk

Mr. J. B. Forgan, in an address before a convention of the American Red Cross, indicated that he felt the members of the audience were more qualified to talk on the subject than he—"like the boy whose father thought he ought to be told something about the facts of life. It took considerable courage, but finally the father invited the boy into the living room after dinner, and after some hesitation said, 'Son, I should like to discuss with you some of the facts of life.' The boy said, 'Father, that is fine, what would you like to know?' "

1043 Whose Remarks

Tony dropped a piece of heavy metal on his foot. His employer had to fill out a long blank under the workingmen's compensation plan. He filled everything out down to the last question, which simply said, "Remarks." He was stumped, and went out and asked the foreman, "What do they want in here—Tony's remarks, or mine?" (Can be used in asking an audience whose remarks they want on a specific subject.)

1044 Horticultural

Mrs. Newrich was fond of flowers and especially liked the salvia, but was not very reliable in getting the names right. She was giving directions to her gardener. "On this side of the walk," she said, "I want you to put out some salivas. Now what would you suggest for the other?"

"Well, madam," answered the gardener solemnly, "maybe it would be a good idea to put some spittoonias there."

1045   Not So Romantic

Friend: "Did you get any replies to your advertisement that a lonely maiden sought light and warmth in her life?"
Spinster: "Yes, two from the electric light company and one from the gas company."

1046   Crime

We pay a tremendous crime bill each year, but we do get a lot of crime for our money.

1047   A Few Remarks

If one wishes to make a few unrelated preliminary remarks, he may say in good humor, as the late Dr. Emory W. Luccock said at the beginning of an address: "I should like to make a few remarks before I say anything."

1048   No Laughing Matter

A married couple lived on the third floor. They were in financial difficulties and were unable to pay their rent. Finally they were put out. On the way down the stairs, she carried a lamp under one arm and a bird-cage in the other. He had the baby and a vacuum cleaner. The wife stopped and began to laugh. Finally, the husband said, "Mary, this is no laughing matter." She answered, "Yes, it is: this is the first time we have gone out together in nine years." And so—I am happy to see so many women here tonight with their husbands. (Told by a well-known attorney in beginning an address after a dinner.)

1049   Unaccustomed As I Am

When giving an address, many men appreciate the comment of the college student who was writing an examination and who had simply drawn the design of a tombstone in the upper right-hand corner of his paper. On the tombstone he placed these words—"Sacred to the memory which leaves me on occasions like this."

1050   Beginning an Address

In opening an address one might say: If I lived in this great city (state, splendid community) with its magnificent mountains, beautiful lakes, cultured people, etc., I know I could repeat what the lady from Boston said. She said—"I live in Boston, so I never have to travel, because I am already there."

1051   *Camera-Action*

"Did they take an X-ray photo of your wife's jaw at the hospital?"
"They tried to, but they got a moving picture."

1052   *Misunderstanding*

Little Raymond came home beaming from Sunday school. "The Super-intendent said something awfully nice about me in his prayer this morning. He said, 'O Lord, we thank thee for our food and Raymond.' "

1053   *Sensible*

Boy: "You look like a nice sensible girl. Let's get married."
Girl: "No. I'm just as nice and sensible as I look."

1054   *Ideal?*

"What is your ideal man?"
"One who is clever enough to make money and foolish enough to spend it!"

1055   *Careful*

He was a careful driver. At the railroad crossing he stopped, looked, and listened. All he heard was the car behind him crashing into his gas tank.

1056   *She Tried*

The young man sneaked up behind her, covered her eyes with his hands, and announced:
"I'm going to kiss you if you can't tell who this is in three guesses."
"George Washington, Thomas Jefferson, Abraham Lincoln," she guessed.

1057   *Honest Answer*

Golfer to caddy: "Why didn't you watch where my ball went?"
Caddy: "I'm sorry. Your ball doesn't usually go anywhere, and this took me completely by surprise."

1058   *Courtesy*

In one German city a foreign motorist who is guilty of a minor offense receives a card which reads: "You have broken the traffic regulations but we want you to feel at home in——."

1059 Could Be

After several synonyms had been given for the word "jubilant," one little boy added: "Oh, I know what it means now—it's like jubilant delinquency!"

1060 Frankness

"Thanks very much for the beautiful necktie," said Junior, kissing Grandma dutifully on the cheek.

"Oh, that's nothing to thank me for," she murmured.

"That's what I thought, but mother said I had to."

1061 Sanity

A ruler of Holland once said, "This country stands for sanity."

Well, we stand for a little of it over here now and then, but we don't especially like it.

1062 Is That Clear?

Smart young man to the simple young girl: "Why does a black cow that eats green grass give white milk that makes yellow butter?"

Said the simple young girl: "For the same reason that black raspberries are red when they are green."

1063 Success

A little girl had a birthday party and it was a highly successful event. She said, "It was wonderful. Nineteen out of twelve came."

1064 Good Prospects

"What makes you think the baby is going to be a great politician?" asked the young mother, anxiously.

"I'll tell you," answered the young father, confidently. "He can say more things that sound well and mean nothing at all than any youngster I ever saw."

1065 English in Australia

Australian entering hospital:

" 'Ullow, Steve."

" 'Ullow, Jim."

"Come in to die?"

"No, yesterdy."

1066 *Taking No Chances*

A kind old gentleman seeing a small boy who was carrying a lot of newspapers under his arm said: "Don't all those papers make you tired, my boy?"

"Naw, I don't read 'em," replied the lad.

1067 *In the Press*

We clip the following for the benefit of those who doubt the power of the press:

"Owing to the overcrowded conditions of our columns, a number of births and deaths are unavoidably postponed this week."

1068 *Be Careful*

"When I was a young man," said Mr. Jones, "I thought nothing of working twelve or fourteen hours a day."

"Father," replied the young man, "I wish you wouldn't mention it. Those non-union sentiments are liable to make you unpopular."

1069 *Why*

Two mosquitoes were watching blood donors giving their blood in a mobile truck. Said one to the other: "Just fancy. They'll come in here and lie down placidly while someone takes a pint of their blood, but they'll yell blue murder if we just take a couple of nips!"

Witticisms and Epigrams

1070   In government, the next step after planned economy is planned extravagance.

1071   With the exception of world unrest, nothing breaks out in more places than an old garden hose.

1072   Thirty minutes is long enough for any man to tell what he knows, but he doesn't become interesting until after that when he tells what he doesn't know.

1073   In some Latin American countries any man with a good voice, a large vocabulary, and a microphone is certain to develop into a political party.

1074   You can't fool all the people all the time but most of us try.

1075   A typical American is one who has his home mortgaged, owes 30 instalments on his car, plays golf when he ought to work, and looks forward to a happy old age with social security.

1076   One of the benefits of inflation is that children no longer get sick on a nickel's worth of candy.

1077   In fairness, it ought to be conceded that the old-fashioned dime novel which is now selling for $3 is printed on better paper.

1078   The motive power for government machinery is supplied by the taxpayer harnessed to a treadmill.

1079   Another good test of blood pressure is to watch a man being liberal with the money he owes you.

1080   If you build a big business, you're a sinister influence; if you don't, you're a failure.

1081   The modern idea of roughing it is to have no television in the camp.

1082   A political plank is what a candidate stands on before election and sits down on afterwards.

1083   Children have become so expensive that only the poor can afford them.

1084   In the old days, it was two chickens in every pot, and now it's two government employees for every taxpayer.

1085   What we need is a child labor law to keep them from working their parents to death.

1086   If all the college boys who slept in class were placed end to end, they would be much more comfortable.

1087   In every one of our universities, there are a number of aggressive, clean-cut young men who are diligently working their dads through college.

1088   The worst thing about football is that none of the cheerleaders ever gets injured.

1089   It's easy to pick out the best people. They'll help you do it.

1090   With modern schools constructed largely of glass, we suppose the whole class doesn't have to stand to see the fire engine go by.

1091   If biologists are right in their assertion that there is not a perfect man today on the face of the globe, a lot of personal opinions here and there will have to be altered.

1092   It's easy to tell when you've got a bargain—it doesn't fit.

1093   The only thing that can keep on growing without nourishment is an ego.

1094   A college education seldom hurts a man if he's willing to learn a little something after he graduates.

1095   As a rule, a man who doesn't know his own mind hasn't missed so much at that.

1096   A woman doesn't hire domestic help now; she marries it.

1097   Oftentimes it's the mink in the closet that is responsible for the wolf at the door.

1098   Profits, not prophets, foretell the future.

1099   Looking at modern art is like trying to follow the plot in a bowl of alphabet soup.

1100   A few more deductions and your take-home pay isn't going to be enough to get you there.

1101   It doesn't matter whose pay roll you are on, you are working for yourself.

1102   When contentment enters, progress ceases.

1103   If you would like to live a quiet, peaceful, uneventful life, you are living at the wrong time.

1104   You have heard of the old woman who said she always felt bad even when she felt good, for fear she would feel worse tomorrow.

1105   Education is not given for the purpose of earning a living. Education is learning what to do with a living after you earn it.

1106   Everyone now works for the government, either on the payroll or on the tax roll.

1107   New pitfalls in all-number calling turn up all the time. One fellow dialed the wrong number and found himself talking to his social security account.

1108   The weaker the argument, the stronger the words.

1109   We like a man who comes right out and says what he thinks, when he agrees with us.

1110   A simple fact that is difficult to learn is that the time to save money is when you have some.

1111   There are two sides to every question that we're not interested in.

1112   Many an argument is sound—merely sound.

1113   Too much of the world is run on the theory that you don't need road manners if you are a five-ton truck.

1114   According to Frank Case's *Tales of a Wayward Inn,* the following saying originated with Wilson Mizner: "When you take stuff from one writer, it's plagiarism, but when you take it from many writers, it's called research."

1115   He had been dead long enough to be great.

1116   There are two sides to every question and if you want to be popular you take both.

1117   There is only one man living who can make a man out of you— that's you.

1118   By the time father gets the vacation bills paid, it is time to think about Christmas presents.

1119   If you want to find out what's wrong with a man, elect him to public office.

1120   Only possible reason we can see why old fools are the biggest fools is because they have had more practice.

1121   A real football fan is one who knows the nationality of every player on the All-American team.

1122   Friends are folks who excuse you when you have made a fool of yourself.

1123   We expect modern youth to be strong, courageous, and prepared to pay even more taxes than their fathers.

1124   Occasionally you see a man driving a car so carefully that you conclude it must be paid for.

1125   An honest confession is good for the soul, but bad for the reputation.

1126   Note to hunters: If it stands on its hind legs and has a pipe in its mouth, it isn't a squirrel.

1127   Trimming expenses is a government's last resort when the tax-payers can stand no more trimming.

1128   There is a lot of history that isn't fit to repeat itself.

1129   The law presumes a man innocent until he is found guilty, and then if he has any money left, his lawyer continues the presumption.

1130   The fact that Congress is no better and no worse than the country is something to worry about.

1131   Among all the nations, we certainly play a loan hand.

1132   Benjamin Franklin wrote: "Only two things in this life are certain—death and taxes." What the taxpayer resents is that they don't come in that order.

1133   When you see a married couple coming down the street, the one who is two or three steps ahead is the one that's mad.

1134   Youth should have its day, because it ages rapidly when tax paying begins.

1135   Indians on a western reservation are reported to be showing symptoms of uneasiness. Maybe someone has been telling them that the whites want to give the country back to them.

1136   There's a bright side to everything, but there's no joy when it's on your blue suit.

1137   Headline: "Husband Leaves in Midst of Wife's Bridge Party; Disappears." Just a fugitive from the chin gang.

1138   When people remove their bills from the envelopes, economic conditions are good.

1139   If the milk business ever becomes a public utility, we suppose that will make a cow a holding company.

1140   The average citizen works 70 days a year to earn enough money to pay his taxes, and he does it because he loves his country, is patriotic, and can't figure out any way of getting out of them.

1141   One nice thing about spending an evening at home is that you never have to redeem your hat after it's over.

1142   After the government takes enough to balance the budget, the citizen has the job of budgeting the balance.

1143   Nature is wonderful! A million years ago she didn't know we were going to wear spectacles, yet look at the way she placed our ears.

1144   The only trouble with doing your Christmas shopping early is to get your wherewithal on the same schedule.

1145   A cynic says that a saver is a far-sighted person who lays money aside for the government's rainy day.

1146   When a person says he wants to give you constructive criticism, he is really constructing skids for you.

1147   You may get along at Christmas time without the holly, but you must have the berries.

1148   Bragging may not bring happiness, but no man having caught a large fish goes home through an alley.

1149   Money is an article which may be used as a universal passport to everywhere except heaven, and as a universal provider of everything except happiness.

1150   A sharp tongue and a dull mind are usually found in the same head.

1151   The character of a man is his principles drawn out and woven into himself.

1152   It is better to remain silent and appear a fool, than to speak and remove all doubt.

1153   Defeat is for those who acknowledge it.

1154   Common sense is the ability to detect values.

1155   The meanest habit in the world is that of self-pity.

1156   Our grandchildren are going to have a hard time paying for the good times we didn't have.

1157   Any idea a college professor has about money is almost certain to be theoretical.—*Grand Rapids Press*

1158   You can't fool all of the people all the time, but somebody is trying.

1159   Talent knows *what* to do, tact knows *how* to do it.

1160   The government makes surveys constantly to find out what people do with their money besides paying for government surveys.

1161   You are born in a hospital, marry in a church, die in a car— what do you need a home for?

1162   Don't put off what you can do today, for the tax on it will be higher tomorrow.

1163   A physician says the way to keep young is to work, and that's just what we've been afraid of all the time.

1164   Talent makes a man *respectable*, tact makes him *respected*. Talent is *wealth*, tact is *ready money*.

1165   No sooner do they get the athletes off the gridiron than they begin putting the coaches on the pan.

1166   And now and then a collision occurs when two motorists go after the same pedestrian.

1167 Nothing influences a congressman like ten thousand telegrams written by the same man.

1168 We are inclined to agree with the Connecticut newspaper which affirms that Barnum never said of suckers, "One is born every minute." The great showman seldom was guilty of understatement.

1169 Law gives the pedestrian the right of way, but makes no provision for flowers.

1170 You can't fool all the people all the time, but it isn't necessary. A majority will do.

1171 The main thing we have learned from our short-wave set is that nearly every country in the world is full of sopranos.

1172 Physician recommends for the middle-aged light exercise and a siesta each day. Daily dozen and daily dozing.

1173 An astronaut said the earth looked blue from space. Well, it often looks that way on the ground also.

1174 Blessed are the peacemakers; they will never be unemployed.

1175 Voice over the phone: "Pop, guess who just got kicked out of college?"

1176 "Those who have hobbies rarely go crazy," asserts a psychiatrist. Yeah, but what about those who have to live with those who have hobbies?

1177 The dramatic critic's meat is the ham actor.

1178 The trouble with a husband who works like a horse is that all he wants to do evenings is hit the hay.

1179 The steps of the dining hall have become considerably worn by the treading of so many heels.—*Prof. Botts, Notre Dame University*

1180 Human diseases are the same as they were a thousand years ago, says an authority. Yes, but doctors have selected more expensive names for them.

1181 The man who boasts he never made a mistake is often married to a woman who did.

1182 Many a fellow comes out of his shell when a wife eggs him on.

1183 The fellow who gets on a high horse is riding for a fall.

1184 One hitchhiker to the other—"That's right, just sit there and let me work my finger to the bone."

1185   Another danger about one-arm driving is that a man may skid right down the center aisle of a church.

1186   Taking my economic theory course may not keep you off the bread lines, but at least you'll know why you're there.—*Prof. Robert-Michel, Hunter (N.Y.) College*

1187   Never miss an opportunity to make others happy—even if you have to let them alone to do it.

1188   You may write your term papers in any manner you choose—only, please observe the copyright laws.—*Prof. F. G. Marsh, San Francisco Junior College*

1189   A man never gets so confused in his thinking that he can't see the other fellow's duty.

1190   A dull person is one with too much polish.

1191   He who laughs last may laugh best, but he soon gets a reputation for being a dummy.

1192   Dad may not be able to appraise the worth of a college career, but he can tell you the cost.

1193   She was all will and a yard wide.

1194   The nice thing about a dull party is that you get to bed at a decent hour.

1195   Many of us spend half our time wishing for the things we could have if we didn't spend so much time wishing for them.

1196   A man laughs at a woman who puts on eyebrow make-up, but he spends ten minutes trying to comb two hairs across a bald spot.

1197   Actually there is no distinct class trodden underfoot except those who hold aisle seats.

1198   An Iowa professor says he finds five different kinds of dumbness. It seems incredible that a prominent man like that should have met so few people.

1199   The real problem concerning your leisure is how to keep other people from using it.

1200   Rip Van Winkle slept for twenty years, but, of course, his neighbors didn't have television.

1201   A sports-writer says there are 300 kinds of games played with balls. There are more than that many played with golf balls alone.

1202   It should be easy to make an honest living—there's so little competition.

1203   Many a woman who goes on a diet finds that she is a poor loser.

1204   The political pot never boils much. The old applesauce is only warmed over.

1205   There are two kinds of voters. Those who will vote for your candidate, and a lot of ignorant prejudiced fools.

1206   Social tact is making your company feel at home, even though you wish they were.

1207   All kinds of social knowledge and graces are useful, but one of the best is to be able to yawn with your mouth closed.

1208   A politician is a person who urges you to vote for him and then sends you a bill for doing it.

1209   There isn't much practical advice to be given the hopeful young graduate, except to marry the first girl he finds who has a steady job.

1210   A Communist is a person who has given up hope of becoming a capitalist.

1211   We can't understand why goods sent by ship is called a cargo, while goods sent in a freight car is a shipment.

1212   If both sides make you laugh, you are broad-minded.

1213   When you sell yourself, be sure that you don't misrepresent the goods.

1214   Some folks would rather blow their own horn than listen to the Marine band.

1215   When you argue with a fool, be sure he isn't similarly engaged.

1216   An election year restores your faith in humanity because you see important men who love everyone.

1217   The two most important muscles which operate without the direction of the brain are the heart and the tongue.

1218   "A vegetarian diet is best for those who would be beautiful," we read. Well, it does not seem to have done much for the elephant.—*Punch (London)*

1219   All we know about "hard" and "easy" money is that any kind is both—hard to get and easy to spend.

1220   Clothes don't make a man, but they can break a husband.

1221   The Smithsonian Institution reveals that there is 45 trillion dollars' worth of gold in the ocean, but we don't suppose it will comfort a seasick guy much to know he's rolling in wealth.—*Boston Herald*

1222   What this country needs is a dollar which will be not so much elastic as adhesive.

1223   In giving till it hurts, some people are extremely sensitive to pain.

1224   The meanest guy in the world is the fellow who was deaf and never told his barber.

1225   The new computers do everything but think, which we must admit makes them almost human.

1226   It is much more dignified to say we're moving in cycles rather than running around in circles, although it comes to about the same thing.

1227   Man is the only animal that laughs. He is also the only animal that has a legislature.

1228   Don't worry about what people think about you, because they aren't thinking about you.

1229   A whale's tongue is found to contain 8 per cent of the oil in his system. In politicians the proportion is even heavier.

1230   One can't help admiring the fellow who is stupid and knows it.

1231   It takes at least forty-eight rabbits to make a sealskin coat for a woman.

1232   Ideas are such funny things; they never work unless you do.

1233   A woman who can spot a blonde hair on a man's coat across the room can't always see a pair of garage doors ten feet wide.

1234   A politician gets money from the rich and votes from the poor with the argument that he is protecting each one from the other.

1235   The fact that silence is golden may explain why there is so little of it.

1236   By the time a man learns to stand up for his rights, his arches have caved in.

1237   A boy goes four years to college because it takes about that long to develop an all-American football player.

1238   Worry is the interest you pay on trouble before it comes.

1239   If you think chickens are dumb, try planting some vegetables.

1240   Experience is one thing you can't get on the easy payment plan.

1241   He called his wife Echo. She always had the last word.

1242   One touch of scandal makes the whole world chin.

1243   Time wounds all heels.

1244   What constitutes a living wage depends upon whether you are giving it or getting it.

1245   Doctors have discovered that hay fever can be either positive or negative. Sometimes the eyes have it and sometimes the nose.

1246   There are two kinds of people, the good and the bad, and the good ones are like you and me.

1247   Sometimes we're not sure whether the people are light-hearted or light-headed.

1248   A medical journal advances the theory that "man is slightly taller in the morning than he is in the evening." We have never tested this, but we have certainly noticed a tendency to become "short" toward the end of the month.

1249   One person in every eight has an accident. The other seven have accident insurance.

1250   There are two sides to every question, and a politician usually takes both.

1251   Sign in Salina, Kansas, grocery store: "If you think the price of beef is high, cigarettes are $6.49 a pound."

1252   There are only two kinds of pedestrians—the quick and the dead.

1253   Restaurant version—One man's meat is another man's croquette.

1254   The car to watch is the car behind the car in front of you.

1255   You really have insomnia if you can't sleep when it's time to get up.

1256   An article in an English journal tells how to start an amateur glee club. The real need, however, is an article telling how to stop one.

1257   A movie patron arose from his seat while viewing a picture and shot himself. We believe we have seen that picture.

1258   With a rear engine car you aren't sure whether it's your car or the traffic policeman just behind you.

1259   Everything in the modern home is controlled by switches except the children.

1260   To tell the temperature in summer you can count the number of times a tree cricket chirps in a second and add forty, or you can look at the thermometer.

1261   Instruments have been invented that will throw a speaker's voice more than a mile. Now we need an instrument that will throw the speaker an equal distance.

1262   They call it the sea of matrimony because husbands have such a hard job keeping their heads above water.

1263   On a bus a man gave his seat to a woman. She fainted. On recovering, she thanked him. Then he fainted.

1264   When a reporter has nothing to write about, he writes about nothing to write about.

1265   Many a man who does not know his own mind would be surprised to learn how well his acquaintances know it.

1266   A person seldom makes the same mistake twice. Generally it's three times or more.

1267   Patent medicine ads are so attractive that it makes a man who has his health feel as though he were missing something.

1268   The cost of living is always about the same—all a fellow has.

1269   An English neurologist says that a man who owns a car seldom walks in his sleep. If he has a family, he does it when he's awake.

1270   Home is where part of the family waits until the rest of them bring back the car.

1271   They say that every bride who is married isn't happy—just triumphant.

1272   When a man begins to realize the truth about himself, it frequently retards his program for reforming his neighbors.

1273   So much down usually means so much to keep up.

1274   Some coeds said they intend to marry "men of brains, character, adequate incomes, and a nice sense of humor." It sounds like bigamy.

1275   Thirty is a nice age for a woman, especially if she happens to be forty.

1276 A recent bride had six bridesmaids in hyacinth blue silk and two pages in rich crimson velvet, with gold lace. A pale bridegroom completed the color scheme.

1277 There are only a few nations left that are so backward they mind their own business.

1278 If all the candid camera fiends were placed end to end, they would probably take a picture.

1279 According to a doctor, singing warms the blood. We have heard some that has made ours positively boil.

1280 Love at first sight is possible, but it is always well to take a second look.

1281 Now and then one picks up a magazine on the stands that makes one curious to see the stuff the editor rejected.

1282 So far no one has invented an intelligence test to equal matrimony.

1283 Sign in wallpaper and paint store: "Husbands choosing colors must have note from wives."

1284 An optimist sees only the initial payment; the pessimist sees the future installments and the upkeep.

1285 A good deal of our prosperous appearance is due to driving a mortgaged car over a bonded road.

1286 It may be understandable if Junior believes in Santa Claus, but it's unpardonable if a politician leads Grandpa to believe it.

1287 A child who is tied to his mother's apron-strings isn't tied to his mother.

1288 Only Americans have mastered the art of being prosperous though broke.

1289 An advertisement for a lecturer says he "speaks straight from the shoulder." Too bad some of these talks can't originate a little higher up.

1290 Punctuality is the art of guessing how late the other fellow is going to be.

1291 Reforms come from below. No man with four aces howls for a new deal.

1292 We have the highest standard of living in the world. Too bad we can't afford it.

1293   When a man says, "I run things at my house," he may mean the washing machine, the vacuum cleaner, and the furnace.

1294   The world will beat a path to your door if you make a better mousetrap. It will do the same thing if you balance the federal budget.

1295   Many a man stays home nights because he has the house to himself.

1296   A man who sits in a swamp all day waiting to shoot a duck will kick if his wife has dinner ten minutes late.

1297   There's no justice. If you make out your income tax correctly, you go to the poorhouse. If you don't you go to jail.

1298   Probably the world's greatest humorist was the man who called "installments" "easy payments."

1299   The paramount question before the country today is, "How much is the down payment?"

1300   A teacher asked a precocious youngster what he was going to be when he grew up and he said a taxpayer.

1301   Our laundryman has the wisdom of a Solomon. When he can't decide to whom a certain shirt belongs, he splits it in half.

1302   A man left the bulk of his fortune to his lawyer. If everybody did this, a lot of time would be saved.

1303   Everything comes to him who waits except the time he lost waiting.

1304   "To think," exclaimed the enthusiastic young husband, "that by the time we get all this furniture paid for we shall have genuine antiques!"

1305   What labor really needs in these days of installment payments is not a thirty hour week but a forty day month.

1306   Golf liars have one advantage over the fishing kind—they don't have to show anything to prove it.

1307   About the time one learns how to make the most of life, the most of it is gone.

1308   Travel broadens you, especially that rich foreign food you eat.

1309   Some motorists are in such a hurry to get into the next town that they go right on into the next world.

1310   Among the things that seem to grow by leaps and bounds are the children in the apartment overhead.

1311   The best things in life are free. It's the worst things that are so expensive.

1312   You may not know when you are well off, but the Internal Revenue Service does.

1313   What this country needs is a man who can be right and President at the same time.

1314   "An Eskimo woman is old at forty," says an explorer. An American woman is not old at forty. In fact, she's not even forty.

1315   Behind every successful man, there's a woman telling him he doesn't amount to much.

1316   It takes three generations or one good guess in the stock market to make a gentleman.

1317   A wizard is the person who can keep up with the neighbors and the installments, too.

1318   It is very difficult to stand prosperity, especially your neighbor's.

1319   Statistics show Americans spent several billions on vacations last year, but they don't say at which resort hotel.

1320   Well, there's still a sucker being born every minute. The trouble is he hasn't got anything you can take away from him.

1321   It's nice to have four years between elections. It takes people that long to regain their faith.

1322   Only an average person is always at his best.

1323   You can fool some of the people all of the time and all of the people some of the time and the rest of the time somebody else will fool them.

1324   We used to worry about future generations becoming soft, but no more. Not when we think of the bond issues they're going to have to pay off.

1325   A college professor declares that contrary to scientific opinion, the interior of the earth is not so hot. In our opinion, the same thing is true of the exterior.

1326   One trouble with the world is that there are always more victors than spoils.

1327   Another change the game of bridge needs is a cross-bar under the table.

1328　If you want economy, never let an economic question get into politics.

1329　Problems in marriage often arise because a man too often shows his worst side to his better half.

1330　It's sort of depressing to think that most of us are just like the rest of the people.

1331　What any government needs is more pruning and less grafting.

1332　A good many human dynamos are short-circuited in a few years.

1333　Some day we hope to be wise enough to get the vitamins that wild animals get by eating what they like.

1334　A politician doesn't stand on his record; he jumps on the other fellow's.

1335　The optimist may be wrong but he has a lot more fun than the pessimist.

1336　The two agencies that redistribute great fortunes are taxation and offspring.

1337　The human race seems to have improved everything except people.

1338　The great leader is one who never permits his followers to discover that he is as dumb as they are.

1339　We wonder if the eloquent founders of this nation would have talked so glowingly of posterity, if they had known we were going to be it.

1340　On the political menu, too, applesauce is served with pork.

1341　A small town is one where the folks know all the news before the paper comes out, but take it to see whether the editor got the stories the way they heard them.

1342　Some persons have nothing to say, but you have to listen a long time to find out.

1343　"The first lie detector," says Sam Hill in the Cincinnati *Enquirer*, "was made out of the rib of a man." And no improvement has ever been made on the original machine.

1344　Man is like a car. Just so much mileage in him, whether he runs it out in forty years or eighty.

1345　The idea of fingerprinting children is a good one. It will settle the question as to who used the guest towel in the bathroom.

1346   A kiss is a peculiar proposition. Of no use to one, yet absolute bliss to two. The small boy gets it for nothing, the young man has to lie for it, and the old man has to buy it. The baby's right, the lover's privilege, and the hypocrite's mask. To a young girl, faith; to a married woman, hope; and to an old maid, charity.

1347   The great difficulty in amplifiers is that they amplify the speaker's voice, but not his ideas.

1348   When a boy marries, two opinions prevail at the home he is leaving: His mother thinks he is throwing himself away, and his sisters think the girl is.

1349   All work and no play makes jack for the nerve specialist.

1350   Some people are like French bread—little dough, but lots of crust.

1351   A businessman is judged by the company he keeps solvent.

1352   Inflation or no inflation, the cost of living seems to remain about the same—all that we earn.

1353   Every man is a hero in his own home—until the company leaves.

1354   Contentment has one big advantage over wealth; friends don't try to borrow it from you.

1355   The young man who worked so hard to graduate later wonders what the hurry was.

1356   We send our actors to England and England sends her actors to us. It's getting to be hams across the sea.

1357   One thing all nations have in common is the ability to see each other's faults.

1358   It's a good thing that politicians are generally paid by the year. They would starve to death on piecework.

1359   When everybody tends to his own business, news is scarce.

1360   One reason we are a great nation is because we have been unable to exhaust our natural resources in spite of our best efforts.

1361   Pat a man on the back and you may make his head swell.

1362   Some time the restaurants may retaliate by putting in a line of drugs and toilet articles.

1363   The man who saves money nowadays isn't a miser; he's a wizard.

1364   You should try to save something while your salary is small. It is almost impossible to save after you begin earning more.

1365   The bigger the bankroll, the tighter the rubber band.

1366   The trouble with self-made men is that they quit the job too early.

1367   A sordid money-grabber is anybody who grabs more money than you can grab.

1368   The subways are so crowded that even the men can't all get seats.

1369   More times than not a woman is responsible for her husband's success because of the money she makes it necessary for him to make.

1370   Never bet on a sure thing unless you can afford to lose.

1371   If all the autos in the world were laid end to end, it would be Sunday afternoon.

1372   A pessimist is one who, when given the choice between two evils, chooses both of them.

1373   The trouble with these "Do You Want Money?" ads is that when you read them you always discover you either have to work for it or mortgage something to get it.

1374   It's worth the taxi fare to feel you don't care what happens to the fenders.

1375   An average woman's vocabulary is said to be about 500 words. Small inventory, but think of the turnover.

1376   There are tens of millions of telephones in the United States, so when you make it in two dials you aren't doing so badly at that.

1377   A lot of nice, fat turkey gobblers would strut less if they could see into the future.

1378   The theater at the present time is not holding a mirror up to life, but a keyhole.

1379   The camera never lies, and it takes a family album to convince some people that the truth is a terrible thing.

1380   The broad general rule is that a man is about as big as the things that make him mad.

1381   The greatest consolation for many vacationists is that they have found where to stay away from next time.

1382   The polls are places where you stand in line for a chance to decide who will spend your money.

1383   Man wants but little here below, but he usually gets along on less.

1384   Most people agree with the person who keeps his mouth shut.

1385   A resort is a place where the natives live on your vacation until next summer.

1386   The greatest paradox of them all is still civilized warfare.

1387   One trouble with the country is that it wants to raise nothing but cotton and wear nothing but silk.

1388   The poet Heine once said to a caller, "My head today is perfectly barren, and you will find me stupid enough; for a friend has been here, and we exchanged ideas."

1389   U.S. now stands for Unlimited Spending.—*Tampa Tribune*

1390   If all the road-hogs were laid end to end, that would be Utopia.

1391   The bigger a man's head gets, the easier it is to fill his shoes.

1392   The fact that no one knows anything about the future makes a business forecaster more confident.

1393   Don't be afraid of having too many irons in the fire, if the fire is hot enough.

1394   Evolution: Dress, $5.75; frock, $19.98; gown, $65; creation, $225.

1395   A man can blow his own horn nowadays before he completes all the payments.

1396   A fool and his money sooner or later wind up in college.

1397   A woman's tears are the greatest water power known to man.

1398   All things come to him who waits, but they are apt to be pretty well shop-worn.

1399   Money may not bring happiness, but it is nice to find out for yourself.

1400   Someone has observed that it takes a student 20 minutes longer to say what he thinks than to tell what he knows.

1401   The man's insomnia was so bad that the sheep were picketing him for shorter hours.

1402   Judging from the amount of the public debt, it is no longer much of a compliment to tell a lady she looks like a million dollars.

1403   If you can spend a perfectly useless afternoon in a perfectly useless manner, you have learned how to live.—*Lin Yutang*

1404   The diploma you get from the school of experience is inscribed in marble, but you won't be able to read it.

1405   He made a nickel go so far the buffalo got sore feet.

1406   A woman is a man's solace, but if it wasn't for her, he wouldn't need any solace.

1407   According to a survey, the most dangerous traffic hour is between seven and eight o'clock at night. That's when everyone is through supper and hurrying to get nowhere.

1408   Hanging out the family wash to dry is a simple problem to the trailer housewife. If it rains, they move over into the next county.

1409   He's so stingy that when the boys give three cheers, he only gives two.

1410   To enjoy garden work, put on a wide hat and gloves, hold a little trowel in one hand, and tell the man where to dig.

1411   There will always be a multitude who are congenitally unable to think straight.—*Charles Evans Hughes*

1412   A golf player is a person who can drive 70 miles an hour in any traffic with perfect ease, but blows up on a two-foot putt if somebody coughs.

1413   It is getting harder and harder to find a courteous person who isn't trying to sell you something.

1414   A real friend will not visit you in prosperity unless he is invited, but when you are in adversity he will call without invitation.

1415   The cautious suitor who stays on the fence too long usually ends up getting the gate.

1416   An honest fisherman is a pretty uninteresting person.

1417   The greatest inspiration is often born of desperation. The fellow who thinks he can't is probably right.

1418   One guy who always goes to the top is a barber.

1419   The advantage about working day and night is that you earn enough to pay the doctor when you break down.

1420   When a fellow's too much in love with himself, he's not likely to have much competition.

1421   When a wife explores a man's pockets, she generally gets what the average explorer does—enough material for a lecture.

1422   Toastmaster: "And now, our featured speaker is a man who needs no introduction—he didn't show up."

1423   It's the fellow in the office who blows his horn the loudest who is generally in a fog.

1424   Almost every after-dinner speech has a happy ending—everyone is glad when it's over.

1425   Sixty million people go to the movies every week, and almost all of them file past our seats at the most exciting part of the picture.

1426   You can't fall out of bed if you sleep on the floor.

1427   When Uncle Sam plays Santa Claus, it's the taxpayer who holds the bag.

1428   Professor Warren of Harvard Law School concedes modern youth a little: "An A.B. degree nowadays means that the holder has mastered the first two letters of the alphabet."

1429   The trick in campaigning is to give them platitudes without fear or favor and straight-from-the-shoulder generalities.

1430   A senator tells us the average American is not tax conscious yet, and this is doubtless so. If he shows signs of coming to, he is struck by another.

1431   One advantage in being stupid is that you never get lonely.

1432   Many persons do not leave their footprints on the sands of time, but they leave their skidmarks at the traffic intersections.

1433   *Some Answers from Sophomores*

"James I claimed the throne of England through his grandmother because he had no father."
"Benjamin Franklin produced electricity by rubbing cats backward. Benjamin Franklin was the founder of electricity."

"America was discovered by the Spinach."

"In 1865 the Pilgrims crossed the ocean, and this was known as Pilgrim's Progress."

"An Ibex is where you look at the back part of a book to find out anything you want."

"A deacon is the lowest kind of a Christian."

"A monastery is a place of monsters."

"False doctrine is when a doctor gives wrong stuff to a man."

1434   A perpetual optimist is a person who has nothing to worry about because he has nothing to worry with.

1435   When success turns a man's head, he faces failure.

1436   Some people have tact, others tell the truth.

1437   There are two kinds of fishermen; those who fish for sport and those who catch something.

1438   Buying what you do not need is an easy road to needing what you cannot buy.

1439   Weak knees come from a weak head.

1440   At a certain age some people's minds close up. They live on their intellectual fat.—*William Lyon Phelps*

1441   Riches are no menace if we do not divorce dollars from sense.

1442   The chief fault of American audiences is that they see the point before you get there, which is disconcerting.—*Jerome K. Jerome*

1443   The man whose conscience never troubles him must have it pretty well trained.

1444   Some persons pray for more things than they are willing to work for.

1445   Tomorrow never comes, but the morning after certainly does.

1446   We would be glad to pay as we go if we could catch up paying for where we have been.

1447   At a banquet of firemen, recently, the chief proposed the toast: "The ladies! Their eyes kindle the only flame which we cannot extinguish, and against which there is no insurance."

1448   The real test of golf and in life is not keeping out of the rough . . . but getting out after we are in.

1449   Life has a way of evening up things. For every woman who makes a fool out of some man there's another who makes a man out of some fool.

1450   The difference between a groove and a grave is only a matter of depth.

1451   A luxury on which you can make the down payment becomes a necessity.

1452   Nothing handicaps you so much in golf as honesty.

1453   The only reason a great many American families don't own an elephant is that they have never been offered an elephant for a dollar down and a dollar a week.

1454   A politician thinks of the next election; a statesman of the next generation. To preserve peace, we need guns of smaller and men of larger caliber.

1455   There are some who call it the Sock Market.

1456   No matter how bad prose is it might be verse.

1457   Everytime he looks in the mirror he takes a bow.

1458   The difference between most men is small, but that little difference is large.

1459   The difference between a prejudice and a conviction is that you can explain a conviction without getting mad.

1460   As a man grows wiser, he talks less and says more.

1461   The average American works himself to death so he can live.

1462   Some marriages crack up when the instalment collector cracks down.

1463   Someone wants to know if there is any cure for waking up with a severe headache? We can only think of insommia.

1464   An optimist is a person who thinks he knows a friend from whom he can borrow, and a pessimist is one who has tried.

1465   When a girl reduces, she is going out of her weigh to please some man.

1466   By the streets of "by and by," one arrives at the house of "never."
—*Cervantes*

1467   If you wish to be miserable, you must think about yourself, what you want, what you like, what respect people ought to pay you, and what people think of you.

1468   Truth is the opinion that still survives.

1469   An automobile is always as drunk as the driver.

1470   Minimize friction and create harmony. You can get friction for nothing, but harmony costs courtesy and self-control.

1471   Genius may have its limitations, but stupidity is not thus handicapped.

1472   The modern idea of roughing it is to do without a radio in each room.

1473   Another great danger of one-arm driving is that you're so likely to skid into a church.

1474   It should be easy for any government to please the people. All they want is lower taxes and larger appropriations.

1475   A man may have more money than brains, but not for long.

1476   It is commendable, to be sure, for a college to offer a course in "What Contemporary Civilization Is," but a little information as to where it is would help a lot too.

1477   A careful driver approached a railroad; he stopped, looked, and listened. All he heard was the car behind him crashing into his gas tank.

1478   If you want to flatter somebody, just look serious and ask him what he thinks of the general situation.

1479   Most wives wonder how their husbands know so much about economics and money without having any.

1480   A court held that the slot machine is not a lottery. Certainly there is little of the element of chance about it.

1481   If the colleges continue to get more and more finicky, pretty soon an amateur won't be able to make a decent living in any sport.

1482   Sign at library: Only low talk permitted here.

1483   We live in a free country where a man can say what he thinks if he isn't afraid of his wife, his neighbors, his boss, his customers, or the government.

1484   Making a fool of yourself is not so bad if you realize who did it.

1485 Chili today and hot tamale.

1486 Man isn't so smart. Thousands of years before he began to have afternoon headaches from trying to think, the turtle had a stream-lined body, hard top, retractable landing gear, and a mobile house.

1487 Money talks and it never says anything so often as "good-bye."

1488 The first essential for leadership is a group of dumb guys to follow you.

1489 There is nothing more difficult than the art of making advice agreeable.

1490 At twenty the will reigns, at thirty the wit, and at forty the judgment.

1491 The only person who gets paid for being disagreeable is a traffic cop.

1492 This is a free country and a good many people are getting it that way by agreeing to pay later.

1493 A rabbit's foot is a poor substitute for horse sense.

1494 It is possible that the man who wakes up to find himself famous has been sleeping all the while with one eye open.

1495 A friend forgives your defects, and if he is very fond of you, he doesn't see any.

1496 Unless you can look interested when you are bored, you will never be a success socially.

1497 No postage stamp sticks better than the one on an envelope with the wrong address.

1498 Nowadays every man wants life, liberty, and two cars in which to pursue happiness.

1499 Broadmindedness is the ability to smile when you learn that the ten bucks you lent your roommate is taking your girl to the prom.

1500 The man who says that he is the boss at home and in his office probably doesn't tell the truth in other matters either.

1501 Simile—R is silent as in Harvard.

1502 Our eyes are placed in front because it is more important to look ahead than look back.

1503   If you can't think of any other way to flatter a man, tell him he's the kind that can't be flattered.

1504   If parents haven't learned something from experience, they can always learn it from their children.

1505   A rich uncle always has nieces and nephews named after him.

1506   Sign at Jonestown, Pa., store on New York to Harrisburg highway: "Modern Antiques."

1507   It certainly pays to advertise. There are twenty-six mountains in Colorado higher than Pike's Peak.

1508   Some people just can't unbend and be human until misfortune has taken the starch out of them.

1509   Some people are born great, some achieve greatness, and some just grate.

1510   In the old days a bad man would go around with nicks in his gun handle, instead of in his fenders.

1511   You might as well do your Christmas hinting early.

1512   The man who thinks he has no faults has at least one.

1513   I had a little dog. I called him August. August was fond of jumping at conclusions, especially at the wrong conclusion. One day he jumped at a mule's conclusion. The next day was the first of September.

1514   Why does a man say he has been fishing when he hasn't caught a thing?

1515   There are three applause periods in a speech. Applause by the audience at the beginning of a speech expresses faith. Applause in the middle of a speech expresses hope. Applause at the end of a speech expresses charity.

1516   A student makes his bed and has to lie in it; a professor makes his bunk and has to lie out of it.

1517   We have often wondered why Nature didn't construct a man so he could kick himself occasionally.

1518   A recession is a period in which you tighten up your belt. A depression is a time in which you have no belt to tighten. When you have no trousers to hold up, it's a panic.

1519   In some cities they tear down buildings to save taxes. They might try tearing down some taxes to save buildings.

1520 We never could understand why other people do not profit from their mistakes.

1521 The government not only has the bad habit of living beyond its income, but also beyond ours.

1522 It's hard to keep up with the neighbors without falling behind with the creditors.

1523 Think of the different ways of saying "Good morning." Someone says it one way and they put a punch in you. They say it in another way, and you want to punch them.

1524 "Many of the compositions that have been handed in are trite— or should I say tripe!" (Professor in English class)

1525 Want Ad—"Young man who gets paid on Monday and is broke by Wednesday would like to exchange small loans with a young man who gets paid on Wednesday and is broke by Monday."

1526 Customer (to headwaiter): "Just for a point of information, did the waiter who took my order leave any family?"

1527 If they ever close up the Metropolitan Opera, where will society go to talk while opera is being sung?

1528 A good many car drivers don't need seat belts as much as they need strait jackets.

1529 Men who are run down generally wind up in a hospital.

1530 We have far too many divorces. Too many persons marry in haste and repent at leisure. A wedding is the only prerequisite for a divorce now.

1531 The other day, the newspapers were showing the pictures of an old man who had reached the age of ninety-eight. But there is nothing so wonderful about that. Look at the time it took him to get there.

1532 The reason some of us find it difficult to think is that we haven't had any previous experience.

1533 "The surtax on any amount of surtax net income not shown in the table is computed by adding to the surtax for the largest amount shown which is less than the income, the surtax upon the excess over the amount of the rate indicated in the table." Instruction on income-tax blank. We contend that the government should supply a slide rule, prayer book, and ouija board with each income-tax return form.

1534 He who hesitates probably turned into a one-way street.

1535 When you hear some folks you know blow and brag, you are reminded of the time the flea said to the elephant, "Boy, didn't we shake that bridge when we crossed it?"

1536 A thoughtful economist has just written a 100-page "Short History of Money." We could write a history of ours in six words: "Here it is; There it goes!"

1537 It is not only unkind to speak of a wasteful bureaucracy—it is also repetitious.

1538 Found on a Freshman's registration card: Name of parents: "Mamma and Papa."

1539 "A Toast," exclaimed the hobo lifting his tomato can. "Here's to de holidays! Bless de hull t'ree hundred and sixty-five of 'em!"

1540 Sign in a self-service elevator: "Eighth Floor Button Out of Order. Please Push Three and Five instead."

1541 Most of us are confident we could move the mountains if somebody would clear the hills out of our way.

1542 Making love is like making pie. All you need is a lot of crust and some applesause. (Then mix it with a spoon).

1543 A famous old inn claims to own a sixty-year old cheese. It is, of course, still going strong.

1544 Sign on a Scottish golf course: Members will refrain from picking up lost balls until they have stopped rolling.

1545 In the old days child guidance was something parents were expected to provide and not submit to.

1546 If a conservative doesn't understand something he opposes it, whereas a liberal supports it.

1547 "Multiple births are more frequent in larger families," declares a statistician. It's mighty hard to fool these statisticians.

1548 In trying to convey an important idea to another person, the Irishman said, "If I can get this one idea into your head, you will have it in a nutshell."—*Dr. Emory W. Luccock.*

1549 A good speech has a good beginning and a good ending, both of which are kept very close together.

1550 Nothing gives you quite the thrill of treading in the darkness on a step that isn't there.

1551   How is it possible for women to understand politics when they have to depend almost entirely on their husbands for their political education?

1552   It is just as well that justice is blind; she might not like some of the things done in her name if she could see them.

1553   A doctor gives us the cheerless news that women are too weak for housework. Well, the men are not strong for it, either.

1554   On the first of the month there is no female or anything else more deadly than the mail.

1555   The habit of going to the bottom of things usually lands a man on top.

1556   The world has facilities enough now for transmitting intelligence rapidly—that is, until we get more intelligence to transmit.

1557   Somebody always backs down when the public gets its back up.

1558   Early to bed and early to rise is a sure sign that you don't care for television.

1559   "The slow-thinkers live longest," says a prominent psychologist. Not if they cross the street.

1560   If a man wants his dreams to come true, he must wake up.

1561   The difficulty in turning immigrants into good Americans is to find a model to work by.

1562   A magazine writer says we need a new religion. But let's not do anything rash until we try the old ones.

1563   If he dodges cars, he is a pedestrian; if he dodges taxes, he is a financier; if he dodges responsibility, he is a statesman.

1564   The modern girl may have her little weaknesses, but she isn't effeminate.

1565   The matrimonial bark is wrecked by the matrimonial barking.

1566   Many a man keeps his nose to the grindstone so his wife can turn hers up at the neighbors.

1567   There is nothing but ill-fortune in a habit of grumbling, which requires no talent, no self-denial, no brains, no character.—*O. S. Marden*

1568   Samuel Johnson demolished a loquacious bore with: "You talk like a watch which ticks away minutes but never strikes the hour."

1569　A marital expert says that when you see a man polishing a woman's car you may be sure they are engaged; and when you see a woman polishing a man's car you may be sure they are married.

1570　One advantage of being poor is that it doesn't take much to improve your situation.

1571　A depression is a period when people do without the things their parents never had.

1572　One nice thing about a one-way street is that you can only be bumped in the rear.

1573　If you make a better mousetrap now, you're just in the old rat race.

1574　A sensible girl is not so sensible as she looks because a sensible girl has more sense than to look sensible.

1575　The huge national debt they will inherit should keep our children from one indulgence—ancestor worship.

1576　He can compress the most words into the smallest ideas of any man I ever met.—*Lincoln,* of a fellow lawyer.

1577　One half of knowing what you want is knowing what you must give up before you get it.—*Sidney Howard*

1578　A seventh-grade pupil won first prize in his class for the best short baseball story: "Rain, no game."

1579　When prices are high, money doesn't talk; it whispers.

1580　Experience is what you get when you're looking for something else.

1581　Snobbery is the pride of those who are not sure of their position. —*Berton Braley*

1582　The longest way home is on the old expense account.

1583　Be pretty if you can, be witty if you must, be agreeable if it kills you.—*Elsie De Wolfe*

1584　Some folk seem to get the idea they're worth a lot of money just because they have it.

1585　A young girl came into a bank to buy some savings bonds. When the teller asked her what denomination, she replied, "Presbyterian."

1586   The average fire is put out before any considerable damage is done by the fire department.

1587   Before television no one ever knew what a headache looked like.

1588   A foreigner who killed himself because he was unable to learn English in New York seems to have thought it was spoken there.

1589   If we should lock up all the feeble-minded, who would write our song hits?

1590   Alarmists seemingly regard the rising generation as a falling one.

1591   Remember the old days when people killed time by working instead of by coffee breaks?

1592   Man is an able creature, but he has made 32,600,000 laws and hasn't yet improved on the Ten Commandments.

1593   The world never will be wholly civilized. Some outlying portions have no natural resources worth seizing.

1594   The members of the smart set never get that way by listening to one another.

1595   The evil that men do lives after them. The saxophone was made in 1846.

1596   Success is getting what you want; happiness is wanting what you get.

1597   The greatest service that could be rendered the Christian peoples would be to convert them to Christianity.

1598   When the sales clerk tells you the price of the article, you can grin and bear it, or smile and charge it.

1599   If you think trifles won't be noticed, just let a catsup bottle drip on white flannel trousers at a picnic.

1600   Scientists say we are what we eat. Nuts must be a commoner diet than we had thought.

1601   The reason ideas die quickly in some heads is because they can't stand solitary confinement.

1602   It's queer that men should take up a life of crime when there are so many legal ways to be dishonest.

1603   Some are bent with toil, and some get crooked trying to avoid it.

1604   Patrick Henry said, "Give me liberty or give me death," but now we leave out the words liberty and death.

1605 Francis Scott Key deserved fame because he knew all the verses of "The Star-Spangled Banner."

 1606 Next to automation nothing beats a wastebasket for speeding up work.

1607 If you are sure you are right, you can afford to keep quiet.

1608 A conceited person never gets anywhere because he thinks he is already there.

1609 It's surprising how many persons unselfishly will neglect their own work in order to tell you how to run your affairs.

Amusing Definitions

1610   *Acrobat*—The only person who can do what everyone else would like to do—pat himself on the back.

1611   *Adam*—The one man in the world who couldn't say, "Pardon me, haven't I seen you before?"

1612   *Adolescence*—The period when children are certain they will never be as stupid as their parents.

1613   *Advice*—What you take for a cold. The suggestions you give someone else which you believe will work to your benefit. Something most of us "give until it hurts."

1614   *Alimony*—A man's cash surrender value.

1615   *All-expense tour*—The perfect example of truth-in-advertising.

1616   *Amateur athlete*—An athlete who is paid in cash—not by check.

1617   *Amateur carpenter*—A carpenter who resembles lightning. He never strikes twice in the same place.

1618   *Amateur golfer*—The man who moves heaven and earth to play golf.

1619   *American*—A person who is always ready to discuss the Constitution although he has never read it.

1620   *Antique collector's song*—"You take the highboy and I'll take the lowboy."

1621   *Baby sitter*—A girl you pay to invite her friends to your house to keep your children awake.

1622   *Bachelor*—A bachelor is a man who gives in when he is wrong; a married man gives in when he is right. He is the only man who never lied to his wife. The difference between a married man and a bachelor is that when a bachelor walks the floor with a baby at midnight he is dancing. The fellow who never says hasty things he has to regret afterward. It has been said, "Not all men are fools—some are bachelors." A man who gets all the credit for what he accomplishes.

1623   *Bargain*—When two people are sure they got the better of each other.

1624   *Beauty*—The one thing a woman may lose and never know it's gone.

1625   *Beginner's luck*—A college freshman with an idea.

1626   *Big game hunter*—A man who can spot a leopard.

1627   *Blessed event*—When a man's mother-in-law goes home.

1628   *Block*—The distance between some people's ears.

1629   *Blotter*—A porous substance you spend your time looking for while the ink is drying.

1630   *Bop*—Just Stravinsky played on an empty stomach.—*Florian Zabach*

1631   *Bottoms up*—A toast you never make to the crew in a boat race.

1632   *Bridge*—Next to hockey the most dangerous shin-bruising game in America.

1633   *Buffer state*—One between two biffer states.

1634   *Bus driver*—The person who tells you where to get off at.

1635   *Business*—Like riding a bicycle. Either you keep moving or you fall down.—*John David Wright*

1636   **Business economy**—A reduction in some other employee's salary.

1637   *Busy doctor*—A doctor who has so many patients that when there is nothing the matter with you, he will tell you so.

1638   *Canoe*—An object that acts like a small boy—it behaves better when paddled from the rear.

1639   *Careful driver*—The fellow who has made the last payment on his car.

1640   *Centenarian*—A person who has lived to be 100 years old. He never smoked or he smoked all his life. He used whiskey for eighty years or he never used it. He was a vegetarian or he wasn't a vegetarian. Follow these rules carefully, and you too can be a centenarian.

1641   *Charm*—The ability to make someone else think that both of you are quite wonderful.

1642   *Chiropodist*—A fellow who, when given an inch, will take a foot. A man who is down at the heel even when he is prosperous.

1643   *Christian nation*—A nation that has churches from which its people may stay away on Sunday. A pagan nation has no churches to which those who might like to attend may go.

1644   *Christmas*—The time when father owes best.

1645   *Club secretary*—The person who keeps the minutes and wastes the hours.

1646   *Cold feet*—The ailment you get when you know what the consequences are going to be.

1647   *College*—The land of the midnight sons.

1648   *College English department*—The chamber of commas.

1649   *College football team*—An organization the American boy joins in order to see the United States.

1650   *Commuter*—A person who has a complaint of long-standing.

1651   *Conscience*—The sixth sense that comes to our aid when we are going wrong and tells us that we are about to get caught.

1652   *Convictions*—What you have when you know what the boss thinks.

1653   *Cooperation*—Doing with a smile what you are compelled to do.

1654   *Courage*—Fear that has said its prayers.—*Karle Baker, as reported in Better Homes and Gardens, June 1955*

1655   *Crooked dough*—Something handled by counterfeiters and pretzel manufacturers.

1656 *Dangerous surgical operation*—An operation that costs more than $500.

1657 *Deaf and dumb couple*—The only married people who can settle a quarrel at night by turning out the lights.

1658 *Defeated politician*—The candidate who never has to explain why he is unable to keep his campaign promises.

1659 *Delegate-at-large*—A man who goes to a convention without his wife.

1660 *Delicatessen operator*—A man who has women eat out of his hand.

1661 *Dentist*—A man who runs a filling station. A collector of old magazines.

1662 *Depression*—A period when you can't spend money you don't have.

1663 *Detour*—The roughest distance between two points.

1664 *Diplomat*—An honest man sent abroad to lie for his country.

1665 —A person who straddles an issue when he isn't dodging one.

1666 *Discretion*—When you are sure you are right and then ask your wife.

1667 *Doctor*—A man who has his tonsils, adenoids and appendix.

1668 *Dough*—A misnomer for money; dough sticks to your fingers.

1669 *Drama critic*—A man who gives the best jeers of his life to the theater.

1670 *Draw*—A term used to describe the result of a battle between a dentist and a patient.

1671 *Dutch treat*—When two businessmen have dinner and each uses his own expense account.

1672 *Eager beaver*—A person who works twice as hard but doesn't know why.

1673 *Economist*—A person who can tell you what is going to happen next month and explain later why it didn't.

1674 —One who tells you what to do with your money after you have done something else with it.

1675   —A person who knows all about money but hasn't any.

1676   —An unemployed financier with a Phi Beta Kappa key on one end of his watch chain and no watch on the other.—*Alben Barkley*

1677   *Education*—"The inculcation of the incomprehensible into the ignorant by the incompetent."—*Sir Josiah Stamp*. The only thing a man is willing to pay for, and hopes he doesn't get. Training that helps one to make more money unless he becomes an educator.

1678   *Egotism*—The anesthetic that dulls the pain of stupidity.—*Frank Leahy, in Look Magazine, January 10, 1955*

1679   *Egotist*—A person who is fascinated with himself.

1680   *Election year*—One year in four when the great dish is apple-sauce.

1681   *Electrician*—A man who wires for money.

1682   *Elephant*—A useful animal with a vacuum-cleaner in front and a rug-beater at the back.

1683   *Error in judgment*—A man who thinks he has an open mind when it's merely vacant.

1684   *Example*—To give an illustration. The teacher asked the student to give an example of the word "boycott." The student said, "The wind blew down my brother's neck and the boycott an awful cold."

1685   *Executive*—A person who can without the facts make quick decisions which occasionally are right.

1686   —A person who never even dreamed of earning the salary he can't get along on today.

1687   *Executive ability*—The faculty of earning your bread by the work of other people.

1688   *Farm*—A portion of land covered by a mortgage.

1689   *Farsighted*—A term used to describe a man who wouldn't take a chance on an auto raffle because he didn't have a garage. When one buys two lawn mowers—one for the neightbors to use. To order three eggs in a restaurant—one for your vest.

1690   *Fatalist*—A person who jumps just as far as the rest of us when a car honks in his ear.

1691   *Father*—A fellow who is put on the pan if he doesn't bring home the bacon.

1692   *Female archer*—A girl who works on eyebrows in a beauty parlor.

1693   *Fifth marriage*—The triumph of hope over experience.

1694   *Fisherman*—One who drops the fish a line but seldom hears from them.

1695   *Flaw*—What the Harvard graduate thinks you walk on in a house.

1696   *Floating debt*—A yacht that hasn't been paid for.

1697   *Folk singer*—A person who sings through his nose by ear.

1698   *Fox*—A wolf who sends flowers.—*Ruth Weston*

1699   *Frog*—The only living thing that has more lives than a cat. It croaks every night.

1700   *Genius*—The ability to evade work by doing something right the first time it has been done.

1701   *Gentleman*—Any man who wouldn't hit a woman with his hat on.—*Fred Allen*

1702   —A person who could tell you about his operation but doesn't.

1703   *Golf*—A game that has produced more liars than anything else except the income tax. Most golfers have taken up the wrong sport. They should have taken up trap shooting.

1704   *Golf optimist*—The fellow who said he made fifteen on the first hole, fourteen on the second, thirteen on the third, and then blew up.

1705   *Guest towel*—A towel you look at but never use.

1706   *Hamburger*—The last round-up.

1707   *Happiness*—The result of being too busy to be miserable.

1708   *Havana tobacco*—A product you find in Cuba in a few cigars.

1709   *Hero*—The person who moves that the minutes of the last meeting be accepted without reading them.

1710   *Hide and sick*—A game played on any ocean liner by the passengers.

1711   *Hitch-hiker*—The only person who could be completely incapacitated by the loss of his thumb.

1712   *Home*—The place where you can enjoy corn on the cob and soup.

1713   *Honesty*—The biggest handicap in golf.

1714   *Hospital*—A place where people who are run down, wind up.

1715   *Human nature*—The thing which makes some men hewers of wood and others drawers of dividends.

1716   *Humor-in-advertising*—"We welcome complaints." "We trust You." "Home Cooking."

1717   *Imagination*—What makes some politicians think they are statesmen.

1718   *I owe it all to*—An expression commonly used in connection with one's wife, landlord, or pawnbroker.

1719   *In the money*—A condition many men hope for, but only a bank teller experiences.

1720   *Insomnia*—A sad condition in which you can't sleep when it's time to get up. When you keep a lot of innocent sheep jumping over a fence all night because you can't go to sleep.

1721   *Intuition*—What enables a woman to contradict her husband before he says anything.

1722   *Jack*—A thing that lifts a car and also keeps it going.

1723   *Janitor*—A man who never puts out any excess hot air.

1724   *Jay*—A bird of the crow family, which can be found in fields and meadows. A jaywalker, on the other hand, is a bird of the Schmoe family who can be found in traffic jams and morgues.—*Phyllis Battelle, in New York Journal American, November 28, 1955*

1725   *June*—The month for weddings—when you have perfect daze.

1726   *Jury*—The only thing that doesn't work right when it's fixed.

1727   *Kangaroo*—Nature's initial effort to produce a cheer leader.

1728   *Kibitzer*—A person with an inferiority complex.

1729   *Lame duck*—A politician whose goose has been cooked.

1730   *Laughter*—The sound you hear when you stumble, or lose your hat in the wind.

1731   *Law of diminishing returns*—An economic law familiar to laundrymen.

1732   *Lean years ahead*—What every woman hopes for.

1733   *Lend me your ears*—A phrase used by Marc Antony and by the mothers of ten million six-year-olds.

1734   *Library*—A place where the dead live.

1735   *Life insurance*—A plan that keeps you poor all your life so you can die rich.

1736   *Love at first sight*—The world's greatest time-saver.

1737   *Luxury*—Something you don't really need and can't do without.

1738   *Major general*—An army officer who has his men behind him before the battle and ahead of him during it.

1739   *Man*—The only animal with brains enough to find a cure for the diseases caused by his own folly.

1740   *Man of few words*—One who takes three hours to tell you he is a man of few words. Husband.

1741   *Married life*—A period when you make progress if you break even. The most dangerous year in married life is the first; then comes the second, third, fourth, fifth, etc. Has three stages—cooing—wedding—billing.

1742   *Microscope expert*—A person who magnifies everything.

1743   *Middle age*—The period when you begin to wonder what it was you ate the day before yesterday.

1744   *Minor operation*—One performed on someone else.

1745   *Monologue*—A conversation between a man and his wife.

1746   *Mouth*—The grocer's friend, the dentist's fortune, the orator's pride, and the fool's trap.

1747 *Naïve person*—Anyone who thinks you are interested when you ask how he is.

1748 *Necessary evil*—One we like so much we refuse to do away with it.

1749 *New idea*—An impossibility until it is born.

1750 *New York*—The city where the people from Oshkosh look at the people from Dubuque in the next theater seats and say, "These New Yorkers don't dress any better than we do."

1751 *Obesity*—The mother of invention.

1752 *Oculist*—A man with an eye for business.

1753 *On the rocks*—A phrase meaning a person is either bankrupt or working in jail. The difference is inconsequential.

1754 *Open mind*—The mind of a man who has the will power to get rid of his present prejudices and take on a new set of prejudices. Sometimes, a case of a person merely rearranging his prejudices.

1755 *Operation*—Something that took a surgeon an hour to perform and the patient years to describe.

1756 *Optimist*—One who takes a frying pan on a fishing trip.

1757 —A businessman who believes his customers will pay their bills by air mail or special delivery.

1758 —One who thinks he will never do anything stupid again.

1759 —One who thinks he can get by with saying "Thanks" to the head waiter.

1760 —A person who thinks there are some big berries in the bottom of the box.

1761 *Overeating*—The destiny that ends our shapes.

1762 *Parking space*—An unoccupied space about seven feet wide and fifteen feet long next to the curb—on the other side of the street. The place where you take your car to have little dents put in the fenders.

1763 *Pedestrian*—A person who isn't safe even when he is riding.

1764 *Perfection*—An alarm clock that doesn't ring.

1765   *Perspiration*—The best solvent of all for solving your problems.

1766   *Pessimism*—The determination to see less than there is in anything, and optimism is the ability to see more than there is in everything.

1767   *Pessimist*—A person who would commit suicide if he could do it without killing himself.

1768   *Pickpocket*—A man who generally lives alone, but occasionally goes out in a crowd for a little change. The optimist in a crowd.

1769   *Playing by note*—To learn to play the piano by note instead of by ear. Twelve payments on the note and the piano is yours to learn to play.

1770   *Political plum*—One result of careful grafting.

1771   *Politician*—A fellow who shakes your hand before the election and shakes you after the election.

1772   *Precocious child*—The child who took his nose apart to see what made it run.

1773   *Prejudice*—Being down on what you are not up on.

1774   *Profanity*—A way of escape for the man who runs out of ideas.

1775   *Prosperity*—A period when there are a lot of after-dinner speakers after dinners to speak after.

1776   *Proverb*—Any short saying that states a great truth. Examples: "A soft answer turneth away wrath, but hath little effect on a door-to-door salesman." "Birds of one feather catch a cold." "A thing of beauty keeps you broke forever."

1777   *Public library building*—The tallest building in town—it has more stories than any other.

1778   *Rabbit*—A little animal that grows the fur other animals get credit for when it's made into a lady's coat.

1779   *Reception*—An ordinary party without chairs.

1780   *Reckless driver*—A person who passes you when you are exceeding the speed limit.

1781   —The other motorist.

1782   —Do not confuse a reckless driver with a wreckless driver.

1783   *Reckless driving*—A woman with a hammer and some nails working on a freshly painted living room wall.

1784   *Reducing machine*—A machine that costs so much you have to starve yourself to keep up the payments.

1785   *Reformer*—One who insists on his conscience being your guide. One who makes his associates feel miserable about their pleasures.

1786   *Rejected play manuscript*—A case of all work and no play.

1787   *Revenge*—A dish that should be eaten cold.—*King Victor Emmanuel II of Italy, reported in Time Magazine, January 31, 1955*

1788   *Rich man*—Only a poor man with money.

1789   —A man who has so much money he doesn't even know his son is in college.

1790   *Roughing it*—To camp out without a television set.

1791   *Rounder*—The fellow who can't look his wife squarely in the eye.

1792   *Rush hour*—When the traffic stands still.

1793   *Salary*—An amount of money that, no matter how large it is, some people spend more than.

1794   *Scandal*—A breeze stirred up by a couple of windbags.

1795   *Scotsman*—The only golfer who wouldn't knock a golf ball out of sight.

1796   *Self-confidence*—A personal quality that is closely related to conceit.—*Herbert V. Prochnow*

1797   *Self-made man*—An individual who might have done better by letting out the contract. An admission that one is a self-made man makes one a martyr; it relieves the conscience of the rest of the world.

1798   *Sickness*—Means not to feel well. There are three stages: 1. Ill; 2. Pill; 3. Bill. Sometimes there is another: 4. Will.

1799   *Silence*—What would follow if the average politician spoke his mind.

1800   *Small town*—A place where everybody knows whose check is good.

1801   *Smallest man in history*—The soldier who went to sleep on his watch.

1802 *Smart fellow*—A man who says what he thinks, provided, of course, he agrees with us.

1803 *Snorer*—A sound sleeper.

1804 *Snoring*—The last of the personal liberties.

1805 *Socialist*—An unsuccessful person who figures his last chance to get something is to get a part of yours.

1806 *Sophistication*—To be too smart to feel guilty about anything you do.

1807 *Soviet Russia*—A nation which owns everything. In the United States, it's the finance companies.

1808 *Spendthrift*—A person who gets more out of life than there is in it.

1809 *Statistician*—A man who can go directly from an unwarranted assumption to a preconceived conclusion.

1810 *Success*—Being able to afford spending what you are already spending.

1811 —To get as much money as the other fellow wishes he could have got. A country retail merchant retired with a fortune of $100,000. That was success. His ability to retire with $100,000 after 40 years, was due to hard work, strict attention to duty, absolute honesty, economical living, and to the death of his uncle who left him $98,500.

1812 *Successful man*—One who can earn more than his wife can spend.

1813 *Successful wife's motto*—If at first you don't succeed, cry, cry again.

1814 *Sugar daddy*—A fellow who calls his sweetie a little sugar and later pays her a lump sum.

1815 *Summer resort*—A town where the inhabitants live on your vacation money until the next summer.

1816 *Synonym*—A word to use when you can't spell the other word.

1817 *Tax cut*—The kindest cut of all.

1818 *Taxpayer*—A person who has the whole government on his payroll.

1819 *The meek*—The people who are going to inherit the earth and pay off the mortgage we leave them.

1820 *Third putt*—The most difficult shot in golf.

1821 *Toot ensemble*—Two hundred cars waiting for a green light at a busy intersection on a Sunday afternoon.

1822 *Tourist*—A person who drives 1,000 miles to see some beautiful scenery and litters the road all the way.

1823 *Tradition*—The widespread acceptance of something which was at first of questionable merit—and still is.

1824 *Traffic policeman*—A man who never loses an argument.

1825 *Tragedy*—A bride without a can opener.

1826 —A California citizen dying in Florida.

1827 —The man who wanted to become a great public speaker and wound up as toastmaster in a restaurant.

1828 *Truth-in-advertising*—Examples: "They Groaned When I Reached for my Saxophone." "Nobody Laughed When He Stepped to the Piano. He Had Come for the Second Installment."

1829 *Truthful woman*—A woman who does not lie about anything except her age, her weight, and her husband's salary.

1830 *Typographical error*—A misstatement. Illustration: A newspaper carried the notice that John Doe was a "defective" on the police force. This was a typographical error. It should have said, "Mr. John Doe is a detective on the police farce."

1831 *Umpire*—A retired baseball player whose eyesight fails him.

1832 *Vacation resort*—Where you go when you are worn out and where you come back from a complete wreck.

1833 —A place that overlooks a lake, and also overlooks comfortable beds and good food.

1834 *Velocity*—What a person puts a hot plate down with.

1835 *Vice-president*—A title given to a bank officer in place of a raise in salary.

1836 *Wastebasket*—A labor-saving device.

1837 *Noah Webster*—The author who had the biggest vocabulary.

1838   *Winter*—The time of the year when it gets later earlier.

1839   *Woman's ambition*—To be weighed and found wanting.

1840   *Woman's crowning glory*—A rich man's scalp.

1841   *Women*—Persons who think more with their hearts than with their heads.

1842   *Yes*—The answer to any question your employer asks.

1843   *Yours*—Anything which up to the present others have not been able to get away from you.

Interesting Lives and Interesting Facts

1844 No Vacation

The late columnist Arthur Brisbane declined to accept William Randolph Hearst's offer of a six months' paid vacation in appreciation for his good work.

"There are two reasons why I will not accept your generous offer, Mr. Hearst," said Brisbane. "The first is that if I quit writing my column for half a year, it might affect the circulation of your newspapers. The second reason is that it might *not!*"

1845 Say It

When you've got a thing to say, say it—don't take half a day; life is short, a fleeting vapor—don't you fill the entire paper with a tale, which at a pinch, could be cornered in an inch. Boil her down until she simmers. Polish her until she glimmers.

When you've got a thing to say, say it—don't take half a day.—*Sunshine Magazine*

1846 Teaching

Carlyle once received a letter from a young man which read like this: "Mr. Carlyle, I wish to be a teacher. Will you tell me the secret of successful teaching?" Carlyle immediately wrote back: "Be what you would

have your pupils be. All other teaching is unblessed mockery and apery."
—*Dr. F. Russell Purdy*

1847 *Mark Twain*

Mark Twain once asked a neighbor if he might read a set of his books. The neighbor replied ungraciously that he was welcome to read them in his library, but he had a rule never to let a book leave the house. Some weeks later the same neighbor sent over to ask for the loan of his lawn-mower.

"I shall be very glad to lend you my lawn-mower," said Mark Twain, "but since I made it a rule never to let it leave my lawn, you will be obliged to use it there."

1848 *Work Break*

A harried businessman reflecting on the coffee break, pasted this notice on the company's bulletin board:

"Due to increased competition, and a keen desire to remain in business, we find it necessary to institute a new policy. We are asking that somewhere between starting and quitting time, and without infringing on the time devoted to lunch, coffee breaks, rest periods, story telling, ticket selling, vacation planning, and re-hashing of gossip, each employee endeavor to find some time that can be set aside and known as the 'Work Break.' This may seem a radical innovation, but we believe that the idea has possibilities. It can conceivably be an aid to steady employment and regular pay checks. While adoption of the 'Work Break' is not compulsory, it is hoped that each employee will find time to give it a fair trial."

1849 *Discipline for Freedom*

Lovers of freedom often overlook this paradox: There is no true freedom without discipline. An ordered and disciplined life gives us freedom to do the things we want to do. . . .

Life offers a choice between self-discipline and imposed discipline. The advocates of dictators would have all discipline imposed by outside force to produce efficient lives. But those of us who love the freedom of democracy do not care to have our lives regulated by some dictator.

Yet discipline is essential. Have it we must, whether we like it or not. If we do not want dictators, we must impose upon ourselves discipline to bring order out of social chaos.

1850 *What's in a Man*

Longfellow was once introduced to a man named Longworth and when the latter commented on the similarity of names, the poet said: "Here is a case, I fear, where Pope's line will apply—'worth makes the man—want of it the fellow.' "

1851   Disraeli

Disraeli, when Prime Minister of England, was known among many other things, as having an excellent memory. One day he was asked how he managed to remember all those names and never offend anyone by appearing not to recognize members of Parliament on sight. The Prime Minister replied: "When I meet a man whose name I cannot remember, I give myself two minutes; then if it is a hopeless case, I always say: 'and how is the old complaint'?"

1852   Darrow

The late Clarence Darrow, eminent Chicago criminal lawyer, was one evening the principal speaker at a meeting of a women's club in a middle western city. After his speech, which had been greeted with salvos of applause, the lawyer found himself engaged in conversation with a couple of ladies who insisted on discussing birth control.

"Now, Mr. Darrow," said one, "what do you think of birth control for the masses?"

"My dear lady," replied the famous lawyer, "whenever I hear people discussing birth control, I always remember that I was the fifth."

1853   Patience

Infinite patience is the price that many a man has paid for success. Gibbon worked twenty years on his *Decline and Fall of the Roman Empire*. Noah Webster spent thirty-six years on his dictionary. George Bancroft spent twenty-six years on his *History of the United States*.

1854   Schubert

Schubert's C-Major Symphony, familiarly known as the Sixth Symphony, is conceded by many musicians to be his masterpiece. This work was first performed in Vienna in 1828, but London and Paris did not hear it until thirty years later. The Paris Orchestra, under Habeneck, refused to play it, and the London Philharmonic laughed at the composition. The conductor withdrew it from rehearsal. Sir August Manns placed it on a program in London in 1856, and after the first movement was finished the horn player called to the first violin sitting close to him:

"Tom, have you been able to discover a tune yet?"

"Heck, no. This hasn't any tune," the violinist replied.

1855   *Hawthorne*

The greatest literary artist in American history, our foremost novelist, Nathaniel Hawthorne, not only owed his success to the daily inspiration of his wife, but also his only opportunity to compose first his mind, and then his masterpiece. If it had not been for Sophia, perhaps we should not now remember Nathaniel. He lost his job in the customhouse. A broken-hearted man, he went home to tell his wife that he was a failure. To his amazement, she beamed with joy, and said: "Now you can write your book!" To his bitter rejoinder, "Yes, and what shall we live on while I am writing it?" the astounding woman opened a drawer and took out an unsuspected hoard of cash. "Where on earth did you get that?" She answered, "I have always known that you were a man of genius. I knew that some day you would write an immortal masterpiece. So every week, out of the money you have given me for housekeeping, I have saved something; here is enough to last us one whole year." Hawthorne sat down and wrote one of the finest books ever written in the Western Hemisphere—*The Scarlet Letter.*

1856   *His Greatest Thought*

Daniel Webster, when asked what was the greatest thought that had ever entered his mind, replied: "My accountability to Almighty God."

1857   *Lincoln*

The Battle of Gettysburg had just been fought. Lincoln sensed an opportunity to end the war by driving hard against Lee's rear in retreat. A swift, daring attack might do it. As commander-in-chief of the army, he ordered General Meade to pursue. A friendly note in the President's handwriting accompanied the instructions:

"The order I enclose is not of record. If you succeed, you need not publish the order. If you fail, publish it. Then, if you succeed, you will have all the credit of the movement. If not, I'll take all the responsibility."

That was Abraham Lincoln, brave, self-effacing, a nobleman in thought and deed.

1858   *Benjamin Franklin*

Printer, editor, publisher, businessman, financier, economist, and teacher of thrift, philosopher, moralist, and advocate of the simple life, scientist and patron of education, philanthropist, statesman, diplomat— and above all a man and a patriot, he is claimed as their own by more groups than any other person in our history. With truth he has been characterized as: "A Man" so various, that he seemed not one but all mankind's epitome. Someone has called him a typical American; rather might we think of him as a composite American. Born in poverty, he was apprenticed in a print shop and always thought of himself as a printer. "He that hath a trade, hath an estate" is one of his famous maxims. By thrift and industry he accumulated a competency which enabled him to devote the latter half of his life to public service. By one fitted to judge, Franklin has been referred to as "the greatest of all diplomatic representatives of this country." As the collector of funds for the Revolutionary War, he might be known as the originator of the Liberty Loan. He has been called the Father of our Navy; and as Postmaster General of the Colonies founded the first adequate postal system here. Not only does our government recognize his great services, but more and more are we coming to realize how much we owe to Benjamin Franklin's genius in all manner of human relationships and endeavors.—*Calvin Coolidge*

1859   Tact

Charles Schwab walked through a factory. He saw three men smoking. He did not reprimand them. He merely reached in his pocket, took out three cigars and said, "Boys, have a cigar on me, but I should appreciate it if you would not smoke it during working hours."

1860   Winston S. Churchill

A story of Winston S. Churchill—told by Gertrude Atherton:
"Shortly after he left the Conservative side of the House (of Commons) for the liberal, he was taking a certain young woman down to dinner, when she looked up at him coquettishly, and remarked with the audacity of her kind:
" 'There are two things I don't like about you, Mr. Churchill.'
" 'And what are they?'
" 'Your new politics and mustache.'
" 'My dear madam,' he replied suavely, 'pray do not disturb yourself. You are not likely to come in contact with either.' "—*Atlanta Journal*

1861   What I Ought to Do

I am only one, but I *am* one;
I cannot do everything
But I can do something.
What I can do, I ought to do
And what I ought to do
By the grace of God, I *will* do.—*Canon Farrar*

1862   Lord Chesterfield

Lord Chesterfield, attending an entertainment in France, appeared to be gazing about at the brilliant circle of ladies which surrounded him, when he was approached by Voltaire.

"My lord," laughingly remarked the great Frenchman, "I know you are a well-qualified judge. Tell me, who are more beautiful—the English or the French ladies?"

In the face of such a ticklish question most men might have quailed; but not the adroit Chesterfield. Looking about at the sea of feminine faces made lovely by the liberal use of rouge and other artificial colorings, he replied, "Upon my word, I cannot tell. I am really no connoisseur of paintings."

1863   Benjamin Franklin

Did you ever stop to wonder who invented the old-fashioned stove—or bifocal glasses—who first advocated the use of copper for roofs—who conceived of a damper for chimneys—who first pointed out that white is the coolest thing to wear in summer—who invented the long pole that is now used in grocery stores to reach articles on top shelves—who thought of a combined chair and step-ladder—who was responsible for the paving and lighting of streets—who thought it would be nice to have trees bordering both sides of streets—who formed the first library company—the first fire company—the first American fire insurance company—who founded the dead letter office and the penny post—who was responsible for American university education? Well, it was Benjamin Franklin, who incidentally was the first president of one of America's oldest universities —the University of Pennsylvania.—*The Fusion Point*

1864   Discovery

> Who never walks save
>   where he sees
> Men's tracks, makes no
>   discoveries.—*J.G. Holland*

1865   Charles I

Although it was Ferdinand V of Spain who dispatched Hernando Cortez on an exploration of the New World, it was to his son, Charles I, that the redoubtable explorer returned to make his report. Cortez recommended that a passage to India be effected by digging a canal across the Isthmus of Panama.

Charles consulted his advisers and then rejected the recommendation. Asked to explain the reason for his decision, the King sternly replied,

"It would be a violation of the Biblical injunction: 'What God hath joined together let no man put asunder.' "

1866   Lafayette

One day at a public function, the admirers of General Lafayette, desiring to show the love and admiration they felt for their idol, un-hitched his horses from the carriage and pulled the vehicle to the hotel themselves.

Some weeks later, a friend of the General, recalling the stirring event, remarked, "You must have been very much pleased."

Lafayette regarded him quietly for a moment, then, with a whimsical smile, replied, "Yes, it was delightful, delightful; but one thing disturbs me a little—I never saw anything more of my horses."

1867   Sir Walter Scott

Long after Sir Walter Scott had gained renown as a writer, he en-deavored to conceal his literary fame from his children, even attempting to keep them from reading his works.

One day his publisher, Ballantyne, came to congratulate him upon the success of his *Lady of the Lake*, and, seeing the author's twelve-year-old daughter alone in the library, said, "And how do you like *The Lady of the Lake?*"

"Oh," she replied, "I haven't read it. Father says that nothing is so harmful for young people as reading bad books."

1868   Respect

Charles V admired and respected the great Titian. One day, when the brush dropped from Titian's hand, Charles V picked it up for him, saying, "You deserve to be served by an emperor."

1869   Mozart and Haydn

Mozart once said to a critic, "If you and I were both melted down together, we should not furnish materials for one Haydn."

And Haydn said of Mozart that if every friend of music, and great men in particular, appreciated Mozart's genius as he did, "Nations would vie with each other to possess such a jewel within their frontiers."

1870   Your Neighbor

Sometimes a neighbor whom we have disliked a lifetime for his arro-gance and conceit lets fall a single commonplace remark that shows us another side, another man, really; a man uncertain, puzzled, and in the dark like ourselves.—*Willa Cather*

1871   Respect a Burden

One time when Napoleon was walking at St. Helena with Mrs. Balcombe, some servants approached carrying a load. Mrs. Balcombe ordered them out of the way, but Napoleon interrupted and said, "Respect the burden, madam."

1872   A Livelihood and Letters and Arts

Many writers, scientists, and distinguished men have had to make a living in business, government, and various fields while they pursued their other interests as time permitted. Chaucer was a soldier and later comptroller of petty customs. Spencer was secretary to the Lord Deputy of Ireland; Bacon was a lawyer before he became Lord Keeper and Lord Chancellor. Addison was Secretary of State. Shakespeare managed a theater and was but an ordinary actor. Dante and Boccaccio were in embassies. Galileo was a physician; Schiller a surgeon. Defoe was a brick- and tile-maker and a shopkeeper. John Stuart Mill was an examiner in the East India House, and Charles Lamb also worked there. Macaulay wrote the *Lays of Ancient Rome* while holding the position of Secretary of War. Ricardo was a banker. Sir Isaac Newton was a Master of the Mint.

1873   An Estimate of the Value of Character and Leadership

In 1798, Washington was an old man living in retirement at Mount Vernon. It seemed possible that France might declare war against us. President Adams wrote Washington, "We must have your name, if you will permit us to use it; there will be more efficacy in it than in many an army." Here was an estimate of the great esteem in which the people held Washington's character and leadership.

1874   Men and Movements

Great institutions and movements grow out of men of great character. So we think of Quakerism and Fox, Methodism and Wesley, Puritanism and Calvin, Jesuitism and Loyola.

1875   Mothers

George Herbert said a good mother equaled a hundred schoolmasters. George Washington, the eldest of five children, was only eleven years old when his father died. His mother was a woman of extraordinary ability who handled her responsibilities with such success that her children grew up to reflect honor upon themselves and upon her. Goethe, Scott, Gray, Schiller, Wesley, Bacon, Erskine, all were particularly influenced by the intelligent guidance of their mothers.

1876 Counting the House

At the end of a concert at Carnegie Hall, Walter Damrosch asked Rachmaninoff what sublime thoughts had passed through his head as he stared out into the audience during the playing of his concerto. Said Rachmaninoff: "I was counting the house."—*David Ogilvy*

1877 Absent-Minded

Henry Erskine, Lord Advocate of Scotland toward the close of the eighteenth century, had a tutor who was very absent-minded. So much so that Erskine, who thought a great deal of the old man, was one day flabbergasted to hear him say: "I was very sorry, my dear boy, you have had the fever in your family; was it you or your brother who died of it?" "It was I," Erskine replied. "Ah, dear me, I thought so—very sorry for it—very sorry for it." And the old man walked away.

1878 In God We Trust

The motto, "In God We Trust," first appeared on a coin of the United States in 1864. It was on a two-cent piece, and two years later, it was placed on the nickel, quarter, half, and silver dollar. It was added to the penny in 1909, to the dime in 1916, and having been dropped from the nickel in 1883, it was restored to that coin in 1938. Originally it was used because of high religious sentiment during the Civil War. The Secretary of the Treasury authorized it after receiving a number of appeals from devout citizens urging that the Deity be recognized suitably on our coins.

1879 No Reason for Dislike

Years on Wall Street failed to rob the late Dwight Morrow of a shy, whimsical humor. Being told that a certain business acquaintance had acquired a marked dislike for him, Mr. Morrow lapsed into a puzzled silence, then plaintively exclaimed, "I don't see why he should feel hard toward me. I don't remember ever doing anything for him."

1880 Only Lacked Poverty

A nobleman, who was an enthusiastic amateur painter, once took a sample of his best work to the great Turner for his candid opinion of it. The artist examined it carefully and, turning to the gentleman said: "My lord, you lack nothing but poverty to become a very excellent painter."

1881 Who Owns America?

Not the politicians. They are public servants, paid by the people to serve the people.

Not the rich. The corporations of America are owned by more than thirty million people.

Not the labor unions, even though some of their leaders act that way.

It is the *savers* who own America. By doing without things, by self-denial, they built homes and started stores, bought government bonds, invested money in American industry—money which buys machines and provides jobs. Most of what their savings earn is taken away from them in taxes, but because it is in their character never to waste, they still save. If they ever stopped, there would be no new capital to create new jobs, no new machinery to make better jobs, no profitable enterprise whose taxes help keep America going.

It is indeed the *savers* who keep America alive. Let's be sure the laws keep *savers* alive, too.—*Warner & Swasey, Cleveland*

1882   Inspiration

Boswell and Johnson were at Drury Lane Theatre together watching the great actor, Garrick. Boswell said to Johnson, "Garrick is not himself tonight" and the great man replied, "No."

All at once Garrick commenced to act superbly, and Boswell remarked, "Do you notice how he has changed and changed for the better?" "Yes," said the old sage, "and did you notice at what point he changed? He took a higher style when Edmund Burke came into the theatre."

1883   Youth

Alfred Tennyson wrote his first volume at eighteen.

Alexander was a mere youth when he rolled back the Asiatic hordes that threatened to overwhelm European civilization almost at its birth.

Napoleon had conquered Italy at twenty-five.

Byron, Raphael, and Poe died at thirty-seven after writing their names among the world's immortals.

Newton made some of his greatest discoveries before he was twenty-five.

It is said that no English poet ever equaled Chatterton at twenty-one.

Victor Hugo wrote a tragedy at fifteen. Many of the world's greatest geniuses never saw forty years.

1884   Sorrow

To live through a period of stress and sorrow with another human being creates a bond which nothing seems able to break. People can be happy together and look back on their contacts very pleasantly, but such contacts will not make the same kind of bond that sorrow lived through together will create.—*Eleanor Roosevelt*

1885 Benjamin Franklin

Famous was the toast given by Benjamin Franklin when he was dining, as the American emissary, with the English Ambassador and the French Minister at Versailles. The story was first published in 1797.

"George the Third," proposed the British Ambassador, "who, like the sun in its meridian, spreads a luster throughout and enlightens the world."

"The illustrious Louis the Sixteenth," proposed the French Minister, "who like the moon, sheds his mild and benignant rays on and influences the globe."

"George Washington," thereupon proposed witty Benjamin Franklin, "commander of the American armies, who, like Joshua of old, commanded the sun and the moon to stand still, and they obeyed him."

1886 Webster and Crockett

After hearing Daniel Webster speak, David Crockett said to him: "I had heard that you were a very great man, but I don't think so. I heard your speech and understood every word you said."

1887 Mark Twain

Mark Twain, as Samuel Langhorne Clemens (1835-1910) chose to call himself, was known to be eccentric—Mrs. Clemens called him "careless"—in his dress. As many a man did before him, and many another has done since, Mark Twain went calling one day without his necktie. He had been visiting Harriet Beecher Stowe, of "Uncle Tom" fame, and he was not aware of his lack of haberdashery until Mrs. Clemens called attention to it on his return.

A little later Mrs. Stowe answered her door to find a messenger, who gave her a small package. Opening it, she found a black silk necktie inside and a brief note:

"Here is a necktie. Take it out and look at it. I think I stayed half an hour this morning without this necktie. At the end of that time, will you kindly return it, as it is the only one I have. Mark Twain."

1888 Rudyard Kipling

When the report went around that Rudyard Kipling was getting a shilling a word for his writings, some Oxford students sent him a shilling, accompanied by this message:

"Please send us one of your words."

And right back came the unexpected answer:

"Thanks."

1889 Houdini

Florenz Ziegfeld and Charles Dillingham, the famous Broadway producers, were pallbearers at the funeral of Houdini, the great magician. As they carried the coffin of the famed handcuff and escape wizard out of the church, Dillingham leaned over and said, "Ziggie, I bet you a hundred dollars he ain't in here!"—*Ladies' Home Journal*

1890 A Difference

A musical student visited Mozart one day and said, "I want to write a concerto. Will you tell me how to go about it?"

"You are too young," replied the great composer. "Wait until you are a few years older."

"But," objected the young man, "you composed when you were seven or eight."

"Yes," agreed Mozart, "but I didn't have to ask anyone how to do it."

1891 Not His Attire

For some reason Bret Harte frequently found himself credited with the authorship of the popular poem, "Little Breeches," a distinction properly belonging to John Hay.

"My dear Mr. Harte, I am so delighted to meet you," exclaimed a gushing young lady. "I want to tell you how much I enjoyed reading your 'Little Breeches'."

"I thank you very kindly, madam," replied Harte, "but permit me to say—you have put the little breeches on the wrong man."

1892 Frederick the Great

Frederick the Great was a master diplomat, and able to compliment those whom he wished to please. In 1770, when the interviews were being held at court, he noticed General Laudohn, one of his most able adversaries seated across the table. Speaking up in a loud voice, he said: "Pray, sir, take place here at my right; I do not feel at ease to have you opposite me even at the table."

1893 Wellington

At the Battle of Waterloo, the colonel commanding the British artillery observed to the Duke of Wellington: "I have got the exact range of the spot where Bonaparte and his staff are standing. If your grace will allow me, I think I can pick some of them off." "No, no," replied Wellington, "Generals-in-chief have something else to do in a great battle besides firing at each other."

1894   *Brandeis*

Louis D. Brandeis, Associate Justice of the United States Supreme Court, was one evening attending a dinner party, and a discussion of lawsuits and trials came about. After listening for several minutes to the discussion, which centered on the causes of arguments which wound up in the court for termination, the Justice said: "Arguments seem so futile to me, for behind every argument I have ever heard lies the astounding ignorance of someone."

1895   *Being Different*

Woolworth conceived the idea of the five and ten cent store.

That was *different*. His fortune was measured by millions when he passed away.

Wanamaker conceived the idea of one-price to everybody in his retail stores.

That was *different*, for at the time he put this policy into effect it was directly contrary to the accepted practice throughout the country.

Ford determined to build a light, cheap car for the millions.

That was *different*. His reward came in the greatest automobile output in the world.

Human progress has often depended on the courage of a man who dared to be different.

1896   *The Challenge of Tom Dooley*

The late Dr. Thomas Dooley, who gained world acclaim in sacrifices to relieve suffering in the outer reaches of the world, wrote as follows to a young doctor, challenging him to spend his life in service:

"Dedicate some of your life to others. Your dedication will not be a sacrifice. It will be an exhilarating experience because it is intense effort applied toward a meaningful end."

1897   *Failures*

Lord Bulwer's life was a succession of failures, crowned with final triumph. His first novel was a *failure*; his first drama was a *failure*; so were his first speeches and poems. But he fought both defeat and ridicule and finally won a place with Thackeray and Dickens.

Savonarola's first efforts were dismal *failures*. His brave heart eventually made him Italy's greatest orator.

Daniel Webster could not make a speech until after years of persistent effort. Finally, he became one of America's greatest orators.

Washington lost more battles than he won. But he triumphed in the end.

Franklin, Patrick Henry, Clay, Jackson, Douglas, Lincoln, Grant, all were sons of poor parents. They faced many obstacles, but they finally surmounted them successfully.

1898   Time

Voltaire, the famous Frenchman, was a dwarf in body and a giant in intellect.

In his *Zadig, a Mystery of Fate,* is found the following question put to Zadig by the Grand Magi:

"What, of all things in the world, is the longest and the shortest, the swiftest and the slowest, the most divisible and the most extended, the most neglected and the most regretted, without which nothing can be done, which devours all that is little, and enlivens all that is great?"

Here is Zadig's answer:

"Time."

"Nothing is longer, since it is the measure of eternity.

"Nothing is shorter, since it is insufficient for the accomplishment of your projects.

"Nothing is more slow to him that expects; nothing more rapid to him that enjoys.

"In greatness it extends to infinity, in smallness it is infinitely divisible.

"All men neglect it; all regret the loss of it; nothing can be done without it.

"It consigns to oblivion whatever is unworthy of being transmitted to posterity, and it immortalizes such actions as are truly great."

Time is man's most precious asset.

1899   No Passes

In the days when the late Colonel Edward H. R. Green, railroad industrialist and banker, was managing the Texas Midland Railroad for his mother, the astute Hetty Green—known to fame as the "richest woman in America"—he was having a lot of trouble with applicants for passes over the line, and so consulted his mother about it. She mentioned the matter to her friend Chauncey M. Depew, who knew all about railroads, being a high official of the New York Central. Depew gave her a list of Biblical quotations, which she forwarded to her son.

The list was arranged as a calendar in this manner:

Monday—"Thou shalt not pass." (Num. 20:18)

Tuesday—"Suffer not a man to pass." (Judg. 3:28)

Wednesday—"The wicked shall no more pass." (Nah. 1:15)

Thursday—"This generation shall not pass." (Mark 13:30)

Friday—"By a perpetual decree it cannot pass." (Jer. 5:22)

Saturday—"None shall pass." (Isa. 34:10)
Sunday—"So he paid the fare thereof and went." (Jonah 1:3)

1900 Parental Praise

When Edward Bok asked Lockwood Kipling, the father of Rudyard Kipling, what he thought of his son's work, the elder Kipling replied, "Creditable."

Surprised, Bok persisted, "But surely you must consider that Rud has done some great work?" He was thinking of *The Jungle Book*, "If," *Captains Courageous*, and other immortal works.

"Creditable," repeated Kipling's father briefly.

Bok was almost ready to give up. "But you think him capable of great work, do you not?"

"He has a certain grasp of the human instinct," Lockwood Kipling admitted. "That some day will lead him to write a great work."

Kipling was never in danger of meaningless praise from his father.—*Christian Science Monitor*

1901 One Must Eat

Daniel Webster, the great American statesman, was once sued by his butcher for a bill of long standing. Before the suit was settled he met the butcher on the street, and to that worthy's embarrassment said: "Why have you not sent around for my order?" "Why, Mr. Webster," said the man. "I did not think you wanted to deal with me when I brought this suit."

"Tut, tut," said Webster, "sue all you wish, but for heaven's sake, don't try to starve me to death."

1902 A Long Speech

In an early American Congress, General Alexander Smythe of Virginia and Henry Clay were members. Smythe was a studious man, but a very laborious speaker, who worried the House with prolonged speeches. One day, in particular, he was being very tedious, and turning to Mr. Clay, said: "You, sir, speak for the present generation; but I speak for posterity." Clay without smiling, retorted: "Yes and you seem resolved to speak until the arrival of your audience."

1903 Joseph Choate

When Joseph Choate was American ambassador to Great Britain, many amusing incidents arose. For one, he had gained quite a lot of weight while in England. When he returned to this country, some of his friends, remembering his slight build, remarked about his corpulence. "Why,

Mr. Choate," said one, "you have been getting stout since you went abroad." "Oh, yes," replied he, "I found it necessary to meet the Englishmen halfway."

1904   *Westinghouse*

Two freight trains collided, and a young man set to work to prevent a repetition of such an accident. The result was the invention of the air brake and the beginning of a great industry.

Railroad executives took the attitude of Commodore Vanderbilt, who, when George Westinghouse explained the superiority of the air brake over the dangerous hand brakes, exclaimed, "Do you mean to tell me that you expect to stop a train with wind? I have no time to waste on damn fools."

Westinghouse did not give up and complain that his ability was not appreciated. He invented a railroad frog which appealed to the railroad officials and eventually gave him an opportunity to have the air brake tested. It is that air brake and Westinghouse's system of railway signaling which made all travel safer.

1905   *Ole Bull*

When Ole Bull, the famous Norwegian violinist, came to play in America, there were some jealous musicians here who attacked him through the press. Mr. James Gordon Bennett very graciously offered him the columns of the *Herald,* so that he might make his reply. But wise Ole Bull knew that he possessed a far better weapon than a printing press.

"I tink, Mr. Bennett," he replied in his broken English, "it is best tey writes against me, and I plays against tem."

The great acclaim he received at the hands of the American public proved that he was right.

1906   *Einstein*

Professor Albert Einstein gave what he considered the best formula for success in life. "If a is success in life, I should say the formula is a equals X plus y plus z, x being *WORK* and y being play."

"And what is z?" inquired the interviewer.

"That," he answered, "is keeping your mouth shut."—*Christian Register*

1907   *Madame de Staël*

Madame de Staël, whose plain features and blunt manner caused many men discomfiture, one night was dining at the home of the beautiful Madame Recamier. The astronomer, Lalande, found himself seated between these two women. Thinking he would please both, he exclaimed: "How happy I am to find myself between wit and beauty."

Not lacking in spirit was Madame de Staël, whose prompt reply was: "And without possessing either."

1908   Royalty

Nicholas I of Russia had asked Liszt, the great pianist, to play at court. Right in the middle of the opening number, the great musician looked at the Czar and saw him talking to an aide. He continued playing, but was very much irritated. As the Czar did not stop, Liszt finally quit playing. The Czar sent a messenger to ask why he was not playing and Liszt said: "When the Czar speaks, everyone should be silent." Thereafter there was no interruption in the concert.

1909   Dr. Everett's Advice

An indignant Bostonian once rushed to Dr. Everett's house. One of the local papers had published an article severely criticizing this man. Should he demand a public apology, or file a suit for damages?

Dr. Everett listened quietly, then interrupted. "What should you do? My dear sir, do nothing. Half the people who read that paper never saw that article. Half of those who read it do not understand it. Half of those who did understand it did not believe it. Half of those who believed it were of no consequence anyway."—*Christian Science Monitor*

1910   The Truly Wise

> The man who knows not that
> he knows not aught—
> He is a fool; no light can
> ever reach him.
> Who knows he knows not and
> would fain be taught—
> He is but simple; take thou
> him and teach him.
> And whoso, knowing, knows
> not that he knows—
> He is asleep; go thou to
> him and wake him.
> The truly wise both knows
> and knows he knows—
> Cleave thou to him and never—
> more forsake him.—*Arabian Proverb*

1911   Simple or Complex Economy

We are told that when Washington, Jefferson, and company originally assigned tasks to governmental and business leaders, we had in this country a "simple economy" and that now we have a "complex economy," though I have never been able to see why one is complex and the other is simple. When my grandmother had to build a fire out of buffalo chips and make a pot of soup out of nothing, that wasn't so simple. My daughter can turn on the gas, open up a tin can, and there is the soup. I would like to know which is the complex and which is the simple.—*B. E. Heacock*

1912 *Thrift*

One hundred average men start their productive life at age 25. At age 65 one is wealthy; four are well-to-do; 54 are not self-supporting; 36 have died. At age 75, 33 of the 100 are still living, and of these, three are entirely self-supporting and thirty are dependent.—*U. S. Treasury Dept. Textbook on Thrift*

1913 *Compound Interest*

Here are four rules that will help anyone who wants to know just what money will do:

At 4 per cent compound interest, money will double itself in a little less than eighteen years.

At 5 per cent compound interest, money will double itself in approximately fourteen years.

At 6 per cent compound interest, money will double itself in approximately twelve years.

At 8 per cent compound interest, money will double itself in about nine years.

When these facts are understood, large fortunes are not so wonderful after all, and a person only wonders that more families do not possess them.

1914 *Epitaph*

A tombstone in an English village cemetery has the following inscription:

> "Here lies a miser who lived for himself,
> And cared for nothing but gathering pelf,
> Now, where he is or how he fares,
> Nobody knows and nobody cares."

1915 *Code of Conduct*

Written in 1858 for the four employees of Carson, Pirie & Company, now Carson, Pirie, Scott & Company, Chicago.

"Store must be open from 6 A.M. to 9 P.M. the year round. Store must be swept; counter base and showcases dusted, lamps trimmed, filled and chimneys cleaned; pens made; doors and windows opened; a pail of water, also a bucket of coal brought in before breakfast (if there is time to do so and attend to customers who call).

"Store must not be opened on the Sabbath, *unless necessary to do,* and then only for a few minutes.

"The employee who is in the habit of smoking Spanish cigars, being shaved at the barber shop, going to dances and other places of amusement, will surely give his employer reason to be suspicious of his integrity and honesty.

"Each employee must pay not less than $5 per year to the church and must attend Sunday school regularly.

"Men employees are given one evening a week for courting and two if they go to prayer meeting.

"After fourteen hours of work in the store, the leisure hours should be spent mostly in reading."

Some of these rules may seem a bit humorous now, but there are great lessons in this code for all of us.

1916   Words

Of the 400,000 words in the English language, the working journalist is accredited with use of the largest number, something less than 20,000. Clergymen, lawyers, and doctors use an average of about 10,000 words. Skilled workers of ordinary education know about 5,000, farm laborers about 1,600. The sciences and professions have large numbers of words the layman never hears of. For instance, medical men and women must know the names of 433 muscles, 193 veins, 707 arteries, 500 pigments, 295 poisons, 109 tumors, 700 tests, over 200 diseases, and over 1,300 bacteria.

Yet with all these words, think of the people who still have trouble expressing themselves. Think of the people who constantly wonder what they are all about.

1917   Evolution of a Man

To be a circus clown.
To be like dad.
To be a fireman.
To do something noble.
To get wealthy.
To make ends meet.
To get the old age pension.

1918   *America in the Early Nineteenth Century*

There was not a public library in the United States.

Almost all the furniture was imported from England.

An old copper mine in Connecticut was used as a prison.

There was one hat factory, and that made cocked hats.

Every gentleman wore a queue, and powdered his hair.

Crockery plates were objected to because they dulled the knives.

Virginia contained a fifth of the whole population of the country.

A gentleman bowing to a lady always scraped his foot on the ground.

The whipping post and pillory were still standing in Boston and New York.

Beef, pork, salt fish, potatoes, and hominy were the staple diet all the year round.

Buttons were scarce and expensive, and the trousers were fastened with pegs or laces.

When a man had enough to eat he placed his spoon across his cup, to indicate that he wanted no more.

The church collection was taken in a bag at the end of a pole, with a bell attached to arouse sleepy contributors.

1919   *Premonition*

Georges Bizet was ill. At the opera house his own *Carmen* was being performed. Madame Galli-Marie, in the title role, was shuffling the cards in that scene where Carmen has a premonition of her death.

Two hours later Bizet, the composer, was dead!

1920   *Giving*

The grave of Christopher Chapman in Westminster Abbey, bearing the date 1680, says:

> "What I gave, I have,
> What I spent, I had,
> What I left, I lost
> By not giving it."

1921   *Cold Feet*

Measuring six feet four himself, Lincoln once met a soldier several inches taller than himself. "Say, friend," said the President, looking up in admiration, "does your head know when your feet are cold?"

1922   *Epitaph—1827*

A seventeenth-century tombstone in an English churchyard contains this inscription:

"Here lies the body of Ethan Bevan,
Killed by lightning sent from heaven
For trading horses on Sunday, June eleven,
In the year Eighteen Hundred Twenty-seven."

1923   *Free Men*

Thomas Jefferson, with all his brilliance and great confidence in the future of the Republic, thought it would take a thousand years to settle the West. He underestimated what free men can accomplish, given the opportunity to create for themselves with minimum government interference and restrictions.—*William A. Patterson, President, United Air Lines*

1924   *The End in View*

Thackeray knew how to puncture the ego of a snob as well with his tongue as with his famous pen.

One day, at his club, he was accosted by an officer of the Guards notorious for both his vanity and his pomposity, who, in a tone of patronizing familiarity, exclaimed, "Haw, Thackeray, old boy, I hear Lawrence has been painting your portrait!"

"So he has," replied Thackeray.

"Haw! Full length?"

"No. Full-length portraits are for soldiers that we may see their spurs. But with authors, the other end of the man is the principal thing."—*Wall Street Journal*

1925   *Outwitted*

Rufus Choate, in association with Daniel Webster, was handling an important case for a Boston shipping house. Before him in the witness box was an Irish shipowner, whom he was trying to confuse by asking him a long and involved question. According to a spectator, the question wound all round the case and straggled through every street in Boston. But the witness remained calm and unruffled.

When Mr. Choate had finished, the Irishman leaned forward and quietly asked, "Mr. Choate, will ye be afther repating that question again?"—*Wall Street Journal*

1926   *A Great Debt*

During forty-seven years of intermittent government service, Herbert Hoover turned all of his federal salary checks over to charitable causes and institutions, including his $20,000 annual pension as a former President. He made his fortune as a mining engineer early in his career. He has given away all his governmental income, he once explained, to acknowledge "a great debt" to his country for the many advantages and opportunities that it has conferred upon him.

1927   Lincoln's Measure

At a White House reception the Russian Ambassador was talking to President Lincoln, when the Chief Executive asked, "Would you have taken me for an American if you had met me anywhere else than in this country?"

The Muscovite, who was something of a wag, surveyed the President's tall frame, and replied, "No, I should have taken you for a Pole."

"And so I am," exclaimed Lincoln, drawing himself up to his full height, "and a Liberty Pole at that."—*Wall Street Journal*

1928   Sympathetic Hammerstein

When Oscar Hammerstein seemed to be encountering financial difficulties in his grand opera undertaking at the Metropolitan Opera House, it was his habit to go to other theaters and console himself for his own trouble by gazing on the spectacle of the empty seats in the other fellow's playhouse.

One night he hied himself over to a theater where a prominent star was holding forth; Hammerstein began to sympathize with the manager of the star, saying, "Really it is too bad you are not drawing better houses."

"I don't need your sympathy; why there's twelve hundred dollars in this house tonight," said the house manager.

"Whew!" exclaimed Oscar, "that's an honest usher you have here."

"What do you mean?" demanded the manager.

"I mean that if there is twelve hundred dollars in the house tonight someone has dropped a thousand on the floor"—and Oscar departed in triumph.

1929   Equipped for a Lecture Tour

A good story concerns Erich Maria Remarque, the author of *All Quiet on the Western Front,* and a pretty American girl to whom he was introduced in Berlin.

The American, speaking in German, asked Remarque why he had never visited the United States. His answer was that he knew only a few sentences in English.

"What are the sentences?" inquired the girl.

Whereupon Remarque, speaking slowly in somewhat guttural English, said: "How do you do? I love you. Forgive me. Forget me. Ham and eggs, please."

"Sakes alive!" ejaculated the girl. "Why, with that vocabulary you could tour my country from Maine to California."

1930   How's That?

Anyone can do any amount of work provided it isn't the work he is supposed to be doing at that moment.—*Robert Benchley, Think*

1931   Depew's Choice

At a dinner given in his honor Chauncey Depew was the recipient of many compliments from various speakers.

Replying, Mr. Depew began, "It's pleasant to hear these nice words while I'm still alive. I'd rather have the taffy than the epitaphy."

1932   Misplaced

Bernard Shaw is a past master at the ready retort. A young woman sitting next to him at dinner remarked: "What a wonderful thing is youth!"

"Yes—and what a crime to waste it on children," G.B.S. replied sagely.

1933   Disengaged

At one time during the American Civil War, General George B. McClellan, then in command of the Union forces, was conducting a waiting campaign. He was so careful to avoid mistakes that little headway was evident. President Lincoln thereupon wrote him a letter:

"My dear McClellan: If you don't want to use the Army, I should like to borrow it for a while. Yours respectfully, A. Lincoln."

1934   Woodrow Wilson

Someone asked Woodrow Wilson how long he would prepare for a ten-minute speech. He said, "Two weeks." "How long for an hour speech?" "One week." "How long for a two-hour speech?" "I am ready now."

1935   Charles Lamb and Whist

Charles Lamb tells of a chronic grumbler who always complained at whist because he had so few trumps. By some artifice his companions managed to deal him the whole thirteen, hoping to extort some expression of satisfaction, but he only looked more wretched than ever as he examined his hand. "Well, Tom," said Lamb, "haven't you trumps enough this time?" "Yes," grunted Tom, "but I've no other cards."

1936   Fulton and Napoleon

An American inventor had come to Paris and had offered the French Admiralty two inventions: one of them a ship to be propelled by steam power instead of by the wind; the other, a submarine boat which was to sink ships by the discharge of a kind of torpedo. "The man is a charlatan," was Napoleon's comment on Fulton, after an experiment in which the inventor's "plunging boat" had had a partial success; and he brushed the whole matter aside. If the American had brought him models of a machine gun and field telegraph, he would have opened his purse.—*Emil Ludwig, in Napoleon*

1937   Humility

Tho I am truly sensible of the high honor done me in this appointment, yet I feel great distress from a consciousness that my abilities and military experience may not be equal to the extensive and important trust. However, as the Congress desire it, I will enter upon the momentous duty, and exert every power I possess in their service and for the support of the glorious cause. I beg they will accept my most cordial thanks for this distinguished testimony of their approbation.

But lest some unlucky event should happen unfavorable to my reputation, I beg it may be remembered by every gentleman in the room that I this day declare, with the utmost sincerity, I do not think myself equal to the command I am honored with.

As to pay, sir, I beg leave to assure the Congress that as no pecuniary consideration could have tempted me to accept this arduous employment at the expense of my domestic ease and happiness, I do not wish to make any profit from it. I will keep an exact account of my expenses. Those, I doubt not, they will discharge, and that is all I desire.—*George Washington, on his appointment as Commander-in-Chief.*

1938   Harvard College

The first college in this country was Harvard College, now Harvard University. Established in Cambridge, Mass., in 1636, the college was surrounded by a tall fence to keep out wolves and Indians.

1939   Humble Beginnings

Even after the J. C. Penney Company was doing a volume of business of hundreds of thousands of dollars, its office equipment remained cheap and austere. Mr. Penney recalls in his book, *Fifty Years with the Golden Rule*, that the office was a room measuring 30 by 35 feet, with a cement floor, one flat-top desk loaned to him by a friend, and one old-fashioned standing desk. Merchants in the early days devised this type of desk on the principle that a bookkeeper who had to stand up at his work would not likely fall asleep.

When mail came in, Mr. Penney personally slit the envelopes and used the blank sides for scratch paper. There was no typewriter, and all work was done in longhand. When a pencil was needed, one of the men went out and bought one for a penny. They bought ink a bottle at a time, and a nickel's worth of pen points.

They kept all overhead expenses down so that the price of all merchandise could remain as low as possible. Eventually, of course, they learned that in modern merchandising it is necessary to make use of the newest and most efficient office equipment. But they showed in the beginning that poverty and poor equipment are never barriers if people work hard and employ right principles.—*Sunshine Magazine*

1940 *Cleanliness*

It has always been called "the White House." But it was not until 1850 that the first bathtub was installed in the Presidential residence. Millard Fillmore was the brave executive who took this great step toward cleaner politics.

1941 *Failure*

Bizet, the great composer, died at the age of thirty-seven, broken-hearted over the supposed failure of his opera, *Carmen*.

1942 *The Ten Commandments*

Someone has tabulated that we have put 35 million laws on the books trying to enforce the Ten Commandments.—*Bert Masterson, in Wall Street Journal*

1943 *Middle Age*

Middle age is when a man figures he has enough financial security to wear the flashy sports coats he didn't have the courage to wear when he was young.—*Bill Vaughan, in Milwaukee Journal*

1944 *Easy*

Clarence Darrow, noted criminal lawyer, and dissenter since youth, was to participate in a debate with another attorney.

"Are you familiar with the subject?" Darrow was asked.

"No," he confessed.

"Then how can you engage in a debate?"

"Easily," said Darrow. "I'll take the negative side. I can argue AGAINST anything."

1945 *Sounds Expensive*

We live in a land where a lazy loafer is often referred to as an "under-achiever," and the smallest size olive on the shelf is described as "medium." Hence it won't surprise anyone to hear of a dentist who refers to the new set of choppers he gives his clients when their teeth wear out as an "aesthetic restoration."—*Presbyterian Life*

1946   God and Man

The Founding Fathers believed devoutly that there was a God and that the unalienable rights of man were rooted—not in the state, nor the legislature, nor in any other human power—but in God alone.—*Tom G. Clark, Associate Justice, U.S. Supreme Court*

1947   Home

Booth Tarkington traveled widely but home to him was his native Indiana.

One night, when he was on a Pacific cruise, a companion said to him: "Why don't you turn in? It's midnight."

"I'm not sleepy," said the author. "It's only eight o'clock in Indiana."

1948   Don't Interrupt

Sir Winston Churchill rehearsed his speeches at every opportunity.

One morning, when Sir Winston was in his tub, his valet heard his voice above the splashing. Opening the door, he asked:

"Were you speaking to me, sir?"

"No," replied Churchill, annoyed at the interruption, "I was addressing the House of Commons."

1949   Not Easy

The late Justice Cardozo, it seems, was a bad sailor. An acquaintance found him leaning over the rail of a ship as it swayed to the heavy roll of the sea.

"Can I do something for you, Judge?" the friend asked.

"Yes," pleaded the Justice. "Overrule the motion."

1950   Common Sense

Dr. Carl Compton of M.I.T. used to tell the story of his sister who lived in Burma.

She was having some wiring installed by a native electrician. Again and again he would come to her for instructions and finally, in exasperation, she said, "You know what I want done. Why don't you use your common sense and do it?"

He made a grave bow and said, "Madam, common sense is a rare gift of God. I have only a technical education."

1951 *The Bible*

A skeptic in London said, in speaking of the Bible that it was quite impossible in these days to believe in any book whose authority was unknown. A Christian asked him if the compiler of the multiplication table was known. "No," he answered.

"Then, of course, you do not believe in it?"

"Oh, yes, I believe it because it works so well."

"So does the Bible," was the rejoinder, and the skeptic had no answer.
—*Katherine Bevis, in Watchman-Examiner*

1952 *Sir Josiah Stamp*

The late Sir Josiah Stamp, in a speech at the Chicago Club, expressed a hope that he wasn't talking too long. "I shouldn't like to be in the position of the parson," he explained, "who, in the midst of an interminable sermon, suddenly broke off his discourse to chide: 'You know I don't mind a bit having you look at your watches to see what time it is, but it really annoys me when you put them up to your ears to hear if they are still running!' "

1953 *A Difference of Only Two Commas*

Margaret Anglin, the story goes, left this message stuck in the mirror of Mrs. Fiske's dressing room:

"Margaret Anglin says Mrs. Fiske is the best actress in America."

Mrs. Fiske read it, added two commas, stuck it in an envelope, and sent it back to Miss Anglin. It read: "Margaret Anglin, says Mrs. Fiske, is the best actress in America."

Similes

1954 About as active as a left-over fly in January.

1955 Adroit as a rhinoceros.—*Franklin P. Adams*

1956 Ambition is like a treadmill; it knows no limits; you no sooner get to the end of it than you begin again.—*Josh Billings*

1957 Hard as a pawnbroker's smile.—*Herbert V. Prochnow*

1958 He had crumbled like an old ruin.

1959 Bashful as a ten-year-old girl.

1960 Beautiful as a drug-store blonde.

1961 Beautiful as a rustic bridge over a mountain stream.

1962 Black as a coal shaft.

1963 He went through things like a customs inspector.

1964 Quiet as a monastery.

1965 As inert as an oyster on the beach in August.

1966 A man of oak and rock.

1967 He is as cosmopolitan as a comet.

1968 He was a man with a mind like an accounting ledger.

1969   He had all the qualities of a fireplace poker except its occasional warmth.

1970   He talks like a man who is unable to keep up with his thoughts no matter how rapidly he speaks.

1971   You will find angling to be like the virtue of humility, which has a calmness of spirit and a world of other blessings attending upon it. —*Izaak Walton*

1972   He is a steam roller in a pair of pants.

1973   Coolidge's perpetual expression was of smelling something burning on the kitchen stove.—*Sherwin L. Cook*

1974   A rude man of the open.—*Lynn H. Hough*

1975   A face with lines as fine as old parchment.

1976   Government by stampede.

1977   Her face was as white and colorless as an icicle.

1978   As uncompromising as a policeman's club.

1979   As companionable as a cat and a goldfish.

1980   An unambitious snore, like a slow leak in an old tire.

1981   As never ending as a brook.

1982   He was as welcome as a monthly bill.

1983   As cynical as Diogenes.

1984   As desolate as a cemetery.

1985   Avarice is like a pig, which seeks its food in the mud, without caring where it comes from.—*Jean B. M. Vianney*

1986   Absence, like death, sets a seal on the image of those we have loved.—*Goldsmith*

1987   Could tell the hour by his movements as accurately as by a sun-dial.—*Washington Irving*

1988   Advancing like the shadow of death.—*Ruskin*

1989   Sweet are the uses of adversity,
                Which, like the toad, ugly and venomous,
                Wears yet a precious jewel in his head.
                                        —*Shakespeare*

1990   Aimless as an autumn leaf
               Borne in November's idle winds afar.
                              —*P. H. Hayne*

1991 Ambition is like hunger; it obeys no law but its appetite.
—*Josh Billings*

1992 Ancient as the stars.—*Voltaire*

1993 An army, like a serpent, goes upon its belly.—*Frederick the Great*

1994 Attracted about as much attention in the artistic world as the advent of another fly in a slaughter house.—*James L. Ford*

1995 Blighted and forlorn, like Autumn waiting for the snow.
—*Whittier*

1996 Bright as mountain snow.—*Southey*

1997   Calm as a child to slumber soothed,
               As if an Angel's hand had smoothed
               The still, white features into rest.
                              —*Whittier*

1998 Changeless as heaven.—*Ibid*

1999 Childhood shows the man, as the morning shows the day.
—*Milton*

2000 Clear as a bell.—*Chaucer*

2001 Her faded beauty was like summer twilight.—*Henry James*

2002 Beautiful as a flower in a seed catalogue.—*Robert H. Davis*

2003 Contagious, like the gladness of a happy child.—*Bulwer-Lytton*

2004 Cool as a snow bank.—*Louisa M. Alcott*

2005 Countless as the desert sands.—*Bayard Taylor*

2006 Crisp as new bank notes.—*Dickens*

2007 A critic is a legless man who teaches running.—*Channing Pollock*

2008 Critics are like brushers of noblemen's clothes.—*Sir Henry Wotton*

2009 Cry of anguish, like the last dying wail of some dumb, hunted creature.—*Adelaide A. Procter*

2010 Cunning as Satan.—*Philip Freneau*

2011   Dark as the grave.—*Cowley*

2012   Dead as a herring.—*Samuel Butler*

2013   She was delicate and fair as moonlight.—*Hans Christian Andersen*

2014   His speech was like a tangled chain; nothing impaired, but all disordered.—*Shakespeare*

2015   Driven . . . like leaves before the autumnal wind.—*Southey*

2016   Blind as ignorance.—*Beaumont and Fletcher*

2017   The slow mists of the evening dropped,
                Dropped as a cloth upon a dead man's face.
                                            —*Kipling*

2018   As modest as a violet.

2019   It is as dignified and beautiful as a Beethoven Sonata.—*Israel Zangwill*

2020   Eyes, brilliant and humid like the reflection of stars in a well. —*Edmondo de Amicis*

2021   These lovely lamps, these windows of the soul.—*Du Bartas*

2022   As hollow as a villain's laugh.—*Herbert V. Prochnow*

2023   Her eyes are blue and dewey as the glimmery Summer-dawn. —*James Whitcomb Riley*

2024   In her hazel eyes her thoughts lay clear
                As pebbles in a brook.—*Alexander Smith*

2025   He was oilier than a kerosene lamp.

2026   He had a face like a benediction.—*Cervantes*

2027   His face looked like a face that had refused to jell and was about to run down on his clothes.—*Irvin S. Cobb*

2028   'Tis not that she paints so ill but, when she has finished her face, she joins so badly to her neck, that she looks like a mended statue, in which the connoisseur may see at once that the head is modern, though the trunk's antique.—*Richard B. Sheridan*

2029   His face had as many wrinkles as an old parchment.—*Herbert V. Prochnow*

2030   Faded like a dream of youth.—*O. W. Holmes*

2031   Faint as a glimmering taper's wasted light.—*Sir William Jones*

2032   As welcome as a collect telegram.

2033   A room without books is like a body without a soul.—*Cicero*

2034   As fair a thing as e'er was form'd of clay.—*Byron*

2035   A face as fair as the summer dawn.—*James Whitcomb Riley*

2036   Fall off, like the leaves from a withered tree.—*Voltaire*

2037   It is with feelings as with waters: the shallow murmur, but the deep are dumb.—*Sir Walter Raleigh*

2038   His face fell like a cookbook cake.—*Joseph C. Lincoln*

2039   My head rang like a fire station gong.

2040   Like the mower's grass at the close of day.—*Byron*

2041   Fits as a shell fits a crab.—*Sir A. Conan Doyle*

2042   As flabby as a sponge.—*Guy de Maupassant*

2043   Flexible as figures in the hands of the statistician.—*Israel Zangwill*

2044   Follow, as the night the day.—*Shakespeare*

2045   Folds up like a crush hat or a concertina.—*Irvin S. Cobb*

2046   Shall fold their tents like the Arabs and as silently steal away. —*Longfellow*

2047   A forehead more pure than the Parian stone.—*Whittier*

2048   Poor and forgotten like a clod upon the field.—*Victor Hugo*

2049   Good fortune, like ripe fruit, ought to be enjoyed while it is present.—*Epictetus*

2050   Rattled like window shutters in a cyclone.

2051   As deceptive as the new paint on a second-hand car.—*Herbert V. Prochnow*

2052   The fragrance of her rich and delightful character still lingered about the place where she had lived, as a dried rosebud scents the drawer where it has withered and perished.—*Hawthorne*

2053   Free as mountain winds.—*Shakespeare*

2054   The feeling of friendship is like that of being comfortably filled with roast beef.—*Dr. Johnson*

2055   As frightened as Macbeth before the ghost of Banquo.—*Louis Veuillot*

2056   Fruitless as the celebrated bee who wanted to swarm alone. —*G. K. Chesterton*

2057   Futile as a tenor in a boiler shop.—*Henry Irving Dodge*

2058   She had more ornaments than a circus band wagon.—*Herbert V. Prochnow*

2059   Genius, like a torch, shines less in the broad daylight of the present than in the night of the past.—*J. Petit Senn*

2060   Ghastly as a laugh in hell.—*Thomas Hardy*

2061   As regular as the roll of an army drum.

2062   Gleamed upon the water like a bride at her looking-glass.— *R. D. Blackmore*

2063   His eyes dilated and glistened like the last flame that shoots up from an expiring fire.—*Guy de Maupassant*

2064   Glitter . . . like the bayonets of a regiment on parade.—*John C. Van Dyke*

2065   Going as if he had trod upon eggs.—*Robert Burton*

2066   Gossip, like ennui, is born of idleness.—*Ninon de Lenclos*

2067   As busy as a Swiss Admiral.

2068   Graceful as a faun.—*Samuel Rogers*

2069   Her eyes are grey like morning dew.—*W. B. Yeats*

2070   Genuine grief is like penitence, not clamorous, but subdued.— *Josh Billings*

2071   Gush like a fountain at its source.—*Donald G. Mitchell*

2072   His speech came in gusts, like linnets in the pauses of the wind. —*William De Morgan*

2073   He returned as often as the postman.

2074   Hairless as an egg.—*Robert Herrick*

2075   He had a hand like a bunch of bananas.—*R. F. Outcault*

2076   Happy as birds in the spring.—*William Blake*

2077   Fingers, hard as a lobster's claws.—*Guy de Maupassant*

2078   Hard as a pine-knot.—*James K. Paulding*

2079   As hard as for an empty sack to stand upright.—*Benjamin Franklin*

2080   The head of a woman is like a weather cock on the top of a house, which turns with the slightest wind.—*Molière*

2081   The head, like the stomach, is most easily infected with poison when it is empty.—*Richter*

2082   Calm as an iceberg.—*Gelett Burgess*

2083   As shallow as a pie pan.

2084   A noble heart, like the sun, showeth its great countenance in its lowest estate.—*Sir Philip Sidney*

2085   Heaves . . .
                Like a mighty ship in pain,
                Facing the tempest with struggle and strain.
                      —*Elizabeth Barrett Browning*

2086   Lies heavy . . . like murder on a guilty soul.—*Schiller*

2087   The sea hissed like twenty thousand kettles!—*Joseph Conrad*

2088   Hissing like a snake.—*Hugo*

2089   He stuck to it about as long as a drug-store cowboy on a bronco.

2090   Holds . . . together as the shell does the egg.—*John C. Van Dyke*

2091   As much at home . . . as a fish in water.—*Balzac*

2092   Our hopes, like withered leaves, fall fast.—*Longfellow*

2093   Hopeful as the break of day.—*T.B. Aldrich*

2094   Hot as Hell-fire.—*Dryden*

2095   Hover—like a moth intoxicated with light.—*John Galsworthy*

2096   Howlings, like a herd of ravenous wolves disappointed of their prey.—*William H. Prescott*

2097   Huddled like beasts beneath the drovers' whips.—*John Masefield*

2098   Humility like darkness reveals the heavenly lights.—*Henry D. Thoreau*

2099   Hungry as the chap that said a turkey was too much for one, not enough for two.—*O.W. Holmes*

2100 Hungry as a wolf.—*John Palgrave*

2101 A true Christian is like the ripening corn; the riper he grows the more lowly he bends his head.

2102
        The nations narrow and expand,
        As tides that ebb, or tides that flow.
            —*Lord de Tabley*

2103 As hopeful as a Spring morning.

2104 Natural to die as to be born.—*Bacon*

2105 Neglected, as the moon by day.—*Swift*

2106 Obstinate as death.—*Dryden*

2107 Opportunitays, like eggs, don't kum but one at a time.—*Josh Billings*

2108 No more conscience than a fox in a poultry farm.—*G. B. Shaw*

2109 Pains like a horrible vulgarism.—*Lafcadio Hearn*

2110 He was as polished, and as hard, as the brass plate upon which his name was etched.—*Herbert V. Prochnow*

2111 God pardons like a mother who kisses away the repentant tears of her child.—*H. W. Beecher*

2112 Pathetic as an autumn leaf.—*George Moore*

2113 Patiently as the spider weaves the broken web.—*Bulwer-Lytton*

2114 As innocent as a child.

2115 Pleading like a frightened child.—*Robert Louis Stevenson*

2116 Pliable as wax.—*James Shirley*

2117 Poignant and silent like the terrible questioning of one's conscience.—*Joseph Conrad*

2118 I was not accustomed to flattery. I was rather like the Hoosier with the gingerbread—who reckoned he loved it better than any man, and got less of it.—*Abraham Lincoln*

2119 She was as pretty as the spring time.—*Balzac*

2120 Prim as a Quaker.—*G. P. Morris*

2121 Kings will lose their privilege, as stars which have completed their time lose their splendor.—*Dumas, Père*

2122　Puffed himself up like a ship in full sail.—*Hans Christian Andersen*

2123　As soft as a Southern wind.

2124　Punctual—like morning.—*James Whitcomb Riley*

2125　Conversation should be like a salad, composed of various ingredients, and well stirred with salt, oil, and vinegar.—*Joquin Setanti*

2126　She is as pure, as good, and as beautiful as an angel.—*Guy de Maupassant*

2127　Receded, as mists fade before a morning sun.—*Barrett Wendell*

2128　Red as the Baldinsville skool-house.—*Artemus Ward*

2129　Ruddy and fresh as the waking morn.—*Eugene Field*

2130　Fell slowly into ruin, like all dwellings to which the presence of man no longer communicates life.—*Hugo*

2131　As illusive as a dream.

2132　Sad as twilight.—*George Eliot*

2133　Saunters . . . like an idle river very leisurely strolling down a flat country to the sea.—*Dickens*

2134　In scandal, as in robbery, the receiver is always as bad as the thief.—*Chesterfield*

2135　Sealed as the voice of a frost-bound stream.—*Swinburne*

2136　Serene as night.—*Byron*

2137　Set, as a piece of sculpture.—*Dickens*

2138　It stuck tighter than bark on a tree.

2139　Shone like the evening star.—*O. W. Holmes*

2140　Shrink as though Death were passing in his shroud.—*John Masefield*

2141　Shun him like the plague.—*Robert Browning*

2142　Delicate as the play of moonbeams on a field of snow.—*Robert P. Downs*

2143　Sifted like great snowdrifts o'er the landscape.—*Longfellow*

2144　Sighed with such a sigh as drops from agony to exhaustion.—*E. B. Browning*

2145   Sighs as men sigh relieved from care.—*J.R. Lowell*

2146   Men, like peaches and pears, grow sweet a little while before they begin to decay.—*O.W. Holmes*

2147   Great men are like meteors; they glitter and are consumed to enlighten the world.—*Napoleon*

2148   Marriage is not like the hill of Olympus, wholly clear, without clouds.—*Thomas Fuller*

2149   As restless as the wind.

2150   Melancholy sound . . . like the weeping of a solitary, deserted human heart.—*Guy de Maupassant*

2151   Swell menacingly like the first whisper of a rising wind.—*Joseph Conrad*

2152   Merciless as ambition.—*Joubert*

2153   As freely as the firmament embraces the world, so mercy must encircle friend and foe.—*Schiller*

2154   As expressionless as a row of empty mail boxes.—*Herbert V. Prochnow*

2155   Monotonous as mutton.—*Richard Le Gallienne*

2156   Motionless as a king's mummy in a catacomb.—*Flaubert*

2157   A voice as mournful as the dying light in the west—for a vague reminder of Death is divinely set in the heavens, and the sun above gives the same warning that is given here on earth by the flowers and the bright insects of the day.—*Balzac*

2158   Moved one like the finest eloquence.—*Alexander Smith*

2159   Multitudinous tongues, like the whispering leaves of a wind-stirred oak.—*Hawthorne*

2160   Murmurs . . . like a bell that calls to prayer.—*John Ruskin*

2161   Muscular as dogmeat.—*Rex Beach*

2162   As mute as the tomb.—*Dumas, Père*

2163   As mute as Pygmalion.—*James Smith*

2164   Hysterical as a tree full of chickens.—*Irvin S. Cobb*

2165   As frivolous as April.—*Herbert V. Prochnow*

2166   As idle as a painted ship upon a painted ocean.—*Coleridge*

2167   He makes his ignorance pass for reserve, and, like a hunting-nag, leaps over what he cannot get through.—*Samuel Butler*

2168   Immortal as the stars.—*Mathilde Blind*

2169   Impersonal as the justice of God.—*Hugo*

2170   Imposing as a set of solid gold teeth.—*Rex Beach*

2171   Indolent as an old bachelor.—*Goethe*

2172   The highest intellects, like the tops of mountains, are the first to catch and reflect the dawn.—*Macaulay*

2173   Irrevocable as death.—*Charlotte Brontë*

2174   Ended abruptly like a rabbit's tail.

2175   As languid as a lillied pond.—*Norman Gale*

2176   A lie is like a snow-ball; the longer it is rolled, the larger it is. —*Luther*

2177   Life is like a tale ended ere 'tis told.—*T. B. Aldrich*

2178   Lifeless as a string of dead fish.—*G.K. Chesterton*

2179   Comfortable as a toothache.—*Mark Twain*

2180   Light and feathery as a squirrel's tail.—*John Muir*

2181   A face as wrinkled as a dried plum.

2182   Lingering like an unloved guest.—*Shelley*

2183   I wandered lonely as a cloud
                  That floats on high o'er vales and hills.
                                    —*Wordsworth*

2184   He looked like a composite picture of five thousand orphans too late to catch a picnic steamboat.—*O. Henry*

2185   He was as wise as Solomon, but as humble as Uriah Heep. —*Herbert V. Prochnow*

2186   Majestic in its movements as a sonnet of Milton.—*Israel Zangwill*

2187   Silent as a country churchyard.—*Macaulay*

2188   Silent as the grave.—*Schiller*

2189   As greedy as the jaws of hell.

2190   Sobbing, as if the body and soul were torn.—*Bulwer-Lytton*

2191   Society, like the Roman youth at the circus, never shows mercy to the fallen gladiator.—*Balzac*

2192   Soft as is the falling thistle downe.—*Joseph Hall*

2193   Soft and still, like birds half hidden in a nest.—*Longfellow*

2194   Walked as softly as the ghost in Hamlet.—*Dickens*

2195   As hard-boiled as an Easter egg.

2196   Sparkle like brooks in the morning sun.—*William Cullen Bryant*

2197   Stood spellbound, like a child to whom his nurse is telling some wonderful story.—*Balzac*

2198   As shriveled as an old prune.

2199   Melancholy as a defeated politician.—*Herbert V. Prochnow*

2200   Staggered away as a defeated man staggers away from the field of battle.—*Joseph Conrad*

2201   Stealthily like rocks that tear a ship's life out under the smooth sea.—*Ibid*

2202   He stood . . . stiff as a marble statue.—*Goethe*

2203   As harmless as a meadow lark.

2204   Struggling like a man led towards death and crucifixion.—*Carlyle*

2205   Swayed like a bird on a twig.—*Arnold Bennett*

2206   Hesitating like an animal at bay.

2207   Talent, like gout, sometimes skips two generations.—*Balzac*

2208   Tenderly, as round the sleeping infant's feet,
                        We softly fold the cradle-sheet.
                                        —*William Cullen Bryant*

2209   Terrifying as the monologue of a storm.—*Hugo*

2210   He was as short and stubby as a hedge fence.

2211   Human thought is like a monstrous pendulum: it keeps swinging from one extreme to the other.—*Eugene Field*

2212   Tossed . . . like a cork on the waves.—*Thomas Hardy*

2213   As frank as a mirror.

2214 Turned like a weather cock with every wind.—*Guy de Maupassant*

2215 As inflexible as a marble pillar.

2216 Unconquerable as chewing gum.—*Arnold Bennett*

2217 Demoralizing as a holiday.—*Abe Martin*

2218 Stand unmoved, like a rock 'mid raging seas.—*Calderon*

2219 As inseparable as a baseball fan and a bag of peanuts.

2220 Upright as a wooden sentinel at the door of a puppet-show.—*Sir Walter Scott*

2221 Vagrant as the wind.—*John Ford*

2222 Pranced around like a colt in a pasture.

2223 Vanished altogether, like the last spark on a burnt piece of paper.—*Hans Christian Andersen*

2224 Vanished like the furrow cut by a ship's keel in the sea.—*Balzac*

2225 Vices, like beasts, are fond of none but those that feed them.—*Samuel Butler*

2226 Lies like a man with a secondhand car to sell.

2227 Virtue is like the polar star, which keeps its place, and all stars turn towards it.—*Confucius*

2228 Void of sense as the movement of the trees and the sound of the winds.—*Hugo*

2229 A wail, as of a babe new-born.—*George Meredith*

2230 She walked with a proud, defiant step, like a martyr to the Coliseum.—*Balzac*

2231 Elusive as a wet fish.

2232 Wandered up and down there like an early Christian refugee in the catacombs.—*Joseph Conrad*

2233 Wandered about at random, like dogs that have lost the scent.—*Voltaire*

2234 His purse was as full as his head was empty.

2235 Warm as a sunned cat.—*Thomas Hardy*

2236 Watchful as a spider sits in his web.—*Bulwer-Lytton*

2237   As faultless as a spring flower.

2238   Withered and pale as an old pauper.—*Dickens*

2239   His words, like so many nimble and airy servitors, trip about him at command.—*Milton*

2240   The world is like a great staircase, some go up and others go down.—*Hipponax*

2241   He floundered around like a fish on the beach.

2242   Yawns like a grave in a cemetery.—*Hugo*

2243   Zeal without knowledge is like expedition to a man in the dark. —*Newton*

2244   As fresh as the dawn.

2245   Adroit as a dinosaur.

2246   His cheek was like a rose in the snow.—*O.W. Holmes*

2247   A face that looks like it had worn out four bodies.

2248   His head was as empty as a politician's speech.

2249   Desolate looking as a summer resort in midwinter.—*Richard Harding Davis*

2250   He stood as erect as a Grecian pillar.

2251   Her eyes looked like two rainy autumn moons.—*Henry James*

2252   He felt like the symptoms on a medicine bottle.—*George Ade*

2253   He was as exacting as a top sergeant.

2254   Freckles, like rust spots.—*Willa Cather*

2255   The human mind should be like a good hotel—open the year around.—*William Lyon Phelps*

2256   His face was as expressionless as a smoked herring.

2257   A white mustache, cut short like a worn-out brush.—*Henry James*

2258   Unremembered as old rain.—*Edna St. Vincent Millay*

2259   As changeable as a woman's mood.

2260   Vanish as raindrops which fall in the sea.—*Susan Coolidge*

2261   I could see the man's very soul writhing in his body like an impaled worm.—*Joseph Conrad*

2262   His joints creaked like those of an old weather-beaten wooden farm gate.—*Herbert V. Prochnow*

2263   As unemotional as a baseball umpire

2264   As unsatisfied as a boy's appetite.

2265   He was as patient as a cigar store Indian.

2266   Gentle as the falling tear.—*Thomas Chatterton*

2267   Hollow as the ghastly amiabilities of a college reunion.—*Raymond M. Weaver*

2268   Intolerant as a sinner newly turned saint.—*Anon.*

2269   Marriage is like a department store. It is all over when you buy.

2270   Marriage is like twirling a baton, turning handsprings, or eating with chopsticks; it looks so easy till you try it.—*Helen Rowland*

2271   The heart of man is like a creeping plant, which withers unless it has something around which it can entwine.—*Charles James Apperley*

2272   An irritable man is like a hedgehog rolled up the wrong way, tormenting himself with his own prickles.—*Thomas Hood*

2273   Money is in some respects like fire; it is a very excellent servant, but a terrible master.—*P.T. Barnum*

Colorful Phrases for Sparkling Speech

2274   *Abraham's bosom*—A figure of speech from the Bible. To rest in Abraham's bosom. A place of reward after death for the blessed and righteous. There was an old custom of allowing a good friend to recline at dinner on one's bosom. John reclined on the bosom of Jesus. The beggar died and was taken by the angels into Abraham's bosom.

2275   *Au fait*—To be a thorough master of; skillful. One may be *au fait* in certain matters.

2276   *Achilles' heel*—A vulnerable spot. Achilles' mother, to make him invulnerable, dipped him into the Styx River. She failed to immerse the heel by which she held him. Paris wounded him mortally by striking him in the heel with an arrow. Everyone may be said to have his Achilles' heel—his weakness.

2277   *A sulking Achilles*—One who withdraws from a part in an important enterprise or undertaking because he holds a personal grievance. In mythology it is said that Achilles sulked in his tent because of an argument with Agamemnon and declined for some time to take part in the battle of the Greeks against the Trojans.

2278   *An Adonis*—An exceptionally handsome man. In mythology he was a handsome young man loved by Venus.

2279   *After me, the deluge*—Means that "I shall keep on doing what pleases me regardless of what happens and even if I am overcome; after me, the deluge." The origin of the phrase is uncertain. Madame Pompadour, a favorite of Louis XV, was one among several who were credited with having used this phrase. She was extravagant and refused to listen to her counselors who said she would ruin the country. She made light of their warnings, saying in French, "After us, the flood."

2280   *All my swans are geese*—To have your plans fail you. To be disappointed. If one says, "All her swans are turned to geese," it means her plans or boasts have failed her. The swan is beautiful; the goose far less attractive.

2281   *Alpha and Omega*—The beginning and the end of anything. In the Greek alphabet, alpha is the first letter, and omega the last. In the Bible the Lord said, "I am Alpha and Omega, the beginning and the ending."

2282   *He cannot bend Ulysses' bow*—The person is not equal to the task. Ulysses had a bow so great ordinary men could not bend it.

2283   *An Odyssey*—The story of great adventure. An epic attributed to Homer describing the ten years' wanderings of Ulysses in returning home after the siege of Troy.

2284   *An Amazon*—A woman of unusual physical strength. Sometimes also used to describe a woman of masculine boldness. The Amazons in mythology were a nation of fighting women.

2285   *Greek gifts or a case of the Greeks bearing gifts*—This means a fatal gift which is presented under friendly guise. In Virgil's *Aeneid* there is a line which says, "I fear the Greeks even when they bear gifts." This refers to the well-known "gift" of the wooden horse which the Trojans offered to the gods. The Greeks had left it outside of the city of Troy and apparently had departed. The Trojans took it within the city's walls and at night Greek soldiers hidden within the horse came out, capturing the city by morning.

2286   *To feed on ambrosia and nectar*—To have excellent food and drink. To the ancient Greeks, "ambrosia" meant the food which the gods ate. Now it means anything delicious to taste or fragrant in perfume. "Nectar" is the drink of the gods.

2287   *To make the amende honorable*—According to *Webster's New Collegiate Dictionary*, this term means "a formal and humiliating acknowledgment of offense and apology made to another, originally in reparation of his injured honor." The punishment was used under the Roman, Dutch, French, and other legal systems. An apology in church or court might require the person to appear with bare feet and head, dressed in white, and carrying a torch.

2288   *An Ulysses*—A person who is clever in developing schemes. Ulysses was one of the Greek heroes in the Trojan War, famous for his craft, intelligence, and eloquence.

2289   *To work or fight like a Trojan*—To fight with great courage or to work with exceptional energy. The ancient Trojans were noted for endurance and pluck.

2290   *A Cassandra utterance*—A prophecy foretelling evil which is not heeded. Cassandra, a daughter of King Priam, was given the power to prophesy by Apollo, according to Greek mythology. Becoming displeased with her, Apollo changed the power Cassandra had to prophesy so she could still prophesy truly, only to be laughed at by those who heard her.

2291   *To hector someone*—To annoy a person. Hector was greatly concerned over the shame brought upon his family and city by his brother, Paris, according to Greek legend, and consequently found fault with him.

2292   *An apple of discord*—A reason for dispute. According to mythology, Discord threw a golden apple on the table "for the most beautiful." Juno, Minerva, and Venus claimed it. Paris awarded it to Venus, thus bringing upon him the vengeance of Juno and Minerva which helped to cause the Trojan War.

2293   *Argonaut*—One of those who sailed with Jason, in the ship *Argo*, to Colchis to search for the Golden Fleece, according to Greek mythology. An adventurer who seeks fame or fortune in unexplored lands.

2294   *Argus-eyed*—Extraordinarily watchful. An Argus-eyed committee may watch the counting of the money or the ballots. Argus, a monster in Greek mythology, had one hundred eyes, only two of which were said to sleep at once. Argus-eyed means to see a great deal.

2295   *Halcyon days*—Days of peace and happiness. Greek legends tell of a girl named Halcyone whose husband perished. Juno, a goddess, did everything in her power to lessen Halcyone's grief and give her serenity of mind and happiness.

2296   *Ark of the covenant*—According to Jewish history, the chest in the most sacred place in the temple in which were placed the two tables of stone with the Ten Commandments written upon them. Anything which is exceptionally sacred. The Constitution of the United States and the Declaration of Independence might each be spoken of as an American ark of the covenant.

2297   *Armageddon*—The place where a titanic battle will be fought on "the great day of God," between the powers of good and evil, according to the Bible. Any great battle, political contest, or climactic conflict.

2298   *To work the oracle*—To attempt to influence some powerful agency so it will bestow a favor upon you.

2299   *Janus-headed*—An early Italian god, Janus, had two faces—one in front and one behind. Presumably he could see backward and forward at the same time. One may say of a committee with two heads that it is Janus-headed.

2300   *Janus-faced*—Means two-faced or deceptive. Janus-faced might be interpreted two ways.

2301   *A saturnine smile*—A smile which is not cheerful, perhaps because the idea of gloominess is connected with the planet Saturn.

2302   *A mercurial temperament*—The Greek god Mercury was light-hearted, clever, changeable, and even a little deceptive; so a mercurial temperament would be of that character.

2303   *Apollo*—In Greek mythology, the god of manly beauty and youth. An unusually handsome man.

2304   *Palladium of our liberty*—A safeguard. The safety of the ancient city of Troy was supposed to depend upon the preservation of a certain wooden statue of Pallas Athena. "Our constitution is the palladium of our liberty."

2305   *Extending the olive branch of peace*—The goddess Minerva was closely connected with the olive tree, having given it to Greece as a gift. She ruled over the arts of peace. An olive-branch policy is a policy of peace.

2306   *A Bacchanalian revel*—Bacchus was the god of wine. Bacchanalian means riotous merriment resulting from the use of too much liquor. A wild orgy. Frenzied dancing, singing, and revelry.

2307   *A mere bagatelle*—The word bagatelle comes from the French who took it from the Italian "bagattella," meaning a trifle. A man may spend his money on bagatelles.

2308   *Mounting Pegasus*—Describes the efforts of a person who hopes or attempts to write poetry or deliver orations. Pegasus was the winged horse of the Muses, to spring from Mount Helicon. Therefore, poetic inspiration. Sometimes the airplane is called a modern Pegasus.

2309   *Is there no balm in Gilead?*—This means "Is there no remedy or consolation, even in religion, for our troubles?" In the Book of Jeremiah in the Bible, the prophet, sorrowing over the sins and troubles of his people asked, "Is there no balm in Gilead; is there no physician there? Why then is not the health of the daughter of my people recovered?"

2310　*Stygian darkness*—Gloomy darkness or deep night. It may also mean infernal darkness. The Styx in mythology was the river of the dark underworld. It flowed seven times around Hades.

2311　*Barkis is willin'*—When an individual especially desires to do something, we may say of him, "Barkis is willin'." In the story, *David Copperfield*, by Charles Dickens, Barkis loved Clara Peggotty. He asked young David to tell Clara Peggotty, after David had said she had no sweethearts, that "Barkis is willin'."

2312　*An Elysium*—In classical mythology, the place where the good dwelt after death. A state of delight and happiness.

2313　*A task of Sisyphus*—A task that is never completed. In Greek mythology, Sisyphus was a crafty king who was condemned in Hades to roll up a hill a huge stone, which constantly rolled back.

2314　*Beggar on horseback*—A person who has risen to wealth and position, forgets his previous poverty, and lords it over his former poorer friends.

2315　*The waters of Lethe*—Implies forgetfulness. An experience that makes one forget care. In mythology, a river of Hades whose waters when drunk caused forgetfulness of the past.

2316　*To beg the question*—To assume the truth of something in question. To assume as true something you are supposed to prove, and to argue from that point. Aristotle first used the phrase.

2317　*A Danaidean task*—An impossible task. King Danaus had fifty daughters (the Danaides), of whom forty-nine slew their husbands at their father's request. The forty-nine were doomed forever to draw water with a sieve in Hades, according to mythology.

2318　*A Pandora's box*—Surprises which are generally unpleasant and in the form of trouble, but sometimes are pleasant. A legislative act may turn out to be a Pandora's box of surprises, unpleasant and pleasant. In Greek mythology, Pandora was a woman sent by Zeus as punishment for the human race because Prometheus had stolen fire from heaven. Zeus gave her a box in which were all human ills; they escaped when she opened the box. In the box also was hope, which remained.

2319　*Belling the cat*—To take it upon one's self to undertake a great risk for friends and associates. The expression comes from the old story in which a mouse suggested that someone should hang a bell on the cat so the mice would know when she was coming. The only problem was "who is to bell the cat?"

2320   *Belshazzar's Feast*—When one takes part in a "feast of Belshazzar," he does so in the spirit of "eat, drink, and be merry, for tomorrow we die." The feast of Belshazzar is described in the fifth chapter of the Book of Daniel in the Bible. "In that night was Belshazzar the king of the Chaldeans slain." At that feast Belshazzar saw the fateful "handwriting on the wall" which told him that the days of his kingdom were numbered, that he had been found wanting, and that his kingdom would be divided and assigned to others.

2321   *To yearn for the flesh pots*—Means to long for the material things of life. In the Book of Exodus in the Bible, it is related how the children of Israel regretted their deliverance from Egypt and the hardships of the wilderness. They wished they could have died in Egypt when they "sat by the flesh pots" and "did eat bread to the full."

2322   *A Cadmean victory*—A victory which involves the victor in even greater danger than that from which he escaped. In Greek mythology, Cadmus slew a dragon, and sowed its teeth, but armed warriors sprang from the teeth and attacked him.

2323   *To sow dragon's teeth*—To do things out of which troubles are certain to spring. Cadmus sowed dragon's teeth and warriors sprang up threatening trouble for him. People may do things out of which troubles for themselves will almost certainly spring.

2324   *A bonanza*—Anything yielding a large return in money. There were several Americans in our earlier history who made great fortunes from the gold and silver mines of the West. They were the original "Bonanza Kings."

2325   *A herculean task*—A task which only Hercules could accomplish. We sometimes speak also of a herculean feat, or herculean labors; these are extraordinary exertions. Hercules was a Grecian hero noted for unusual strength and for achieving twelve great tasks or "labors" imposed on him as the result of the hatred of Juno.

2326   *Hydra-headed difficulties or evils*—A hydra-headed evil is one which, if it is overcome in one case, breaks out in several places. An evil having many sources, which cannot be overcome by a single effort. In Greek mythology, Hydra was a nine-headed monster slain by Hercules. When any one of its nine heads was cut off, it was succeeded by two others, unless the wound was cauterized.

2327   *Born to the purple*—To be born to a position of great wealth or to an exalted station. In Cicero's time, wool dyed purple was very expensive because the dye came in small quantities from a Mediterranean fish.

Purple was, therefore, a highly sought after color and symbolized royal power. Today, purple dye has become inexpensive, but the phrase is still used.

2328   *Buncombe*—Anything said or written for mere show; hence, nonsense. "Bunk" is an abbreviation. In the early days of this country there was a member of Congress from the part of North Carolina including Buncombe county. The representatives were anxious to vote on an issue, but the member from Buncombe insisted on speaking. He refused to stop speaking when urged by members of Congress and said he was "bound to talk for Buncombe."

2329   *An Augean task*—A seemingly impossible task. An enormous job. In Greek mythology, King Augeas was said to have had an enormous stable containing many oxen. The stable had not been cleaned for years. Hercules cleaned it by diverting two rivers through it.

2330   *One cannot seize the club of Hercules*—It is impossible to steal the power and ability of one who is great. Hercules was noted for his strength.

2331   *Byzantine luxury*—A lavish and almost barbaric display of wealth and riches. Pertains to the Byzantine empire, Byzantium being the former name of Constantinople, now Istanbul. The Byzantine empire was rich and powerful.

2332   *To wear the cap and bells*—To play the part of a jester. Many years ago the court jesters wore bells attached to their caps.

2333   *A shirt of Nessus*—A gift which is harmful or causes trouble. According to mythology, Dejanira sent her husband, Hercules, a garment dipped in blood which had been given to her in a bottle by a centaur named Nessus. The garment poisoned Hercules.

2334   *Caviar to the general*—"General" means the "common run" of human beings. "Caviar to the general" means anything above the taste or appreciation of "ordinary" people. Caviar is roe of the sturgeon and other fish. It is a delicacy, an expensive appetizer, desired by those who acquire a taste for it. Shakespeare says in *Hamlet*, "The play, I remember, pleased not the million; 'twas caviar to the general." One could say also, "It was caviar to the masses."

2335   *Cheating the devil*—To believe that you can follow evil methods, particularly in making money unscrupulously, and then compromise with your conscience by giving part of your monetary gain to charity, the church, or some other worthy objective. That is an attempt to "cheat the devil."

2336   A Cincinnatus—One who puts aside his regular work to serve his country. Indicates unselfish patriotism. Cincinnatus was a Roman who was called from the field he was plowing to lead the Roman army. After the enemy was overcome, he put aside any personal ambition and returned to the plow. George Washington might be called an American Cincinnatus.

2337   Hoc opus, hic labor est (Latin)—This is the real difficulty; this is the task; there's the rub.

2338   A Minotaur—One who will sacrifice youths for his personal ambition. A ruler who will lead young men to death to satisfy his own ambition. In mythology, the Minotaur was a monster that devoured young men and women.

2339   A Circe—A beautiful woman whose charms are so great they cannot be resisted. In the *Odyssey*, Circe was a sorceress who turned her victims by magic into beasts, but she was thwarted by Odysseus with the herb moly given to him by Hermes.

2340   A stentorian voice—A very loud voice. Stentor was a herald in the *Iliad* with a very loud voice.

2341   A Helen or a Helen of Troy—A woman of extraordinary beauty. In mythology, Helen was the beautiful daughter of Jupiter and Leda.

2342   Cordelia's gift—A soft voice. Cordelia was the youngest of King Lear's three daughters in Shakespeare's play, *King Lear*. Shakespeare says in that play, "Her voice was ever soft, gentle and low; an excellent thing in woman."

2343   Cornelia's jewels—Children. Cornelia was the mother of the famous Gracchi. An old Roman story relates that a woman was displaying her jewels to Cornelia and asked to see the latter's jewels. Cornelia called her two sons and said, "These are my jewels, in which alone I delight."

2344   A lotus-eater—A person who lives a life without ambition or effort and in ease and idleness. In the *Odyssey*, one of a people who subsisted on the lotus and lived in the dreamy indolence it induced.

2345   To give a sop to Cerberus—To give a gift to some person who might make trouble, in order to keep him quiet. In mythology, Cerberus was a three-headed dog which guarded the entrance to Hades fiercely.

2346   Rich as Croesus—A very rich person. Croesus was a king of Lydia in the 6th century B.C., and had vast wealth.

2347   *Under the aegis of*—To have the power or authority of some strong person or institution back of one. In Greek mythology, Jupiter was said to have permitted Minerva to wear his terrible aegis, a covering for the breast with the head of Medusa in the center, which was so awful to behold that even the strong were terrified upon seeing it.

2348   *Between Scylla and Charybdis*—When a person must choose between two great dangers. Scylla is a rock on the Italian coast opposite the whirlpool Charybdis off the Sicilian coast. In early legends, Scylla and Charybdis were monsters who lived in caves in the strait between Italy and Sicily. They preyed upon vessels which passed and wrecked them.

2349   *A protean artist*—One who can take various roles successfully. In mythology, Proteus was a sea-god who could assume various shapes.

2350   *A Penelope*—A wife who remains faithful to her husband. Penelope was the wife of Ulysses. During his absence she was importuned by suitors, but postponed her decision until she had finished weaving a funeral pall for her father-in-law. Every night she unraveled what she had woven by day, and so deferred making any choice until Ulysses returned, when the unwelcome suitors were sent away.

2351   *An Icarian adventure*—A bold adventure which comes to a fatal end. In Greek mythology, Icarus fell into the sea when he attempted to escape from the Cretan Labyrinth by means of wings made from feathers. He flew too near the sun, the wax of his wings melted, and he fell into the sea.

2352   *To cut up didoes*—To make mischief; to cut up; to play tricks. Dido was a queen of Carthage. When Dido was obtaining land for her city, she was told she could have as much land as an ox hide would cover. She cut the hide into pieces so it would cover more ground.

2353   *Suffering the punishment of Tantalus*—To come close to attaining one's objectives and yet never reach them. According to mythology, Tantalus was punished in Hades by the sight of food and water which he could never quite reach.

2354   *To look to one's laurels*—To be careful that one's position or rank be not lost. The ancient Greeks used the foliage of the laurel to crown victors in the Pythian games and as a mark of distinction for certain offices. Later a crown of laurels was used for academic honors.

2355   *To win laurels*—To secure fame as a result of some significant accomplishment.

2356   *Coup de grace*—In French, a blow of mercy. The death blow by which the executioner ended the suffering of the condemned. A decisive, finishing stroke which mercifully puts an end to the sufferings of a victim.

2357   *A siren*—A fascinating woman who entices one to destruction. In mythology, the Sirens were beautiful women who lured mariners to their destruction by singing.

2358   *A Triton among minnows*—One who excels his competitors. The Tritons, in mythology, were sea-gods.

2359   *A fidus Achates*—A faithful friend. Achates was a faithful companion of Aeneas in Virgil's *Aeneid*.

2360   *Coup d'état*—A sudden decisive use of force by which an existing government is subverted. Power is seized and an existing government is overthrown. Napoleon III in 1851 dissolved the French Assembly by force and seized the supreme rule over France, becoming emperor; that was a coup d'état.

2361   *A Ganymede*—A handsome boy. In mythology, Ganymede was a beautiful Trojan boy who took the place of Hebe as a cup-bearer of the gods.

2362   *Crossing the Rubicon*—To take an important or decisive step. At the beginning of the civil war with Pompey, Caesar crossed a river called the Rubicon, and exclaimed, "the die is cast." By crossing this river contrary to government orders, Caesar precipitated the war.

2363   *Apollo serving Admetus*—A person of special ability who is compelled by necessity to do a menial task. Admetus was a king in Thessaly whom Apollo at one time served as a shepherd.

2364   *To feel the sword of Damocles hanging over one's head*—A sense of impending disaster. Damocles was a flatterer at the court of Dionysius of Syracuse. Damocles constantly called attention to the happiness of kings, so Dionysius invited him to a banquet, seating him under a sword hung by a single hair to show what dangers were present in the fancied happiness of kings. It showed how foolish it was to long for happiness which might end so soon.

2365   *To drink from the fountain of Hippocrene*—To obtain inspiration for a literary work. Hippocrene was a fountain on Mount Helicon in Boeotia whose water was said in Greek mythology to impart poetic inspiration.

2366   *A titanic effort*—An exceptional effort. The Titans in mythology were deities of enormous strength.

2367   *The Dark Ages*—One may say that a terrible war will drive civilization back into the Dark Ages. The Dark Ages represent a period in the history of the world characterized by the decline or eclipse of the arts, letters, and sciences. The Dark Ages are considered as the period between ancient and modern times, as between the fall of the Roman Empire and the revival of letters; the period from about 400 to 1400 A.D.

2368   *Olympian anger*—Anger such as the gods might display. In Greek mythology, the gods were supposed to dwell upon a mountain called Olympus; Olympian implies something that is godlike.

2369   *A harpy*—A very greedy person who will do anything to obtain wealth. In Greek mythology, a Harpy was one of a group of foul creatures, part woman, part bird, that snatched away the souls of the dead or seized or defiled the food of their victims.

2370   *In the doldrums*—State of listlessness, boredom, or indifference. The doldrums are a part of the ocean near the equator, abounding in calms, squalls, and baffling winds, making it difficult for a sailing vessel to make progress. A person may be "in the doldrums"—bored and listless, uninterested in progress.

2371   *As riotous as Donnybrook Fair*—A riotous disorder or occasion. Donnybrook Fair was an annual fair, noted for fighting and disorder, formerly held in Donnybrook, Ireland.

2372   *To dragoon someone*—To compel one, or try to force one, to follow a certain course by harsh means. To harass by, or as if by, dragoons. A dragoon was formerly a mounted infantryman heavily armed; and the name dragoon came from the dragoons, or short muskets, which were said to spout fire like dragons.

2373   *To draw a red herring across the track*—To draw attention from the principal question to some secondary matter. To divert one's attention. The phrase is said to have arisen two or three centuries ago when a red herring or a dead cat or animal was drawn across the track to train dogs in hunting.

2374   *To play ducks and drakes*—To throw away heedlessly or squander foolishly. May be used in connection with money; for example, to show how an unworthy heir squanders his estate. Ducks and drakes refers to the sport of throwing flat stones or shells so that they will skim or bound along the water.

2375   *A Dulcinea*—A sweetheart. Dulcinea was one of the most famous sweethearts in all literature, being Don Quixote's lady-love in Cervantes' novel of that name.

2376   *A Xanthippe*—Xanthippe was Socrates' wife. Her peevish scold-ing and quarrelsome temper have become proverbial. A woman with these characteristics is a Xanthippe.

2377   *Utopia*—Any place of ideal perfection. In a book written in 1516, Sir Thomas More described an imaginary ideal commonwealth, enjoying perfection in politics, law and in every way. The word "Utopia" comes from two Greek words meaning "no place." Utopian schemes are impractical and impossible of realization.

2378   *To cut the Gordian knot*—To solve a problem or to get rid of a difficulty in a fearless, determined manner. Gordius, the king of Phrygia, tied a knot no one could loosen. An oracle declared that whoever untied the knot would be master of Asia. Alexander the Great cut it with his sword.

2379   *To eat crow*—To be forced to eat one's own words; to confess one was wrong; to accept what one has fought against. The crow is not considered fit for human food; one would only eat it against his will.

2380   *An El Dorado*—A place of fabulous richness. El Dorado refers to a legendary rich king of a South American tribe or his imaginary kingdom, having a great deal of gold.

2381   *To tilt at windmills*—To fight against imaginary wrongs, evils, or opponents. The phrase comes from *Don Quixote* by Cervantes. Don Quixote declared thirty or forty windmills were giants and, riding his horse, he drove at one of the windmills with his lance.

2382   *On tenterhooks*—In suspense, or under a distressing strain. Cloth may be stretched or tenterhooked, a tenterhook being a sharp hooked nail used for fastening cloth on a tenter. A tenter is a frame for stretching cloth.

2383   *A stormy petrel*—A harbinger of trouble. One who may cause trouble. The petrel is a bird which it is believed is active before a storm at sea and so foretells the storm.

2384   *She is stately as Juno*—A complimentary remark to a woman. Juno in mythology was the wife of Jupiter and the queen of heaven.

2385   *Eureka*—An expression of triumph over a discovery. To cry out "Eureka" means one has found something after much effort, or that is greatly desired. "I have found it" is the exclamation attributed to Archimedes upon discovering a method of determining the purity of gold.

2386   *To speak or write ex cathedra*—To speak from the chair—the chair of power and knowledge; to speak with authority. Sometimes used to comment sarcastically on the remarks of a dogmatic writer or speaker as "Mr. Jones certainly spoke in an ex cathedra manner on a subject about which he was little informed." In the Roman Catholic church, the Pope may speak ex cathedra in his pontifical character—from his throne as the representative of Saint Peter.

2387   *To cudgel one's brains*—To make a painful effort to remember or understand something.

2388   *Star chamber proceedings*—A secret or irresponsible tribunal. In early English history, the star chamber was a high court exercising wide civil and criminal jurisdiction; it could proceed on mere rumor and could apply torture. One might say, "The committee applied star chamber methods in its examination of witnesses."

2389   *Neither fish, flesh, nor good red herring*—Means not one thing or another—no particular thing—nothing at all. Many years ago, "not fish" meant not food for monks; "not flesh" meant not food for people; not "good red herring" meant not food for the poor. So anything that did not fit one of these groups was nothing.

2390   *He can hear the pipes of Pan*—He is sensitive to the wind, the waves, and nature. He is at one with nature. In mythology, Pan was the god of pastures, forests and their wild life, and patron of shepherds and hunters.

2391   *A stalking horse*—A mask or pretense. Something put forward as the apparent reason of a person or group whereas the real purpose remains hidden, temporarily at least. In politics, a candidate put forward to divide the opposition or to conceal someone's real candidacy.

2392   *Sons of Belial*—Wicked, evil, immoral, or corrupt persons. In the New Testament the name "Belial" became identified with Satan; in Milton's *Paradise Lost*, one of the fallen angels.

2393   *In the Slough of Despond*—In the depths of despair or discouragement. In *Pilgrim's Progress*, the Slough of Despond was a deep quagmire which Christian, the pilgrim, had to cross.

2394   *A fool's paradise*—A condition of illusive happiness. A person who indulges in vain hopes lives in a fool's paradise.

2395   *A fool's errand*—A ridiculous, profitless undertaking.

2396   *The fourth estate*—Newspapers; the public press. It has been said that Burke originated the term when he spoke of three estates in Parliament and then added that the reporters' gallery was the fourth estate, the most important of all. Macaulay used it also. The first three estates were the lords spiritual, the lords temporal, and the commons.

2397 *An Iliad of ills or an Iliad of woes*—A long series of evils or woes. Many evils experienced at the same time. The *Iliad* is a Greek epic poem ascribed to Homer. It narrates events of the last year of the Trojan War, and is filled with many tragic experiences.

2398 *A Frankenstein's monster*—A work or agency that ultimately destroys its originator. Frankenstein was a student of physiology in Mrs. Shelley's romance of the same name. He constructed a monster and gave it a kind of life. The monster inflicted the most terrible retribution upon his creator. The name now is used to indicate someone destroyed by his own works.

2399 *A gay Lothario*—A man who trifles with women's affections. In Rowe's drama, *The Fair Penitent,* Lothario was a gay and unscrupulous seducer. The name is also found in stories by Cervantes and Goethe.

2400 *At sixes and sevens*—A condition when affairs, matters, or things are in disorder and confusion. The origin of the phrase is not certain, but Shakespeare and other writers have used it.

2401 *Simon-pure*—Genuine; authentic. In the comedy, a *Bold Stroke for a Wife* (1718), by Mrs. S. Centlivre, a Colonel Feignwell poses as Simon Pure, a Pennsylvania Quaker. He wins the heart of Miss Lovely, and when Simon Pure himself arrives, he is at first treated as an imposter until he identifies himself as the true Simon Pure.

2402 *A Scrooge or an Ebenezer Scrooge*—A hard, greedy person. In the *Christmas Carol* by Dickens, Ebenezer Scrooge was an avaricious man visited by spirits on Christmas Eve and made kindly when they showed him the meaning of consideration and generosity to others.

2403 *To find a Golconda*—To discover a source of great wealth. Golconda is the name of a city in India which was famous for its great riches.

2404 *A Sinon*—A skillful liar. Sinon was a Greek through whose lies the Trojans were led to take the wooden horse, in which were concealed Greek warriors, into the city of Troy.

2405 *A Golgotha*—A place of torment or martyrdom; a cemetery. In the New Testament, the place where Christ was crucified.

2406 *A Saturnalia of crime*—An unusually large number of crimes. Saturnalia was the old Roman festival beginning December 17 in honor of the god Saturn. It was a time of much rejoicing, but was also marked by excesses and periods of general license.

2407   *A round robin*—A written petition or protest with the signatures in a circle so as not to indicate who signed first. The origin of the phrase is not certain, some believing that it came from the French.

2408   *A Rosetta stone*—A key by which a mystery or difficult problem may be solved. The Rosetta stone was found in 1799 near the Rosetta mouth of the Nile. It contains an inscription in hieroglyphic characters which gave the first clue for deciphering the Egyptian hieroglyphics.

2409   *To commit political hara-kiri*—To commit political suicide. Hara-kiri was formerly a Japanese method of suicide practiced in cases of disgrace or by government order.

2410   *Hobson's choice*—A choice in which one has no alternative; one must take the thing offered or nothing. Thomas Hobson was an Englishman (1631) who let out horses in Cambridge; he had many horses, but every customer had to take the horse nearest the door.

2411   *Wealthy as a nabob*—To have great riches. A nabob is a native deputy or viceroy in India, or a Mogul provincial governor. These men have great wealth.

2412   *To be proud as Lucifer*—To be proud or rebellious in spirit even in the face of power that may not be challenged. Lucifer is the name sometimes used for Satan as identified with the rebel archangel before his fall.

2413   *Homeric laughter*—Loud and uncontrolled laughter. The Greek epic poet Homer is said to have written the famous *Iliad*, and this phrase refers to a passage in that poem.

2414   *On the hustings*—Any place where political speeches are being made. The Hustings is the platform from which candidates for Parliament were formerly nominated.

2415   *On the horns of a dilemma*—A dilemma is an argument which gives an antagonist two or more alternatives (or horns), but equally against him. One has a choice between equally undesirable and unsatisfactory alternatives. The horns probably refer to a bull which may toss an object from one horn to the other.

2416   *Pons asinorum*—A Latin phrase meaning an asses' bridge. The phrase is used to mean some obstacle to be overcome which is difficult for beginners to comprehend. The asses' bridge is a proposition from geometry which it is not always easy for beginners to understand. To illustrate the phrase: The pons asinorum that worried the sidewalk onlookers was how engineers could build a subway under streets over which heavy traffic was moving.

2417   *A jackanapes*—A conceited or impertinent person. The word is said to have come from a jack (monkey or ape) from napes (Naples in Italy).

2418   *The Pierian spring*—A source of knowledge. The poet Pope wrote: "A little learning is a dangerous thing; drink deep, or taste not the Pierian spring." To drink from the Pierian spring, according to Greek legends, was to obtain knowledge. The spring was in Pieria, a region of ancient Macedonia, one of the earliest seats of the worship of the Muses, who were the goddesses of the arts, history and music.

2419   *From Dan to Beersheba*—From limit to limit. From one end of the land to the other. A candidate for office might carry the election from Dan to Beersheba, that is, from one end of the state or nation to the other. Dan and Beersheba were formerly the northern and southern limits of Palestine.

2420   *A Jason's quest*—A difficult search. According to Greek mythology, Jason was sent by Pelias in search of the Golden Fleece. Jason met very difficult conditions, but obtained the fleece. To be asked to find a Shakespeare among today's playwrights might be said to be a Jason's quest. When one goes in search of the golden fleece, it may also mean to try to find one's fortune.

2421   *Quid pro quo*—A Latin phrase meaning something for something. *Webster's New Collegiate Dictionary* defines it as "something for something: something given or received for something else."

2422   *Job's comforter*—One who maliciously injures with words which supposedly are meant to comfort. A person who pretends he feels sorry for you and sympathizes with you, but who blames you for your troubles. The phrase comes from the experience Job had, as related in the Bible, with his friends when he was in great trouble.

2423   *Robbing Peter to pay Paul*—To pay one person with something to which another person has a prior right. To satisfy one obligation by leaving another unsatisfied. The expression is said to have originated as follows: About 300 years ago the Abbey Church of St. Peter, Westminster, London, was made a cathedral; a decade later it became a part of the diocese of London and a large part of its property was taken over by St. Paul's Cathedral. Someone writing at the time implied it was not right to rob St. Peter's altar to build one for St. Paul's Cathedral.

2424   *Namby pamby*—Weakly sentimental; insipid. One may speak, for example, of namby pamby writing or talk. Ambrose Phillips was an English poet whose verses for children were ridiculed. Namby came from a baby way of pronouncing Ambrose and pamby merely rhymed with namby.

2425   *Peripatetic*—The word comes from the Greek and means to walk about. Aristotle and his followers were called peripatetics because they taught or discussed matters while walking or moving about.

2426   *Knight-errant*—One who travels looking for opportunities to exhibit skill, prowess and generosity. May also be used to indicate one who goes about attempting to correct conditions or actions he believes are wrong. In ancient legends the knights-errant went about seeking to set free imprisoned kings, right wrongs and aid the oppressed as they saw the need. They are mentioned in Don Quixote. A tourist from this country in a Central American country might be considered a knight-errant if he expressed his opinion about correcting what he thought was wrong in the social life and customs of the people of the foreign country.

2427   *Pickwickian*—An adjective relating to or characteristic of Mr. Pickwick of Dickens' *Pickwick Papers*. Mr. Pickwick was simple and goodhearted.

2428   *A jingo*—One who is in favor of a belligerent or warlike policy in foreign affairs. A chauvinist. The phrase was used in England about 1877 when some people wanted England to assist Turkey against Russia. A popular song at that time said,
   "We don't want to fight; but by jingo, if we do,
   "We've got the ships, we've got the men, and got the money too."

2429   *A patriarch*—A father, leader, chief. A venerable old man. In Biblical history before Moses, the father and ruler of a family or tribe. A person regarded as the father or founder, as of a race, science, religion. Adam Smith might be called the patriarch of political economy. The monarch oak might be called the patriarch of the trees.

2430   *Pecksniffian*—To resemble the hypocrisy or suave insincerity of Pecksniff who was a canting rascal in Dickens' story *Martin Chuzzlewit*.

2431   *To hunt with the lantern of Diogenes*—Diogenes was a Greek Cynic philosopher who was said to have gone about the streets of Corinth in broad daylight with a lighted lantern looking for an honest man. To illustrate the expression: It would take a Diogenes hunting with a lantern to find an honest man in a graft-ridden municipal government.

2432   *A Macedonian cry*—A call for help or assistance. The expression is of Biblical origin. In Chapter 16 of the Book of Acts, verses 9 and 10, it is recorded that a vision appeared to Paul by night, the vision of a Macedonian standing and appealing to him with the words, "Cross over to Macedonia and help us," from which it was inferred that "God had called us to preach the gospel to them." As soon as Paul saw the vision, "we made efforts to start for Macedonia."

2433　*Patient as Griselda*—A very patient woman. In romantic stories of medieval days, Griselda was a lady who was proverbial for virtue and patience. Her husband put her to severe trials, and she became a model of patience.

2434　*Out-Herod Herod*—To surpass in violent treatment or in wickedness. Shakespeare uses the expression in *Hamlet*. Herod was the king of Judea (37 B.C.) who destroyed the infants of Bethlehem.

2435　*Machiavellian*—Political cunning or bad faith; unscrupulous. Machiavelli was a Florentine statesman (1469-1527) who believed that any means, however unscrupulous, may be properly employed by a ruler in order to maintain a strong central government.

2436　*A Mugwump*—An independent in politics; one who reserves the right to bolt the candidate or platform of his party. The term was originally used to describe a bolter from the Republican party in the Presidential campaign of 1884.

2437　*A Mississippi bubble*—A visionary and fantastic financial scheme in which many people are financially interested and which later collapses. The reference is to a scheme a Scotsman, John Law, had for colonizing along the Mississippi River. Law lived in Paris. Ridiculous stories of gold mines were circulated. The mint of France was even involved in Law's schemes. The shares of his company increased greatly, but eventually the whole financial structure crashed.

2438　*To pile Ossa upon Pelion*—To pile one problem or difficulty upon another. In Greek mythology, the giants, striving to attack the Olympians, piled Pelion, a high wooded mountain, on Mount Olympus and Ossa, a steep mountain, on Pelion.

2439　*A Munchausen*—One who tells fantastic and impossible stories; a liar. Baron Munchausen was the pretended author of a book of travels (by Rudolph Eric Raspe, 1785) filled with extravagar⁺ fictions.

2440　*A Mrs. Malaprop*—One who makes blunders in the use of words. "Malapropism" means the ridiculous misuse of a word. Mrs. Malaprop was a character in Sheridan's *The Rivals*, noted for her blunders in the use of words.

2441　*Aliquando bonus dormitat Homerus* (Latin)—Sometimes even the good Homer nods, that is, the greatest are sometimes caught napping. Homer, the Greek poet, was said to be the author of the famous *Iliad*.

2442　*A mare's nest*—According to *Webster's New Collegiate Dictionary*, a mare's nest is something believed to be wonderful, but turning out to be imaginary or a hoax. To find a mare's nest is to make what you think is an important discovery, but which actually turns out to be a hoax.

2443   *A mess of pottage*—A mess is a confused or disagreeable mixture; a muddle or hodge-podge. A pottage is a thick soup or a dish of vegetables, sometimes including meat. The reference is to the book of Genesis in the Bible where it is related that Esau sold his birthright to Jacob for bread and pottage. To sell something of value for a mess of pottage would obviously be very unwise. A mess of pottage would be something of little value.

2444   *The mills of God*—In literature the idea has often been conveyed of God ruling over a great mill which grinds out the destinies of men. One finds the expression, "The mills of God grind slowly, yet they grind exceeding small." One may escape punishment for a time for wrongdoing, but eventually it comes. Justice may be a long time coming, but its coming is inevitable.

2445   *Bourgeois* (French)—Middle class; ordinary; humdrum.

2446   *Cliché* (French)—Stereotyped expression; hackneyed phrase.

2447   *Commencement de la fin* (French)—Beginning of the end.

2448   *Caveat emptor*—Let the purchaser beware. The buyer should keep his eyes open.

Biblical Quotations

Old Testament

Genesis

2449   God created man in his own image.—*1:27*

2450   It is not good that man should be alone.—*2:18*

2451   In the sweat of thy face shalt thou eat bread.—*3:19*

2452   For dust thou art, and unto dust shalt thou return.—*3:19*

2453   Am I my brother's keeper?—*4:9*

2454   There were giants in the earth in those days.—*6:4*

2455   Whoso sheddeth man's blood, by man shall his blood be shed.—
9:6

2456   The voice is Jacob's voice, but the hands are the hands of Esau.—
27:22

Exodus

2457   Who made thee a prince and a judge over us?—*2:14*

2458   A land flowing with milk and honey.—*3:8*

2459   The land of Egypt, when we sat by the flesh-pots, and when we
did eat bread to the full.—*16:3*

The Ten Commandments—20:3-17

2460 I. Thou shalt have no other gods before me.

2461 II. Thou shalt not make unto thee any graven image, or any likeness of any thing that is in heaven above, or that is in the earth beneath, or that is in the water under the earth: thou shalt not bow down thyself to them, nor serve them: for I the Lord thy God am a jealous God, visiting the iniquity of the fathers upon the children unto the third and fourth generation of them that hate me; and shewing mercy unto thousands of them that love me, and keep my commandments.

2462 III. Thou shalt not take the name of the Lord thy God in vain; for the Lord will not hold him guiltless that taketh his name in vain.

2463 IV. Remember the sabbath day, to keep it holy. Six days shalt thou labor, and do all thy work; but the seventh day is the sabbath of the Lord thy God: in it thou shalt not do any work, thou, nor thy son, nor thy daughter, thy manservant, nor thy maidservant, nor thy cattle, nor thy stranger that is within thy gates: for in six days the Lord made heaven and earth, the sea, and all that in them is, and rested the seventh day: wherefore the Lord blessed the sabbath day, and hallowed it.

2464 V. Honor thy father and thy mother: that thy days may be long upon the land which the Lord thy God giveth thee.

2465 VI. Thou shalt not kill.

2466 VII. Thou shalt not commit adultery.

2467 VIII. Thou shalt not steal.

2468 IX. Thou shalt not bear false witness against thy neighbor.

2469 X. Thou shalt not covet thy neighbor's house, thou shalt not covet thy neighbor's wife, nor his manservant, nor his maidservant, nor his ox, nor his ass, nor anything that is thy neighbor's.

Deuteronomy

2470 Man doth not live by bread only.—*8:3*

2471 Eye for eye, tooth for tooth, hand for hand, foot for foot.—*19:21*

2472 Thou shalt not muzzle the ox when he treadeth out the corn.—*25:4*

Joshua

2473 I am going the way of all the earth.—*23:14*

Judges

2474   The stars in their courses fought against Sisera.—*5:20*

First Samuel

2475   Be strong, and quit yourselves like men.—*4:9*

2476   A man after his own heart.—*13:14*

Second Samuel

2477   How are the mighty fallen! Tell it not in Gath, publish it not in the streets of Askelon.—*1:19, 20*

2478   And Nathan said to David, Thou art the man.—*12:7*

First Kings

2479   How long halt ye between two opinions? if the Lord be God follow him: but if Baal, then follow him.—*18:21*

2480   A still small voice.—*19:12*

First Chronicles

2481   Our days on the earth are as a shadow.—*29:15*

2482   And he died in a good old age, full of days, riches, and honour.—*29:28*

Job

2483   One that feared God, and eschewed evil.—*1:1*

2484   The Lord gave, and the Lord hath taken away; blessed be the name of the Lord.—*1:21*

2485   Skin for skin, yea all that a man hath will he give for his life.—*2:4*

2486   Shall a man be more pure than his Maker?—*4:17*

2487   Although affliction cometh not forth of the dust, neither doth trouble spring out of the ground: yet man is born unto trouble as the sparks fly upward.—*5:6, 7*

2488   Man that is born of a woman is of few days, and full of trouble.—*14:1*

2489   I am escaped with the skin of my teeth.—*19:20*

2490   The price of wisdom is above rubies.—*28:18*

2491 Behold, my desire is . . . that mine adversary had written a book. —*31:35*

2492 He was righteous in his own eyes.—*32:1*

2493 He multiplieth words without knowledge.—*35:16*

2494 He saith among the trumpets, Ha, ha; and he smelleth the battle afar off.—*39:25*

Psalms

2495 Yea, though I walk through the valley of the shadow of death, I will fear no evil: for thou art with me; thy rod and thy staff they comfort me.—*23:4*

2496 Many are the afflictions of the righteous: but the Lord delivereth him out of them all.—*34:19*

2497 The wicked borroweth, and payeth not again: but the righteous showeth mercy, and giveth.—*37:21*

2498 He heapeth up riches, and knoweth not who shall gather them.— *39:6*

2499 Blessed is he that considereth the poor.—*41:1*

2500 As the hart panteth after the water brooks.—*42:1*

2501 Deep calleth unto deep.—*42:7*

2502 Oh that I had wings like a dove! for then would I fly away, and be at rest.—*55:6*

2503 We took sweet counsel together.—*55:14*

2504 The words of his mouth were smoother than butter, but war was in his heart; his words were softer than oil, yet were they drawn swords.— *55:21*

2505 Cast thy burden upon the Lord, and he shall sustain thee: he shall never suffer the righteous to be moved.—*55:22*

2506 Vain is the help of man.—*60:11*

2507 For a thousand years in thy sight are but as yesterday when it is past, and as a watch in the night.—*90:4*

2508 As for man, his days are as grass: as a flower of the field, so he flourisheth.—*103:15*

2509 They that go down to the sea in ships, that do business in great waters; these see the works of the Lord, and his wonders in the deep.— *107:23, 24*

2510   The stone which the builders refused is become the head stone of the corner.—*118:22*

2511   Lo, children are an heritage of the Lord: happy is the man that hath his quiver full of them.—*127:3, 5*

2512   Behold, how good and how pleasant it is for brethren to dwell together in unity!—*133:1*

2513   If I forget thee, O Jerusalem, let my right hand forget her cunning.—*137:5*

2514   I am fearfully and wonderfully made.—*139:14*

2515   Man is like to vanity: his days are as a shadow that passeth away.—*144:4*

Proverbs

2516   Surely in vain the net is spread in the sight of any bird.—*1:17*

2517   Whom the Lord loveth he correcteth.—*3:12*

2518   Go to the ant, thou sluggard; consider her ways, and be wise.—*6:6*

2519   As an ox goeth to the slaughter.—*7:22*; Jer. *11:19*

2520   A wise son maketh a glad father.—*10:1*

2521   In the multitude of counsellors there is safety.—*11:14; 24:6*

2522   He that is surety for a stranger shall smart for it.—*11:15*

2523   A virtuous woman is a crown to her husband.—*12:4*

2524   The way of the transgressors is hard.—*13:15*

2525   He that walketh with wise men shall be wise: but a companion of fools shall be destroyed.—*13:20*

2526   He that spareth his rod hateth his son.—*13:24*

2527   Righteousness exalteth a nation.—*14:34*

2528   A soft answer turneth away wrath: but grievous words stir up anger.—*15:1*

2529   A merry heart maketh a cheerful countenance.—*15:13*

2530   Pride goeth before destruction, and an haughty spirit before a fall.—*16:18*

2531   The hoary head is a crown of glory, if it be found in the way of righteousness.—*16:31*

2532   He that is slow to anger is better than the mighty: and he that ruleth his spirit than he that taketh a city.—*16:32*

2533   He that repeateth a matter separateth very friends.—*17:9*

2534   He that hath knowledge spareth his words.—*17:27*

2535   Even a fool, when he holdeth his peace, is counted wise.—*17:28*

2536   A man's gift maketh room for him, and bringeth him before great men.—*18:16*

2537   He that hath pity upon the poor lendeth unto the Lord.—*19:17*

2538   Wine is a mocker, strong drink is raging.—*20:1*

2539   It is naught, it is naught, saith the buyer—but when he is gone his way, then he boasteth.—*20:14*

2540   A good name is rather to be chosen than great riches.—*22:1*

2541   Train up a child in the way he should go: and when he is old, he will not depart from it.—*22:6*

2542   The rich ruleth over the poor, and the borrower is servant to the lender.—*22:7*

2543   Seest thou a man diligent in his business? he shall stand before kings; he shall not stand before mean men.—*22:29*

2544   As he thinketh in his heart, so is he.—*23:7*

2545   Drowsiness shall clothe a man with rags.—*23:21*

2546   If thou faint in the day of adversity, thy strength is small.—*24:10*

2547   Rejoice not when thine enemy falleth, and let not thine heart be glad when he stumbleth.—*24:17*

2548   Debate thy cause with thy neighbor himself; and discover not a secret to another.—*25:9*

2549   A word fitly spoken is like apples of gold in pictures of silver. —*25:11*

2550   Whoso boasteth himself of a false gift is like clouds and wind without rain.—*25:14*

2551   Seest thou a man wise in his own conceit? there is more hope of a fool than of him.—*26:12*

2552   The sluggard is wiser in his own conceit than seven men that can render a reason.—*26:16*

2553   As coals are to burning coals, and wood to fire; so is a contentious man to kindle strife.—*26:21*

2554   Boast not thyself of tomorrow; for thou knowest not what a day may bring forth.—*27:1*

2555   The wicked flee when no man pursueth: but the righteous are bold as a lion.—*28:1*

2556   He that maketh haste to be rich shall not be innocent.—*28:20*

2557   He that giveth unto the poor shall not lack: but he that hideth his eyes shall have many a curse.—*28:27*

2558   A fool uttereth all his mind: but a wise man keepeth it in till afterward.—*29:11*

2559   The ants are a people not strong, yet they prepare their meat in the summer.—*30:25*

2560   Favor is deceitful, and beauty is vain.—*31:30*

Ecclesiastes

2561   One generation passeth away, and another generation cometh; but the earth abideth forever.—*1:4*

2562   All the rivers run into the sea; yet the sea is not full.—*1:7*

2563   In much wisdom is much grief.—*1:18*

2564   Better is an handful with quietness, than both hands full with travail and vexation of spirit.—*4:6*

2565   A living dog is better than a dead lion.—*9:4*

2566   The race is not to the swift, nor the battle to the strong, neither yet bread to the wise, nor yet riches to men of understanding, nor yet favour to men of skill; but time and chance happeneth to them all.—*9:11*

2567   He that diggeth a pit shall fall into it.—*10:8*

2568   Cast thy bread upon the waters: for thou shall find it after many days.—*11:1*

2569   Remember now thy Creator in the days of thy youth, while the evil days come not.—*12:1*

2570   Of making many books there is no end; and much study is a weariness of the flesh.—*12:12*

Song of Solomon

2571   Many waters cannot quench love.—*8:7*

Isaiah

2572 The ox knoweth his owner, and the ass his master's crib.—*1:3*

2573 Bring no more vain oblations; incense is an abomination unto me.—*1:13*

2574 They shall beat their swords into plough shares, and their spears into pruning hooks.—*2:4*

2575 Grind the faces of the poor.—*3:15*

2576 Woe unto them that are wise in their own eyes!—*5:21*

2577 The wolf also shall dwell with the lamb, and the leopard shall lie down with the kid.—*11:6*

2578 How art thou fallen from heaven, O Lucifer, son of the morning!—*14:12*

2579 Babylon is fallen, is fallen.—*21:9*

2580 Watchman, what of the night?—*21:11*

2581 Let us eat and drink, for tomorrow we shall die.—*22:13*

2582 We have made a covenant with death.—*28:15*

2583 Behold, the nations are as a drop of a bucket, and are counted as the small dust of the balance.—*40:15*

2584 Shall the clay say to him that fashioneth it, What makest thou? —*45:9*

2585 A man of sorrows and acquainted with grief.—*53:3*

2586 We all do fade as a leaf.—*64:6*

Jeremiah

2587 Saying, Peace, peace; when there is no peace.—*6:14*

Lamentations

2588 She that was great among the nations, and princess among the provinces, how is she become tributary!—*1:1*

Hosea

2589 For they have sown the wind, and they shall reap the whirlwind. —*8:7*

Joel

2590 Your sons and your daughters shall prophesy, your old men shall dream dreams, your young men shall see visions.—*2:28*

Zechariah

2591   Prisoners of hope.—*9:12*

2592   I was wounded in the house of my friends.—*13:6*

New Testament

The Gospel According to St. Matthew

2593   And now also the axe is laid unto the root of the trees.—*3:10*

2594   Man shall not live by bread alone.—*4:4 (also Luke 4:4)*

2595   Blessed are the poor in spirit: for theirs is the kingdom of heaven.

2596   Blessed are they that mourn: for they shall be comforted.

2597   Blessed are the meek: for they shall inherit the earth.

2598   Blessed are they which do hunger and thirst after righteousness: for they shall be filled.

2599   Blessed are the merciful: for they shall obtain mercy.

2600   Blessed are the pure in heart: for they shall see God.

2601   Blessed are the peacemakers: for they shall be called the children of God.

2602   Blessed are ye, when men shall revile you, and persecute you, and shall say all manner of evil against you falsely, for my sake.

2603   Rejoice, and be exceeding glad: for great is your reward in heaven: for so persecuted they the prophets which were before you. —*5:312*

2604   Ye are the salt of the earth: but if the salt have lost his savour, where-with shall it be salted? *(See Mark 9:50; Luke 14:34)*—*5:13*

2605   Ye are the light of the world. A city that is set on an hill cannot be hid.—*5:14*

2606   Neither do men light a candle, and put it under a bushel. *(See Mark 4:21)*—*5:15*

2607   Whosoever is angry with his brother without a cause shall be in danger of the judgment.—*5:22*

2608   An eye for an eye, and a tooth for a tooth.—*5:38*

2609   Whosoever shall smite thee on thy right cheek, turn to him the other also. *(See Luke 6:20)*—*5:39*

2610 Give to him that asketh thee, and from him that would borrow of thee turn not thou away.—*5:42*

2611 Love your enemies. (*See* Luke *6:27*)—*5:44*

2612 Let not thy left hand know what thy right hand doeth.—*6:3*

2613 Use not vain repetitions.—*6:7*

2614 Where moth and rust doth corrupt, and where thieves break through and steal.—*6:19*

2615 For where your treasure is, there will your heart be also. (*See* Luke *12:34*)—*6:21*

2616 No man can serve two masters. (*See* Luke *16:13*)—*6:24*

2617 Ye cannot serve God and mammon. (*See* Luke *16:13*)—*6:24*

2618 Consider the lilies of the field, how they grow; they toil not, neither do they spin: And yet I say unto you, That even Solomon in all his glory was not arrayed like one of these. (*See* Luke *12:27*)—*6:28, 29*

2619 Take therefore no thought for the morrow: for the morrow shall take thought for the things of itself. Sufficient unto the day is the evil thereof.—*6:34*

2620 Judge not, that ye be not judged. (*See* Luke *6:37*)—*7:1*

2621 Ask, and it shall be given you; seek, and ye shall find; knock, and it shall be opened unto you: for every one that asketh receiveth; and he that seeketh findeth; and to him that knocketh it shall be opened. —*7:7, 8*

2622 What man is there of you, whom if his son ask bread, will he give him a stone? (*See* Luke *11:11*)—*7:9*

2623 Therefore all things whatsoever ye would that men should do to you, do ye even so to them. (*See* Luke *6:31*)—*7:12*

2624 Wide is the gate, and broad is the way, that leadeth to destruction.—*7:13*

2625 Beware of false prophets, which come to you in sheep's clothing, but inwardly they are ravening wolves.—*7:15*

2626 Ye shall know them by their fruits.—*7:16*

2627 A foolish man, which built his house upon the sand. (*See* Luke *6:49*)—*7:26*

2628 I am a man under authority, having soldiers under me: and I say to this man, Go, and he goeth; and to another, Come, and he cometh. —*8:9*

2629   The foxes have holes, and the birds of the air have nests; but the Son of man hath not where to lay his head.—*8:20*

2630   Follow me; and let the dead bury their dead. (*See* Luke *9:60*)—*8:22*

2631   No man putteth a piece of new cloth unto an old garment. (*See* Mark *3:21*)—*9:16*

2632   The harvest truly is plenteous, but the labourers are few. (*See* Luke *10:2*)—*9:37*

2633   The very hairs of your head are all numbered. (*See* Luke *21:18*)—*10:30*

2634   A man's foes shall be they of his own household.—*10:36*

2635   Come unto me, all ye that labour and are heavy laden.—*11:28*

2636   He that is not with me is against me. (*See* Mark *9:40*; Luke *9:50*; *11:23*)—*12:30*

2637   The tree is known by his fruit. (*See* Luke *6:44*)—*12:33*

2638   Out of the abundance of the heart the mouth speaketh. (*See* Luke *6:45*)—*12:34*

2639   Whosoever hath, to him shall be given, and he shall have more abundance: but whosoever hath not, from him shall be taken away even that he hath.—*13:12*

2640   When he had found one pearl of great price.—*13:46*

2641   If the blind lead the blind, both shall fall into the ditch.—*15:14*

2642   Get thee behind me Satan. (*See* Mark *8:33*)—*16:23*

2643   For what is a man profited, if he shall gain the whole world and lose his own soul? (*See* Mark *8:36*; Luke *9:25*)—*16:26*

2644   What therefore God hath joined together, let not man put asunder. (*See* Mark *10:9*)—*19:6*

2645   It is easier for a camel to go through the eye of a needle, than for a rich man to enter into the kingdom of God. (*See* Mark *10:25*)—*19:24*

2646   But many that are first shall be last; and the last shall be first. (*See* Mark *10:31*; Luke *13:30*)—*19:30*

2647   For many are called, but few are chosen.—*22:14*

2648   Render therefore unto Caesar the things which are Caesar's; and unto God the things that are God's. (*See* Mark *12:17*; Luke *20:25*)—*22:21*

2649   And whosoever shall exalt himself shall be abased; and he that shall humble himself shall be exalted. (*See* Luke *14:11*)—*23:12*

2650   Ye blind guides, which strain at a gnat, and swallow a camel. —*23:24*

2651   Ye are like unto whited sepulchres, which indeed appear beautiful outward, but are within full of dead men's bones, and of all uncleanness.—*23:27*

2652   Wars and rumours of wars.—*24:6*

2653   Well done, thou good and faithful servant.—*25:21*

2654   Reaping where thou hast not sown, and gathering where thou hast not strawed. (*See* Luke *19:21*)—*25:24*

2655   For unto everyone that hath shall be given. (*See* Mark *4:25*) —*25:29*

2656   I was a stranger, and ye took me in.—*25:35*

2657   Inasmuch as ye have done it unto one of the least of these my brethren, ye have done it unto me.—*25:40*

2658   So the last error shall be worse than the first.—*27:64*

2659   Lo, I am with you always, even unto the end of the world. —*28:20*

The Gospel According to St. Mark

2660   He that hath ears to hear, let him hear.—*4:9*

2661   Lord, I believe; help thou mine unbelief.—*9:24*

2662   Whosoever shall offend one of these little ones that believe in me, it is better for him that a millstone were hanged about his neck, and he were cast into the sea.—*9:42*

2663   Suffer the little children to come unto me, and forbid them not: for of such is the kingdom of God. (*See* Matt. *19:13*; Luke *18:15*) —*10:14*

2664   Which devour widows' houses, and for a pretence make long prayers. (*See* Matt. *23:14*)—*12:40*

The Gospel According to St. Luke

2665   On earth peace, good will towards men.—*2:14*

2666   Be content with your wages.—*3:14*

2667   Physician, heal thyself.—*4:20*

2668   The labourer is worthy of his hire.—*10:7*

2669   He passed by on the other side.—*10:31*

2670   Go, and do thou likewise.—*10:37*

2671   Take thine ease, eat, drink, and be merry.—*12:19*

2672   Friend, go up higher.—*14:10*

2673   I have married a wife, and therefore I cannot come.—*14:20*

2674   Wasted his substance with riotous living.—*15:13*

2675   How hardly shall they that have riches enter into the kingdom of God!—*18:24*

2676   God be merciful to me a sinner.—*18:13*

2677   The Son of Man is come to seek and to serve that which was lost.—*19:10*

The Gospel According to St. John

2678   He came unto his own, and his own received him not.—*1:11*

2679   Can there any good thing come out of Nazareth?—*1:46*

2680   Men loved darkness rather than light, because there deeds were evil.—*3:19*

2681   He was a burning and a shining light.—*5:35*

2682   Judge not according to the appearance.—*7:24*

2683   The truth shall make you free.—*8:32*

2684   The night cometh, when no man can work.—*9:4*

2685   Let not your heart be troubled.—*14:1*

2686   In my father's house are many mansions.—*14:2*

2687   I am the way, the truth, and the life.—*14:6*

2688   Greater love hath no man than this, that a man lay down his life for his friends.—*15:13*

2689   What I have written I have written.—*19:22*

Acts of the Apostles

2690   Your sons and your daughters shall prophesy, and your young men shall see visions; and your old men shall dream dreams.—*2:17*

2691   Of a truth I perceive that God is no respecter of persons: but in every nation he that feareth him, and worketh righteousness, is accepted with him.—*10:34, 35*

2692   It is more blessed to give than to receive.—*20:35*

2693   Much learning doth make thee mad.—*26:24*

Epistle to the Romans

2694   To be carnally minded is death.—*8:6*

2695   He that giveth, let him do it with simplicity; he that ruleth, with diligence; he that sheweth mercy, with cheerfulness.—*12:8*

2696   Abhor that which is evil; cleave to that which is good.—*12:9*

2697   Mind not high things, but condescend to men of low estate. Be not wise in your own conceits.—*12:16*

2698   If it be possible, as much as lieth in you, live peaceably with all men.—*12:18*

2699   Vengeance is mine; I will repay, saith the Lord.—*12:19*

2700   In so doing thou shalt heap coals of fire on his head. (*See* Proverbs *25:22*)—*12:20*

2701   Owe no man anything.—*13:8*

2702   The night is far spent, the day is at hand: let us therefore cast off the works of darkness, and let us put on the armour of light.—*13:12*

2703   None of us liveth to himself, and no man dieth to himself.—*14:7*

First Epistle to the Corinthians

2704   Eye hath not seen, nor ear heard, neither have entered into the heart of man, the things which God hath prepared for them that love him—*2:9*

2705   The wisdom of this world is foolishness with God.—*3:19*

2706   Absent in body, but present in spirit.—*5:3*

2707   A little leaven leaveneth the whole lump.—*5:6*

2708   The fashion of this world passeth away.—*7:31*

2709   Knowledge puffeth up, but charity edifieth.—*8:1*

2710   Let him that thinketh he standeth take heed lest he fall.—*10:12*

2711   The earth is the Lord's and the fullness thereof.—*10:26, 28*

2712   Though I bestow all my goods to feed the poor, and though I give my body to be burned, and have not charity, it profiteth me nothing. —*13:3*

2713   Charity suffereth long, and is kind; charity envieth not; charity vaunteth not itself, is not puffed up, doth not behave itself unseemly, seeketh not her own, is not easily provoked, thinketh no evil; rejoiceth not in iniquity, but rejoiceth in the truth; beareth all things, believeth all things, hopeth all things, endureth all things.—*13:47*

2714   Charity never faileth.—*13:8*

2715   When I was a child, I spake as a child, I understood as a child, I thought as a child: but when I became a man, I put away childish things.—*13:11*

2716   And now abideth, faith, hope, charity, these three; but the greatest of these is charity.—*13:13*

2717   Christ died for our sins.—*15:3*

2718   Let us eat and drink; for tomorrow we die.—*15:32*

Second Epistle to the Corinthians
2719   A thorn in the flesh.—*12:7*

Epistle to the Galatians
2720   Ye are all the children of God by faith in Christ Jesus.—*3:26*

2721   Whatsoever a man soweth, that shall he also reap.—*6:7*

2722   Let us not be weary in well-doing: for in due season we shall reap, if we faint not.—*6:9*

Epistle to the Ephesians
2723   Carried about with every wind of doctrine.—*4:14*

2724   Let not the sun go down upon your wrath.—*4:26*

2725   Let no man deceive you with vain words.—*5:6*

2726   Children, obey your parents in the Lord: for that is right.—*6:1*

Epistle to the Philippians
2727   For to me to live is Christ, and to die is gain.—*1:21*

2728   The peace of God, which passeth all understanding.—*4:7*

2729   Whatsoever things are true, whatsoever things are honest, whatsoever things are just, whatsoever things are pure, whatsoever things are lovely, whatsoever things are of good report; if there be any virtue, and if there be any praise, think on these things.—*4:8*

2730   I have learned, in whatsoever state I am, therewith to be content.—*4:11*

2731   I can do all things through Christ which strengthened me.—*4:13*

Second Epistle to the Thessalonians

2732   Be not weary in well-doing.—*3:13*

First Epistle to Timothy

2733   Every creature of God is good.—*4:4*

2734   Neglect not the gift that is in thee.—*4:14*

2735   And having food and raiment let us be therewith content.—*6:8*

2736   For the love of money is the root of all evil.—*6:10*

2737   Rich in good works.—*6:18*

Second Epistle to Timothy

2738   I have fought the good fight, I have finished the course, I have kept the faith.—*4:7*

Epistle to the Hebrews

2739   Faith is the substance of things hoped for, the evidence of things not seen.—*11:1*

2740   Whom the Lord loveth he chasteneth, and scourgeth every son whom he receiveth. If ye endure chastening, God dealeth with you as with sons; for what son is he whom the father chasteneth not?—*12:6, 7*

Epistle of James

2741   Let every man be swift to hear, slow to speak, slow to wrath.—*1:19*

2742   Faith without works is dead.—*2:20*

2743   For what is your life? It is even a vapour, that appeareth for a little time and then vanisheth away.—*4:14*

First Epistle of Peter

2744   Love covereth a multitude of sins.—*4:8*

Second Epistle of Peter

2745   The dog is turned to his own vomit again; and the sow that was washed to her wallowing in the mire.—*2:23*

First Epistle of John

2746   The world passeth away, and the lust thereof: but he that doeth the will of God abideth forever.—*2:17*

The Revelation

2747   Be thou faithful unto death, and I will give thee a crown of life. —*2:10*

2748   I am Alpha and Omega, the beginning and the end, the first and the last.—*22:13*

A Rich Treasure House of Selected Quotations

Ability

2749   One machine can do the work of fifty ordinary men. No machine can do the work of one extraordinary man.—*Elbert Hubbard*

2750   He is always the severest censor of the merits of others who has the least worth of his own.—*E.L. Magoon*

2751   The winds and waves are always on the side of the ablest navigators.—*Edward Gibbon*

Abuse

2752   Abuse is the weapon of the vulgar.—*S.G. Goodrich*

Achievement

2753   First say to yourself what you would be; and then do what you have to do.—*Epictetus*

2754
        Heaven is not reached at a single bound;
        But we build the ladder by which we rise
        From the lowly earth to the vaulted skies,
        And we mount to its summit round by round.
                —*Josiah Gilbert Holland*

2755   Oh may I join the choir invisible
Of those immortal dead who live again
In minds made better by their presence.
—Marian Evans Cross

2756   An ill-favoured thing, sir, but mine own.—*Shakespeare*

2757   Finish every day and be done with it. You have done what you could; some blunders and absurdities crept in; forget them as soon as you can. Tomorrow is a new day; you shall begin it well and serenely and with too high a spirit to be encumbered with your old nonsense.
—Emerson

2758   We judge ourselves by what we feel capable of doing; others judge us by what we have done.— *Longfellow*

2759   Men at some time are masters of their fates:
The fault, dear Brutus, is not in our stars.
But in ourselves, that we are underlings.
—Shakespeare

2760   Nothing will come of nothing.—*Shakespeare*

2761   No great thing is created suddenly, any more than a bunch of grapes or a fig. If you tell me that you desire a fig, I answer you that there must be time. Let it first blossom, then bear fruit, then ripen.
—Epictetus

2762   My greatest inspiration is a challenge to attempt the impossible.
—Albert A. Michelson

2763   "Give me a standing place," said Archimedes, "and I will move the world"—Goethe has changed the postulate into the precept. "Make good thy standing place, and move the world."—*S. Smiles*

2764   A brain is known by its fruits.—*H.G. Wells*

Action

2765   Awake, arise, or be forever fallen!—*John Milton*

2766   Thought is the seed of action.—*Emerson*

Admiration

2767   Admiration: our polite recognition of another man's resemblance to ourselves.—*Ambrose Bierce*

2768   Admiration is the daughter of ignorance.—*Benjamin Franklin*

Adversity

2769 I'll say this for adversity: people seem to be able to stand it, and that's more than I can say for prosperity.—*Kin Hubbard*

2770 You can bear anything if it isn't your own fault.—*K. F. Gerould*

2771 Happy those who knowing they are subject to uncertain changes, are prepared and armed for either fortune; a rare principle, and with much labor learned in wisdom's school.—*Massinger*

2772 In this thing one man is superior to another, that he is better able to bear prosperity or adversity.—*Philemon*

2773 Most of our comforts grow up between our crosses.—*Young*

2774 The greater the difficulty, the more glory in surmounting it.— Skillful pilots gain their reputation from storms and tempests.—*Epicurus*

2775 Let us be of good cheer, remembering that the misfortunes hardest to bear are those which never come.—*J.R. Lowell*

2776 It has done me good to be somewhat parched by the heat and drenched by the rain of life.—*Longfellow*

2777 Adversity has the effect of eliciting talents which in prosperous circumstances would have lain dormant.—*Horace*

2778   Sweet are the uses of adversity,
    Which like the toad, ugly and venomous,
    Wears yet a precious jewel in his head;
    And this our life, exempt from public haunt,
    Finds tongues in trees, books in the running brooks,
    Sermons in stones, and good in every thing.
          —*Shakespeare*

Advice

2779 A bad cold wouldn't be so annoying if it weren't for the advice of our friends.—*Kin Hubbard*

2780 "Be yourself!" is about the worst advice you can give to some people.—*Tom Masson*

2781 When a man comes to me for advice, I find out the kind of advice he wants, and I give it to him.—*Josh Billings.*

Age

2782 When one finds company in himself and his pursuits, he cannot feel old, no matter what his years may be.—*A.B. Alcott*

2783   To me, old age is always fifteen years older than I am.—*Bernard M. Baruch*

2784   Age will not be defied.—*Francis Bacon*

2785   Men of age object too much, consult too long, adventure too little, repent too soon.—*Francis Bacon*

2786   It is not by the gray of the hair that one knows the age of the heart.—*Sir Henry Bulwer*

2787   It is usual to associate age with years only because so many men and women somewhere along in what is called middle age stop trying.—*Henry Ford*

2788   A poor, infirm, weak, and despised old man.—*Shakespeare*

2789   The ripest fruit first falls.—*Shakespeare*

2790   Crabbed age and youth cannot live together.—*Shakespeare*

2791   Nobody loves life like an old man.—*Sophocles*

2792   We hope to grow old, yet we fear old age; that is, we are willing to live, and afraid to die.—*La Bruyère*

2793   Age is a quality of mind;
                    If you've left your
                    Dreams behind,
                    If hope is cold,
                    If you no longer look ahead
                    If your ambitious fires
                    Are dead,
                    Then, you are old!

Ambition

2794   Every man is said to have his peculiar ambition . . . I have no other so great as that of being truly esteemed of my fellow-men, by rendering myself worthy of their esteem.—*Lincoln*

2795   'Tis not what man does which exalts him, but what man would do!—*Robert Browning*

2796   Most people would succeed in small things if they were not troubled by great ambitions.—*Longfellow*

2797   Hitch your wagon to a star.—*Emerson*

2798   When that the poor have cried, Caesar hath wept: Ambition should be made of sterner stuff.—*Shakespeare*

America

2799 There is nothing wrong with America that the faith, love of freedom, intelligence, and energy of her citizens cannot cure.—*Dwight D. Eisenhower*

2800 America lives in the heart of every man everywhere who wishes to find a region where he will be free to work out his destiny as he chooses.—*Woodrow Wilson*

2801 Our greatness is built upon our freedom—is moral, not material. We have a great ardor for gain; but we have a deep passion for the rights of man.—*Woodrow Wilson*

Ancestors

2802 Every man is an omnibus in which his ancestors ride.—*O.W. Holmes*

Anticipation

2803 Nothing is so good as it seems beforehand.—*George Eliot*

2804 Uncertainty and expectation are the joys of life. Security is an insipid thing, though the overtaking and possessing of a wish discovers the folly of the chase.—*William Congreve*

Appetite

2805 Any young man with good health and a poor appetite can save up money.—*J.M. Bailey*

Applause

2806 Applause is the echo of a platitude.—*Ambrose Bierce*

Appreciation

2807 Next to excellence is the appreciation of it.—*William M. Thackeray*

2808 I have yet to find the man, however exalted his station, who did not do better work and put forth greater effort under a spirit of approval than under a spirit of criticism.—*Charles Schwab*

Argument

2809 Behind every argument is someone's ignorance.—*Louis D. Brandeis*

Art

2810   Real art is illumination. . . . It adds stature to life.—*Brooks Atkinson*

2811   In art the hand can never execute anything higher than the heart can inspire.—*Emerson*

Baby

2812   Here we have a baby. It is composed of a bald head and a pair of lungs.—*Eugene Field*

Beauty

2813   A thing of beauty is a joy for ever.—*John Keats*

2814   In all ranks of life the human heart yearns for the beautiful; and the beautiful things that God makes are his gift to all alike—*Harriet Beecher Stowe*

Bible

2815   I call the Book of Job, apart from all theories about it, one of the grandest things ever written with pen.—*Thomas Carlyle*

2816   The Bible is a window in this prison-world, through which we may look into eternity—*Timothy Dwight*

2817   The English Bible—a book which, if everything else in our language should perish, would alone suffice to show the whole extent of its beauty and power.—*Thomas B. Macaulay*

Biography

2818   Biography is the only true history.—*Carlyle*

2819   Every great man nowadays has his disciples, and it is always Judas who writes the biography.—*Oscar Wilde*

Books

2820   All that Mankind has done, thought, gained or been: it is lying as in magic preservation in the pages of books. They are the chosen possession of men.—*Carlyle*

2821   Everywhere I have sought rest and found it not except sitting apart in a nook with a little book.—*Thomas Kempis*

2822   As good almost kill a man as kill a good book: who kills a man kills a reasonable creature, God's image; but he who destroys a good book kills reason itself, kills the image of God, as it were, in the eye.—*Milton*

Bore

2823   Society is now one polished horde,
Formed of two mighty tribes, the *Bores* and *Bored*.
—*Lord Byron*

2824   He says a thousand pleasant things,—
But never says "Adieu."—*J.G. Saxe*

Brevity

2825   This is the short and the long of it.—*Shakespeare*

2826   Brevity is the soul of wit.—*Shakespeare*

Bribery

2827   Few men have virtue to withstand the highest bidder.—*George Washington*

Business

2828   We demand that big business give people a square deal; in return we must insist that when anyone engaged in big business honestly endeavors to do right, he shall himself be given a square deal.—*Theodore Roosevelt*

2829   The greatest meliorator of the world is selfish, huckstering trade.—*Emerson*

2830   It is a socialist idea that making profits is a vice. I consider the real vice is making losses.—*Sir Winston Churchill*

2831   To my mind the best investment a young man starting out in business could possibly make is to give all his time, all his energies to work, just plain, hard work.—*C.M. Schwab*

Care

2832   The night shall be filled with music
And the cares that infest the day
Shall fold their tents like the Arabs,
And as silently steal away.—*Longfellow*

Caution

2833   Little boats should keep near shore.—*Franklin*

2834   Caution is the eldest child of wisdom.—*Victor Hugo*

Change

2835   The world goes up and the world goes down,
And the sunshine follows the rain;
And yesterday's sneer and yesterday's frown
Can never come over again.—*Charles Kingsley*

Character

2836   The end of a dissolute life is, most commonly, a desperate death.—*Bion*

2837   It is hardly respectable to be good nowadays.—*Edith Sitwell*

2838   We boil at different degrees.—*Emerson*

2839   Condemn the fault, and not the actor of it?—*Shakespeare*

2840   Make it thy business to know thyself, which is the most difficult lesson in the world.—*Cervantes*

2841   Be such a man, and live such a life, that if every man were such as you, and every life a life like yours, this earth would be God's Paradise.—*Phillips Brooks*

2842   I would to God thou and I knew where a commodity of good names were to be bought.—*Shakespeare*

2843   Smooth runs the water where the brook is deep.—*Shakespeare*

2844   To reform a man, you must begin with his grandmother.—*Victor Hugo*

2845   He has a face like a benediction.—*Cervantes*

2846   What the heart has once owned and had, it shall never lose.—*H.W. Beecher*

2847   The holiest of all holidays are those kept by ourselves in silence and apart, the secret anniversaries of the heart, when the full tide of feeling overflows.—*Longfellow*

2848   Envy's memory is nothing but a row of hooks to hang up grudges on. Some people's sensibility is a mere bundle of aversions; and you hear them display and parade it, not in recounting the things they are attached to, but in telling you how many things and persons "they cannot bear."—*John Foster*

2849   The hardest trial of the heart is, whether it can bear a rival's failure without triumph.—*Aikin*

2850   Our deeds still travel with us from afar,
And what we have been makes us what we are.

—George Eliot

2851   Secret, and self-contained, and solitary as an oyster.—*Charles Dickens*

2852   Be and continue poor, young man, while others around you grow rich by fraud and disloyalty; be without place or power, while others beg their way upward; bear the pain of disappointed hopes, while others gain the accomplishment of theirs by flattery; forego the gracious pressure of the hand for which others cringe and crawl. Wrap yourself in your own virtue, and seek a friend and your daily bread. If you have in such a course grown gray with unblenched honor, bless God, and die.—*Heinzelmann*

2853   Talents are best nurtured in solitude; character is best formed in the stormy billows of the world.—*Goethe*

2854   Our character is but the stamp on our souls of the free choices of good and evil we have made through life.—*Geikie*

2855   In the destiny of every moral being there is an object more worthy of God than happiness.—It is character.—And the grand aim of man's creation is the development of a grand character—and grand character is, by its very nature, the product of probationary discipline.—*Austin Phelps*

2856   Leaves seem light, useless, idle, wavering and changeable—they even dance; yet God has made them part of the oak.—So he has given us a lesson, not to deny stout-heartedness within, because we see lightsomeness without.—*Leigh Hunt*

Charity

2857   My poor are my best patients. God pays for them.—*Boerhaave*

2858   He who waits to do a great deal of good at once, will never do anything.—*Samuel Johnson*

Children

2859   Children are the anchors that hold a mother to life.—*Sophocles*

2860   How sharper than a serpent's tooth it is to have a thankless child!—*Shakespeare*

2861   If I could get to the highest place in Athens, I would lift up my voice and say: "What mean ye, fellow citizens, that ye turn every stone to scrape wealth together, and take so little care of your children, to whom ye must one day relinquish all?"—*Socrates*

2862   Childhood has no forebodings; but then it is soothed by no memories of outlived sorrow.—*George Eliot*

2863   The first duty to children is to make them happy.—If you have not made them so, you have wronged them.—No other good they may get can make up for that.—*C. Buxton*

Choice

2864   There's small choice in rotten apples.—*Shakespeare*

2865   The question is this: Is man an ape or an angel? I, my lord, I am on the side of the angels.—*Disraeli*

Christ

2866   If the life and death of Socrates were those of a sage, the life and death of Jesus were those of a God.—*J.-J. Rousseau*

Civilization

2867   3 Fish.: "Master, I marvel how the fishes live in the sea." 1 Fish.: "Why, as men do a-land: the great ones eat up the little ones."—*Shakespeare*

2868   Better fifty years of Europe than a cycle of Cathay.—*Tennyson*

2869   Yet I doubt not through the ages one increasing purpose runs,
And the thoughts of men are widened with the process of the suns.—*Tennyson*

2870   The history of the world is the record of man in quest of his daily bread and butter.—*Hendrik Willem Van Loon*

2871   A conviction that what is called fashionable life was compound of frivolity, of fraud and vice.—*Disraeli*

2872   Ring in the nobler modes of life with sweeter manners, purer laws.—*Tennyson*

2873   Ring out old shapes of foul disease,
Ring out the narrowing lust of gold;
Ring out the thousand wars of old,
Ring in the thousand years of peace!—*Tennyson*

2874   The true test of civilization is, not the census, nor the size of cities, nor the crops, but the kind of man that the country turns out.— *Emerson*

2875   No true civilization can be expected permanently to continue which is not based on the great principles of Christianity.—*Tryon Edwards*

Clothes

2876   Good clothes open all doors.—*Thomas Fuller*

2877   She wears her clothes as if they were thrown on her with a pitchfork.—*Jonathan Swift*

Common Sense

2878   Good health and good sense are two of life's greatest blessings. —*Publius Syrus*

2879   Common sense does not ask an impossible chessboard, but takes the one before it and plays the game.—*Wendell Phillips*

Communism

2880   The theory of Communism may be summed up in one sentence: Abolish all private property.—*Karl Marx and Friedrich Engels*

2881   Communism is the exploitation of the strong by the weak. In Communism, inequality springs from placing mediocrity on a level with excellence.—*Proudhon*

Conceit

2882   He who is always his own counsellor will often have a fool for his client.—*Hunter*

2883   He was like a cock who thought the sun had risen to hear him crow.—*George Eliot*

2884   I am not in the roll of common men.—*Shakespeare*

2885   An egotist is a man who talks so much about himself that he gives me no time to talk about myself.—*H.L. Wayland*

2886   Conceit in weakest bodies strongest works.—*Shakespeare*

2887   Truly, this world can get on without us, if we would but think so.—*Longfellow*

Conduct

2888　We are growing serious, and, let me tell you, that's the very next step to being dull.—*Addison*

2889　Sometimes we may learn more from a man's errors, than from his virtues.—*Longfellow*

2890　It is not enough that you form, and even follow the most excellent rules for conducting yourself in the world; you must, also, know when to deviate from them, and where lies the exception.—*Greville*

2891　A bone to the dog is not charity. Charity is the bone shared with the dog, when you are just as hungry as the dog.—*Jack London*

Conquest

2892　I came, I saw, I conquered.—*Julius Caesar*

2893　Self-conquest is the greatest of victories.—*Plato*

Conscience

2894　A guilty conscience never feels secure.—*Publius Syrus*

2895　Guilty consciences always make people cowards.—*Pilpay*

2896　A peace above all earthly dignities, a still and quiet conscience. —*Shakespeare*

2897　Conscience is merely your own judgment of the right or wrong of our actions, and so can never be a safe guide unless enlightened by the word of God.—*Tryon Edwards*

2898　There is no class of men so difficult to be managed in a state as those whose intentions are honest, but whose consciences are bewitched. —*Napoleon I*

2899　It is astonishing how soon the whole conscience begins to unravel if a single stitch drops.—One single sin indulged in makes a hole you could put your head through.—*C. Buxton*

Conservatism

2900　A statesman who is enamored of existing evils, as distinguished from the Liberal, who wishes to replace them with others.—*Ambrose Bierce*

Contentment

2901　Poor and content is rich and rich enough.—*Shakespeare*

2902   The despotism of custom is on the wane.—We are not content to know that things are; we ask whether they ought to be.—*J.S. Mill*

2903   One should be either sad or joyful. Contentment is a warm sty for eaters and sleepers.—*Eugene O'Neill*

2904   Since we cannot get what we like, let us like what we can get.— *Spanish Proverb*

Conversation

2905   His words, like so many nimble and airy servitors, trip about him at command.—*John Milton*

2906   Let thy speech be better than silence, or be silent.—*Dionysius the Elder*

2907   Gratiano speaks an infinite deal of nothing; his reasons are as two grains of wheat hid in two bushels of chaff; you shall seek all day ere you find them, and when you have them they are not worth the search.—*Shakespeare*

2908   Know how to listen, and you will profit even from those who talk badly.—*Plutarch*

2909   Men of few words are the best men.—*Shakespeare*

2910   Language is the dress of thought.—*Samuel Johnson*

2911   And when you stick on conversation's burrs,
             Don't strew your pathway with those dreadful urs.
                                      —*Oliver Wendell Holmes*

2912   A kind of excellent dumb discourse.—*Shakespeare*

Courage

2913   We should do by our cunning as we do by our courage,—always have it ready to defend ourselves, never to offend others.—*Greville*

2914   Cowards do not count in battle; they are there, but not in it.— *Euripides*

2915   Courage is grace under pressure.—*Ernest Hemingway*

2916   No man is worth his salt who is not ready at all times to risk his body . . . to risk his well-being . . . to risk his life . . . in a great cause. —*T. Roosevelt*

2917   For courage mounteth with occasion.—*Shakespeare*

2918   The better part of valour is discretion.—*Shakespeare*

2919   I will utter what I believe today, if it should contradict all I said yesterday.—*Wendell Phillips*

2920   No man can answer for his own valor or courage, till he has been in danger.—*La Rochefoucauld*

2921   The brave man is not he who feels no fear, for that were stupid and irrational; but he whose noble soul subdues its fear, and bravely dares the danger nature shrinks from.—*Joanna Baillie*

2922   At the bottom of a good deal of the bravery that appears in the world there lurks a miserable cowardice.—Men will face powder and steel because they cannot face public opinion.—*E.H. Chapin*

Create

2923   Originality is nothing but judicious imitation.—The most original writers borrowed one from another. The instruction we find in books is like fire. We fetch it from our neighbor's, kindle it at home, communicate it to others, and it becomes the property of all.—*Voltaire*

2924   It is better to create than to be learned; creating is the true essence of life.—*Niebuhr*

2925   If you would create something, you must be something.—*Goethe*

Crime

2926   Punishment is lame, but it comes.—*Herbert*

2927   Those who are themselves incapable of great crimes, are ever backward to suspect others.—*La Rochefoucauld*

2928   The devil knoweth his own, and is a particularly bad paymaster. —*F.M. Crawford*

2929   The consequences of our crimes long survive their commission, and, like the ghosts of the murdered, forever haunt the steps of the malefactor.—*Sir Walter Scott*

2930   Nor florid prose, nor honied lines of rhyme,
            Can blazon evil deeds, or consecrate a crime.—*Byron*

Criticism

2931   Sarcasm is the language of the devil; for which reason I have long since as good as renounced it.—*Carlyle*

2932   The pleasure of criticism takes from us that of being deeply moved by very beautiful things.—*La Bruyère*

2933   If we had no failings ourselves, we should not take so much pleasure in finding out those of others.—*La Rochefoucauld*

2934   There is an unfortunate disposition in man to attend much more to the faults of his companions that offend him, than to their perfections which please him.—*Greville*

2935   Endeavor to be always patient of the faults and imperfections of others; for thou hast many faults and imperfections of thine own that require forbearance. If thou are not able to make thyself that which thou wishest, how canst thou expect to mold another in conformity to thy will?—*Thomas à Kempis*

2936   For I am nothing, if not critical.—*Shakespeare*

2937   Animals are such agreeable friends—they ask no questions, they pass no criticisms.—*George Eliot*

Curiosity

2938   Where necessity ends, desire and curiosity begin; no sooner are we supplied with everything nature can demand, than we sit down to contrive artificial appetites.—*S. Johnson*

Death

2939   Out of the jaws of death.—*Shakespeare*

2940   He that dies pays all debts.—*Shakespeare*

2941   When death, the great reconciler, has come, it is never our tenderness that we repent of, but our severity.—*George Eliot*

2942   Let's talk of graves, of worms, and epitaphs.—*Shakespeare*

2943   Did any man at his death, ever regret his conflicts with himself, his victories over appetite, his scorn of impure pleasure, or his sufferings for righteousness' sake?—*W.E. Channing*

2944   But oh for the touch of a vanished hand,
            And the sound of a voice that is still!—*Tennyson*

2945   Each in his narrow cell forever laid, the rude forefathers of the hamlet sleep.—*Thomas Gray*

2946   Cowards die many times before their deaths; the valiant never taste of death but once.—*Shakespeare*

2947   Dear as remembered kisses after death.—*Tennyson*

2948   Vicissitude of fortune which spares neither man nor the proudest of his works, but buries empires and cities in a common grave.—*Gibbon*

2949   Why fear death? It is the most beautiful adventure in life.— *Charles Frohman*

2950   Man wants but little, nor that little long. How soon must he resign his very dust, which frugal nature lent him for an hour.—*Young*

2951   The boast of heraldry, the pomp of pow'r, and all that beauty, all that wealth e'er gave, await alike the inevitable hour; the paths of glory lead but to the grave.—*Gray*

2952   In every parting, there is an image of death.—*George Eliot*

2953   Who knows but life be that which men call death, and death what men call life?—*Euripides*

2954   I know of but one remedy against the fear of death that is effectual and that will stand the test either of a sick-bed or of a sound mind— that is, a good life, a clear conscience, an honest heart, and a well-ordered conversation; to carry the thoughts of dying men about us, and so to live before we die as we shall wish we had when we come to it.— *Norris*

2955   Death has nothing terrible which life has not made so. A faithful Christian life in this world is the best preparation for the next.—*Tryon Edwards*

2956   A dislike of death is no proof of the want of religion. The instincts of nature shrink from it, for no creature can like its own dissolution.—But though death is not desired, the result of it may be, for dying to the Christian is the way to life eternal.—*W. Jay*

2957   Time for him had merged itself into eternity; he was, as we say, no more.—*Thomas Carlyle*

2958   The grave buries every error, covers every defect, extinguishes every resentment.—From its peaceful bosom spring none but fond regrets and tender recollections.—Who can look down upon the grave of an enemy, and not feel a compunctious throb that he should have warred with the poor handful of dust that lies moldering before him.—*Washington Irving*

Debt

2959   If you want the time to pass quickly, just give your note for 90 days.—*R.B. Thomas*

Deception

2960   Half the work that is done in the world is to make things appear what they are not.—*E.R. Beadle*

2961   The very essence of assumed gravity is design, and consequently deceit; a taught trick to gain credit with the world for more sense and knowledge than a man is worth.—*Laurence Sterne*

2962   The cunning livery of hell.—*Shakespeare*

2963   It is a shameful and unseemly thing to think one thing and speak another, but how odious to write one thing and think another.—*Seneca*

2964   It goes far toward making a man faithful to let him understand that you think him so; and he that does but suspect I will deceive him, gives me a sort of right to do it.—*Seneca*

Decision

2965   Decision of character will often give to an inferior mind command over a superior.—*W. Wirt*

2966   Tomorrow I will live, the fool does say: today itself's too late; the wise lived yesterday.—*Martial*

Deeds

2967   We have left undone those things which we ought to have done; and we have done those things which we ought not to have done.—*Book of Common Prayer*

Defeat

2968   What is defeat? Nothing but education, nothing but the first step to something better.—*Wendell Phillips*

Desire

2969   Our desires always increase with our possessions. The knowledge that something remains yet unenjoyed impairs our enjoyment of the good before us.—*Samuel Johnson*

2970   There are two tragedies in life. One is not to get your heart's desire. The other is to get it.—*George Bernard Shaw*

Determination

2971   I'll not budge an inch.—*Shakespeare*

2972   The best lightning-rod for your protection is your own spine.—*Emerson*

2973   Man has his will,—but woman has her way.—*O. W. Holmes*

2974   He who is firm and resolute in will moulds the world to himself. —*Goethe*

2975   Either I will find a way, or I will make one.—*Sir Philip Sidney*

2976   The truest wisdom, in general, is a resolute determination.—*Napoleon I*

2977   Toil, feel, think, hope; you will be sure to dream enough before you die, without arranging for it.—*J. Sterling*

Discontent

2978   Discontent is the first step in the progress of a man or a nation.—*Wilde*

Doing

2979   Do not then be afraid of defeat.—You are never so near to victory as when defeated in a good cause.—*H. W. Beecher*

2980   None are so busy as the fool and knave.—*John Dryden*

2981   If to do were as easy as to know what were good to do, chapels had been churches, and poor men's cottages princes' palaces.—*Shakespeare*

2982   Our grand business is not to see what lies dimly in the distance, but to do what lies clearly at hand.—*Carlyle*

2983   Doing is the great thing. For if resolutely, people do what is right, in time they come to like doing it.—*Ruskin*

Doubt

2984   Our doubts are traitors
        And make us lose the good we oft might win
        By fearing to attempt.—*Shakespeare*

Duty

2985   He on whom Heaven confers a sceptre knows not the weight till he bears it.—*Corneille*

2986   I do perceive here a divided duty.—*Shakespeare*

2987   Every duty which we omit, obscures some truth which we should have known.—*Ruskin*

2988   We live in a world which is full of misery and ignorance, and the plain duty of each and all of us is to try to make the little corner he can influence somewhat less miserable and somewhat less ignorant than it was before he entered it.—*Huxley*

2989   An ambassador is an honest man sent to lie and intrigue abroad for the benefit of his country.—*Sir H. Wotton*

2990   Not once or twice in our rough-island story
              The path of duty was the way to glory.—*Tennyson*

Earnestness

2991   Earnestness is the salt of eloquence.—*V. Hugo*

2992   Earnestness is enthusiasm tempered by reason.—*Pascal*

Economy

2993   Socrates said, "Those who want fewest things are nearest to the gods."—*Diogenes Laertius*

2994   He seldom lives frugally who lives by chance. Hope is always liberal, and they that trust her promises make little scruple of revelling today on the profits of tomorrow.—*Johnson*

2995   A sound economy is a sound understanding brought into action. It is calculation realized; it is the doctrine of proportion reduced to practice; it is foreseeing contingencies and providing against them; it is expecting contingencies and being prepared for them.—*Hannah More*

2996   Nothing is cheap which is superfluous, for what one does not need, is dear at a penny.—*Plutarch*

2997   There are but two ways of paying a debt; increase of industry in raising income, or increase of thrift in laying out.—*Carlyle*

Education

2998   There is a time in every man's education when he arrives at the conviction that envy is ignorance; that imitation is suicide; that he must take himself for better, for worse, as his portion; that though the wide universe is full of good, no kernel of nourishing corn comes to him but through his toil bestowed on that plot of ground which is given him to till. The power which resides in him is new in nature, and none but he knows what that is which he can do, nor does he know until he has tried. —*Emerson*

2999   Aristotle said that education was an ornament in prosperity and a refuge in adversity.—*Diogenes Laertius*

3000   The great end of education is, to discipline rather than to furnish the mind; to train it to the use of its own powers, rather than fill it with the accumulations of others.—*Tryon Edwards*

3001   He is to be educated not because he is to make shoes, nails, and pins, but because he is a man.—*Channing*

3002   Culture is "To know the best that has been said and thought in the world."—*Matthew Arnold*

3003   A mixture of misery and education is highly explosive.—*Herbert Samuel*

3004   Out of monuments, names, words, proverbs, traditions, private records and evidences, fragments of stories, passages of books and the like, we do save and recover somewhat from the deluge of time.—*Bacon*

3005   The real object of education is to give children resources that will endure as long as life endures; habits that time will ameliorate, not destroy; occupations that will render sickness tolerable, solitude pleasant, age venerable, life more dignified and useful, and death less terrible.—*Sidney Smith*

3006   All who have meditated on the art of governing mankind have been convinced that the fate of empires depends on the education of youth.—*Aristotle*

Eloquence

3007   Eloquence is the child of knowledge.—*Disraeli*

3008   The manner of speaking is full as important as the matter, as more people have ears to be tickled than understandings to judge.—*Chesterfield*

Enemy

3009   Observe thyself as thy greatest enemy would do, so shalt thou be thy greatest friend.—*Jeremy Taylor*

3010   He makes no friend who never made a foe.—*Tennyson*

3011   If we could read the secret history of our enemies, we should find in each man's life sorrow and suffering enough to disarm all hostility.—*Longfellow*

3012   It is much safer to reconcile an enemy than to conquer him; victory may deprive him of his poison, but reconciliation of his will.—*Feltham*

3013   However rich or powerful a man may be, it is the height of folly to make personal enemies; for one unguarded moment may yield you to the revenge of the most despicable of mankind.—*Lyttleton*

3014   If you want enemies, excel others; if friends, let others excel you.
—*Colton*

Enthusiasm

3015   Violent zeal even for truth has a hundred to one odds to be either petulancy, ambition, or pride.—*Swift*

3016   Every production of genius must be the production of enthusiasm.
—*Disraeli*

3017   Every man is enthusiastic at times. One man has enthusiasm for thirty minutes—another man has it for thirty days, but it is the man who has it for thirty years who makes a success in life.—*Edward B. Butler*

Equality

3018   Your levelers wish to level *down* as far as themselves; but they cannot bear leveling *up* to themselves.—*Samuel Johnson*

3019   As men, we are all equal in the presence of death.—*Publius Syrus*

Error

3020   When every one is in the wrong, every one is in the right.—*La Chaussée*

3021   The man who makes no mistakes does not usually make anything.—*Edward J. Phelps*

Evil

3022   He will give the devil his due.—*Shakespeare*

3023   The devil can cite Scripture for his purpose.—*Shakespeare*

3024   The world is grown so bad, that wrens make prey where eagles dare not perch.—*Shakespeare*

3025   All the perfumes of Arabia will not sweeten this little hand.—*Shakespeare*

3026   There is some soul of goodness in things evil, would men observingly distil it out.—*Shakespeare*

3027   There is this good in real evils,—they deliver us, while they last, from the petty despotism of all that were imaginary.—*Colton*

Example

3028   I am a part of all that I have met.—*Tennyson*

3029   My advice is, to consult the lives of other men as we would a looking-glass, and from thence fetch examples for our own imitation.—*Terence*

3030   If you would convince a man that he does wrong, do right. Men will believe what they see. Let them see.—*Thoreau*

3031   Man is an imitative creature, and whoever is foremost leads the herd.—*Schiller*

3032   People seldom improve when they have no other model but themselves to copy after.—*Goldsmith*

3033   No man was ever great by imitation.—*Samuel Johnson*

3034   No man is so insignificant as to be sure his example can do no hurt.—*Lord Clarendon*

3035   We are all of us more or less echoes, repeating involuntarily the virtues, the defects, the movements, and the characters of those among whom we live.—*Joubert*

Experience

3036   I had rather have a fool to make me merry than experience to make me sad.—*Shakespeare*

3037   You take all the experience and judgment of men over 50 out of the world and there wouldn't be enough left to run it.—*Henry Ford*

3038   I know the past, and thence will assay to glean a warning for the future, so that man may profit by his errors, and derive experience from his folly.—*Shelley*

3039   There is no merit where there is no trial; and till experience stamps the mark of strength, cowards may pass for heroes, and faith for falsehood.—*A. Hill*

3040   No man was ever endowed with a judgment so correct and judicious, but that circumstances, time, and experience, would teach him something new, and apprise him that of those things with which he thought himself the best acquainted, he knew nothing; and that those ideas which in theory appeared the most advantageous were found, when brought into practice, to be altogether impracticable.—*Terence*

Eyes

3041   Eyes will not see when the heart wishes them to be blind.—
Desire conceals truth, as darkness does the earth.—*Seneca*

Faith

3042   For they conquer who believe they can.—*Virgil*

3043   Howe'er it be, it seems to me,
                'Tis only noble to be good.
                Kind hearts are more than coronets,
                And simple faith than Norman blood.—*Tennyson*

3044   Here I stand; I can do no otherwise. God help me. Amen!—
Martin Luther

3045   It is cynicism and fear that freeze life; it is faith that thaws it
out, releases it, sets it free.—*Harry Emerson Fosdick*

3046   When faith is lost, and honors dies, the man is dead.—*John G.
Whittier*

3047   Fanatic faith, once wedded fast to some dear falsehood, hugs it
to the last.—*Moore*

3048   Goodness thinks no ill where no ill seems.—*Milton*

3049   Strike from mankind the principle of faith, and men would have
no more history than a flock of sheep.—*Bulwer*

3050   All the scholastic scaffolding falls, as a ruined edifice, before one
single word—faith.—*Napoleon I*

3051   Faith in order, which is the basis of science, cannot reasonably
be separated from faith in an ordainer, which is the basis of religion.—
Asa Gray

Falsehood

3052   A lie never lives to be old.—*Sophocles*

3053   Lie not, neither to thyself, nor man, nor God.—It is for cowards
to lie.—*Herbert.*

3054   The practice of politics in the East may be defined by one word—
dissimulation.—*Disraeli*

3055   The most terrible of lies is not that which is uttered but that
which is lived.—*W. G. Clarke*

3056   Never chase a lie; if you let it alone, it will soon run itself to death.—You can work out a good character faster than calumny can destroy it.—*E. Nott*

3057   A liar should have a good memory.—*Quintilian*

Fame

3058   Toil, says the proverb, is the sire of fame.—*Euripides*

3059   Those who despise fame seldom deserve it.—We are apt to undervalue the purchase we cannot reach, to conceal our poverty the better.—It is a spark that kindles upon the best fuel, and burns brightest in the bravest breast.—*Jeremy Collier*

3060   To judge of the real importance of an individual, we should think of the effect his death would produce.—*Levis*

3061   How men long for celebrity!—Some would willingly sacrifice their lives for fame, and not a few would rather be known by their crimes than not known at all.—*Sinclair*

3062   Our admiration of a famous man lessens upon our nearer acquaintance with him; and we seldom hear of a celebrated person without a catalogue of some of his weaknesses and infirmities.—*Addison*

Family

3063   Who serves his country well has no need of ancestors.—*F. Voltaire*

3064   As are families, so is society. If well ordered, well instructed, and well governed, they are the springs from which go forth the streams of national greatness and prosperity—of civil order and public happiness.—*Thayer*

3065   It is a wise father that knows his own child.—*Shakespeare*

3066   A man cannot leave a better legacy to the world than a well-educated family.—*Thomas Scott*

3067   It is indeed a desirable thing to be well descended, but the glory belongs to our ancestors.—*Plutarch*

3068   Every man is his own ancestor, and every man is his own heir. He devises his own future; and he inherits his own past.—*H. F. Hedge*

3069   Mere family never made a man great.—Thought and deed, not pedigree, are the passports to enduring fame.—*Skobeleff*

Farming

3070   Those who labor in the earth are the chosen people of God, if He ever had a chosen people, whose breasts He has made His peculiar deposit for substantial and genuine virtue.—*Jefferson*

3071   A farmer is always going to be rich next year.—*Philemon*

Fashion

3072   Fashion is a form of ugliness so intolerable that we have to alter it every six months.—*Wilde*

Fault

3073   When a man is wrong and won't admit it, he always gets angry.—*Haliburton*

3074   The absent are never without fault, nor the present without excuse.—*Franklin*

3075   Men do not suspect faults which they do not commit.—*Samuel Johnson*

3076   But friend, to me
He is all fault who hath no fault at all.
For who loves me must have a touch of earth.—*Tennyson*

Fear

3077   No one loves the man whom he fears.—*Aristotle*

3078   One of the greatest artifices the devil uses to engage men in vice and debauchery, is to fasten names of contempt on certain virtues, and thus fill weak souls with a foolish fear of passing for scrupulous, should they desire to put them in practice.—*Blaise Pascal*

3079   The two great movers of the human mind are the desire of good, and the fear of evil.—*Johnson*

3080   They are slaves who fear to speak
For the fallen and the weak.—*J. R. Lowell*

3081   They are slaves who dare not be
In the right with two or three.—*J. R. Lowell*

Flag

3082   Let it rise! let it rise, till it meet the sun in his coming: let the earliest light of the morning gild it, and the parting day linger and play on its summit.—*Daniel Webster*

Flattery

3083   If we would not flatter ourselves, the flattery of others could not harm us.—*La Rochefoucauld*

3084   When our vices quit us, we flatter ourselves with the belief that it is we who quit them.—*La Rochefoucauld*

Flowers

3085   Flowers have an expression of countenance as much as men or animals. Some seem to smile; some have a sad expression; some are pensive and diffident; others again are plain, honest and upright, like the broad-faced sunflower and the hollyhock.—*H. W. Beecher*

Folly

3086   He has spent all his life in letting down empty buckets into empty wells, and he is frittering away his age in trying to draw them up again.— *Sydney Smith*

Food

3087   He hath eaten me out of house and home.—*Shakespeare*

3088   One meal a day is enough for a lion, and it ought to be for a man.—*G. Fordyce*

3089   They are as sick that surfeit with too much, as they that starve with nothing.—*Shakespeare*

Fools

3090   As if anything were so common as ignorance! The multitude of fools is a protection to the wise.—*Cicero*

3091   Fortune, to show us her power, and abate our presumption, seeing she could not make fools wise, has made them fortunate.— *Montaigne*

3092   Ridicule is the first and last argument of fools.—*C. Simmons*

3093   A fool flatters himself; the wise man flatters the fool.—*Bulwer*

3094   In all companies there are more fools than wise men, and the greater part always gets the better of the wiser.—*Rabelais*

3095   Young men think old men fools, and old men know young men to be so.—*Metcalf*

3096   Haint we got all the fools in town on our side? And ain't that a big enough majority in any town?—*Mark Twain*

3097   A learned fool is more foolish than an ignorant fool.—*Molière*

3098   He who thinks himself wise, O heavens! is a great fool.—*Voltaire*

Forgiveness

3099   It is easier for the generous to forgive, than for the offender to ask forgiveness.—*Thomson*

3100   They who forgive most, shall be most forgiven.—*Bailey*

3101   Nothing in this lost and ruined world bears the meek impress of the Son of God so surely as forgiveness.—*Alice Cary*

Forgotten

3102   Who is the Forgotten Man? He is the clean, quiet, virtuous, domestic citizen, who pays his debts and his taxes and is never heard of out of his little circle.—*William Graham Sumner*

Fortune

3103   Fortune is not on the side of the faint-hearted.—*Sophocles*

3104   Fortune is like glass, the brighter the glitter, the more easily broken.—*Publius Syrus*

3105   There is a tide in the affairs of men
Which taken at the flood, leads on to fortune:
Omitted, all the voyage of their life
Is bound in shallows and in miseries.—*Shakespeare*

Frankness

3106   There are few, very few, that will own themselves in a mistake.
—*Swift*

3107   I can promise to be candid, though I may not be impartial.—*Goethe*

Freedom

3108   The cause of freedom is the cause of God.—*Samuel Bowles*

3109   Personal liberty is the paramount essential to human dignity and human happiness.—*Bulwer-Lytton*

Friendship

3110   What you dislike in another, take care to correct in yourself.—*Sprat*

3111　Reprove thy friend privately; commend him publicly.—*Solon*

3112　The greatest comfort of my old age, and that which gives me the highest satisfaction, is the pleasing remembrance of the many benefits and friendly offices I have done to others.—*Cato*

3113　We gain nothing by being with such as ourselves: we encourage each other in mediocrity.—I am always longing to be with men more excellent than myself.—*Charles Lamb*

3114　If a man does not make new acquaintances as he advances through life, he will soon find himself left alone; one should keep his friendships in constant repair.—*Johnson*

3115　Thou mayest be sure that he that will in private tell thee of thy faults, is thy friend, for he adventures thy dislike, and doth hazard thy hatred; there are few men that can endure it, every man for the most part delighting in self-praise, which is one of the most universal follies that bewitcheth mankind.—*Sir Walter Raleigh*

3116　We take care of our health, we lay up money, we make our roof tight and our clothing sufficient, but who provides wisely that he shall not be wanting in the best property of all—friends?—*Emerson*

Future

3117　When all else is lost, the future still remains.—*Bovee*

3118　The present is great with the future.—*Leibnitz*

Genius

3119　The true genius is a mind of large general powers, accidentally determined to some particular direction.—*Samuel Johnson*

3120　Doing easily what others find difficult is talent; doing what is impossible for talent is genius.—*Henri-Frédéric Amiel*

3121　Every man who observes vigilantly, and resolves steadfastly, grows unconsciously into genius.—*Bulwer*

3122　Times of general calamity and confusion have ever been productive of the greatest minds. The purest ore is produced from the hottest furnace, and the brightest thunderbolt is elicited from the darkest storm. —*Colton*

3123　There is no great genius without tincture of madness.—*Seneca*

3124　Men give me credit for some genius. All the genius I have lies in this: When I have a subject in hand, I study it profoundly. Day and night it is before me. My mind becomes pervaded with it. Then the effort which I have made is what people are pleased to call the fruit of genius. It is the fruit of labor and thought.—*Alexander Hamilton*

Gentlemen

3125   Good manners are made up of petty sacrifices.—*Emerson*

3126   Men of courage, men of sense, and men of letters are frequent: but a true gentleman is what one seldom sees.—*Steele*

3127   Good-breeding shows itself most, where to an ordinary eye it appears the least.—*Addison*

Giving

3128   Give what you have. To some one it may be better than you dare to think.—*Longfellow*

3129   There was a man, though some did count him mad,
The more he cast away the more he had.—*John Bunyan*

3130   Shall we call ourselves benevolent, when the gifts we bestow do not cost us a single privation?—*Degerando*

3131   He who is not liberal with what he has, does not deceive himself when he thinks he would be liberal if he had more.—*W. S. Plumer*

God

3132   A mighty fortress is our God,
A bulwark never failing;
Our helper He amid the flood
Of mortal ills prevailing.—*Martin Luther*

3133   Though the mills of God grind slowly, yet they grind exceeding small;
Though with patience He stands waiting, with exactness grinds He all.—*Friedrich Von Logau*

3134   That is best which God sends; it was his will; it is mine.—*O. Meredith*

3135   There's a divinity that shapes our ends, rough-hew them how we will.—*Shakespeare*

3136   The world is God's epistle to mankind—his thoughts are flashing upon us from every direction.—*Plato*

3137   God tempers the wind to the shorn lamb.—*Sterne*

3138   One on God's side is a majority.—*Wendell Phillips*

3139   Anything that makes religion a second object makes it no object.
—He who offers to God a second place offers him no place.—*Ruskin*

3140   How often we look upon God as our last and feeblest resource!
We go to Him because we have nowhere else to go. And then we learn
that the storms of life have driven us, not upon the rocks, but into the
desired haven.—*George Macdonald*

3141   Two men please God—who serves Him with all his heart because he knows Him; who seeks Him with all his heart because he knows
Him not.—*Panin*

Gossip

3142   We cannot control the evil tongues of others; but a good life
enables us to disregard them.—*Cato*

3143   Done to death by slanderous tongues.—*Shakespeare*

3144   And there's a lust in man no charm can tame
             Of loudly publishing our neighbor's shame;
             On eagles' wings immortal scandals fly,
             While virtuous actions are but born and die.—*Stephen Harvey*

Government

3145   Democracy is based upon the conviction that there are extraordinary possibilities in ordinary people.—*Harry Emerson Fosdick*

3146   As I sat opposite the Treasury Bench, the Ministers reminded me
of those marine landscapes not unusual on the coasts of South America.
You behold a range of exhausted volcanoes.—*Disraeli*

3147   Freedom of religion, freedom of the press, and freedom of person
under the protection of the habeas corpus, these are principles that have
guided our steps through an age of revolution and reformation.—*Jefferson*

3148   A State to prosper, must be built on foundations of a moral
character; and this character is the principal element of its strength and
the only guaranty of its permanence and prosperity.—*J. Currie*

3149   The greater the power the more dangerous the abuse.—*Edmund
Burke*

3150   What is the best government?—That which teaches us to govern
ourselves.—*Goethe*

3151   Every wanton and causeless restraint of the will of the subject, whether practised by a monarch, a nobility, or a popular assembly, is a degree of tyranny.—*William Blackstone*

3152   The four pillars of government . . . religion, justice, counsel and treasure.—*Francis Bacon*

3153   In that fierce light which beats upon a throne.—*Tennyson*

3154   A man must first govern himself ere he is fit to govern a family; and his family ere he be fit to bear the government of the commonwealth. —*Sir W. Raleigh*

3155   Our rulers will best promote the improvement of the nation by strictly confining themselves to their own legitimate duties, by leaving capital to find its most lucrative course, commodities their fair price, industry and intelligence their natural reward, idleness and folly their natural punishment, by maintaining peace, by defending property and by observing strict economy in every department of the state. Let the Government do this—the people will assuredly do the rest.—*Thomas Babington Macaulay*

Gratitude

3156   Ingratitude, thou marble-hearted fiend!—*Shakespeare*

3157   Most men remember obligations, but not often to be grateful; the proud are made sour by the remembrance and the vain silent.—*Simms*

3158   It is generally true that all that is required to make men unmindful of what they owe to God for any blessing, is, that they should receive that blessing often and regularly.—*Whately*

3159   He who receives a benefit should never forget it; he who bestows should never remember it.—*Charron*

Greatness

3160   The way of a superior man is threefold; virtuous, he is free from anxieties; wise, he is free from perplexities; bold, he is free from fear.— *Confucius*

3161   From the sublime to the ridiculous there is but one step.— *Napoleon I*

3162   The mightiest powers by deepest calms are fed.—*B. W. Procter*

3163   No man is so great as mankind.—*Theodore Parker*

3164   Let him that would move the world, first move himself.—*Socrates*

3165 In the heraldry of heaven goodness precedes greatness, and so on earth it is more powerful.—The lowly and lovely may often do more good in their limited sphere than the gifted.—*Bp. Horne*

3166 Lives of great men all remind us, we can make our lives sublime. —*Longfellow*

3167 Speaking generally, no man appears great to his contemporaries, for the same reason that no man is great to his servants—both know too much of him.—*Colton*

3168 The greatest man in history was the poorest.—*Emerson*

3169 A great many men—some comparatively small men now—if put in the right position, would be Luthers and Columbuses.—*E. H. Chapin*

3170 I would much rather that posterity should inquire why no statues were erected to me, than why they were.—*Cato*

Grief

3171 If you have tears, prepare to shed them now.—*Shakespeare*

3172 There is no grief which time does not lessen and soften.—*Cicero*

Habit

3173 How use doth breed a habit in man!—*Shakespeare*

3174 Sow an act, and you reap a habit; sow a habit, and you reap a character; sow a character, and you reap a destiny.—*G. D. Boardman*

Happiness

3175 How bitter a thing it is to look into happiness through another man's eyes!—*Shakespeare*

3176 Silence is the perfectest herald of joy: I were but little happy, if I could say how much.—*Shakespeare*

3177 The most unhappy of all men is he who believes himself to be so. —*Hume*

3178 Only the spirit of rebellion craves for happiness in this life. What right have we human beings to happiness?—*Henrik Ibsen*

3179 The fountain of content must spring up in the mind; and he who has so little knowledge of human nature as to seek happiness by changing anything but his own disposition, will waste his life in fruitless efforts, and multiply the griefs which he purposes to remove.—*Johnson*

Hardship

3180 There are some defeats more triumphant than victories.—*Michel de Montaigne*

3181 Fire is the test of gold; adversity of strong men.—*Seneca*

3182 Nature is upheld by antagonism. Passions, resistance, danger, are educators. We acquire the strength we have overcome.—*Emerson*

Health

3183 God heals, and the doctor takes the fee.—*Franklin*

3184 Life is not to live, but to be well.—*Martial*

3185 He who has health, has hope; and he who has hope, has everything.—*Arabian Proverb*

Heart

3186   Still stands thine ancient sacrifice—
        An humble and a contrite heart.
            —*Rudyard Kipling*

Heaven

3187 Earth hath no sorrow that Heaven cannot heal.—*Thomas Moore*

3188 God has two dwellings: one in heaven, and the other in a meek and thankful heart.—*Izaak Walton*

3189 Men are all groping for infinity—every effort to prove there is no God is in itself an effort to reach for God.—*Bishop Charles Edward Locke*

3190 There's none but fears a future state; and when the most obdurate swear they do not, their trembling hearts belie their boasting tongues. —*John Dryden*

History

3191 History, a distillation of rumor.—*Carlyle*

3192 There is properly no history, only biography.—*Emerson*

3193 History is indeed little more than the register of the crimes, follies, and misfortunes of mankind.—*Edward Gibbon*

Home

3194 The strength of a nation, especially of a republican nation, is in the intelligent and well-ordered homes of the people.—*Mrs. Sigourney*

3195   To most men their early home is no more than a memory of their early years. The image is never marred. There's no disappointment in memory, and one's exaggerations are always on the good side. —*George Eliot*

Honesty

3196   Make yourself an honest man, and then you may be sure that there is one rascal less in the world.—*Carlyle*

3197   Money dishonestly acquired is never worth its cost, while a good conscience never costs as much as it is worth.—*J. P. Senn*

3198   For Brutus is an honourable man;
              So are they all, all honourable men.
                            —*Shakespeare*

3199   Great honours are great burdens.—*Ben Jonson*

Hope

3200   He who loses hope, may then part with anything.—*Congreve*

3201   Hope is the only good that is common to all men; those who have nothing else possess hope still.—*Thales*

Humanity

3202   After all there is but one race—humanity.—*George Moore*

3203   Humanity is the Son of God.—*Theodore Parker*

Humility

3204   Humility is the solid foundation of all the virtues.—*Confucius*

3205   I believe the first test of a truly great man is his humility. —*John Ruskin*

Humor

3206   Honest good humor is the oil and wine of a merry meeting, and there is no jovial companionship equal to that where the jokes are rather small and the laughter abundant.—*Washington Irving*

3207   Where judgment has wit to express it, there is the best orator. —*Penn*

3208   Wit loses its respect with the good, when seen in company with malice; and to smile at the jest which places a thorn in another's breast, is to become a principal in the mischief.—*Richard B. Sheridan*

3209   The little foolery that wise men have makes a great show.
—*Shakespeare*

Ideas

3210   No army can withstand the strength of an idea whose time has come.—*Victor Hugo*

3211   It is only liquid currents of thought that move men and the world.—*Wendell Phillips*

Ignorance

3212   Against stupidity the very gods themselves contend in vain.
—*J.C.F. von Schiller*

3213   An ass may bray a good while before he shakes the stars down.
—*George Eliot*

3214   The more we study the more we discover our ignorance.
—*Shelley*

3215   The common curse of mankind,—folly and ignorance.—*Shakespeare*

Immortality

3216   Immortality is the glorious discovery of Christianity.—*William Ellery Channing*

3217   Life is the childhood of our immortality.—*Goethe*

3218   The nearer I approach the end, the plainer I hear around me the immortal symphonies of the worlds which invite me. It is marvelous, yet simple.—*Victor Hugo*

Injury

3219   If the other person injures you, you may forget the injury; but if you injure him, you will always remember.—*Kahlil Gibran*

Insult

3220   Of all the griefs that harass the distressed,
Sure the most bitter is a scornful jest;
Fate never wounds more deep the generous heart,
Than when a blockhead's insult points the dart.
                    —*Samuel Johnson*

Intentions

3221 Good intentions are very mortal and perishable things; like very mellow and choice fruit they are difficult to keep.—*C. Simmons*

3222 In the works of man as in those of nature, it is the intention which is chiefly worth studying.—*Goethe*

Jealousy

3223 In jealousy there is more of self-love, than of love to another. —*La Rochefoucauld*

3224 All jealousy must be strangled in its birth, or time will soon make it strong enough to overcome the truth.—*Davenant*

Judgment

3225 We always like those who admire us, but we do not always like those whom we admire.—*La Rochefoucauld*

3226 Young in limbs, in judgment old.—*Shakespeare*

3227 I never knew so young a body with so old a head.—*Shakespeare*

Justice

3228 As to be perfectly just is an attribute of the divine nature, to be so to the utmost of our abilities is the glory of man.—*Addison*

3229 Man is unjust, but God is just; and finally justice triumphs.— *Longfellow*

3230 How much easier it is to be generous than just! Men are sometimes bountiful who are not honest.—*Junius*

3231 Justice and power must be brought together, so that whatever is just may be powerful, and whatever is powerful may be just.—*Pascal*

Kindness

3232 Rich gifts wax poor when givers prove unkind.—*Shakespeare*

3233 I expect to pass through life but once.—If therefore, there be any kindness I can show, or any good thing I can do to any fellow-being, let me do it now, and not defer or neglect it, as I shall not pass this way again.—*Penn*

3234 To cultivate kindness is a valuable part of the business of life. —*Johnson*

3235 This was the most unkindest cut of all.—*Shakespeare*

Knowledge

3236   To despise theory is to have the excessively vain pretension to do without knowing what one does, and to speak without knowing what one says.—*Fontenelle*

3237   If you have knowledge, let others light their candles by it. —*Margaret Fuller*

3238   If a little knowledge is dangerous, where is the man who has so much as to be out of danger?—*Thomas Henry Huxley*

3239   New ideas can be good or bad, just the same as old ones.— *Franklin D. Roosevelt*

3240   Common sense is the knack of seeing things as they are, and doing things as they ought to be done.—*C.E. Stowe*

3241   Socrates said that there was one only good, namely, knowledge; and one only evil, namely, ignorance.—*Diogenes Laertius*

3242   Ignorance never settles a question.—*Disraeli*

3243   Who are a little wise, the best fools be.—*John Donne*

3244   Have the courage to be ignorant of a great number of things, in order to avoid the calamity of being ignorant of everything.—*Sydney Smith*

3245   Command large fields, but cultivate small ones.—*Virgil*

3246   We know accurately only when we know little; with knowledge doubt increases.—*Goethe*

3247   Who so neglects learning in his youth, loses the past and is dead for the future.—*Euripides*

3248   Wearing all that weight
                    Of learning lightly like a flower.
                                    —*Tennyson*

3249   Lack of confidence and lack of information sleep in the same bed, locked in the closest kind of embrace. When a man has confidence he gets along in business, but without confidence he might just as well not enter business at all. For confidence is the son of vision, and is sired by information.—*Cornelius Vanderbilt, Jr.*

3250   He who has no inclination to learn more will be very apt to think that he knows enough.—*Powell*

3251   Knowledge is of two kinds. We know a subject ourselves, or we know where we can find information upon it.—*Samuel Johnson*

3252   Every branch of knowledge which a good man possesses, he may apply to some good purpose.—*C. Buchanan*

3253   The more extensive a man's knowledge of what has been done, the greater will be his power of knowing what to do.—*Disraeli*

3254   Nothing in this life, after health and virtue, is more estimable than knowledge,—nor is there anything so easily attained, or so cheaply purchased,—the labor, only sitting still, and the expense but time, which, if we do not spend, we cannot save.—*Sterne*

3255   All wish to possess knowledge, but few, comparatively speaking, are willing to pay the price.—*Juvenal*

3256   To be proud of learning, is the greatest ignorance.—*Jeremy Taylor*

Labor

3257   If you divorce capital from labor, capital is hoarded, and labor starves.—*Daniel Webster*

3258   Whatever there is of greatness in the United States, or indeed in any other country, is due labor. The laborer is the author of all greatness and wealth. Without labor there would be no government, and no leading class, and nothing to preserve.—*U.S. Grant*

Language

3259   Words should be employed as the means, not as the end; language is the instrument, conviction is the work.—*Sir J. Reynolds*

3260   The knowledge of words is the gate of scholarship.—*Wilson*

3261   It makes a great difference in the force of a sentence whether a man be behind it or no.—*Emerson*

Laughter

3262   Laff every time you pheel tickled, and laff once in awhile enyhow. —*Josh Billings*

3263   They laugh that win.—*Shakespeare*

3264   Men show their character in nothing more clearly than by what they think laughable.—*Goethe*

3265   If we consider the frequent reliefs we receive from laughter, and how often it breaks the gloom which is apt to depress the mind, one would take care not to grow too wise for so great a pleasure of life. —*Addison*

Law

3266   No people were ever better than their laws, though many have been worse.—*J. B. Priestley*

3267   Good laws make it easier to do right and harder to do wrong. —*William E. Gladstone*

3268   We should never create by law what can be accomplished by morality.—*Montesquieu*

3269   Laws are the very bulwarks of liberty; they define every man's rights, and defend the individual liberties of all men.—*J.G. Holland*

Liberty

3270   Eternal vigilance is the price of liberty.—*Jefferson*

3271   The true danger is, when liberty is nibbled away, for expedients, and by parts.—*Edmund Burke*

3272   I know not what course others may take; but as for me, give me liberty or give me death!—*Patrick Henry*

3273   Liberty and union, now and forever, one and inseparable.— *Daniel Webster*

3274   Free will is not the liberty to do whatever one likes, but the power of doing whatever one sees ought to be done, even in the very face of otherwise overwhelming impulse. There lies freedom, indeed. —*G. Macdonald*

3275   It is a stronge desire, to seek power, and to lose liberty.— *Francis Bacon*

3276   Liberty is the right to do what the laws allow; and if a citizen could do what they forbid, it would be no longer liberty, because others would have the same powers.—*Montesquieu*

3277   O Liberty, how many crimes are committed in thy name!— *Mme. Roland*

3278   The people never give up their liberties but under some delusion. —*Burke*

Library

3279   A great library contains the diary of the human race.—The great consulting room of a wise man is a library.—*G. Dawson*

3280   The true university of these days is a collection of books.— *Carlyle*

3281   We enter our studies, and enjoy a society which we alone can bring together. We raise no jealousy by conversing with one in preference to another; we give no offense to the most illustrious by questioning him as long as we will, and leaving him as abruptly. Diversity of opinion raises no tumult in our presence; each interlocutor stands before us, speaks or is silent, and we adjourn or decide the business at our leisure. —*Landor*

Life

3282   The smallest worm will turn, being trodden on.—*Shakespeare*

3283   I have had my day and my philosophies.—*Tennyson*

3284   The web of our life is of a mingled yarn, good and ill together. —*Shakespeare*

3285   Press not a falling man too far!—*Shakespeare*

3286   The pleasantest things in the world are pleasant thoughts, and the great art in life is to have as many of them as possible.—*C.N. Bovee*

3287   The shell must break before the bird can fly.—*Tennyson*

3288   There is more to life than increasing its speed.—*Mahatma Gandhi*

3289   Life is a quarry, out of which we are to mold and chisel and complete a character.—*Goethe*

3290   Though we seem grieved at the shortness of life in general, we are wishing every period of it at an end. The minor longs to be at age, then to be a man of business; then to make up an estate, then to arrive at honors, then to retire.—*Addison*

3291   If I could get the ear of every young man but for one word, it would be this; make the most and best of yourself.—There is no tragedy like a wasted life—a life failing of its true end, and turned to a false end. —*T.T. Munger*

3292   Life is the childhood of our immortality.—*Goethe*

3293   Hope writes the poetry of the boy, but memory that of the man. Man looks forward with smiles, but backward with sighs. Such is the wise providence of God. The cup of life is sweetest at the brim, the flavor is impaired as we drink deeper, and the dregs are made bitter that we may not struggle when it is taken from our lips.—*A. Monod*

3294   Of all the words of tongue and pen,
The saddest are, "It might have been,"
More sad are these we daily see
"It is, but it hadn't ought to be!"
—*Bret Harte*

3295   Life resembles the banquet of Damocles; the sword is ever suspended.—*Voltaire*

3296   The vocation of every man and woman is to serve other people——*Count Leo Nikolaevich Tolstoi*

3297   The measure of a man's life is the well spending of it, and not the length.—*Plutarch*

3298   My life is like the summer rose
That opens to the morning sky,
But ere the shades of evening close
Is scattered on the ground—to die.
—*Richard Henry Wilde*

3299   It matters not how long you live, but how well.—*Publius Syrus*

3300   Roaming in thought over the Universe, I saw the little that is Good steadily hastening towards immortality, and the vast that is evil I saw hastening to merge itself and become lost and dead.—*Walt Whitman*

3301   One life; a little gleam of time between two eternities; no second chance for us forever more.—*Carlyle*

3302   Why all this toil for the triumphs of an hour?—*Young*

3303   While we are reasoning concerning life, life is gone; and death, though perhaps they receive him differently, yet treats alike the fool and the philosopher.—*David Hume*

3304   We never live; we are always in the expectation of living.—*Voltaire*

3305   You know how little while we have to stay, and, once departed, may return no more.—*Edward FitzGerald*

3306   The Wine of Life keeps oozing drop by drop, the Leaves of Life keep falling one by one.—*FitzGerald*

3307   A Book of Verses underneath the Bough,
A Jug of Wine, a Loaf of Bread—and Thou
Beside me singing in the Wilderness—
Oh, Wilderness were Paradise enow!
—*FitzGerald*

3308   Oh threats of Hell and Hopes of Paradise!
        One thing at least is certain—*This* life flies;
        One thing is certain, and the rest is Lies;
        The Flower that once has blown for ever dies.
                        —*FitzGerald*

3309   The Moving Finger writes; and, having writ,
        Moves on: nor all your Piety nor Wit
        Shall lure it back to cancel half a Line,
        Nor all your Tears wash out a Word of it.
                        —*FitzGerald*

Literature

3310   In science, read, by preference, the newest works; in literature the oldest. The classic literature is always modern.—*Bulwer*

3311   The decline of literature indicates the decline of a nation; the two keep pace in their downward tendency.—*Goethe*

3312   Nothing lives in literature but that which has in it the vitality of creative art; and it would be safe advice to the young to read nothing but what is old.—*E.P. Whipple*

3313   Literature is the immortality of speech.—*Schlegel*

Love

3314   To do him any wrong was to beget
        A kindness from him for his heart was rich—
        Of such fine mould that if you sowed therein
        The seed of Hate, it blossomed Charity.
                        —*Tennyson*

3315   The course of true love never did run smooth.—*Shakespeare*

3316   No man at one time can be wise and love.—*Robert Herrick*

3317   To be rich in admiration and free from envy; to rejoice greatly in the good of others; to love with such generosity of heart that your love is still a dear possession in absence or unkindness—these are the gifts of fortune which money cannot buy and without which money can buy nothing. He who has such a treasury of riches, being happy and valiant himself, in his own nature, will enjoy the universe as if it were his own estate; and help the man to whom he lends a hand to enjoy it with him.—*Robert Louis Stevenson*

3318   And on her lover's arm she leant,
        And round her waist she felt it fold,

And far across the hills they went
In that new world which is the old.
—*Tennyson*

3319 Then, must you speak of one that loved not wisely but too well;
of one not easily jealous, but being wrong perplex'd in the extreme.
—*Shakespeare*

3320 There's beggary in the love that can be reckon'd.—*Shakespeare*

3321 Men have died from time to time, and worms have eaten them,
—but not for love.—*Shakespeare*

3322 'Tis better to have loved and lost than never to have loved at all.
—*Tennyson*

3323 Drink to me only with thine eyes,
And I will pledge with mine;
Or leave a kiss but in the cup,
And I'll not look for wine.
—*Ben Jonson*

3324 I do not love thee, Sabidius, nor can I say why; this only I can
say, I do not love thee.—*Martial*

3325 Next to God, thy parents.—*Penn*

3326 Never to judge rashly; never to interpret the actions of others
in ill-sense, but to compassionate their infirmities, bear their burdens,
excuse their weaknesses, and make up for their defects—to hate their
imperfections, but love themselves, this is the true spirit of charity.
—*Caussin*

3327 The conqueror is regarded with awe; the wise man commands
our respect; but it is only the benevolent man that wins our affection.
—*Howells*

3328 Courtship consists in a number of quiet attentions, not so pointed
as to alarm, nor so vague as not to be understood.—*Sterne*

3329 In charity there is no excess.—*Francis Bacon*

3330 I am not one of those who do not believe in love at first sight,
but I believe in taking a second look.—*H. Vincent*

3331 Man's love is of man's life a part; it is woman's whole existence.
—*Byron*

3332 There is nothing half so sweet in life as love's young dream.
—*T. Moore*

3333   It is astonishing how little one feels poverty when he loves.
—*Bulwer*

Luxury

3334   Luxury makes a man so soft, that it is hard to please him, and easy to trouble him; so that his pleasures at last become his burden. Luxury is a nice master, hard to be pleased.—*Mackenzie*

3335   Avarice and luxury, those pests which have ever been the ruin of every great state.—*Livy*

3336   On the soft bed of luxury most kingdoms have expired.—*Young*

3337   War destroys men, but luxury destroys mankind; at once corrupts the body and the mind.—*Crown*

Majority

3338   The voice of the majority is no proof of justice.—*Schiller*

3339   It never troubles the wolf how many the sheep may be.—*Virgil*

3340   We go by the major vote, and if the majority are insane, the sane must go to the hospital.—*H. Mann*

3341   A man in the right, with God on his side, is in the majority though he be alone.—*H.W. Beecher*

Mankind

3342   Let each man think himself an act of God.
            His mind a thought, his life a breath of God.—*Bailey*

3343   We are the miracle of miracles, the great inscrutable mystery of God.—*Carlyle*

3344   When faith is lost, when honor dies,
                The man is dead!—*Whittier*

3345   Man is an animal that makes bargains; no other animal does this—one dog does not change a bone with another.—*Adam Smith*

3346   He that is good for making excuses, is seldom good for anything else.—*Franklin*

3347   Man proposes, but God disposes.—*Thomas à Kempis*

3348   What a piece of work is a man! in form and moving how express and admirable! in action how like an angel! in apprehension how like a god!—*Shakespeare*

3349   Lord, what fools these mortals be!—*Shakespeare*

3350   His life was gentle, and the elements so mix'd in him, that Nature might stand up and say to all the world, "This was a man!"—*Shakespeare*

3351   It takes a clever man to turn cynic and a wise man to be clever enough not to.—*Fannie Hurst*

3352   He was a man, take him for all in all, I shall not look upon his like again.—*Shakespeare*

3353   In counsel it is good to see dangers; but in execution, not to see them unless they be very great.—*Bacon*

3354   The tendency is to be broadminded about other people's security.—*Aristide Briand*

3355   There is no man so good, who, were he to submit all his thoughts and actions to the law, would not deserve hanging ten times in his life.—*Montaigne*

3356   So far is it from being true that men are naturally equal, that no two people can be half an hour together but one shall acquire an evident superiority over the other.—*Johnson*

3357   I do not mean to expose my ideas to ingenious ridicule by maintaining that everything happens to every man for the best; but I will contend, that he who makes the best use of it, fulfills the part of a wise and good man.—*Cumberland*

3358   There is less misery in being cheated than in that kind of wisdom which perceives, or thinks it perceives, that all mankind are cheats. —*E.H. Chapin*

3359   In my youth I thought of writing a satire on mankind, but now in my age I think I should write an apology for them.—*Walpole*

3360   Man is not the creature of circumstances. Circumstances are the creatures of men.—*Disraeli*

3361   Youth is a blunder; manhood is a struggle; old age a regret.— *Disraeli*

3362   Passion often makes fools of the ablest men, and able men of the most foolish.—*La Rochefoucauld*

3363   Nothing is so uncertain as the minds of the multitude.—*Leiz*

3364   The multitude is always in the wrong.—*Roscommon*

3365   The Devil was sick,—the Devil a monk would be;
The Devil was well,—the Devil a monk was he.—*Rabelais*

3366   Were we to take as much pains to be what we ought to be, as we do to disguise what we really are, we might appear like ourselves without being at the trouble of any disguise whatever.—*La Rochefoucauld*

3367   I can make a lord, but only the Almighty can make a gentleman.—*James I*

3368   I do not know what comfort other people find in considering the weakness of great men, but 'tis always a mortification to me to observe that there is no perfection in humanity.—*S. Montague*

3369   Not armies, not nations, have advanced the race; but here and there, in the course of ages, an individual has stood up and cast his shadow over the world.—*E.H. Chapin*

3370   The proper study of mankind is man.—*Alexander Pope*

3371   Man's inhumanity to man makes countless thousands mourn.—*Robert Burns*

3372   Man! thou pendulum betwixt a smile and tear.—*Byron*

3373   We have all sufficient strength to endure the misfortunes of others.—*La Rochefoucauld*

3374   In the adversity of our best friends we often find something that is not exactly displeasing.—*La Rochefoucauld*

Marriage

3375   I chose my wife, as she did her wedding gown, for qualities that would wear well.—*Oliver Goldsmith*

3376   Men should keep their eyes wide open before marriage, and half shut afterward.—*Madame Scuderi*

3377   The sanctity of marriage and the family relation make the cornerstone of our American society and civilization.—*Garfield*

Master

3378   If thou art a master, sometimes be blind; if a servant, sometimes be deaf.—*Fuller*

3379   Men, at some time, are masters of their fates.—*Shakespeare*

Maxims

3380   Maxims are the condensed good sense of nations.—*Sir J. Mackintosh*

3381　All maxims have their antagonist maxims; proverbs should be sold in pairs, a single one being but a half truth.—*W. Matthews*

3382　The two maxims of any great man at court are, always to keep his countenance, and never to keep his word.—*Swift*

Medicine

3383　The best of all medicines are resting and fasting.—*Franklin*

3334　Over the door of a library in Thebes is the inscription, "Medicine for the soul."—*Diodorus Siculus*

Mediocrity

3385　Mediocrity is not allowed to poets, either by the gods or men.—*Horace*

3386　Nothing in the world is more haughty than a man of moderate capacity when once raised to power.—*Wessenburg*

3387　There are certain things in which mediocrity is not to be endured, such as poetry, music, painting, public speaking.—*La Bruyère*

Meditation

3388　Meditation is the nurse of thought, and thought the food of meditation.—*C. Simmons*

3389　It is not the number of books you read, nor the variety of sermons you hear, nor the amount of religious conversation in which you mix, but it is the frequency and earnestness with which you meditate on these things till the truth in them becomes your own and part of your being, that ensures your growth.—*F.W. Robertson*

Memory

3390　Memory tempers prosperity, mitigates adversity, controls youth, and delights old age.—*Lactantius*

3391　Memory is the receptacle and sheath of all knowledge.—*Cicero*

3392　The memory is a treasurer to whom we must give funds, if we would draw the assistance we need.—*Rowe*

3393　Everyone complains of his memory; nobody of his judgment.—*La Rochefoucauld*

3394　Memory seldom fails when its office is to show us the tombs of our buried hopes.—*Lady Blessington*

3395　The true art of memory is the art of attention.—*Johnson*

Mercy

3396 Among the attributes of God, although they are all equal, mercy shines with even more brilliancy than justice.—*Cervantes*

3397 We hand folks over to God's mercy, and show none ourselves.—*George Eliot*

3398 Teach me to feel another's woe, to hide the fault I see; that mercy I to others show, that mercy show to me.—*Pope*

Method

3399 Method is like packing things in a box; a good packer will get in half as much again as a bad one.—*Cecil*

3400 Every great man exhibits the talent of organization or construction, whether it be in a poem, a philosophical system, a policy, or a strategy. And without method there is no organization nor construction.—*Bulwer*

Miser

3401 The prodigal robs his heir; the miser robs himself.—*La Bruyère*

3402 A miser grows rich by seeming poor; an extravagant man grows poor by seeming rich.—*Shenstone*

Misfortune

3403 He that is down needs fear no fall.—*Bunyan*

3404 Little minds are tamed and subdued by misfortune; but great minds rise above it.—*Washington Irving*

Mistake

3405 The sight of a drunkard is a better sermon against that vice than the best that was ever preached on that subject.—*Saville*

3406 A man should never be ashamed to own he has been in the wrong, which is but saying in other words that he is wiser today than he was yesterday.—*Pope*

3407 Any man may make a mistake, but none but a fool will continue in it.—*Cicero*

3408 No man ever became great or good except through many and great mistakes.—*Gladstone*

3409 The only people who make no mistakes are dead people. I saw a man last week who had not made a mistake for four thousand years.

He was a mummy in the Egyptian department of the British Museum.—
H.L. Wayland

Mob

3410   Human affairs are not so happily arranged that the best things please the most men.—It is the proof of a bad cause when it is applauded by the mob.—*Seneca*

3411   A mob is a society of bodies, voluntarily bereaving themselves of reason, and traversing its work. The mob is man, voluntarily descending to the nature of the beast. Its fit hour of activity is night; its actions are insane, like its whole constitution.—*Emerson*

3412   We are all of us imaginative in some form or other, for images are the brood of desire.—*George Eliot*

Moderation

3413   Moderation is the inseparable companion of wisdom, but with it genius has not even a nodding acquaintance.—*Colton*

3414   Everything that exceeds the bounds of moderation, has an unstable foundation.—*Seneca*

Modesty

3415   Bashfulness is an ornament to youth, but a reproach to old age. —*Aristotle*

3416   It is no great thing to be humble when you are brought low; but to be humble when you are praised is a great and rare attainment.— *St. Bernard*

3417   Modesty is a shining light; it prepares the mind to receive knowledge and the heart for truth.—*Guizot*

3418   Modesty seldom resides in a breast that is not enriched with nobler virtues.—*Goldsmith*

3419   The greatest ornament of an illustrious life is modesty and humility, which go a great way in the character even of the most exalted princes.—*Napoleon I*

Money

3420   But the jingling of the guinea helps the hurt that Honour feels.— *Tennyson*

3421   No man but a blockhead ever wrote except for money.—*Samuel Johnson*

3422   All love has something of blindness in it, but the love of money especially.—*South*

3423   Men are seldom more innocently employed than when they are honestly making money.—*Johnson*

3424   The covetous man never has money; the prodigal will have none shortly.—*Ben Jonson*

3425   To despise money is to dethrone a king.—*Chamfort*

3426   Ready money is Aladdin's lamp.—*Byron*

Monument

3427   No man who needs a monument ever ought to have one.— *Hawthorne*

3428   Tombs are the clothes of the dead; a grave is but a plain suit; a rich monument is an embroidered one.—*Fuller*

Morning

3429   The morning hour has gold in its mouth.—*Franklin*

3430   Now from night's gloom the glorious day breaks forth, and seems to kindle from the setting stars.—*D.K. Lee*

Mortality

3431   Oh, why should the spirit of mortal be proud?
Like a fast-flitting meteor, a fast-flying cloud,
A flash of the lightning, a break of the wave,
He passes from life to his rest in the grave.

—*William Knox*

Mother

3432   The mother's heart is the child's schoolroom.—*H.W. Beecher*

3433   Let France have good mothers, and she will have good sons.— *Napoleon I*

3434   My mother's influence in molding my character was conspicuous. She forced me to learn daily long chapters of the Bible by heart. To that discipline and patient, accurate resolve I owe not only much of my general power of taking pains, but the best part of my taste for literature.— *John Ruskin*

3435   A mother is a mother still, the holiest thing alive.—*Coleridge*

3436   All that I am, or hope to be, I owe to my angel mother.—*Lincoln*

3437   A father may turn his back on his child; brothers and sisters may become inveterate enemies; husbands may desert their wives and wives their husbands. But a mother's love endures through all; in good repute, in bad repute, in the face of the world's condemnation, a mother still loves on, and still hopes that her child may turn from his evil ways, and repent; still she remembers the infant smiles that once filled her bosom with rapture, the merry laugh, the joyful shout of his childhood, the opening promise of his youth; and she can never be brought to think him all unworthy.—*Washington Irving*

Music

3438   There is something marvelous in music. I might almost say it is, in itself, a marvel. Its position is somewhere between the region of thought and that of phenomena; a glimmering medium between mind and matter, related to both and yet differing from either. Spiritual, and yet requiring rhythm; material, and yet independent of space.—*H. Heine*

3439   Music is well said to be the speech of angels.—*Carlyle*

Nation

3440   Socrates said he was not an Athenian or a Greek, but a citizen of the world.—*Plutarch*

3441   The primary duty of organized society is to enlarge the lives and increase the standards of living of all the people.—*Herbert Hoover*

3442   Our purpose is to build in this nation a human society, not an economic system.—*Herbert Hoover*

3443   Praise the Power that hath made and preserved us
                  a nation,
         Then conquer we must, for our cause it is just,
         And this be our motto, "In God is our trust."
                                        —*Francis S. Key*

3444   A good newspaper and Bible in every house, a good schoolhouse in every district, and a church in every neighborhood, all appreciated as they deserve, are the chief support of virtue, morality, civil liberty, and religion.—*Franklin*

3445   Patriotism is the last refuge of a scoundrel.—*Samuel Johnson*

3446   Territory is but the body of a nation.—The people who inhabit its hills and valleys are its soul, its spirit, its life.—*Garfield*

3447   No nation can be destroyed while it possesses a good home life.
—*J.G. Holland*

3448   Not that I loved Caesar less, but that I loved Rome more.—
Shakespeare

3449   A horse! A horse! My kingdom for a horse!—*Shakespeare*

3450   The noblest motive is the public good.—*Virgil*

3451   After what I owe to God, nothing should be more dear or more
sacred than the love and respect I owe to my country.—*De Thou*

3452   Republics come to an end by luxurious habits; monarchies by
poverty.—*Montesquieu*

3453   Taxes are the sinews of the state.—*Cicero*

Nature

3454   To him who in the love of nature holds communion with her
visible forms, she speaks a various language.—*William Cullen Bryant*

3455   One touch of nature makes the whole world kin.—*Shakespeare*

3456   Nature is the living, visible garment of God.—*Goethe*

3457   Nature is the most thrifty thing in the world; she never wastes
anything; she undergoes change, but there's no annihilation—the essence
remains.—*T. Binney*

Necessity

3458   Necessity knows no law except to conquer.—*Publius Syrus*

3459   Necessity reforms the poor, and satiety the rich.—*Tacitus*

Newspaper

3460   Were it left to me to decide whether we should have a government without newspapers or newspapers without government, I should
not hesitate a moment to prefer the latter.—*Jefferson*

Night

3461   The death-bed of a day, how beautiful!—*Bailey*

3462   I must become a borrower of the night for a dark hour or twain.
—*Shakespeare*

3463   Ye stars, that are the poetry of heaven!—*Byron*

3464 The stars hang bright above, silent, as if they watched the sleeping earth.—*Coleridge*

3465
> The curfew tolls the knell of parting day,
> The lowing herd winds slowly o'er the lea,
> The ploughman homeward plods his weary way,
> And leaves the world to darkness and to me.
> —*Thomas Gray*

3466 The day is done, and darkness falls from the wings of night.—*Longfellow*

3467 In her starry shade of dim and solitary loveliness, I learn the language of another world.—*Byron*

3468 Wisdom mounts her zenith with the stars.—*Mrs. Barbauld*

Nobility

3469 Tears are the noble language of the eye.—*Robert Herrick*

3470 Virtue is the first title of nobility.—*Molière*

3471 If a man be endued with a generous mind, this is the best kind of nobility.—*Plato*

3472 It is better to be nobly remembered, than nobly born.—*Ruskin*

3473 It seems to me 'tis only noble to be good.—*Tennyson*

Nonsense

3474 No one is exempt from talking nonsense; the misfortune is to do it solemnly.—*Montaigne*

Obedience

3475 Let the child's first lesson be obedience, and the second may be what thou wilt.—*Fuller*

3476 Wicked men obey from fear; good men, from love.—*Aristotle*

Oblivion

3477
> Full many a gem of purest ray serene,
> The dark, unfathomed caves of ocean bear:
> Full many a flower is born to blush unseen.
> And waste its sweetness on the desert air.—*Thomas Gray*

3478 Oblivion is the flower that grows best on graves.—*George Sand*

3479 Fame is a vapor; popularity an accident; riches take wings; the only certainty is oblivion.—*Horace Greeley*

Open-Minded

3480　It is well for people who think to change their minds occasionally in order to keep them clean. For those who do not think, it is best at least to rearrange their prejudices once in a while.—*Luther Burbank*

3481　The great menace to the life of an industry is industrial self-complacency.—*David Sarnoff*

3482　It is always the minorities that hold the key of progress; it is always through those who are unafraid to be different that advance comes to human society.—*Raymond B. Fosdick*

3483　"Can any good come out of Nazareth?"—This is always the question of the wiseacres and knowing ones.—But the good, the new, comes from exactly that quarter whence it is not looked for, and is always something different from what is expected.—Everything new is received with contempt, for it begins in obscurity. It becomes a power unobserved.—*Feuerbach*

Opinion

3484　I have bought golden opinions from all sorts of people.—*Shakespeare*

3485　There is no such thing as modern art. There is art—and there is advertising.—*Albert Sterner*

3486　Predominant opinions are generally the opinions of the generation that is vanishing.—*Disraeli*

3487　The eyes of other people are the eyes that ruin us. If all but myself were blind, I should want neither fine clothes, fine houses, nor fine furniture.—*Franklin*

3488　The men of the past had convictions, while we moderns have only opinions.—*H. Heine*

3489　The history of human opinion is scarcely anything more than the history of human errors.—*Voltaire*

Opportunity

3490　Art is long, life short; judgment difficult, opportunity transient.—*Goethe*

3491　Next to knowing when to seize an opportunity, the most important thing in life is to know when to forego an advantage.—*Disraeli*

3492   Great opportunities come to all, but many do not know they have met them. The only preparation to take advantage of them is simple fidelity to what each day brings.—*A.E. Dunning*

Oratory

3493   Oratory is the power to talk people out of their sober and natural opinions.—*Chatfield*

Pain

3494   Pain is the deepest thing we have in our nature, and union through pain and suffering has always seemed more real and holy than any other.—*Hallam*

3495   He jests at scars that never felt a wound. But, soft! What light through yonder window breaks? It is the east, and Juliet is the sun.—*Shakespeare*

Parent

3496   The first half of our lives is ruined by our parents and the second half by our children.—*Clarence S. Darrow*

3497   Next to God, thy parents.—*William Penn*

Patience

3498   If I have ever made any valuable discoveries, it has been owing more to patient attention, than to any other talent.—*Sir Isaac Newton*

3499   How poor are they that have not patience!—*Shakespeare*

3500   It's easy finding reasons why other folks should be patient.—*George Eliot*

3501   Patience is bitter, but its fruit is sweet.—*Rousseau*

3502   There are times when God asks nothing of his children except silence, patience, and tears.—*C.S. Robinson*

3503   Patience is power; with time and patience the mulberry leaf becomes silk.—*Chinese Proverb*

3504   Steady, patient, persevering thinking will generally surmount every obstacle in the search after truth.—*Emmons*

Peace

3505   God's in His heaven—all's right with the world!—*Robert Browning*

3506   Peace hath her victories no less renown'd than war.—*John Milton*

3507   Peace is such a precious jewel that I would give anything for it but truth.—*M. Henry*

3508   There is but one way to tranquillity of mind and happiness, and that is to account no external things thine own, but to commit all to God. —*Epictetus*

3509   Five great enemies to peace inhabit with us: *viz.*, avarice, ambition, envy, anger, and pride. If those enemies were to be banished, we should infallibly enjoy perpetual peace.—*Petrarch*

Perfection

3510   It is a bad plan that admits of no modification.—*Publius Syrus*

3511   Bachelors' wives and old maids' children are always perfect.— *Chamfort*

3512   Even the worthy Homer sometimes nods.—*Horace*

3513   It takes a long time to bring excellence to maturity.—*Publius Syrus*

3514   It is only imperfection that complains of what is imperfect.— The more perfect we are, the more gentle and quiet we become toward the defects of others.—*Fénelon*

Persistence

3515   Every noble work is at first impossible.—*Carlyle*

3516   The falling drops at last will wear the stone.—*Lucretius*

3517   And many strokes, though with a little axe, hew down and fell the hardest-timbered oak.—*Shakespeare*

3518   Knock and the door will open to you. For it is always the one who asks who receives and the one who searches who finds, and the one who knocks to whom the door opens.—*Goodspeed's Translation of the New Testament*

Philosophy

3519   Three things too much, and three too little are pernicious to man; to speak much, and know little; to spend much, and have little; to presume much, and be worth little.—*Cervantes*

3520   There are more things in heaven and earth, Horatio, than are dreamt of in your philosophy.—*Shakespeare*

3521 It was through the feeling of wonder that men now and at first began to philosophize.—*Aristotle*

3522 There is nothing so ridiculous that has not at some time been said by some philosopher.—*Oliver Goldsmith*

3523 The greatest object in the universe, says a certain philosopher, is a good man struggling with adversity; yet there is a still greater, which is the good man that comes to relieve it.—*Oliver Goldsmith*

3524 The discovery of what is true, and the practice of that which is good, are the two most important objects of philosophy.—*Voltaire*

3525 The first business of a philosopher is to part with self-conceit. —*Epictetus*

3526 Philosophy, when superficially studied, excites doubt; when thoroughly explored, it dispels it.—*Bacon*

Pity

3527 Pity is the feeling which arrests the mind in the presence of whatsoever is grave and constant in human sufferings and unites it with the human sufferer.—*James Joyce*

Pleasure

3528 The generous heart should scorn a pleasure which gives others pain.—*Thomson*

3529 If all the year were playing holidays, to sport would be as tedious as to work.—*Shakespeare*

3530 Consider pleasures as they depart, not as they come.—*Aristotle*

3531 He who can at all times sacrifice pleasure to duty approaches sublimity.—*Lavater*

Poetry

3532 A poet must needs be before his own age, to be even with posterity.—*J.R. Lowell*

3533 Poets utter great and wise things which they do not themselves understand.—*Plato*

3534 One merit of poetry few persons will deny; it says more, and in few words, than prose.—*Voltaire*

Politeness

3535 As charity covers a multitude of sins before God, so does politeness before men.—*Greville*

3536　A polite man is one who listens with interest to things he knows all about, when they are told him by a person who knows nothing about them.—*De Morny*

Politics

3537　A statesman makes the occasion, but the occasion makes the politician.—*G.S. Hillard*

3538　Politics is the art of being wise for others—policy of being wise for self.—*Bulwer*

3539　There is no gambling like politics.—*Disraeli*

3540　Nothing is politically right which is morally wrong.—*Daniel O'Connell*

3541　There is an infinity of political errors which, being once adopted, become principles.—*Abbé Raynal*

3542　Every political question is becoming a social question, and every social question is becoming a religious question.—*R.T. Ely*

Poverty

3543　Meager were his looks, sharp misery had worn him to the bones. —*Shakespeare*

3544　Let not ambition mock their useful toil, their homely joys and destiny obscure; nor grandeur hear with a disdainful smile, the short and simple annals of the poor.—*Thomas Gray*

3545　Poverty is the wicked man's tempter, the good man's perdition, the proud man's curse, the melancholy man's halter.—*Bulwer*

3546　Of all the advantages which come to any young man, I believe it to be demonstrably true that poverty is the greatest.—*J.G. Holland*

3547　Poverty is uncomfortable, as I can testify: but nine times out of ten the best thing that can happen to a young man is to be tossed overboard and compelled to sink or swim for himself.—*Garfield*

3548　He is not poor that has little, but he that desires much.—*Daniel*

Power

3549　But yesterday the word of Caesar might have stood against the world; now lies he there and none so poor to do him reverence.— *Shakespeare*

3550   Power will intoxicate the best hearts, as wine the strongest heads. No man is wise enough, nor good enough, to be trusted with unlimited power.—*Colton*

3551   Self-reverence, self-knowledge, self-control,—these three alone lead life to sovereign power.—*Tennyson*

Praise

3552   Sweet is the scene where genial friendship plays the pleasing game of interchanging praise.—*O.W. Holmes*

3553   Praise undeserved is satire in disguise.—*Broadhurst*

3554   Those who are greedy of praise prove that they are poor in merit.—*Plutarch*

3555   Damn with faint praise.—*Pope*

3556   As the Greek said, many men know how to flatter; few know to praise.—*Wendell Phillips*

Prayer

3557   I pray thee, O God, that I may be beautiful within.—*Socrates*

3558   Her eyes are homes of silent prayer.—*Tennyson*

3559   Our prayers should be for blessings in general, for God knows best what is good for us.—*Socrates*

3560   A strict belief in fate is the worst kind of slavery; on the other hand there is comfort in the thought that God will be moved by our prayers.—*Epicurus*

3561   Certain thoughts are prayers. There are moments when, whatever be the attitude of the body, the soul is on its knees.—*Victor Hugo*

3562   Let not him who prays, suffer his tongue to outstrip his heart; nor presume to carry a message to the throne of grace, while that stays behind.—*South*

3563   A prayer in its simplest definition is merely a wish turned Godward.—*Phillips Brooks*

3564   The Lord's Prayer contains the sum total of religion and morals. —*Wellington*

3565   The Lord's Prayer is not, as some fancy, the easiest, the most natural of all devout utterances. It may be committed to memory quickly, but it is slowly learned by heart.—*Maurice*

Prejudice

3566   To be prejudiced is always to be weak.—*Samuel Johnson*

3567   Never try to reason the prejudice out of a man.—It was not reasoned into him and cannot be reasoned out.—*Sydney Smith*

3568   Prejudice is the reason of fools.—*Voltaire*

3569   Ignorance is less remote from the truth than prejudice.—*Diderot*

3570   Prejudice is the child of ignorance.—*William Hazlitt*

3571   When the judgment is weak, the prejudice is strong.—*O'Hara*

3572   Even when we fancy we have grown wiser, it is only, it may be, that new prejudices have displaced old ones.—*Bovee*

3573   Prejudices are what rule the vulgar crowd.—*Voltaire*

Pride

3574   To be vain of one's rank or place, is to show that one is below it.—*Stanislaus*

3575   Pride is seldom delicate; it will please itself with very mean advantages.—*Johnson*

3576   Of all marvellous things, perhaps there is nothing that angels behold with such supreme astonishment as a proud man.—*Colton*

3577   Haughty people seem to me to have like the dwarfs, the statures of a child and the face of a man.—*Joubert*

Principles

3578   He who merely knows right principles is not equal to him who loves them.—*Confucius*

3579   Expedients are for the hour; principles for the ages.—*H.W. Beecher*

Progress

3580   Progress—the onward stride of God.—*Victor Hugo*

3581   I find the great thing in this world is not so much where we stand, as in what direction we are moving.—*O.W. Holmes*

Promise

3582   The vow that binds too strictly snaps itself.—*Tennyson*

3583   Apt to promise is apt to forget.—*Thomas Fuller*

Property

3584   Property is at once the consequence and the basis of the state.—*Mikhail A. Bakunin*

3585   The instinct of ownership is fundamental in man's nature.—*William James*

3586   The reason why men enter into society is the preservation of their property.—*Locke*

Prosperity

3587   Treason doth never prosper; for if it prosper, none dare call it treason.—*Sir J. Harrington*

3588   Prosperity tries the fortunate, adversity the great.—*Pliny the Younger*

3589   All sunshine makes the desert.—*Arabian Proverb*

3590   Everything in the world may be endured, except continual prosperity.—*Goethe*

Prudence

3591   The one prudence in life is concentration; the one evil is dissipation.—*Emerson*

3592   Rashness is the characteristic of ardent youth, and prudence that of mellowed age.—*Cicero*

Purpose

3593   He who wishes to fulfill his mission in the world must be a man of one idea, that is of one great overmastering purpose, overshadowing all his aims, and guiding and controlling his entire life.

Quotations

3594   Next to the originator of a good sentence is the first quoter of it. —*Emerson*

3595   I quote others only the better to express myself.—*Montaigne*

3596   The wisdom of the wise and the experience of ages may be preserved by quotation.—*Disraeli*

3597   By necessity, by proclivity, and by delight, we quote.—We quote not only books and proverbs, but arts, sciences, religions, customs, and laws; nay, we quote temples and houses, tables and chairs by imitation.—*Emerson*

Reading

3598   Deep versed in books, and shallow in himself.—*Milton*

3599   Read not to contradict and confute; nor to believe and take for granted; nor to find talk and discourse: but to weigh and consider—*Francis Bacon*

3600   Books are men of higher stature, and the only men that speak aloud for future times to hear.—*Elizabeth Barrett Browning*

3601   There is no book so bad but something valuable may be derived from it.—*Pliny*

3602   Some books are to be tasted; others swallowed; and some few to be chewed and digested.—*Bacon*

3603   When a book raises your spirit, and inspires you with noble and manly thoughts, seek for no other test of its excellence.—It is good, and made by a good workman.—*La Bruyère*

3604   Reading maketh a full man; conference a ready man; and writing an exact man; and, therefore, if a man write little, he had need have a great memory; if he confer little, he had need have a present wit; and if he read little, he had need have much cunning, to seem to know that he doth not.—*Bacon*

3605   We should accustom the mind to keep the best company by introducing it only to the best books.—*Sydney Smith*

3606   That is a good book which is opened with expectation, and closed with delight and profit.—*A.B. Alcott*

Reason

3607   Blot out vain pomp; check impulse; quench appetite; keep reason under its own control.—*Marcus Aurelius Antoninus*

3608   We may take Fancy for a companion, but must follow Reason as our guide.—*Samuel Johnson*

3609   O judgment! thou art fled to brutish beasts, and men have lost their reason.—*Shakespeare*

3610   Neither rhyme nor reason.—*Shakespeare*

3611   When passion is on the throne, reason is out of doors.—*M. Henry*

3612   Never reason for what you do not know. If you do, you will soon believe what is utterly against reason.—*Ramsay*

3613   To reason correctly from a false principle, is the perfection of sophistry.—*Emmons*

3614   Neither great poverty nor great riches will hear reason.—*Fielding*

Religion

3615   What greater calamity can fall upon a nation than the loss of worship.—*Carlyle*

3616   A strong and faithful pulpit is no mean safeguard of a nation's life.—*St. John*

3617   Christianity is the companion of liberty in all its conflicts, the cradle of its infancy, and the divine source of its claims.—*De Tocqueville*

3618   A little philosphy inclineth man's mind to atheism; but depth in philosophy bringeth men's minds about to religion.—*Francis Bacon*

3619   Morality without religion has no roots. It becomes a thing of custom, changeable, transient, and optional.—*H.W. Beecher*

3620   The blood of the martyrs is the seed of the church.—*St. Jerome*

3621   Seems it strange that thou shouldest live forever? Is it less strange that thou shouldst live at all?—This is a miracle; and that no more.—*Young*

3622   I have immortal longings in me.—*Shakespeare*

3623   The best theology is rather a divine life than a divine knowledge.—*Jeremy Taylor*

3624   Carry the cross patiently, and with perfect submission; and in the end it shall carry you.—*Thomas à Kempis*

3625   An agnostic is a man who doesn't know whether there is a God or not, doesn't know whether he has a soul or not, doesn't know whether there is a future life or not, doesn't believe that anyone else knows any more about these matters than he does, and thinks it a waste of time to try to find out.—*Dana*

3626   No sciences are better attested than the religion of the Bible.—*Sir Isaac Newton*

3627   The longer you read the Bible, the more you will like it; it will grow sweeter and sweeter; and the more you get into the spirit of it, the more you will get into the spirit of Christ.—*Romaine*

3628   The whole hope of human progress is suspended on the ever-growing influence of the Bible.—*William H. Seward*

3629   Do you know a book that you are willing to put under your head for a pillow when you lie dying? That is the book you want to study while you are living. There is but one such book in the world. The Bible.—*Joseph Cook*

3630   Men will wrangle for religion; write for it; fight for it; die for it; anything but live for it.—*Colton*

3631   If religious books are not widely circulated among the masses in this country, and the people do not become religious, I do not know what is to become of us as a nation.—*Daniel Webster*

3632   Religion cannot pass away. The burning of a little straw may hide the stars of the sky, but the stars are there, and will reappear.—*Carlyle*

3633   Culture of intellect, without religion in the heart, is only civilized barbarism and disguised animalism.—*Bunsen*

3634   Religion is the best armor in the world, but the worst cloak.—*John Newton*

3635   Only truly Christian life will do more to prove the divine origin of Christianity than many lectures. It is of much greater importance to develop Christian character, than to exhibit Christian evidence.—*J.M. Gibson*

3636   He who shall introduce into public affairs the principles of primitive Christianity, will revolutionize the world.—*Franklin*

3637   There's not much practical Christianity in the man who lives on better terms with angels and seraphs, than with his children, servants, and neighbors.—*H.W. Beecher*

3638   A Christian church is a body or collection of persons, voluntarily associated together, professing to believe what Christ teaches, to do what Christ enjoins, to imitate his example, cherish his spirit, and make known his gospel to others.—*R.F. Sample*

Remorse

3639   Remorse is beholding heaven and feeling hell.—*Moore*

3640   Believe me, every heart has its secret sorrows, which the world knows not; and oftentimes we call a man cold when he is only sad.—*Longfellow*

3641   Of all the sad words of tongue or pen, the saddest are these: "It might have been."—*Whittier*

Repentance

3642   Of all acts of man repentance is the most divine.—The greatest of all faults is to be conscious of none.—*Carlyle*

3643   To do so no more is the truest repentance.—*Luther*

3644   There is one case of death-bed repentance recorded, that of the penitent thief, that none should despair; and only one that none should presume.—*St. Augustine*

Reputation

3645   Reputation, reputation, reputation! Oh, I have lost my reputation! I have lost the immortal part of myself, and what remains is bestial.—*Shakespeare*

3646   The way to gain a good reputation, is, to endeavor to be what you desire to appear.—*Socrates*

3647   One may be better than his reputation, but never better than his principles.—*Latena*

3648   Good name in man and woman, dear my lord, is the immediate jewel of their souls: Who steals my purse steals trash; 'tis something, nothing; 'Twas mine, 'tis his, and has been slave to thousands: Robs me of that which not enriches him and makes me poor indeed.—*Shakespeare*

Revenge

3649   In taking revenge a man is but equal to his enemy, but in passing it over he is his superior.—*Bacon*

3650   Revenge is the poor delight of little minds.—*Juvenal*

Revolution

3651   Revolutions begin in the best heads, and run steadily down to the populace.—*Metternich*

3652   Too long denial of guaranteed right is sure to lead to revolution—bloody revolution, where suffering must fall upon the innocent as well as the guilty.—*U.S. Grant*

3653   Revolutions are not made, they come. A revolution is as natural a growth as an oak. It comes out of the past. Its foundations are laid far back.—*Wendell Phillips*

Reward

3654   Recompense injury with justice and unkindness with kindness.—*Confucius*

3655   The evening of a well-spent life brings its lamps with it.—*Joubert*

3656   He who wishes to secure the good of others has already secured his own.—*Confucius*

Riches

3657   We have seen better days.—*Shakespeare*

3658   Most of the luxuries and many of the so-called comforts of life are not only not indispensable, but positive hindrances to the elevation of mankind.—*Thoreau*

3659   Can one desire too much of a good thing?—*Shakespeare*

3660   There are two things needed in these days; first, for rich men to find out how poor men live; and second, for poor men to know how rich men work.—*E. Atkinson*

3661   Riches are apt to betray a man into arrogance.—*Addison*

3662   I am happy in having learned to distinguish between ownership and possession. Books, pictures, and all the beauty of the world belong to those who love and understand them. All of these things that I am entitled to, I have—I own them by divine right. So I care not a bit who possesses them. I used to care very much and consequently was very unhappy.—*James Howard Keller*

3663   My riches consist not in the extent of my possessions, but in the fewness of my wants.—*J. Brotherton*

3664   The pride of dying rich raises the loudest laugh in hell.—*John Foster*

3665   To have what we want is riches, but to be able to do without is power.—*G. Macdonald*

3666   Public sentiment will come to be, that the man who dies rich dies disgraced.—*Andrew Carnegie*

Right

3667   I would rather be right than be President.—*Henry Clay*

3668   Let us have faith that right makes might, and in that faith, let us to the end, dare to do our duty, as we understand it.—*Lincoln*

Sabbath

3669   He who ordained the Sabbath loves the poor.—*J.R. Lowell*

3670   The longer I live the more highly do I estimate the Christian Sabbath, and the more grateful do I feel to those who impress its importance on the community.—*Daniel Webster*

3671   A corruption of morals usually follows a profanation of the Sabbath.—*Blackstone*

Science

3672   Every great advance in science has issued from a new audacity of imagination.—*John Dewey*

3673   Science is simply common sense at its best—that is, rigidly accurate in observation, and merciless to fallacy in logic.—*T.H. Huxley*

Secret

3674   A truly wise man should have no keeper of his secret but himself.—*Guizot*

3675   Three may keep a secret, if two of them are dead.—*Franklin*

Self-Control

3676   Heat not a furnace for your foe so hot.—*Shakespeare*

3677   By taking revenge, a man is but even with his enemy; but in passing over it, he is superior.—*Bacon*

3678   He who reigns within himself and rules his passions, desires, and fears is more than a king.—*Milton*

Silence

3679   Blessed is the man who, having nothing to say, abstains from giving in words evidence of the fact.—*George Eliot*

3680   Speech is great, but silence is greater.—*Carlyle*

3681   Silence never shows itself to so great an advantage as when it is made the reply to calumny and defamation.—*Addison*

3682   'Tis not my talent to conceal my thoughts, or carry smiles and sunshine in my face, when discontent sits heavy at my heart.—*Addison*

3683   Learn to hold thy tongue; five words cost Zacharias forty weeks of silence.—*Fuller*

3684   Speaking much is a sign of vanity, for he that is lavish in words is a niggard in deed.—*Sir W. Raleigh*

Simplicity

3685   The fashion wears out more apparel than the man.—*Shakespeare*

3686   Simplicity of all things, is the hardest to be copied.—*Steele*

3687   Nothing is more simple than greatness; indeed, to be simple is to be great.—*Emerson*

3688   The greatest truths are the simplest; and so are the greatest men. —*Hare*

Sin

3689   Selfishness is the greatest curse of the human race.—*W.E. Gladstone*

3690   I am a man more sinn'd against than sinning.—*Shakespeare*

3691   Some rise by sin, and some by virtue fall.—*Shakespeare*

3692   No man ever became extremely wicked all at once.—*Juvenal*

3693   Of Man's first disobedience, and the fruit of that forbidden tree whose mortal taste brought death into the world, and all our woe.—*John Milton*

3694   Sin is essentially a departure from God.—*Luther*

3695   How immense appear to us the sins that we have not committed. —*Madame Necker*

3696   Sins are like circles in the water when a stone is thrown into it; one produces another.—When anger was in Cain's heart, murder was not far off.—*Philip Henry*

Sincerity

3697   Without earnestness no man is ever great or does really great things. He may be the cleverest of men; he may be brilliant, entertaining, popular; but he will want weight.—*Bayne*

3698   Sincerity and truth are the basis of every virtue.—*Confucius*

Slander

3699   Slander is a vice that strikes a double blow, wounding both him that commits, and him against whom it is committed.—*Saurin*

3700   Slander is the revenge of a coward, and dissimulation his defense. —*Johnson*

3701 We cannot control the evil tongues of others, but a good life enables us to despise them.—*Cato*

Sleep

3702 Sleep that knits up the ravell'd sleave of care, the death of each day's life, sore labour's bath, balm of hurt minds, great nature's second course, chief nourisher in life's feast.—*Shakespeare*

3703 O sleep, O gentle sleep, nature's soft nurse! how have I frightened thee, that thou no more wilt weigh my eyelids down and steep my senses in forgetfulness?—*Shakespeare*

Society

3704 Society is composed of two great classes: those who have more dinners than appetite, and those who have more appetite than dinners.—*Chamfort*

3705 The best cure for worry, depression, melancholy, brooding, is to go deliberately forth and try to lift with one's sympathy the gloom of somebody else.—*Arnold Bennett*

3706 God has made no one absolute.—The rich depend on the poor, as well as the poor on the rich.—The world is but a magnificent building; all the stones are gradually cemented together.—No one subsists by himself alone.—*Feltham*

3707 Society is now one polished horde, formed of two mighty tribes, the bores and bored.—*Byron*

Solitude

3708 No one is so utterly desolate, but some heart, though unknown, responds unto his own.—*Longfellow*

3709 Eating the bitter bread of banishment.—*Shakespeare*

3710 I never found the companion that was so companionable as solitude.—*Thoreau*

3711 A wise man is never less alone than when he is alone.—*Swift*

3712 Conversation enriches the understanding, but solitude is the school of Genius.—*Gibbon*

3713 If from society we learn to live, it is solitude should teach us how to die.—*Byron*

3714   It is easy, in the world, to live after the world's opinion; it is easy, in solitude to live after your own; but the great man is he who, in the midst of the crowd, keeps with perfect sweetness the independence of solitude.—*Emerson*

Sorrow

3715   The deeper the sorrow the less tongue it hath.—*Talmud*

3716   When sorrows come, they come not single spies, but in battalions. —*Shakespeare*

3717   Good night, good night! parting is such sweet sorrow, that I shall say good night till it be morrow.—*Shakespeare*

3718   Men can counsel and speak comfort to that grief which they themselves not feel.—*Shakespeare*

3719   Joys are our wings; sorrows our spurs.—*Richter*

3720   Tearless grief bleeds inwardly.—*Bovee*

3721   Tears are often the telescope by which men see far into heaven. —*H.W. Beecher*

3722   Everyone can master a grief but he that has it.—*Shakespeare*

Soul

3723   Sensuality is the grave of the soul.—*Channing*

3724   It is the mind that makes the man, and our vigour is in our immortal soul.—*Ovid*

3725   Great truths are portions of the soul of man; great souls are portions of eternity.—*J.R. Lowell*

3726   Two souls with but a single thought, two hearts that beat as one. —*E.F.J. von Münch-Bellinghausen*

3727   Build thee more stately mansions, O, my soul,
As the swift seasons roll!
Leave thy low-vaulted past!
Let each new temple, nobler than the last
Shut thee from heaven with a dome more vast,
'Till thou at length art free,
Leaving thine outgrown shell by life's unresting sea!
—*O.W. Holmes*

3728   Whatever that be which thinks, which understands, which wills, which acts, it is something celestial and divine, and on that account must necessarily be eternal.—*Cicero*

3729   I am fully convinced that the soul is indestructible, and that its activity will continue through eternity. It is like the sun, which, to our eyes, seems to set in night; but it has in reality only gone to diffuse its light elsewhere.—*Goethe*

Speech

3730   Charm us, orator, till the lion look no larger than the cat.—*Tennyson*

3731   Speech is a faculty given to man to conceal his thoughts.—*Talleyrand*

3732   Speeches cannot be made long enough for the speakers, nor short enough for the hearers.—*Perry*

3733   Repartee is perfect, when it effects its purpose with a double edge. Repartee is the highest order of wit, as it bespeaks the coolest yet quickest exercise of genius at a moment when the passions are roused.—*Colton*

3734   Rhetoric is nothing but reason well dressed, and argument put in order.—*Jeremy Collier*

3735   "I have heard many great orators." said Louis XIV to Massilon, "and have been highly pleased with them; but whenever I hear you, I go away displeased with myself." This is the highest encomium that could be bestowed on a preacher.—*C. Simmons*

3736   With words we govern men.—*Disraeli*

3737   What too many orators want in depth, they give you in length.—*Montesquieu*

3738   The language of the heart which comes from the heart and goes to the heart—is always simple, graceful, and full of power, but no art of rhetoric can teach it. It is at once the easiest and most difficult language,—difficult, since it needs a heart to speak it; easy, because its periods though rounded and full of harmony, are still unstudied.—*Bovee*

Spring

3739   Winter, lingering, chills the lap of May.—*Goldsmith*

3740   In the spring a livelier iris changes on the burnished dove; in the spring a young man's fancy lightly turns to thoughts of love.—*Tennyson*

Success

3741   Nothing succeeds so well as success.—*Talleyrand*

3742   Benjamin Franklin's secret of success: "I will speak ill of no man, and speak all the good I know of everybody."

3743   Many shining actions owe their success to chance, though the general or statesman runs away with the applause.—*Home*

3744   The way to be nothing is to do nothing.—*Howe*

Tact

3745   It is a very hard undertaking to seek to please everybody.—*Publius Syrus*

3746   Tact comes as much from goodness of heart as from fineness of taste.—*Endymion*

3747   It is a sad thing when men have neither the wit to speak well, nor judgment to hold their tongues.—*La Bruyère*

Taxes

3748   The art of taxation consists in so plucking the goose as to obtain the largest amount of feathers with the least possible amount of hissing.—*Attributed to J. B. Colbert*

3749   The power to tax carries with it the power to embarrass and destroy.—*Supreme Court of the United States—Evans vs. Gore, 1920*

Teacher

3750   The teacher is like the candle which lights others in consuming itself.—*Ruffini*

Temptation

3751   No man is matriculated to the art of life till he has been well tempted.—*George Eliot*

3752   Every temptation is great or small according as the man is.—*Jeremy Taylor*

3753   Better shun the bait than struggle in the snare.—*Dryden*

3754   Some temptations come to the industrious, but all temptations attack the idle.—*Spurgeon*

Thought

3755   True, I talk of dreams, which are the children of an idle brain, begot of nothing but vain fantasy.—*Shakespeare*

3756   Thy wish was father, Harry, to that thought.—*Shakespeare*

3757   Give thy thoughts no tongue.—*Shakespeare*

3758   There is nothing either good or bad, but thinking makes it so.—*Shakespeare*

3759   Thinking is the hardest work there is, which is the probable reason why so few engage in it.—*Henry Ford*

3760   Sit in reverie, and watch the changing color of the waves that break upon the idle seashore of the mind.—*Longfellow*

3761   Every thought which genius and piety throw into the world alters the world.—*Emerson*

3762   They only babble who practise not reflection.—I shall think; and thought is silence.—*Sheridan*

3763   Some persons do first, think afterward, and then repent forever.—*Secker*

3764   A picture is an intermediate something between a thought and a thing.—*Coleridge*

3765   The most important thought I ever had was that of my individual responsibility to God.—*Daniel Webster*

3766   Thinking is the talking of the soul with itself.—*Plato*

3767   It is not strange that remembered ideas should often take advantage of the crowd of thoughts and smuggle themselves in as original.—Honest thinkers are always stealing unconsciously from each other.—Our minds are full of waifs and estrays which we think our own.—Innocent plagiarism turns up everywhere.—*O.W. Holmes*

3768   The men of action are, after all, only the unconscious instruments of the men of thought.—*Heinrich Heine*

Time

3769   The inaudible and noiseless foot of Time.—*Shakespeare*

3770   We burn daylight.—*Shakespeare*

3771   It is hoped that, with all modern improvements, a way will be discovered of getting rid of bores; for it is too bad that a poor wretch can be punished for stealing your handkerchief or gloves, and that no punishment can be inflicted on those who steal your time, and with it your temper and patience, as well as the bright thoughts that might have entered your mind, if they had not been frightened away by the bore.—*Byron*

3772   O, call back yesterday, bid time return!—*Shakespeare*

3773   Come what come may, time and the hour run through the roughest day.—*Shakespeare*

3774   In the posteriors of this day, which the rude multitude call the afternoon.—*Shakespeare*

3775   The great rule of moral conduct is, next to God, to respect time. —*Lavater*

3776   If hours did not hang heavy, what would become of scandal?— *Bancroft*

3777   Dost thou love life?—Then do not squander time, for that is the stuff life is made of.—*Franklin*

3778   No hand can make the clock strike for me the hours that are passed.—*Byron*

3779   Tomorrow is the day when idlers work, and fools reform, and mortal men lay hold on heaven.—*Young*

3780   Every man's life lies within the present; for the past is spent and done with, and the future is uncertain.—*Marcus Antoninus*

3781   Live this day as if it were the last.—*Kerr*

3782   Thou wilt find rest from vain fancies if thou doest every act in life as though it were thy last.—*Marcus Aurelius Antoninus*

3783   Time is a sort of river of passing events, and strong is its current; no sooner is a thing brought to sight than it is swept by and another takes its place, and this too will be swept away.—*Marcus Aurelius Antoninus*

3784   The whole life of man is but a point of time; let us enjoy it, therefore, while it lasts, and not spend it to no purpose.—*Plutarch*

3785   Dionysius the Elder, being asked whether he was at leisure, he replied, "God forbid that it should ever befall me!"—*Plutarch*

3786   As if you could kill time without injuring eternity!—*Thoreau*

3787   Nothing lies on our hands with such uneasiness as time. Wretched and thoughtless creatures! In the only place where covetousness were a virtue we turn prodigals.—*Addison*

3788   All my possessions for a moment of time.—*Queen Elizabeth I's last words*

Tolerance

3789   He who never leaves his own country is full of prejudices.—*Goldoni*

3790   Intolerance has been the curse of every age and state.—*S. Davies*

3791   Tolerance comes with age; I see no fault committed that I myself could not have committed at some time or other.—*Goethe*

Tradition

3792   But to my mind, though I am native here and to the manner born, it is a custom more honoured in the breach than the observance.—*Shakespeare*

3793   Tradition is an important help to history, but its statements should be carefully scrutinized before we rely on them.—*Addison*

Tragedy

3794   The worst is not so long as we can say, "This is the worst."—*Shakespeare*

3795   A perfect tragedy is the noblest production of human nature.—*Addison*

3796   Never morning wore to evening, but some heart did break.—*Tennyson*

Travel

3797   Usually speaking, the worst bred person in company is a young traveller just returned from abroad.—*Swift*

3798   The travelled mind is the catholic mind, educated out of exclusiveness and egotism.—*A.B. Alcott*

Trifles

3799   Small to greater matters must give way.—*Shakespeare*

3800   Good taste rejects excessive nicety; it treats little things as little things, and is not hurt by them.—*Fénelon*

3801   Trifles make perfection, but perfection itself is no trifle.—*Michaelangelo*

3802   He that despiseth small things, shall fall by little and little.—*Ecclesiasticus*

3803 Most of the critical things in life, which become the starting points of human destiny, are little things.—*R. Smith*

3804 It is the little rift within the lute that by and by will make the music mute, and ever widening slowly silence all.—*Tennyson*

Troubles

3805 This world has cares enough to plague us; but he who meditates on others' woe, shall, in that meditation, lose his own.—*Cumberland*

3806 Troubles are often the tools by which God fashions us for better things.—*H.W. Beecher*

Truth

3807 Logic is the art of convincing us of some truth.—*La Bruyère*

3808 Those who exaggerate in their statements belittle themselves. —*C. Simmons*

3809 Truth is truth to the end of reckoning.—*Shakespeare*

3810 The truth is always the strongest argument.—*Sophocles*

3811 A man should never be ashamed to own he has been in the wrong, which is but saying, in other words, that he is wiser today than he was yesterday.—*Pope*

3812 The telling of a falsehood is like the cut of a sabre; for though the wound may heal, the scar of it will remain.—*Saadi*

3813 Truth sits upon the lips of dying men.—*Matthew Arnold*

3814　　　　Truth, crushed to earth, shall rise again:
　　　　　　The eternal years of God are hers;
　　　　　　But Error, wounded, writhes with pain,
　　　　　　And dies among his worshippers.
　　　　　　　　　—*William Cullen Bryant*

3815 Truth is the foundation of all knowledge and the cement of all societies.—*John Dryden*

3816 If the world goes against truth, then Athanasius goes against the world.—*Athanasius*

3817 He who seeks truth should be of no country.—*Voltaire*

Vanity

3818 It is our own vanity that makes the vanity of others intolerable to us.—*La Rochefoucauld*

3819   Vanity is the fruit of ignorance.—*Ross*

3820   There is no arena in which vanity displays itself under such a variety of forms as in conversation.—*Pascal*

3821   There's none so homely but loves a looking-glass.—*South*

Vengeance

3822   The fire you kindle for your enemy often burns yourself more than him.—*Chinese Proverb*

3823   No man ever did a designed injury to another, but at the same time he did a greater to himself.—*Home*

Virtue

3824   Of all virtues magnanimity is the rarest; there are a hundred persons of merit for one who willingly acknowledges it in another.—*Hazlitt*

3825   There is but one virtue—the eternal sacrifice of self.—*George Sand*

3826   True humility, the highest virtue, mother of them all.—*Tennyson*

3827   Confidence in another man's virtue, is no slight evidence of one's own.—*Montaigne*

3828   He that is good will infallibly become better, and he that is bad will as certainly become worse; for vice, virtue, and time are three things that never stand still.—*Colton*

3829   I cannot praise a fugitive and cloistered virtue, unexercised and unbreathed, that never sallies out and sees her adversary. The virtue that knows not the utmost that vice promises to her followers, and rejects it, is but a blank virtue, not a pure.—*Milton*

Voice

3830   The voice of the people is the voice of God.—*Hesiod*

Want

3831   Man wants but little here below,
                        Nor wants that little long.
                                        —*Goldsmith*

War

3832   Take my word for it, if you had seen but one day of war, you would pray to Almighty God, that you might never see such a thing again.—*Wellington*

3833 In disarming Peter, Christ disarmed every soldier.—*Tertullian*

3834 One murder makes a villain; millions a hero.—*Bp. Porteus*

3835 Who overcomes force, hath overcome but half his foe.—*John Milton*

3836 War loves to seek its victims in the young.—*Sophocles*

3837 War! that mad game the world so loves to play.—*Swift*

3838 There never was a good war, or a bad peace.—*Franklin*

3839 War is the business of barbarians.—*Napoleon I*

3840
> Someone had blundered:
> Theirs not to make reply,
> Theirs not to reason why,
> Theirs but to do and die.
> —*Tennyson*

3841
> Cannon to right of them,
> Cannon to left of them,
> Cannon in front of them.
> . . . .
> Into the jaws of death,
> Into the mouth of hell
> Rode the six hundred.
> —*Tennyson*

Wealth

3842 Rich people should consider that they are only trustees for what they possess, and should show their wealth to be more in doing good than merely in having it. They should not reserve their benevolence for purposes after they are dead, for those who give not of their property till they die show that they would not then if they could keep it any longer.—*Bp. Hall*

3843 All that glisters is not gold.—*Shakespeare*

3844 Rank and riches are chains of gold, but still chains.—*Ruffini*

3845 Supine amidst our flowing store, we slept securely, and we dreamt of more.—*John Dryden*

3846 He is richest who is content with the least, for content is the wealth of nature.—*Socrates*

3847 Wealth may be an excellent thing, for it means power, leisure, and liberty.—*J.R. Lowell*

3848   There is no society, however free and democratic, where wealth will not create an aristocracy.—*Bulwer*

3849   Wealth consists not in having great possessions but in having few wants.—*Epicurus*

Wife

3850   All other goods by fortune's hand are given:
        A wife is the peculiar gift of Heav'n.—*Pope*

Will

3851   If weakness may excuse, what murderer, what traitor, parricide incestuous, sacrilegious, but may plead it? All wickedness is weakness; that plea, therefore, with God or man will gain thee no remission. —*Milton*

3852   At twenty years of age the will reigns; at thirty, the wit; and at forty, the judgment.—*Gratian*

3853   He who has a firm will molds the world to himself.—*Goethe*

3854   People do not lack strength; they lack will.—*Hugo*

3855   To deny the freedom of the will is to make morality impossible. —*Froude*

Wind

3856   The gentle wind, a sweet and passionate wooer, kisses the blushing leaf.—*Longfellow*

3857   God tempers the wind to the shorn lamb.—*Sterne*

Wisdom

3858   Never reason from what you do not know.—*Ramsay*

3859   Knowledge comes, but wisdom lingers.—*Tennyson*

3860   A child can ask a thousand questions that the wisest man cannot answer.—*J. Abbott*

3861   Judge of a man by his questions rather than by his answers. —*Voltaire*

3862   The years teach much which the days never know.—*Emerson*

3863   Wise men argue causes; fools decide them.—*Anacharsis*

3864   The fool doth think he is wise, but the wise man knows himself to be a fool.—*Shakespeare*

3865   When he that speaks, and he to whom he speaks, neither of them understand what is meant, that is metaphysics.—*Voltaire*

3866   He draweth out the thread of his verbosity finer than the staple of his argument.—*Shakespeare*

3867   He is truly wise who gains wisdom from another's mishap. —*Publius Syrus*

3868   People generally quarrel because they cannot argue.—*G.K. Chesterton*

3869   If a man will begin with certainties, he shall end in doubts; but if he will be content to begin with doubts, he shall end in certainties. —*Francis Bacon*

3870   A fool may have his coat embroidered with gold, but it is a fool's coat still.—*Rivarol*

3871   A well cultivated mind is made up of all the minds of preceding ages; it is only the one single mind educated by all previous time.— *Fontenelle*

3872   Few minds wear out; more rust out.—*Bovee*

3873   Common-sense in an uncommon degree is what the world calls wisdom.—*Coleridge*

3874   The Delphic oracle said I was the wisest of all the Greeks. It is because that I alone, of all the Greeks, know that I know nothing.— *Socrates*

3875   The first consideration a wise man fixeth upon is the great end of his creation; what it is, and wherein it consists; the next is of the most proper means to that end.—*Walker*

3876   Perfect wisdom hath four parts, viz., wisdom, the principle of doing things aright; justice, the principle of doing things equally in public and private; fortitude, the principle of not flying danger but meeting it; and temperance, the principle of subduing desires and living moderately. —*Plato*

Wit

3877   To leave this keen encounter of our wits.—*Shakespeare*

3878   There's a skirmish of wit between them.—*Shakespeare*

3879   I am not only witty in myself, but the cause that wit is in other men.—*Shakespeare*

Woman

3880   The sum of all that makes a just man happy consists in the well choosing of his wife.—*Massinger*

3881   For a wife take the daughter of a good mother.—*Fuller*

3882   I have no other but a woman's reason: I think him so, because I think him so.—*Shakespeare*

3883   Frailty, thy name is woman!—*Shakespeare*

3884   Her voice was ever soft, gentle, and low,—an excellent thing in woman.—*Shakespeare*

3885   A lion among ladies is a most dreadful thing.—*Shakespeare*

3886   Woman apparently is doing everything possible to destroy in herself those very qualifications which render her beautiful, namely, modesty, purity, and chastity. It is a blindness which can only be explained by the fascination of that vanity of which the Scriptures speak with such severity.—*Pope Pius XI*

3887   No one knows like a woman how to say things which are at once gentle and deep.—*Victor Hugo*

3888   Men have sight; women insight.—*Hugo*

Word

3889   A very great part of the mischiefs that vex this world arises from words.—*Burke*

3890   The word impossible is not in my dictionary.—*Napoleon I*

3891   But yesterday the word of Caesar might
Have stood against the world; now lies he there,
And none so poor to do him reverence.—*Shakespeare*

Work

3892   Rest is the sweet sauce of labor.—*Plutarch*

3893   God gives every bird its food, but he does not throw it into the nest.—*J.G. Holland*

3894   So many worlds, so much to do, so little done, such things to be.
—*Tennyson*

3895   Things don't turn up in this world until somebody turns them up.—*Garfield*

3896   It is a sober truth that people who live only to amuse themselves, work harder at the task than most people do in earning their daily bread.—*H. More*

3897   Light is the task where many share the toil.—*Homer*

3898   Every man is, or hopes to be, an Idler.—*Samuel Johnson*

3899   Few men are lacking in capacity, but they fail because they are lacking in application.—*Calvin Coolidge*

3900   Temptation rarely comes in working hours. It is in their leisure time that men are made or marred.—*W.M. Taylor*

3901   Laziness grows on people; it begins in cobwebs and ends in iron chains. The more business a man has to do the more he is able to accomplish, for he learns to economize his time.—*Sir M. Hale*

3902   If you have great talents, industry will improve them; if moderate abilities, industry will supply their deficiencies. Nothing is denied to well directed labor; nothing is ever to be attained without it.—*Sir Joshua Reynolds*

3903   Every industrious man, in every lawful calling, is a useful man. —And one principal reason why men are so often useless is, that they neglect their own profession or calling, and divide and shift their attention among a multiplicity of objects and pursuits.—*Emmons*

3904   There is only one thing which will really train the human mind, and that is the voluntary use of the mind by the man himself. You may aid him, you may guide him, you may suggest to him, and, above all you may inspire him; but the only thing worth having is that which he gets by his own exertions: and what he gets is proportionate to the effort he puts into it.—*A. Lawrence Lowell*

World

3905   This world is all a fleeting show,
                 For man's illusion given;
                 The smiles of joy, the tears of woe,
                 Deceitful shine, deceitful flow,—
                 There's nothing true but Heaven.—*Moore*

3906   All the world's a stage,
          And all the men and women merely players.—*Shakespeare*

Writing

3907   The wise men of old have sent most of their morality down the stream of time in the light skiff of apothegm or epigram.—*E.P. Whipple*

3908   The two most engaging powers of an author, are, to make new things familiar, and familiar things new.—*Johnson*

3909   A man will turn over half a library to make one book.—*Johnson*

3910   The pen is the tongue of the mind.—*Miguel de Cervantes*

3911   The press is the foe of rhetoric, but the friend of reason.— *Colton*

3912   There are only two powers in the world, the sword and the pen; and in the end the former is always conquered by the latter.—*Napoleon I*

3913   Plagiarists have, at least, the merit of preservation.—*Disraeli*

Wrong

3914   Truth forever on the scaffold, wrong forever on the throne.— *J.R. Lowell*

Youth

3915   So wise so young, they say, do never live long.—*Shakespeare*

3916   He wears the rose of youth upon him.—*Shakespeare*

3917   We have some salt of our youth in us.—*Shakespeare*

3918   The excesses of our youth are drafts upon our old age, payable with interest about thirty years after date.—*Colton*

3919   Girls we love for what they are; young men for what they promise to be.—*Goethe*

Pertinent Proverbs

Ability

3920   No one knows what he can do until he tries.—*Latin*

Absence

3921   He that is absent is soon forgotten.

3922   Greater things are believed of those who are absent.—*Tacitus*

Abundance

3923   Abundance, like want, ruins man.—*Franklin*

Ache

3924   The tongue ever turns to the aching tooth.

Acquaintance

3925   Short acquaintance brings repentance.

Action

3926   Action is the proper fruit of knowledge.

3927   Great actions speak great minds.—*Fletcher*

Advantage

3928   Every advantage has its disadvantage.—*Latin*

Adversity

3929 Adversity makes a man wise, not rich.

3930 There is no education like adversity.—*Disraeli*

3931 Adversity has no friends.—*Tacitus*

Advice

3932 Fools need advice most, but wise men only are the better for it.—*Franklin*

3933 Less advice and more hands.—*German*

3934 When we are well, it is easy to give good advice to the sick.— *Terence*

3935 Hazard not your wealth on a poor man's advice.—*Spanish*

3936 Ask advice, but use your own common sense.—*Yiddish*

Affection

3937 Talk not of wasted affection, affection never was wasted.— *Longfellow*

Age

3938 All would live long, but none would be old.—*Franklin*

3939 Many foxes grow gray, but few grow old.—*Franklin*

3940 No wise man ever wished to be younger.—*Swift*

3941 The old forget, the young don't know.—*German*

3942 It is hard to put old heads on young shoulders.

Ambition

3943 Ambition is the mind's immodesty.—*D'Avenant*

3944 Ambition is the only power that combats love.—*Cibber*

3945   . . . fling away ambition:
By that sin fell the angels.—*Shakespeare*

3946 Would you rise in the world, veil ambition with the forms of humanity.—*Chinese*

3947 There is no eel so small but it hopes to become a whale.— *German*

3948　Ambition destroys its possessor.—*Hebrew*

Amusement

3949　Amusement is the happiness of those who cannot think.—*Pope*

Anger

3950　He that is slow to wrath is of great understanding.—*Old Testament, Proverbs*

3951　Anger is never without a reason, but seldom with a good one.—*Franklin*

3952　When a man grows angry, his reason rides out.

3953　When anger blinds the eye, truth disappears.

3954　The greatest remedy for anger is delay.—*Seneca*

Appearance

3955　All things are less dreadful than they seem.

3956　Men are valued not for what they are, but for what they seem to be.—*Bulwer-Lytton*

3957　O what a goodly outside falsehood hath!—*Shakespeare*

Architecture

3958　Architecture is frozen music.—*Goethe*

Argument

3959　A noisy man is always in the right.

3960　Treating your adversary with respect is giving him an advantage to which he is not entitled.—*Johnson*

3961　You have not converted a man because you have silenced him.

Artist

3962　An artist is a dreamer consenting to dream of the actual world. —*Santayana*

3963　Every artist writes his own autobiography.—*H. Ellis*

3964　The great artist is the simplifier.—*Amiel*

Aspiration

3965　No bird soars too high if he soars with his own wings.—*Blake*

3966　'Tis not what man does which exalts him, but what man would do.—*R. Browning*

3967　Too low they build, who build beneath the stars.—*Young*

Atheism

3968　The fool hath said in his heart, There is no God.—*Old Testament, Psalms*

3969　Atheism is rather in the lip than in the heart of man.—*Bacon*

Bear

3970　Make sure of the bear before you sell his skin.—*Aesop*

Beauty

3971　All heiresses are beautiful.

3972　Beauty and folly are old companions.

3973　Beauty has wings, and too hastily flies.

Begin

3974　All glory comes from daring to begin.

3975　He who begins many things, finishes but few.

Belief

3976　Each man's belief is right in his own eyes.

3977　He does not believe that does not live according to his belief.

3978　They can conquer who believe they can.—*Virgil*

Benefit

3979　To accept a benefit is to sell one's freedom.

3980　When you confer a benefit on a worthy man you oblige all men.

Biography

3981　Biography is the only true history.—*Carlyle*

3982　Biography—one of the new terrors of death.—*Arbuthnot*

Birth

3983　Our birth made us mortal, our death will make us immortal.

3984　I wept when I was born, and every day shows why.

3985 He who is born, yells; he who dies is silent.—*Russian*

Blame

3986 He must be pure who would blame another.—*Danish*

Blind

3987 When the blind man carries the banner, woe to those who follow.
—*French*

Boldness

3988 Great boldness is seldom without some absurdity.—*Bacon*

3989 Boldness has genius, power, and magic in it.—*Goethe*

3990 Fortune assists the bold.—*Latin*

Book

3991 A book may be as great a thing as a battle.—*Disraeli*

3992 A good book is the precious life-blood of the master spirit . . .
—*Milton*

3993 Books, the children of the brain.

3994 Word by word the great books are written.—*Voltaire*

Borrow

3995 Creditors have better memories than debtors.

3996 He who does not have to borrow lives without cares.—*Yiddish*

Bread

3997 His bread is buttered on both sides.

3998 Whose bread I eat, his song I sing.—*German*

Build

3999 To build is to be robbed.

4000 It is easier to pull down than to build.—*Latin*

Burden

4001 Every horse thinks his own pack heaviest.

4002 None knows the weight of another's burden.

4003 The burden is light on the shoulder of another.—*Russian*

Businessman

4004   Everyone lives by selling something.

4005   Keep thy shop and thy shop will keep thee.

4006   The market is a place set apart where men may deceive each other.—*Greek*

Caesar

4007   What millions died—that Caesar might be great!—*Campbell*

Candor

4008   I hate him that my vices telleth me.—*Chaucer*

Cemetery

4009   A piece of a churchyard fits everybody.

Character

4010   A man shows his character by what he laughs at.—*German*

4011   Character is habit long continued.—*Greek*

4012   It matters not what you are thought to be, but what you are.—*Latin*

Charity

4013   He that gives to be seen will relieve none in the dark.

4014   He gives twice who gives quickly.—*Latin*

4015   Do good and ask not for whom.—*Yiddish*

Children

4016   Children are poor men's riches.

4017   Children have wide ears and long tongues.

4018   Little children, little sorrows; big children, big sorrows.

4019   Where children are not, heaven is not.

4020   Children have more need of models than of critics.—*French*

4021   Better the child should cry than the father.—*German*

4022   Our neighbor's children are always the worst.—*German*

Church

4023   A church is God between four walls.—*French*

City

4024   God made the country and man made the town.—*Cowper*

4025   A great city, a great solitude.—*Greek*

Clever

4026   Cleverness is serviceable for everything, sufficient for nothing.—
French

4027   Don't be so clever; cleverer ones than you are in jail.—*Russian*

4028   He who would be too clever makes a fool of himself.—*Yiddish*

Commerce

4029   Commerce is the great civilizer.

4030   The merchant has no country.—*Jefferson*

Conceit

4031   Conceit is God's gift to little men.

4032   Every man has a right to be conceited until he is successful.—
Disraeli

4033   He is so full of himself that he is quite empty.

Conscience

4034   Conscience is the voice of God in the soul.

Content

4035   Content lodges oftener in cottages than in palaces.

4036   Think not on what you lack as much as on what you have.—
Greek

Courage

4037   Courage is the most common and vulgar of the virtues.—
Melville

4038   You can't answer for your courage if you have never been in
danger.—*French*

4039　Fortune favors the brave.

Danger

4040　The danger past and God forgotten.

4041　Fear the goat from the front, the horse from the rear, and man from all sides.—*Russian*

Day

4042　One of these days is none of these days.

Death

4043　The Lord gave, and the Lord hath taken away; blessed be the name of the Lord.—*Old Testament, Job*

4044　Yet a little sleep, a little slumber, a little folding of the hands to sleep.—*Old Testament, Proverbs*

4045　As soon as a man is born he begins to die.

4046　　　Death is but a path that must be trod
　　　　　If man would ever pass to God.—*Parnell*

4047　Six feet of earth make all men equal.—*Italian*

4048　Death—the gate of life.—*Latin*

Debt

4049　That is but an empty purse that is full of other men's money.

Deceit

4050　　　O what a tangled web we weave,
　　　　　When first we practice to deceive!—*Sir Walter Scott*

4051　The easiest person to deceive is one's self.

Democracy

4052　Democracy becomes a government of bullies tempered by editors.—*Emerson*

4053　Democracy substitutes election by the incompetent many for appointment by the corrupt few.—*G.B. Shaw*

Destiny

4054　One meets his destiny often in the road he takes to avoid it.—*French*

Dispute

4055   He who disputes with the stupid must have sharp answers.—
German

Doctor

4056   A man who is his own doctor has a fool for his patient.

4057   In a good surgeon, a hawk's eye; a lion's heart; and a lady's
hand.

4058   Every doctor thinks his pills the best.—*German*

Doubt

4059   Doubt makes the mountain which faith can move.

Dress

4060   If all the world went naked, how could we tell the kings?

4061   No fine clothes can hide the clown.

4062   That man is best dressed whose dress no one observes.

Duty

4063   Duty is what one expects from others.—*O. Wilde*

Early

4064   Get a name to rise early, and you may lie all day.

Economy

4065   Without frugality none can be rich, and with it very few would
be poor.

4066   Frugality is misery in disguise.—*Latin*

Education

4067   Education is an ornament in prosperity and a refuge in adversity.
—*Greek*

4068   There is no royal road to geometry.—*Euclid*

Egoism

4069   Every man is of importance to himself.

4070   When a man tries himself, the verdict is in his favor.

Eloquence

4071   Eloquence is the child of knowledge.

4072   It is the heart which makes men eloquent.—*Latin*

Enemy

4073   A man's greatness can be measured by his enemy.

4074   None but myself ever did me any harm.—*Napoleon I*

4075   Better a good enemy than a bad friend.—*Yiddish*

Envy

4076   Envy is the sincerest form of flattery.

Equality

4077   Equality begins in the grave.—*French*

Error

4078   When the learned man errs, he errs with a learned error.—*Arabian*

4079   Who errs and mends, commends himself to God.—*Spanish*

Eternity

4080   In the presence of eternity, the mountains are as transient as the clouds.

Evil

4081   Evil often triumphs but never conquers.

4082   An evil life is a kind of death.—*Spanish*

Example

4083   A good example is the best sermon.

4084   Example is a lesson that all men can read.

4085   Example is the school of mankind, and they will learn at no other.—*Burke*

Experience

4086   He knows the water best who has waded through it.—*Danish*

4087 It is costly wisdom that is bought by experience.

4088 Experience is the teacher of fools.—*Latin*

Fact

4089 Facts do not cease to exist because they are ignored.

4090 You can't alter facts by filming them over with romance.

Fame

4091 All fame is dangerous: good brings envy; bad, shame.

4092 Fame is but an inscription upon a grave.

4093 Fame . . . that last infirmity of noble minds.—*Milton*

Father

4094 One father is more than a hundred schoolmasters.

Fear

4095 Fear is the offspring of ignorance.

4096 Fear makes lions tame.—*German*

4097 Our fears always outnumber our dangers.—*Latin*

4098 If the thunder is not loud, the peasant forgets to cross himself.
—*Russian*

Fight

4099 We fight to great disadvantage when we fight with those who have nothing to lose.—*Italian*

4100 Do not fight against two adversaries.—*Latin*

Fortune

4101 No one is satisfied with his fortune nor dissatisfied with his intellect.—*French*

4102 Seldom are men blessed with good fortune and good sense at the same time.—*Latin*

Friend

4103 The wretched have no friends.

4104 A faithful friend is an image of God.—*French*

Giving

4105   The wise man does not lay up treasure. The more he gives, the more he has.—*Chinese*

4106   He that gives his heart will not deny his money.

4107   He who can give has many a good neighbor.

God

4108   God often visits us, but most of the time we are not at home.—*French*

4109   God is patient because eternal.—*St. Augustine*

Government

4110   No man is good enough to govern another without that other's consent.—*Lincoln*

4111   Every country has the government it deserves.—*French*

Happiness

4112   Man is not born for happiness.

4113   Happiness is made to be shared.—*French*

Heart

4114   When there is room in the heart there is room in the house.—*Danish*

4115   Every heart hath its own ache.

History

4116   Sin writes histories, goodness is silent.—*Goethe*

Honesty

4117   An honest man does not make himself a dog for the sake of a bone.—*Danish*

4118   They are all honest men, but my cloak is not to be found.—*Spanish*

Honor

4119   The louder he talked of his honor, the faster we counted our spoons.—*Emerson*

4120   When faith is lost, when honor dies,
             The man is dead!—*Whittier*

Hope

4121   Hope is the poor man's income.—*Danish*

4122   Great hopes make great men.

Humility

4123   There is no true holiness without humility.

4124   Humble thyself in all things.—*Thomas à Kempis*

Husband

4125   A good husband makes a good wife.

4126   A good wife makes a good husband.

Ignorance

4127   The tragedy of ignorance is its complacency.

4128   He who knows nothing is confident of everything.

4129   Ignorance is a voluntary misfortune.

Immortality

4130   All men desire to be immortal.

4131   He hath not lived that lives not after death.

Independence

4132   The strongest man in the world is he who stands most alone.—
Ibsen

Industry

4133   The dog that trots about finds a bone.

Justice

4134   Justice is truth in action.—*Joubert*

4135   If all men were just, there would be no need of valor.—*Greek*

Knowledge

4136   A man without knowledge is as one that is dead.

4137   Knowledge in youth is wisdom in age.

4138   The desire for knowledge increases with its acquisition.

4139   Those who really thirst for knowledge always get it.

Labor

4140   To labor is to pray.—*Latin*

4141   Life is in labor.—*Russian*

Language

4142   Language is the dress of thought.—*S. Johnson*

Laugh

4143   And if I laugh at any mortal thing,
'Tis that I may not weep.—*Byron*

4144   Our sincerest laughter
With some pain is fraught.—*Shelley*

Law

4145   Where is there any book of the law so clear to each man as that written in his heart?—*Tolstoi*

Lend

4146   He who lends to the poor gets his interest from God.—*German*

Library

4147   A great library is the diary of the human race.

Life

4148   I wept when I was born, and every day shows why.

4149   The present hour alone is man's.

4150   A useless life is an early death.—*Goethe*

4151   There is more to life than increasing its speed.—*Gandhi*

Lose

4152   Losers are always in the wrong.—*Spanish*

4153   If you've nothing to lose, you can try everything.—*Yiddish*

Man

4154   Man, an animal that makes bargains.—*Adam Smith*

4155   Man is a machine into which we put food and produce thought.

4156

> Though every prospect pleses,
> And only man is vile.—*Heber*

Manners

4157   Good breeding consists in concealing how much we think of ourselves and how little we think of the other person.—*Mark Twain*

Marriage

4158   Every woman should marry, and no man.—*Disraeli*

4159   Marriage halves our griefs, doubles our joys, and quadruples our expenses.

Misfortune

4160   It is the nature of mortals to kick a man when he is down.—*Greek*

4161   Misfortune is friendless.—*Greek*

Money

4162   A golden key opens every lock.

4163

> Money is honey, my little sonny,
> And a rich man's joke is always funny.

4164   The love of money and the love of learning seldom meet.

Mother

4165   Simply having children does not make mothers.

Music

4166   Music—the only universal tongue.

Nature

4167   Nature pardons no mistake.

4168   Nature is the art of God.—*Latin*

Necessity

4169   Necessity makes even the timid brave.—*Latin*

Old

4170　Old foxes want no tutors.

Parent

4171　If parents want honest children, they should be honest themselves.

Patience

4172　He preacheth patience that never knew pain.

4173　Patience is the art of hoping.—*French*

Peace

4174　When a man finds no peace within himself, it is useless to seek it elsewhere.—*French*

People

4175　The mob has many heads but no brains.

4176　No man who depends upon the caprice of the ignorant rabble can be accounted great.—*Cicero*

Philanthropy

4177　The most acceptable service of God is doing good to man.— *Franklin*

4178　I am a man, and nothing human can be indifferent to me.— *Terence*

Pleasure

4179　Pleasures are transient, honors are immortal.—*Greek*

Poor

4180　Poor men seek meat for their stomachs; rich men stomach for their meat.

4181　Whoso stoppeth his ear at the cry of the poor, shall cry himself and not be heard.—*Hebrew*

4182　Not he who has little, but he who wishes for more, is poor.— *Latin*

Poverty

4183　Poverty is the mother of all the arts.

4184   Poverty—the mother of temperance.—*Greek*

4185   No man should praise poverty but he who is poor.—*St. Bernard*

4186   There are many things which ragged men dare not say.—*Latin*

4187   There are only two families in the world, the Haves and the Have-Nots.—*Cervantes*

Praise

4188   Self-praise is no recommendation.

Prayer

4189   And Satan trembles when he sees
                The weakest saint upon his knees.—*Cowper*

4190   God warms his hands at man's heart when he prays.—*Masefield*

4191   Who rises from prayer a better man, his prayer is answered.—*Meredith*

4192   If you pray for another, you will be helped yourself.—*Yiddish*

Prejudice

4193   Prejudice is the child of ignorance.

Prosperity

4194   Prosperity is a great teacher; adversity, a greater.

4195   Prosperity makes friends, adversity tries them.—*Latin*

4196   The prosperous man is never sure that he is loved for himself.—*Latin*

Prudence

4197   That should be long considered which can be decided but once.—*Latin*

Quarrel

4198   When we quarrel, how we wish we had been blameless!

Reading

4199   I love to lose myself in other men's minds.—*Lamb*

4200   The art of reading is to skip judiciously.

Repentance

4201   He who repents his sins is almost innocent.—*Latin*

Revenge

4202   The noblest vengeance is to forgive.

4203   To forget a wrong is the best revenge.

Rich

4204   To gain wealth is easy; to keep it, hard.—*Chinese*

4205   Ill fares the land, to hastening ills a prey,
      Where wealth accumulates, and men decay.—*Goldsmith*

4206   At the door of the rich are many friends.—*Hebrew*

Saint

4207   The way of this world is to praise dead saints and persecute living ones.

Saving

4208   For age and want save while you may:
      No morning sun lasts a whole day.

Scandal

4209   There is nothing that can't be made worse by telling.—*Latin*

Secret

4210   If you wish another to keep your secret, first keep it yourself.—*Latin*

Self-Love

4211   To love oneself is the beginning of a life-long romance.—*O. Wilde*

4212   Self-love is the greatest of all flatterers.—*La Rochefoucauld*

Sickness

4213   The chamber of sickness is the chapel of devotion.

4214   In time of sickness the soul collects itself anew.—*Latin*

4215   Sickness shows us what we are.—*Latin*

Sin

4216   The cat shuts its eyes while it steals cream.

4217   Sin writes histories; goodness is silent.—*Goethe*

4218   There is a sin of omission as well as of commission.—*Greek*

Solitude

4219   Solitude is the best nurse of wisdom.

4220   The strongest man in the world is he who stands alone.—*Ibsen*

Sorrow

4221   Earth has no sorrow that Heaven cannot heal.

4222   The longest sorrow finds at last relief.

Speech

4223   The true use of speech is to conceal our thoughts.

4224   A man's character is revealed by his speech.—*Greek*

Success

4225   Nothing is so impudent as success.

4226   Success makes a fool seem wise.

4227   Everything is subservient to success.

Talk

4228   He who talks much is sometimes right.—*Spanish*

Thought

4229   I would that my tongue could utter
             The thoughts that arise in me.—*Tennyson*

4230   The profound thinker always suspects that he may be superficial.
—*Disraeli*

Time

4231   Nought treads so silent as the foot of time.

4232   All the treasures of earth cannot bring back one lost moment.—
French

Travel

4233   It is not worth while to go round the world to count the cats in Zanzibar.—*Thoreau*

4234   See one mountain, one sea, one river—and see all.—*Greek*

4235   He who never leaves his country is full of prejudices.—*Italian*

Truth

4236   When in doubt, tell the truth.—*Mark Twain*

4237   Individuals may perish; but truth is eternal.—*French*

4238   Time discovers truth.—*Latin*

University

4239   A university is a place where pebbles are polished and diamonds are dimmed.—*Ingersoll*

Unlucky

4240   He falls on his back and breaks his nose.—*French*

Vice

4241   Never open the door to a little vice lest a great one enter with it.

4242   The virtues of society are the vices of the saints.—*Emerson*

Virtue

4243   Virtue is always in a minority.—*French*

4244   Virtue unites man with God.—*Latin*

War

4245   Force and fraud are in war the two cardinal virtues.—*Hobbes*

4246   War never leaves where it found a nation.—*Burke*

4247   War loves to seek its victims in the young.—*Greek*

Wealth

4248   Ill fares the land, to hastening ills a prey,
Where wealth accumulates and men decay.—*Goldsmith*

Wife

4249   A cheerful wife is the joy of life.

4250   An expensive wife makes a pensive husband.

4251   An obedient wife commands her husband.

4252   The wife that loves the looking-glass hates the saucepan.

Wisdom

4253   That man is wisest who realizes that his wisdom is worthless.—*Socrates*

4254   Wisdom comes by suffering.—*Greek*

4255   There is often wisdom under a shabby cloak.—*Latin*

Wise

4256   What's the good of being wise when foolishness serves?—*Yiddish*

Wit

4257   Wit does not take the place of knowledge.

4258   Wit is the salt of conversation, not the food.

Woman

4259   We may live with, but cannot live without 'em.

4260   Kind words and few are a woman's ornament.—*Danish*

4261   A woman can be anything the man who loves her would have her be.—*Barrie*

4262   A handsome woman is always right.—*German*

4263   It is a sad house where the hen crows louder than the rooster.

Work

4264   Blessed is he who has found his work; let him ask no other blessedness.—*Carlyle*

Writing

4265   Either write things worth reading, or do things worth writing.—*Franklin*

4266   Look in thy heart and write.—*Sidney*

Youth

4267   Youth is the season of hope.

4268　The majority of men employ the first portion of their life in making the other portion miserable.—*La Bruyère*

Zeal

4269　Zeal is fit only for wise men but is found mostly in fools.

4270　Zeal without knowledge is the sister of folly.

Quotations from Modern Sources

4271 *Advertising*

Advertising may be described as the science of arresting the human intelligence long enough to get money from it.—*Stephen Leacock*

So far as advertising is concerned, I repeat that it must survive as a thriving dynamic force. Not only does it deserve to continue because of its contributions to our way of life but it has a job to do now.—*Leon Henderson*

4272 *The Flag*

The things that the flag stands for were created by the experience of a great people. Everything that it stands for was written by their lives. The flag is the embodiment, not of sentiment, but of history.—*Woodrow Wilson*

4273 *Vain*

To say that a man is vain means merely that he is pleased with the effect he produces on other people. A conceited man is satisfied with the effect he produces on himself.—*Max Beerbohm*

4274 *Expert*

What's an expert? I read somewhere that the more a man knows, the more he knows he doesn't know. So I suppose one definition of an expert would be someone who doesn't admit out loud that he knows enough about a subject to know he doesn't really know much.—*Malcolm S. Forbes*

4275 Art

For art, if it is to be reckoned with as one of the great values of life, must teach man humility, tolerance, wisdom and magnanimity. The value of art is not beauty, but right action.—*W. Somerset Maugham*

4276 English

I haven't been abroad in so long that I almost speak English without an accent.—*Robert Benchley*

4277 Life

You can't tell how good it is to be alive, till you are facing death, because you don't live till then.—*John Galsworthy*

4278 Tolerance

Tolerance is the key to peace, for there can be no peace unless there is mutual tolerance between differing peoples and systems and cultures.—*Adlai E. Stevenson*

4279 War

There has never been a war yet which, if the facts had been put calmly before the ordinary folk, could not have been prevented. The common man is the greatest protection against war.—*Ernest Bevin*

4280 New England

The swaggering underemphasis of New England.—*Heywood Broun*

4281 Civilizations

So I should say that civilizations begin with religion and stoicism; they end with skepticism and unbelief, and the undisciplined pursuit of individual pleasure. A civilization is born stoic and dies epicurean.—*Will Durant*

4282 Schoolteachers

Emerson advised his fellow-townsmen to manufacture schoolteachers and make them the best in the world.—*Van Wyck Brooks*

4283   Woman Suffrage

Wouldn' th' way things are goin' these days make a fine argyment in favor of woman suffrage if we didn' already have it?—*Frank McKinney Hubbard*

4284   Future

Everyone is interested in the future, in what lies ahead, and particularly is this true in business. Peering into the crystal ball to discern the future can be interesting, frustrating, tedious, sometimes even humorous, but at all times it is an important phase of business leadership. Forecasting has been described as an educated guess.—*Wayne A. Johnston*

4285   Cultured

When you take a bath, you are civilized, when you don't take a bath, you are cultured.—*Lin Yutang*

4286   Occupational Diseases

Arrogance, pedantry, and dogmatism are the occupational diseases of those who spend their lives directing the intellects of the young.—*Henry S. Canby*

4287   Trees

I like trees because they seem more resigned to the way they have to live than other things do.—*Willa Cather*

4288   Elegant Variation

The very limitations of his field drive the sports writer to ingenious devices. . . . How many ways is it possible to say that one football team defeated another? As season follows season with annual and ruthless regularity, the sports writer is confronted with situations and subjects that he has faced not once or twice before, but many times. Almost inevitably, he becomes an expert in what Arthur Quiller-Couch long ago named "the trick of elegant variation, so rampant in the sporting press."—*Chicago Tribune*

4289   Democracy

My political ideal is democracy. Everyone should be respected as an individual, but no one idolized.—*Albert Einstein*

4290   English

By being so long in the lowest form [at Harrow] I gained an immense advantage over the cleverer boys. . . . I got into my bones the essential structure of the ordinary British sentence—which is a noble thing. Naturally I am biassed in favor of boys learning English; and then I would let the clever ones learn Latin as an honor, and Greek as a treat.—*Sir Winston Churchill*

4291 Discontent

Restlessness is discontent—and discontent is the first necessity of progress. Show me a thoroughly satisfied man—and I will show you a failure. —*Thomas A. Edison*

4292 Slogans

Slogans are both exciting and comforting, but they are also powerful opiates for the conscience.—*James Bryant Conant*

4293 Democracy

Democracy is based upon the conviction that there are extraordinary possibilities in ordinary people.—*Harry Emerson Fosdick*

The greatest destroyer of democracy in the world is war itself.—*Harry Emerson Fosdick*

4295 Education

The most important function of education at any level is to develop the personality of the individual and the significance of his life to himself and to others. This is the basic architecture of a life; the rest is ornamentation and decoration of the structure. As such, it is desirable but only in a supplementary sense.—*Grayson Kirk*

The primary concern of American education today is . . . to cultivate in the largest number of our future citizens an appreciation both of the responsibilities and the benefits which come to them because they are American and free.—*James Bryant Conant*

4297 Humanity

It is not tolerable, it is not possible, that from so much death, so much sacrifice and ruin, so much heroism, a greater and better humanity shall not emerge.—*Charles de Gaulle*

4298 United States of Europe

The conception of a United States of Europe is right. Every step to that end, which makes easier the traffic and reciprocal services of Europe, is good for all.—*Sir Winston Churchill*

4299 New Thinker

A "New Thinker" when studied closely, is merely a man who does not know what other people have thought.—*Frank Moore Colby*

4300 New England

New England is a finished place. Its destiny is that of Florence or Venice, not Milan, while the American empire careens onward toward its unpredicted end. . . . It is the first American section to be finished, to achieve stability in the conditions of its life. It is the first old civilization, the first permanent civilization in America.—*Bernard De Voto*

4301 Accounting

> Nobody was ever meant
> To remember or invent
> What he did with every cent.—*Robert Frost*

4302 Human Personality

Christian teaching alone, in its majestic integrity, can give full meaning and compelling motive to the demand for human rights and liberties, because it alone gives worth and dignity to human personality.—*Pope Pius XI*

4303 Arrogance

Early in life I had to choose between arrogance and hypocritical humility. I chose honest arrogance and have seen no occasion to change.— *Frank Lloyd Wright*

4304 Private Wealth

I like to walk about amidst the beautiful things that adorn the world; but private wealth I should decline, or any sort of personal possessions, because they would take away my liberty.—*George Santayana*

4305 Success

Success, which touches nothing that it does not vulgarize, should be its own reward . . . the odium of success is hard enough to bear, without the added ignominy of popular applause.—*Robert Bontine Cunninghame Graham*

4306 Horse's Mouth

We have a phrase in English "straight from the horse's mouth." I never knew why the particular animal chosen was a horse, especially as most horses are generally not very communicative.—*Joseph Clark Grew*

4307 Architecture

The only thing wrong with architecture is architects.—*Frank Lloyd Wright*

4308 Underprivileged

The war on privilege will never end. Its next great campaign will be against the special privileges of the underprivileged.—*Henry L. Mencken*

4309 Undergraduates

The most conservative persons I ever met are college undergraduates.—*Woodrow Wilson*

4310 Biography

Biography, like big game hunting, is one of the recognized forms of sport, and it is as unfair as only sport can be.—*Philip Guedalla*

4311 Old Age

Old age, believe me, is a good and pleasant time. It is true that you are gently shouldered off the stage, but then you are given such a comfortable front stall as spectator, and, if you have really played your part, you are more content to sit down and watch.—*Jane Ellen Harrison*

4312 Attitude

The important and decisive factor in life is not what happens to us, but the attitude we take toward what happens. The surest revelation of one's character is the way one bears one's suffering. Circumstances and situations may color life, but by the grace of God, we have been given the power to choose what that color shall be. The effect that misfortune, handicap, sickness, and sorrow have upon life is determined by the way in which we meet them.—*Charles R. Woodson*

4313 Englishman

An Englishman is a man who lives on an island in the North Sea governed by Scotsmen.—*Philip Guedalla*

4314 American Literature

All modern literature comes from one book by Mark Twain called *Huckleberry Finn.* . . . There was nothing before. There has been nothing as good since.—*Ernest Hemingway*

4315 Law

The Law, wherein, as in a magic mirror we see reflected not only our own lives, but the lives of all men that have been! When I think on this majestic theme my eyes dazzle.—*Oliver Wendell Holmes, Jr.*

4316 Brotherhood

Human brotherhood is not just a goal. It is a condition on which our way of life depends. The question for our time is not whether all men are brothers. That question has been answered by the God who placed us on this earth together. The question is whether we have the strength and the will to make the brotherhood of man the guiding principle of our daily lives.—*John F. Kennedy*

4317 Understanding

It is probably a pity that every citizen of each state cannot visit all the others, to see the differences, to learn what we have in common, and to come back with a richer, fuller understanding of America—in all its beauty, in all its dignity, in all its strength, in support of moral principle. —*Dwight D. Eisenhower*

4318 Professional Work

Whether four years of strenuous attention to football and fraternities is the best preparation for professional work has never been seriously investigated.—*Robert Maynard Hutchins*

4319 Freedom of the Press

Absolute freedom of the press to discuss public questions is a foundation stone of American liberty.—*Herbert Hoover*

4320 Government

For three long years I have been going up and down this country preaching that government . . . costs too much. I shall not stop that preaching.—*Franklin D. Roosevelt*

4321 In those days, the [Roman] government gave them bread and circuses. Today we give them bread and elections, but it is just a change in the style of a periodical amusement.—*Will Durant*

4322 Committee

If you want to kill any idea in the world today, get a committee working on it.—*C. F. Kettering*

4323 Shoes

I do wear a size 13, and I want you to know that size is hard, but not impossible, to get in your mouth.—*Secretary of Labor W. Willard Wirtz*

4324 Taxes

The men who collect taxes are working in one of the oldest professions known. Archaeological evidence dating from 1900 B.C. includes a clay tablet recording a tax for public works and a papyrus scroll which reveals that even 4,000 years ago, taxpayers had some complaints.—*Optimist Magazine*

4325 Progress

Unquestionably, there is progress. The average American now pays out twice as much in taxes as he formerly got in wages.—*Henry L. Mencken*

4326 The Thing We Have to Fear

The thing we have to fear in this country, to my way of thinking, is the influence of the organized minorities, because somehow or other the great majority does not seem to organize. They seem to feel that they are going to be effective because of their own strength, but they give no expression of it.—*Alfred E. Smith*

4327 Education

We do not know what education could do for us, because we have never tried it.—*Robert Maynard Hutchins*

4328 Pity

Pity is the feeling which arrests the mind in the presence of whatsoever is grave and constant in human sufferings and unites it with the human sufferer.—*James Joyce*

4329 Ideas

It is ideas, not vested interests, which are dangerous for good or evil. —*John Maynard Keynes*

4330 Neckties

I like calm hats and I don't wear spats,
But I want my neckties wild!—*Stoddard King*

4331 Governments

Very few established institutions, governments and constitutions . . . are ever destroyed by their enemies until they have been corrupted and weakened by their friends.—*Walter Lippmann*

4332 History

History repeats itself, that's one of the things that's wrong with history.
—*Clarence Darrow*

4333 Responsibility

The nourishing of the American system requires a sense of responsibility, not only on the part of individual citizens, but especially on the part of America's leadership. I am not speaking alone of political leaders, but of the leaders of all phases of our society as well.

To the extent that they do not exercise their power and influence in the direction of the common good, they are undermining the very system that has given them that power and influence.—*Nelson A. Rockefeller*

4334 Libraries

A library is a landmark of civilization, a monument to the people's desire to learn. Whether the place looks monumental or not really doesn't matter. A library is a service organization, not a building. Whether it is a classic-pillared marble temple, a downtown store front or just a bookmobile is not nearly as important as what's inside and how it is used.— *Changing Times*

4335 Young Writers

A good many young writers make the mistake of enclosing a stamped, self-addressed envelope, big enough for the manuscript to come back in. This is too much of a temptation to the editor.—*Ring Lardner*

4336 Ancestors

. . . there is no point in our ancestors speaking to us unless we know how to listen.—*Mortimer J. Adler*

4337 Historian

Any event, once it has occurred, can be made to appear inevitable by a competent historian.—*Lee Simonson*

4338 Emotion

People don't ask for facts in making up their minds. They would rather have one good, soul-satisfying emotion than a dozen facts.—*Robert Keith Leavitt*

4339 To Protect Liberty

Experience should teach us to be most on our guard to protect liberty when the government's purposes are beneficent. Men born to freedom are naturally alert to repel invasion of their liberty by evil-minded rulers. The greatest dangers to liberty lurk in insidious encroachment by men of zeal, well-meaning, but without understanding.—*Louis D. Brandeis*

4340　*Contract*

A verbal contract isn't worth the paper it's written on.—*Samuel Goldwyn*

4341　*Law*

The law and the stage—both are a form of exhibition.—*Orson Welles*

4342　*Education*

Anyone who can read and who owns a dictionary can become an educated person. Hungry minds always become educated and sharpen their mental and emotional tools as they grow in life through experience.—*Dr. Galen Starr Ross*

4343　*Progress?*

Ten years ago the moon was an inspiration to poets and an opportunity for lovers. Ten years from now it will be just another airport.—*Emmanuel G. Mesthene*

4344　*Man*

It isn't the common man at all who is important; it's the uncommon man.—*Lady Nancy Astor*

4345　Men will often say that they have "found themselves" when they have really been worn down into a groove by the brutal and compulsive force of circumstance.—*Thomas Wolfe*

4346　*American Education*

The primary concern of American education today is not the development of the appreciation of the "good life" in young gentlemen born to the purple. Our purpose is to cultivate in the largest number of our future citizens an appreciation both of the responsibilities and the benefits which come to them because they are American and free.—*James Bryant Conant*

4347　*Liberty*

It is true that liberty is precious—so precious that it must be rationed. —*Nikolai Lenin*

4348 Faults

Nature didn't make us perfect so she did the next best thing. She made us blind to our faults.—*Grit*

4349 American Professors

To a true-blue professor of literature in an American university, literature is not something that a plain human being, living today, painfully sits down to produce. No; . . . it is something magically produced by super-human beings who must, if they are to be regarded as artists at all, have died at least one hundred years before the diabolical invention of the typewriter. . . .

Our American professors like their literature clear and cold and pure and very dead.—*From an address given by Sinclair Lewis on receiving the Nobel Prize for Literature, December 12, 1930*

4350 World

The world has different owners at sunrise. Fields belong to hired men opening gates for sows; meadows, to old women with carpetbags, collecting mushrooms. Even your own garden does not belong to you. Rabbits and blackbirds have the lawns; a tortoiseshell cat who never appears in daytime patrols the brick walls, and a golden-tailed pheasant glints his way through the iris spears.—*Anne Morrow Lindbergh*

4351 Americanism

Of "Americanism" of the right sort we cannot have too much. Mere vaporing and boasting become a nation as little as a man. But honest, outspoken pride and faith in our country are infinitely better and more to be respected than the cultivated reserve which sets it down as ill bred and in bad taste ever to refer to our country except by way of deprecation, criticism, or general negation.—*Henry Cabot Lodge*

4352 Communism

Communism is based on the belief that man is so weak and inadequate that he is unable to govern himself, and therefore requires the rule of strong masters.—*Harry S Truman*

4353 Time

Time has no divisions to mark its passage, there is never a thunderstorm or blare of trumpets to announce the beginning of a new month or year. Even when a new century begins it is only we mortals who ring bells and fire off pistols.—*Thomas Mann*

4354 Precept

I forget who it was that recommended men for their soul's good to do each day two things they disliked: ... it is a precept that I have followed scrupulously; for every day I have got up and I have gone to bed.—*W. Somerset Maugham*

4355 Advice

Only when a man is safely ensconced under six feet of earth with several tons of enlauding granite upon his chest, is he in a position to give advice with any certainty, and then he is silent.—*A. Edward Newton*

4356 Snowflakes

Science informs us that no two snowflakes are alike, but along about this time of year I tend to feel that when you've seen one you've seen them all.—*Burton Hillis, in Better Homes & Gardens*

4357 Youth

A society that puts an exaggerated premium upon youth is gravely sick. Of course, any culture needs the leaven of youthful vigor, experiment, irreverence and drive; but it also needs mature judgment, understanding of and respect for its traditions, otherwise it will be all dazzle and no density.—*Stuart Holyroyd*

4358 Family

... Woman knows what Man has too long forgotten, that the ultimate economic and spiritual unit of any civilization is still the family.—*Clare Boothe Luce*

4359 Forgetting the Rugged Virtues

A people bent on a soft security, surrendering their birthright of individual self-reliance for favors, voting themselves into Eden from a supposedly inexhaustible public purse, supporting everyone by soaking a fast-disappearing rich, scrambling for subsidy, learning the arts of political log-rolling and forgetting the rugged virtues of the pioneer, will not measure up to competition with a tough dictatorship.—*Vannevar Bush*

4360 Winter

The mountains in the Wintertime had a stern and demonic quality of savage joy that was, in its own way, as strangely, wildly haunting as all the magic and the gold of April.—*Thomas Wolfe*

4361　How to Live

I wish that some one would give a course in how to live. It can't be taught in the colleges; that's perfectly obvious, for college professors don't know any better than the rest of us.—*A. Edward Newton*

4362　My Country

I believe in the United States of America as a Government of the people, by the people, for the people; whose just powers are derived from the consent of the governed; a democracy in a republic, a sovereign Nation of many sovereign States; a perfect Union one and inseparable; established upon those principles of freedom, equality, justice and humanity for which American patriots sacrificed their lives and fortunes. I therefore believe it is my duty to my country to love it, to support its Constitution, to obey its laws, to respect its flag, and to defend it against all enemies.—*William Tyler Page*

4363　Social Progress

Social progress does not have to be bought at the price of individual freedom.—*John Foster Dulles*

4364　Argument

It is impossible to defeat an ignorant man in argument.—*William G. McAdoo*

4365　American Heritage

Our American heritage is threatened as much by our own indifference as by the most unscrupulous office or by the most powerful foreign threat. The future of this republic is in the hands of the American voter. —*Dwight D. Eisenhower*

4366　Real Messages

The real messages of hope in our generation are not those to be bounced from the moon, but those to be reflected from one human heart to another.—*Kenneth S. Wills*

4367　Humility

He is without humility who sees it within himself.—*William A. Ward, in Meadowbrook (Tex.) Herald*

4368　Ignorance

My father, a good man, told me, "Never lose your ignorance; you cannot replace it."—*Erich Maria Remarque*

4369   Smile

Her smile was not meant to be seen by anyone and served its whole purpose in being smiled.—*Rainer Maria Rilke*

4370   Northwest Passage

On every side of us are men who hunt perpetually for their personal Northwest Passage, too often sacrificing health, strength and life itself to the search; and who shall say they are not happier in their vain but hopeful quest than wiser, duller folks who sit at home, venturing nothing and, with sour laughs, deriding the seekers for that fabled thoroughfare?—*Kenneth Roberts*

4371   Politics

Politics has got so expensive that it takes lots of money to even get beat with.—*Will Rogers*

4372   Reading

I read for pleasure, mark you. In general I like wedding bells at the end of novels. "They married and lived happily ever after"—why not? It has been done.—*A. Edward Newton*

4373   Rover

For the fifth year in succession I have pored over the catalogue of dogs in the show at Madison Square Garden without finding a dog named Rover, Towser, Sport, Spot, or Fido.

Who is the man who can call from his back door at night: "Here, Champion Alexander of Clane o' Wind-Holme! Here, Champion Alexander of Clane o' Wind-Holme"?—*Westbrook Pegler*

4374   Grief

Happiness is beneficial for the body but it is grief that develops the powers of the mind.—*Marcel Proust*

4375   Their Death

I did not know the dignity of their birth, but I do know the glory of their death.—*Douglas MacArthur*

4376   Speech

Of course, sometimes it is not possible to prepare an address fully, but it is much better to do so even if you intend to speak extemporaneously. —*Robert A. Taft*

4377 Army

The army report confined itself to the single sentence: All quiet on the Western Front.—*Erich Maria Remarque*

4378 Oratory

Oratory: the art of making deep noises from the chest sound like important messages from the brain.—*H.I. Phillips*

4379 Four Freedoms

Four freedoms: The first is freedom of speech and expression—everywhere in the world. The second is freedom of every person to worship God in his own way, everywhere in the world. The third is freedom from want . . . everywhere in the world. The fourth is freedom from fear . . . anywhere in the world.—*Franklin D. Roosevelt*

4380 Liberty

I like to walk about amidst the beautiful things that adorn the world; but private wealth I should decline, or any sort of personal possessions, because they would take away my liberty.—*George Santayana*

4381 Americans

What they do, boys, is creep up on you, and I don't mean Indians. I mean Americans, over the radio, over the waves, from platform, pulpit, press and curb.—*William Saroyan*

4382 Dress and Manners

We don't bother much about dress and manners in England, because, as a nation we don't dress well and we've no manners.—*George Bernard Shaw*

4383 War

They wrote in the old days that it is sweet and fitting to die for one's country. But in modern war there is nothing sweet nor fitting in your dying. You will die like a dog for no good reason.—*Ernest Hemingway*

4384 Wars to end wars are an illusion. Wars, more than any other form of human activity, create the conditions which breed more war.—*John Foster Dulles*

4385 . . . never think that war, no matter how necessary, nor how justified, is not a crime. Ask the infantry and ask the dead.—*Ernest Hemingway*

4386 Levity

My method is to take the utmost trouble to find the right thing to say, and then to say it with the utmost levity.—*George Bernard Shaw*

4387 Dignity

Perhaps the only true dignity of man is his capacity to despise himself. —*George Santayana*

4388 The True Joy

This is the true joy in life, the being used for a purpose recognized by yourself as a mighty one; the being thoroughly worn out before you are thrown on the scrap heap; the being a force of Nature instead of a feverish selfish little clod of ailments and grievances complaining that the world will not devote itself to making you happy.—*George Bernard Shaw*

4389 A General's Map

What do I care for the colored pins on a General's map . . . It's not a fair bargain—this exchange of my life for a small part of a colored pin. —*Irwin Shaw*

4390 Monotony

Monotony is the law of nature. Look at the monotonous manner in which the sun rises. . . . The monotony of necessary occupations is exhilarating and life-giving.—*Mahatma Gandhi*

4391 Knowledge

Fullness of knowledge always and necessarily means some understanding of the depths of our ignorance, and that is always conducive to both humility and reverence.—*Robert A. Millikan*

4392 Authors

When audiences come to see us authors lecture, it is largely in the hope that we'll be funnier to look at than to read.—*Sinclair Lewis*

4393 Beauty

Beauty comes and passes, is lost the moment that we touch it, can no more be stayed or held than one can stay the flowing of a river.— *Thomas Wolfe*

4394 Silence

Silence is the most perfect expression of scorn.—*George Bernard Shaw*

4395 Philosopher

The greater philosopher a man is, the more difficult it is for him to answer the foolish questions of common people.—*Henryk Sienkiewicz*

4396 Always the Same

What a bore it is, waking up in the morning always the same person. I wish I were unflinching and emphatic, and had big, bushy eyebrows and a Message for the Age. I wish I were a deep Thinker, or a great Ventriloquist.—*Logan Pearsall Smith*

4397 Life

The significant questions of human destiny are not to be approached with a smile. God, misery, and salvation are no joke.—*Irwin Edman*

4398 I don't want to own anything that won't fit into my coffin.—*Fred Allen*

4399 Eat with the Rich, but go to the play with the Poor, who are capable of Joy.—*Logan Pearsall Smith*

4400 The United States

In the United States there is more space where nobody is than where anybody is.

This is what makes America what it is.—*Gertrude Stein*

4401 Man

Man, unlike any other thing organic or inorganic in the universe, grows beyond his work, walks up the stairs of his concepts, emerges ahead of his accomplishments.—*John Steinbeck*

4402 Democracy

People who want to understand democracy should spend less time in the library with Aristotle and more time on the buses and in the subway. —*Simeon Strunsky*

4403 Criminals

The criminal is the product of spiritual starvation. Someone failed miserably to bring him to know God, love Him and serve Him.— *J. Edgar Hoover*

4404 Listeners

A good listener is not someone who has nothing to say. A good listener is a good talker with a sore throat.—*Katherine Whitehorn, in Daily Herald (London)*

4405 Loneliness

The whole conviction of my life now rests upon the belief that loneliness, far from being a rare and curious phenomenon, peculiar to myself and to a few other solitary men, is the central and inevitable fact of human existence.—*Thomas Wolfe*

4406 Our Fears

We are so largely the playthings of Fate in our fears. To one, fear of the dark, to another, of physical pain, to a third, of public ridicule, to a fourth of poverty, to a fifth of loneliness—for all of us our particular creature lurks in ambush.—*Hugh Walpole*

4407 Dawn

For what human ill does not dawn seem to be an alleviation?—*Thornton Wilder*

4408 Freedom

Freedom is an indivisible word. If we want to enjoy it, and fight for it, we must be prepared to extend it to everyone, whether they are rich or poor, whether they agree with us or not, no matter what their race or the color of their skin.—*Wendell L. Willkie*

4409 Alone

Naked and alone we came into exile. . . . Which of us has known his brother? Which of us has looked into his father's heart? . . . Which of us is not forever a stranger and alone?

4410 Love

. . . the unity that binds us all together, that makes this earth a family, and all men brothers and the sons of God, is love.—*Thomas Wolfe*

4411 Confidence

If Government is to retain the confidence of the people, it must not spend more than can be justified on grounds of national need or spent with maximum efficiency.—*John F. Kennedy*

4412　Belief

A belief is not merely an idea the mind possesses; it is an idea that possesses the mind.—*Robert Bolton*

4413　Cooking Dinner

There is no spectacle on earth more appealing than that of a beautiful woman in the act of cooking dinner for someone she loves.—*Thomas Wolfe*

4414　Beauty of the World

The beauty of the world has two edges, one of laughter, one of anguish, cutting the heart asunder.—*Virginia Woolf*

4415　Experience

Those who disregard the past are bound to repeat it.—*George Santayana*

4416　Play

The play left a taste of lukewarm parsnip juice.—*Alexander Woollcott*

4417　Ideas

The things that a man does not say often reveal the understanding and penetration of his mind even more than the things he says.—*Robert A. Millikan*

4418　Growing Old

Growing old is no more than a bad habit which a busy man has no time to form.—*André Maurois*

4419　No Bigger

A man who is too big to study his job is as big as he will ever be. —*William E. North*

4420　Great Colleges

Great individuals, not great organization men, make a college or university great.—*Harold W. Dodds*

4421　Money

A man who has a million dollars is as well off as if he were rich.—*John Jacob Astor III*

4422 *Brilliance*

To give an accurate and exhaustive account of that period would need a far less brilliant pen than mine.—*Sir Thomas Beecham*

4423 *Dozing*

I had just dozed off into a stupor when I heard what I thought was myself talking to myself. I didn't pay much attention to it, as I knew practically everything I would have to say to myself, and wasn't particularly interested.—*Robert Benchley*

4424 *Travel*

I haven't been abroad in so long that I almost speak English without an accent.—*Robert Benchley*

4425 *Speech*

The wise man thinks once before he speaks twice.—*Robert Benchley*

4426 *Middle of the Road*

We know what happens to people who stay in the middle of the road. They get run over.—*Aneurin Bevan*

4427 *Leader*

I must follow them; I am their leader.—*Andrew Bonar Law*

4428 *Actor*

An actor's a guy who, if you ain't talking about him, ain't listening.—*Marlon Brando*

4429 *Listening*

I was never tired of listening to his wisdom or imparting my own—*Sir Winston Churchill*

4430 *Illness*

I've just learnt about his illness; let's hope it's nothing trivial.—*Irvin S. Cobb.*

4431 No Difference

Why should a worm turn? It's probably just the same on the other side.—*Irvin S. Cobb*

4432 In the Long Run

He (Maynard Keynes) was the first Englishman since Horace Walpole to tell The Long Run to go jump into a lake. "In the long run," said Maynard Keynes, ". . . we are all dead."—*Claud Cockburn*

4433 An Editor

An editor: A person who knows precisely what he wants—but isn't quite sure.—*Walter Davenport*

4434 Ballet

My own personal reaction is that most ballets would be quite delightful if it were not for the dancing.—*Evening Standard*

4435 Family

Our family is not yet so good as to be degenerating.—*Kurt Ewald*

4436 Not All Bad

Anybody who hates children and dogs can't be all bad.—*W. C. Fields*

4437 No Time Left

A big man has no time really to do anything but just sit and be big.—*F. Scott Fitzgerald*

4438 What to Do

"What'll we do with ourselves this afternoon?" cried Daisy, "and the day after that, and the next thirty years?"—*F. Scott Fitzgerald*

4439 Approved Religion

Ronny approved of religion as long as it endorsed the National Anthem, but he objected when it attempted to influence his life.—*E. M. Forster*

4440 People

People are inexterminable—like flies and bed-bugs. There will always be some that survive in cracks and crevices—that's us.—*Robert Frost*

4441 No Serious Hate

I never hated a man enough to give his diamonds back.—*Zsa Zsa Gabor*

4442 Wealth

Wealth has never been a sufficient source of honor in itself. It must be advertised, and the normal medium is obtrusively expensive goods.—*J. K. Galbraith*

4443 Modern Liberal

The modern liberal rallies to protect the poor from the taxes which in the next generation, as the result of a higher investment for their children, would eliminate poverty.—*J. K. Galbraith*

4444 Politicians

I have come to the conclusion that politics are too serious a matter to be left to the politicians.—*General Charles de Gaulle*

4445 Snub

I never snub anybody accidentally.—*Norman Ginsbury*

4446 Definite

I'll give you a definitive maybe.—*Samuel Goldwyn*

4447 Even More

It's more than magnificent—it's mediocre.—*Samuel Goldwyn*

4448 Film and TV

Why should people go out and pay money to see bad films when they can stay at home and see bad television for nothing?—*Samuel Goldwyn*

4449 Burglar

A burglar who respects his art always takes his time before taking anything else.—*O. Henry*

4450 Transition

When our first parents were driven out of Paradise, Adam is believed to have remarked to Eve: "My dear, we live in an age of transition."—*W. R. Inge, Dean of St. Paul's*

4451   Appearance

We tolerate shapes in human beings that would horrify us if we saw them in a horse.—*W. R. Inge, Dean of St. Paul's*

4452   Religion

Among all my patients in the second half of life—that is to say over thirty-five—there has not been one whose problem in the last resort was not that of finding a religious outlook on life.—*C. G. Jung*

4453   Your Country

Ask not what your country can do for you; ask what you can do for your country.—*John F. Kennedy*

4454   Confusion

I had nothing to offer anybody except my own confusion.—*Jack Kerouac*

4455   Labor

Workingmen are at the foundation of society. Show me that product of human endeavor in the making of which the workingman has had no share, and I will show you something that society can well dispense with.—*Samuel Gompers*

4456   Literature

Our American professors like their literature clean and cold and pure and very dead.—*Sinclair Lewis*

4457   Kingfish

I looked around at the little fishes present, and said, "I'm the King-fish."—*Huey Long*

4458   Popular

In high school and college my sister Mary was very popular with the boys, but I had braces on my teeth and got high marks.—*Betty MacDonald*

4459   Our Age

If the nineteenth century was the age of the editorial chair, ours is the century of the psychiatrist's couch.—*Marshall McLuhan*

4460   Poverty

I've worked myself up from nothing to a state of extreme poverty.—*Groucho Marx*

4461   Principle

You can't learn too soon that the most useful thing about a principle is that it can always be sacrificed to expediency.—*W. Somerset Maugham*

4462   My Greatest Friend

My dear, she's been my greatest friend for fifteen years. I know her through and through, and I tell you that she hasn't got a single redeeming quality.—*W. Somerset Maugham*

4463   A Precept He Followed

I forget who it was that recommended men for their soul's good to do each day two things they disliked. . . . It is a precept that I have followed scrupulously; for every day I have got up and I have gone to bed.—*W. Somerset Maugham*

4464   His Opinion

I'll give you my opinion of the human race in a nutshell. . . . Their heart's in the right place, but their head is a thoroughly inefficient organ.—*W. Somerset Maugham*

4465   The Swiss

The Swiss managed to build a lovely country around their hotels.—*George Mikes*

4466   A Good Newspaper

A good newspaper, I suppose, is a nation talking to itself.—*Arthur Miller*

4467   Church

There are many who stay away from church these days because you hardly ever mention God any more.—*Arthur Miller*

4468   Thinking

I wrote somewhere once that the third-rate mind was only happy when it was thinking with the majority, the second-rate mind was only happy when it was thinking with the minority, and the first-rate mind was only happy when it was thinking.—*A. A. Milne*

4469 Prophets

Prophets were twice stoned—first in anger; then, after their death, with a handsome slab in the graveyard.—*Christopher Morley*

4470 Socialism

To the ordinary working man, the sort you would meet in any pub on Saturday night, Socialism does not mean much more than better wages and shorter hours and nobody bossing you about.—*George Orwell*

4471 Work

Work expands so as to fill the time available for its completion. General recognition of this fact is shown in the proverbial phrase, "It is the busiest man who has time to spare."—*C. Northcote Parkinson*

4472 Incompetence

The Peter Principle: In a Hierarchy Every Employee Tends to Rise to His Level of Incompetence.—*Lawrence J. Peter*

4473 In Love with Himself

He fell in love with himself at first sight and it is a passion to which he has always remained faithful. Self-love seems so often unrequited.—*Anthony Powell*

4474 Money

Money is good for bribing yourself through the inconveniences of life.—*Gottfried Reinhardt*

4475 Thinking

You can't think rationally on an empty stomach, and a whole lot of people can't do it on a full one either.—*Lord Reith*

4476 Time

Half our life is spent trying to find something to do with the time we have rushed through life trying to save.—*Will Rogers*

4477 Politics

The more you read about politics, you got to admit that each party is worse than the other.—*Will Rogers*

4478 Ignorance

Everybody is ignorant, only on different subjects.—*Will Rogers*

4479   *Ancestors*

My folks didn't come over on the Mayflower, but they were there to meet the boat.—*Will Rogers*

4480   *Cheaper*

Any time you see him he is generally by himself because being by himself is not apt to cost him anything.—*Damon Runyon*

4481   *Money*

My boy . . . always try to rub up against money, for if you rub up against money long enough, some of it may rub off on you.—*Damon Runyon*

4482   *Friends*

I step over to his table and give him a medium hello, and he looks up and gives me a medium hello right back, for, to tell the truth, Maury and I are never bosom friends.—*Damon Runyon*

4483   *Patriots*

Patriots always talk of dying for their country, and never of killing for their country.—*Bertrand Russell*

4484   *Agony*

They had a passion for getting something for nothing. Every blackberry in the hedgerow was an agony to Lavinia until she had bottled it.—*Victoria Sackville-West*

4485   *Income*

All decent people live beyond their incomes nowadays, and those who aren't respectable live beyond other people's. A few gifted individuals manage to do both.—*"Saki" (H. H. Munro)*

4486   *Young and Old*

The young have aspirations that never come to pass, the old have reminiscences of what never happened.—*"Saki" (H. H. Munro)*

4487   *Strictly Brought Up*

I think she must have been very strictly brought up, she's so desperately anxious to do the wrong thing correctly.—*"Saki" (H. H. Munro)*

4488   *Library*

A library is thought in cold storage.—*Herbert Samuel*

4489   *The Past*

Those who cannot remember the past are condemned to repeat it.—*George Santayana*

4490   *Time*

Three o'clock is always too late or too early for anything you want to do.—*Jean-Paul Sartre*

4491   *An Intellectual*

I too had thoughts once of being an intellectual, but I found it too difficult. (To an African who refused to perform some humdrum duty on the grounds that he was an intellectual.)—*Albert Schweitzer*

4492   *Titles*

Titles distinguish the mediocre, embarrass the superior, and are disgraced by the inferior.—*George Bernard Shaw*

4493   *Respectable*

The more things a man is ashamed of, the more respectable he is.—*George Bernard Shaw*

4494   *Carried Away*

Lying hardly describes it. I overdo it. I get carried away in an ecstasy of mendacity.—*George Bernard Shaw*

4495   *Education*

Education is what survives when what has been learnt has been forgotten.—*B. F. Skinner*

4496   *Prayers*

Prayers are like those appeals of ours. Either they don't get through or they're returned with "rejected" scrawled across 'em.—*A. Solzhenitsyn*

4497   *The United States*

In the United States there is more space where nobody is than where anybody is. That is what makes America what it is.—*Gertrude Stein*

4498 *Finality*

Finality is death. Perfection is finality. Nothing is perfect. There are lumps in it.—*James Stephens*

4499 *Gains and Pains*

Let's talk sense to the American people. Let's tell them the truth, that there are no gains without pains.—*Adlai Stevenson*

4500 *Statesman*

A politician is a statesman who approaches every question with an open mouth.—*Adlai E. Stevenson*

4501 *Early to Rise*

Early to rise and early to bed makes a male healthy and wealthy and dead.—*James Thurber*

4502 *Sleep*

I haven't been to sleep for over a year. That's why I go to bed early. One needs more rest if one doesn't sleep.—*Evelyn Waugh*

4503 *Obsolescence*

Britain today is suffering from galloping obsolescence.—*Anthony Wedgwood Benn*

4504 *Cynicism*

Cynicism is humour in ill-health.—*H. G. Wells*

4505 *Christmas*

To perceive Christmas through its wrapping becomes more difficult with every year.—*E. B. White*

4506 *Fools*

Ninety-nine percent of the people in the world are fools and the rest of us are in great danger of contagion.—*Thornton Wilder*

4507 *Marriage*

Marriage is a bribe to make a housekeeper think she's a house holder.—*Thornton Wilder*

4508   Business

Business underlies everything in our national life, including our spiritual life. Witness the fact that in the Lord's Prayer the first petition is for daily bread. No one can worship God or love his neighbor on an empty stomach.—*Woodrow Wilson*

4509   Cold Accusing Eyes

It was one of those cold, clammy, accusing sort of eyes—the kind that makes you reach up to see if your tie is straight: and he looked at me as if I were some sort of unnecessary product which Cuthbert the Cat had brought in after a ramble among the local ash-cans.—*P. G. Wodehouse*

4510   How He Felt

It must have been about one in the afternoon when I woke. I was feeling more or less like something the Pure Food Committee had rejected.—*P. G. Wodehouse*

4511   Captain of Industry

As a rule, from what I've observed, the American captain of industry doesn't do anything out of business hours. When he has put the cat out and locked up the office for the night, he just relapses into a state of coma from which he emerges only to start being a captain of industry again.—*P. G. Wodehouse*

4512   Life

I spent the afternoon musing on Life. If you come to think of it, what a queer thing Life is! So unlike anything else, don't you know, if you see what I mean.—*P. G. Wodehouse*

4513   Our Past

Each had his past shut in him like the leaves of a book known to him by heart; and his friends could only read the title.—*Virginia Woolf*

4514   Design

The chair . . . was upholstered in one of those flagrant chintzes, designed, apparently, by the art editor of a seed catalog.—*Alexander Woollcott*

4515   Knowledge

Ross, a man who knew nothing . . . and had contempt for anything he didn't understand, which was practically everything.—*Alexander Woollcott*

4516   *Architect*

The physician can bury his mistakes, but the architect can only advise his client to plant vines.—*Frank Lloyd Wright*

4517   *Music Teacher*

The music teacher came twice each week to bridge the awful gap between Dorothy and Chopin.—*George Ade*

4518   *Seldom Lost*

A schoolgirl answered the question, "In what countries are elephants found?" Elephants are very large and intelligent animals, and are seldom lost.—*James Agate*

4519   *Church*

He was of the faith chiefly in the sense that the church he currently did not attend was Catholic.—*Kingsley Amis*

4520   *On Oath*

(After describing himself in a court of law as the greatest living actor, excused his boastfulness with) You see, I am on oath.—*George Arliss*

4521   *Success*

Every man who is high up likes to feel that he has done it all himself; and the wife smiles, and lets it go at that. It's our only joke. Every woman knows that.—*James M. Barrie*

4522   *Crowd Mind*

You cannot make a man by standing a sheep on its hind legs. But by standing a flock of sheep in that position you can make a crowd of men.—*Max Beerbohm*

4523   *Be Still*

To my mind the most pregnant mystical exhortation ever written is "Be still and know that I am God."—*Anon.*

4524   *Ostentation*

I explained to him I had simple tastes and didn't want anything ostentatious, no matter what it cost me.—*Art Buchwald*

4525 Last Judgment

Don't wait for the Last Judgment. It takes place every day.—*Albert Camus*

4526 An Artist

He is an artist, you know, and talks a great deal for his own pleasure.— *Joyce Cary*

4527 Being President

There is one thing about being President—nobody can tell you when to sit down.—*Dwight D. Eisenhower*

4528 Intellectual

An intellectual is a man who takes more words than necessary to tell more than he knows.—*Dwight D. Eisenhower*

4529 Risk

(Asked if as a boy he had ever thought of the possibility he would grow up to be President) Yes, but I just dismissed it as a normal risk that any red-blooded American boy has to take.—*Adlai E. Stevenson*

4530 Redemption of Ignorance

(He once squelched a heckler with) I believe in the forgiveness of sin and the redemption of ignorance.—*Adlai E. Stevenson*

4531 Election

To the victor belong the toils.—*Adlai E. Stevenson*

4532 Politics

Moderate progressivism: Don't just do something—stand there.—*Adlai E. Stevenson*

4533 Speech

Churchill was always rewriting his speeches until he had to give them. But that's where my similarity to Churchill ends.—*Adlai E. Stevenson*

4534 Free Society

My definition of a free society is a society where it is safe to be unpopular.—*Adlai E. Stevenson*

4535 *President*

Some of the Presidents were great and some of them weren't. I can say that, because I wasn't one of the great Presidents, but I had a good time trying to be one, I can tell you that.—*Harry S Truman*

4586 *Failure*

My father was not a failure. After all, he was the father of a President of the United States.—*Harry S Truman*

4537 *Peace*

Peace is the goal of my life. I'd rather have lasting peace in the world than be President. I wish for peace, I work for peace and I pray for peace continually.—*Harry S Truman*

4538 *Favorite Prayer*

O Almighty and Everlasting God, Creator of Heaven, Earth and the Universe:

Help me to be, to think, to act what is right, because it is right; make me truthful, honest and honorable in all things; make me intellectually honest for the sake of right and honor and without thought of reward to me. Give me the ability to be charitable, forgiving and patient with my fellow men—help me to understand their motives and their shortcomings—even as thou understandest mine! Amen, Amen, Amen.—*Harry S Truman*

4539 *Fund-raising*

I am deeply touched—not as deeply touched as you have been by coming to this dinner, but nevertheless, it is a sentimental occasion.— *John F. Kennedy*

4540 *Why He Was a War Hero*

It was absolutely involuntary. They sank my boat.—*John F. Kennedy*

4541 *Welcome*

There is no city in the United States in which I get a warmer welcome and less votes than Columbus, Ohio.—*John F. Kennedy*

4542 *Politics*

Those of you who regard my profession of political life with some disdain should remember that it made it possible for me to move from being an obscure lieutenant in the United States Navy to Commander-in-Chief in fourteen years with very little technical competence.—*John F. Kennedy*

4543 **Learn**

You ain't learnin' nothin' when you're talkin'.—*Lyndon B. Johnson*

4544 **Honest**

At the card ·game one of the boys looked across the table and said: "Now, Reuben, play the cards fair. I know what I dealt you."—*Lyndon B. Johnson*

4545 **Golf**

I don't have any handicap. I am all handicap.—*Lyndon B. Johnson*

4546 **Taxation**

In 1790, the nation which had fought a revolution against taxation without representation discovered that some of its citizens weren't much happier about taxation with representation.—*Lyndon B. Johnson*

4547 **Responsibility**

The Secretary of Labor is in charge of finding you a job, the Secretary of the Treasury is in charge of taking half the money you make away from you, and the Attorney General is in charge of suing you for the other half.—*Lyndon B. Johnson*

4548 **President**

My White House job pays more than public school systems but the tenure is less certain.—*Lyndon B. Johnson*

4549 **Life**

An hour late and a dollar short, that's the way I've been all my life.—*Lyndon B. Johnson*

4550 **Indignation**

On a certain occasion in the House of Commons, Churchill said something which caused another Member to jump to his feet bursting so strongly with disagreement as to be almost unintelligible. "My right honourable friend," said Churchill, "should not develop more indignation than he can contain."—*Sir Winston Churchill*

4551 *Politics*

Politics are almost as exciting as war and quite as dangerous, although in war you can be killed only once, in politics many times.—*Sir Winston Churchill*

4552 **Communism**

Trying to maintain good relations with the Communists is like wooing a crocodile. You do not know whether to tickle it under the chin or beat it over the head. When it opens its mouth you cannot tell whether it is trying to smile or preparing to eat you up.—*Sir Winston Churchill*

4553 *Difficulty*

Don't argue about the difficulties. The difficulties will argue for themselves.—*Sir Winston Churchill*

4554 *Acuteness of Mind*

Neither of his colleagues can compare with him in that acuteness or energy of mind with which he devotes himself to so many topics injurious to the strength and welfare of the State (of Sir Stafford Cripps).—*Sir Winston Churchill*

4555 *Family*

Where does the family start? It starts with a young man falling in love with a girl. No superior alternative has yet been found.—*Sir Winston Churchill*

4556 *Intelligentsia*

The intelligent are to the intelligentsia what a gentleman is to a gent.—*Stanley Baldwin*

4557 *Speech*

Herbert H. Asquith's lucidity of style is a positive disadvantage when he has nothing to say.—*Arthur Balfour*

4558 *Enthusiasm*

It is unfortunate, considering that enthusiasm moves the world, that so few enthusiasts can be trusted to speak the truth.—*Arthur Balfour*

4559 *Truth*

Nothing should impede the truth save a substantial sum of money.—*Hilaire Belloc*

4560 Wealth

Stand not too near the rich man lest he destroy thee—and not too far away lest he forget thee.—*Aneurin Bevan*

4561 Speech

Please don't be deterred in the fanatical application of your sterile logic.—*Aneurin Bevan*

4562 Winston Churchill

His ear is so sensitively attuned to the bugle note of history that he is often deaf to the more raucous clamour of contemporary life, a defect which his Conservative upbringing and background tend to reinforce. The seven-league-boot tempo of his imagination hastens him on to the "sunny uplands" of the future; he is apt to forget that the slow steps of humanity must travel every inch of the weary road that leads there.— *Aneurin Bevan*

4563 Lord Attlee

He seems determined to make a trumpet sound like a tin whistle. . . . He brings to the fierce struggle of politics the tepid enthusiasm of a lazy summer afternoon at a cricket match.—*Aneurin Bevan*

4564 Of a Government Official

A man walking backwards with his face to the future—*Aneurin Bevan*

4565 History

That great dustheap called history.—*Augustine Birrell*

4566 Mind

Sir Stafford (Cripps) has a brilliant mind until it is made up.—*Lady Violet Bonham Carter*

4567 Income Tax

The one thing that hurts more than paying an income tax is not having to pay an income tax.—*Lord Dewar*

4568 Love

Love is an ocean of emotions, entirely surrounded by expenses.—*Lord Dewar*

4569 *Criticism*

To be criticised is not necessarily to be wrong.—*Sir Anthony Eden*

4570 *Highbrow*

A highbrow is the kind of person who looks at a sausage and thinks of Picasso.—*Sir Alan Herbert*

4571 *Confidence*

I do not object to Gladstone always having the ace of trumps up his sleeve but merely to his belief that God Almighty put it there.—*Henry Labouchère*

4572 *Understanding*

Poincaré knows everything and understands nothing—Briand understands everything and knows nothing.—*David Lloyd George*

4573 *Criticism*

I have never found, in a long experience of politics, that criticism is ever inhibited by ignorance.—*Harold Macmillan*

4574 *No Greater Love*

Greater love hath no man than this, that he lay down his friends for his life.—*Jeremy Thorpe*

Quotations and Illustrations
for Special Days

Birthday

4575   My birthday! what a different sound
         That word had in my youthful ears;
         And how each time the day comes round,
         Less and less white its mark appears.
                               —Thomas Moore

4576   You've heard of the three ages of man—youth, age, and "you are looking wonderful."—*Francis Cardinal Spellman*

4577   The older I grow the more I distrust the familiar doctrine that age brings wisdom.—*Henry L. Mencken*

4578   To me, old age is always fifteen years older than I am.—*Bernard M. Baruch*

4579   Of middle age the best that can be said is that a middle-aged person has likely learned how to have a little fun in spite of his troubles.—*Don Marquis*

4580   Old age isn't so bad when you consider the alternative.—*Maurice Chevalier*

4581   When a man has a birthday he takes a day off, but when a woman has a birthday she takes a year off.—*Anon.*

4582   At 19, everything is possible and tomorrow looks friendly.—*Jim Bishop*

Christmas

4583   Many Christmas customs are carryovers from pre-Christian celebrations. Hanging gifts on trees is supposed to stem from the tree worship of the Druids, and the belief that the tree was the giver of all good things. The Druids are also partly responsible for the use of mistletoe at Christmastime. They regarded the mistletoe as sacred, made certain that it never touched the ground, and dedicated it to the Goddess of Love, which explains the kissing that goes on under it. Originally, when a boy kissed a girl, he plucked a berry from the cluster and presented it to her. When the berries were gone, so were the kisses.

4584   For many of us, sadly, the spirit of Christmas is "hurry." And yet, eventually, the hour comes when the rushing ends and the race against the calendar mercifully comes to a close. It is only now perhaps that we truly recognize the spirit of Christmas. It is not a matter of days or weeks, but of centuries—nearly twenty of them now since that holy night in Bethlehem. Regarded in this manner, the pre-Christmas rush may do us greater service than we realize. With all its temporal confusion, it may just help us to see that by contrast, Christmas itself is eternal.—*Burton Hillis*

4585   I heard the bells on Christmas Day
             Their old, familiar carols play,
             And wild and sweet the words repeat
             Of peace on earth, good-will to men!—*Longfellow*

4586   I will honor Christmas in my heart, and try to keep it all the year.—*Charles Dickens*

4587   No Santa Claus! Thank God, he lives, and he lives forever. A thousand years from now, Virginia, nay, ten times ten thousand years from now, he will continue to make glad the heart of childhood.—*Francis P. Church*

4588   A three-year-old gave this reaction to her Christmas dinner: "I don't like the turkey, but I like the bread he ate."

4589   Mother decided that 10-year-old Cathy should get something "practical" for Christmas. "Suppose we open a savings account for you?" mother suggested. Kathy was delighted.

"It's your account, darling," mother said as they arrived at the bank, "so you fill out the application."

Cathy was doing fine until she came to the space for "Name of your former bank." After a slight hesitation, she put down "Piggy."

4590   There was the little boy who approached Santa in a department store with a long list of requests. He wanted a bicycle and a sled, a chemical set, a cowboy suit, a set of trains, a baseball glove and roller skates.

"That's a pretty long list," Santa said sternly. "I'll have to check in my book and see if you were a good boy."

"No, no," the youngster said quickly. "Never mind checking. I'll just take the roller skates."

4591   'Twas the night before Christmas, when all through the house
Not a creature was stirring—not even a mouse:
The stockings were hung by the chimney with care,
In hopes that St. Nicholas soon would be there.
—*Clement C. Moore*

4592   He who has no Christmas in his heart will never find Christmas under a tree.—*Sunshine Magazine*

Columbus Day

4593   Every ship that comes to America got its chart from Columbus.—*Emerson*

4594   It was wonderful to find America, but it would have been more wonderful to miss it.—*Mark Twain*

Easter

4595   Dating from Easter, life took on a newness which made it a different kind of life not known before—life that will not be content until all the world comes alive. Despair is death, and despair faded from the minds of men who believed. Fear is death, and fear no longer invaded the still hours. Cowardice is death, and cowardice ceased to be a part of those who knew Easter.—*Glenn H. Asquith*

4596
>
> Jesus Christ is risen today,
> Our triumphant holy day;
> Who did once upon the cross
> Suffer to redeem our loss
> Hallelujah!
> —*From a Latin hymn of the
> fifteenth century*

4597   This is the promise that He hath promised us, even eternal life.—*I John 2:25*

4598   Easter so longed for is gone in a day.—*James Howell*

4599   The great Easter truth is not that we are to live newly after death—that is not the great thing—but that . . . we are to, and may, live nobly now because we are to live forever.—*Phillips Brooks*

Election Day

4600
>
> A weapon that comes down as still
> As snowflakes fall upon the sod,
> But executes a freeman's will
> As lightning does the will of God,
> And from its force nor doors nor locks
> Can shield you—'tis the ballot-box.
> —*John Pierpont*

4601   As long as I count the votes, what are you going to do about it?—*William M. Tweed*

4602   The one pervading evil of democracy is the tyranny of the majority, or rather of that party, not always the majority, that succeeds, by force or fraud, in carrying elections.—*Lord Acton*

4603   We will spend and spend, and tax and tax, and elect and elect.—*Harry L. Hopkins*

4604   Bad officials are elected by good citizens who do not vote.—*Unknown*

4605   Whatever government is not a government of laws is a despotism, let it be called what it may.—*Daniel Webster*

4606   All free governments are managed by the combined wisdom and folly of the people.—*Garfield*

4607   Republics end with luxury: monarchies with poverty.—*Montesquieu*

4608   Though the people support the government, the government should not support the people.—*Grover Cleveland*

4609   The deterioration of a government begins almost always by the decay of its principles.—*Montesquieu*

Father's Day

4610   One father is more than a hundred schoolmasters.—*Herbert*

4611   Fathers should be neither seen nor heard. That is the only proper basis for family life.—*Oscar Wilde*

4612   A father is a banker provided by nature.—*French proverb*

4613   What a father says to his children is not heard by the world, but it will be heard by posterity.—*Richter*

4614   Directly after God in Heaven comes Papa.—*Mozart as a boy.*

4615   No man is responsible for his father. That is entirely his mother's affair.—*Margaret Trumbull*

4616   The child had every toy his father wanted.—*Robert C. Whitten*

Fourth of July—Independence Day

4617   Yesterday the greatest question was decided which was ever debated in America; and a greater perhaps never was, nor will be, decided among men. A resolution was passed without one dissenting colony, that those United Colonies are, and of right ought to be, free and independent states.—*John Adams*

4618   The Fourth of July marks an epoch in the world's history. It marks the birth of a free nation, with all that implies—a nation in the existence of which the oppressed of all lands rejoice, and of which every true American is justly proud.—*Anon.*

4619   Is life so dear, or peace so sweet, as to be purchased at the price of chains and slavery? Forbid it, Almighty God!—I know not what course others may take; but as for me, give me liberty or give me death!—*Patrick Henry*

4620   The United States is the only country with a known birthday.—*James G. Blaine*

4621   Although it is agreed by most historians that the momentous document, the Declaration of Independence, was adopted on July 4, 1776, there is doubt that it was actually signed on that date. However, it is agreed that John Hancock of Massachusetts, serving as President of the

Continental Congress, was the first to affix his signature to the famous paper. Being a man of wit and humor, as well as patriotism, Hancock remarked as he wielded the pen, "I am signing my name so plain that even King George III can read it without his spectacles!" The signature of John Hancock has been a model of beautiful penmanship for two hundred years.

4622   The cause of Freedom is the cause of God.—*The Reverend W. L. Bowles*

4623   Eternal vigilance is the price of liberty.—*John Philpot Curran*

4624   God grants liberty only to those who love it, and are always ready to guard and defend it.—*Daniel Webster*

4625   To embody human liberty in workable government, America was born.—*Herbert Hoover*

Good Friday

4626   Good Friday . . . in a way . . . is not Good Friday at all. It is Black Friday—a very Black Friday. It is Good Friday only in the sense that we know Easter will follow.—*J. Edward Lantz*

4627   I find no fault in him.—*John 19:6*

4628   Then said Jesus, Father, forgive them; for they know not what they do.—*Luke 23:34*

4629   At the cross her station keeping
                Stood the mournful mother weeping,
                Where He hung, the dying Lord.—*Anon.*

Graduation Day

4630   A college education shows a man how little other people know.—*Sam Slick*

4631   It was a saying of his that education was an ornament in prosperity and a refuge in adversity.—*Diogenes*

4632   But it was in making education not only common to all, but in some sense compulsory on all, that the destiny of the free republics of America was practically settled.—*J. R. Lowell*

4633   The roots of education are bitter, but the fruit is sweet.—*Aristotle*

4634   Human history becomes more and more a race between education and catastrophe.—*H. G. Wells*

4635   A well-trained mind is made up, so to speak, of all the minds of past ages: only a single mind has been educated during all that time.—*Fontenelle*

4636   A university should be a place of light, of liberty, and of learning.—*Disraeli*

4637   To talk in public, to think in solitude, to read and to hear, to inquire and answer inquiries, is the business of a scholar.—*Samuel Johnson*

4638   Colleges hate geniuses, just as convents hate saints.—*Emerson*

4639   What sculpture is to a block of marble, education is to the soul.—*Addison*

4640   A scholar is the favorite of Heaven and earth, the excellency of his country, the happiest of men.—*Emerson*

4641   The foundation of every state is the education of its youth.—*Diogenes*

4642   There is nothing so stupid as an educated man, if you get off the thing that he was educated in.—*Will Rogers*

High Holydays

Rosh Hashanah and Yom Kippur

4643   Every Autumn the Jewish people observe what are known as the High Holydays. This is a period of ten days beginning with Rosh Hashanah, which means New Year, and ending with Yom Kippur, the Day of Atonement. The term New Year is used by the Jews at this time to mean the new effort which they make to correct mistakes they have made in the past. It is a new year of conscience, not the calendar. The observance of Yom Kippur begins at sunset, , with a worship service which includes the singing of the hymn, "Kol Nidre," a plea for forgiveness for decisions made in haste and without regard for the feelings of others. This is Atonement Day, on which the worshiper tries to atone for his faults. Although the High Holydays are the most important religious occasion for the Jewish people, there is nothing about them which does not apply to all people.

Labor Day

4644   He who prays and labors lifts his heart to God with his hands.—*St. Bernard*

4645   A truly American sentiment recognizes the dignity of labor and the fact that honor lies in honest toil.—*Grover Cleveland*

4646   Labor conquers all things.—*Homer*

4647   Labor, if it were not necessary for the existence, would be indispensable for the happiness of man.—*Samuel Johnson*

4648   Labor was the first price, the original purchase money that was paid for all things.—*Adam Smith*

4649   Life gives' nothing to man without labor.—*Horace*

4650   To labor is to pray.—*Motto of the Benedictines*

4651   God sells us all things at the price of labor.—*Leonardo da Vinci*

Lincoln's Birthday

4652
Honesty rare as a man without selfpity,
Kindness as large and plain as a prairie wind.
—*Stephen Vincent Benét*

4653
His heart was as great as the world
but there was no room in it to hold
the memory of a wrong.
—*Emerson*

4654   Now he belongs to the ages.—*Edwin M. Stanton*

4655
Here was a man to hold against the world,
A man to match the mountains and the sea.
—*Edwin Markham*

Memorial Day—Decoration Day

4656   There is a shrine in the temple of ages, where lie forever embalmed the memories of such as have deserved well of their country and their race.—*John Mason Brown*

4657   Here sleeps heroic dust! It is meet that a redeemed nation should come, to pay it homage at such tombs, wreathing the memory of its patriot dead in the emblems of grateful affection. These grass-grown mounds, these flower-decked graves, awake the memories of the past, and the history of our nation's perils and its triumphs come crowding on us here.—*American Wesleyan*

4658   Here rests in honored glory an American soldier known but to God.—*Inscription on the tomb of the Unknown Soldier, Arlington National Cemetery*

4659   The little green tents where the soldiers sleep and the sunbeams play and the women weep, are covered with flowers today.—*Walt Mason*

Mother's Day

4660
> A mother is a mother still,
> The holiest thing alive.
> —*Coleridge*

4661
> Over my slumbers your loving watch keep;
> Rock me to sleep, mother; rock me to sleep.
> —*Elizabeth Chase*

4662
> The hand that rocks the cradle
> Is the hand that rules the world.
> —*W. R. Wallace*

4663   Her children arise up, and call her blessed.—*Proverbs 31:28*

4664   Mother is the name for God in the lips and hearts of little children.—*William M. Thackeray*

4665   The mother's heart is the child's schoolroom.—*H. W. Beecher*

4666   What are Raphael's madonnas but the shadow of a mother's love, fixed in permanent outline forever?—*T. W. Higginson*

Passover

4667   This day (Passover) shall be unto you for a memorial; and ye shall keep it a feast to the Lord throughout your generations.—*Exodus 12:14*

4668   Ye shall observe the feast of unleavened bread.—*Exodus 12:17*

4669   It is the sacrifice of the Lord's passover, who passed over the houses of the children of Israel in Egypt, when he smote the Egyptians, and delivered our houses.—*Exodus 12:27*

4670   The feast of unleavened bread drew nigh, which is called the Passover.—*Luke 22:1*

4671   Passover affirms the great truth that liberty is the inalienable right of every human being.—*M. Joseph*

4672   The Seder nights . . . tie me with the centuries before me.—*L. Frank*

St. Patrick's Day

4673   It is somewhat suggestive that the apostle of Ireland was himself a foreign-born citizen. He acquired a better right to speak for Ireland than any man that was ever born in it, before or since. And that should be a lesson to moderate certain Irish patriots who would have it that there is nothing good that does not come from Ireland. There are good things, always have been and always will be, out of Ireland, as well as every country, as well as in it, and while it is permissible for us on this one day of the year to blow our own horn a little, it is well for us to be modest enough to acknowledge and to be thankful for the apostle who was not an Irishman and yet was the best Irishman that ever lived.—*Dr. Edward McGlynn*

St. Valentine's Day

4674   Oh, if it be to choose and call thee mine,
Love, thou art every day my Valentine!
—*Thomas Hood*

4675   I claim there ain't Another Saint
As great as Valentine.
—*Ogden Nash*

4676   A lovely heart-shaped box of chocolates was received on Valentine's Day by a coed from her newest date. On the enclosed card was the inscription, "To Helen—with all my allowance."

4677   Love me little, love me long,
Is the burden of my song.
—*Old ballad*

4678   And on her lover's arm she leant,
And round her waist she felt it fold,
And far across the hills they went
In that new world which is the old.
—*Tennyson*

Thanksgiving

4679   Thanksgiving Day is one of the most remarkable days of the year. Decreed by a layman, the President of the United States, by authorization of Congress, it is obeyed by Catholic, Jew, and Protestant, and by many who have no church affiliation. The response of more than 200 million people to this call is one of the most encouraging events in our national life. Thankfulness blesses and enriches our daily life. Not only is it deserving of a special day; it merits everyday observance.—*Sunshine Magazine*

4680   Thanksgiving Day comes, by statute, once a year; to the honest man it comes as frequently as the heart of gratitude will allow, which may mean every day, or at least once in seven days.—*Edward Sandford Martin*

4681   Let the people praise thee, O God; let all the people praise thee. —*Psalms 67:3*

4682   Let us come before his presence with thanksgiving.—*Psalms 95:2*

4683   O Lord, that lends me life, lend me a heart replete with thankfulness.—*Shakespeare*

4684   A thankful heart is not only the greatest virtue, but the parent of all the other virtues.—*Cicero*

Veterans Day—Armistice Day

4685   The Federal government should treat with the utmost consideration every disabled soldier, sailor and marine of the World War, whether his disability be due to wounds received in line of action or to health impared in service; and for the dependents of the brave men who died in the line of duty the government's tenderest concern and richest bounty should be their requital.—*Democratic National Platform 1920*

4686   Closer to the truth than he meant to be was the schoolboy who wrote on an exam paper: "The Armistice was signed on the 11th of November in 1918, and since then every year there have been two minutes of peace."

4687   Soldier, rest! thy warfare o'er,
                    Sleep the sleep that knows not breaking;
                    Dream of battled fields no more,
                    Days of danger, nights of waking.
                                                    —*Scott*

4688   The nation which forgets its defenders will be itself forgotten.— *Calvin Coolidge*

Washington's Birthday

4689   Washington is the mightiest name on earth—long since mightiest in the course of civil liberty; still mightiest in moral reformation. On that name an eulogy is expected. Let none attempt it. In solemn awe pronounce the name and in its naked, deathless splendor leave it shining on.—*Lincoln*

4690   A gentleman of one of the first fortunes upon the continent . . . sacrificing his ease, and hazarding all in the cause of his country.—*John Adams*

4691   His memory will be adored while liberty shall have votaries, his name will triumph over time and will in future ages assume its just station among the most celebrated worthies of the world.—*Jefferson*

4692   When Washington declined a military escort on the occasion of his inauguration (1789), he said, "I require no guard but the affections of the people."—*Dr. Edward Everett*

4693   'Tis substantially true that virtue or morality is a necessary spring of popular government.—*George Washington*

Wedding Day

4694   What woman, however old, has not the bridal-favours and raiment stowed away, and packed in lavender, in the inmost cupboards of her heart?—*William M. Thackeray*

4695   The smallest piece of silver which can qualify as a wedding gift is a marmalade spoon.—*Charles W. Morton*

4696   To have and to hold from this day forward, for better for worse, for richer for poorer, in sickness and in health, to love and to cherish, till death us do part.—*Book of Common Prayer*

4697   There is something about a wedding-gown prettier than any other gown in the world.—*Douglas Jerrold*

4698   The kindest and the happiest pair
                        Will find occasion to forbear,
                        And something every day they live
                        To pity, and perhaps forgive.
                                            —*Cowper*

Index

All numbers in this index refer to numbers placed in numerical order at the left-hand margins of the pages. The 4,698 items of source material are completely indexed so that it is possible quickly to find all the items throughout the book which relate to a particular idea. To illustrate, under the classification, *marriage*, in the index, one can immmediately locate the numbers of all quotations, epigrams, humorous stories, definitions and other items relating to this subject. In addition, almost every one of the 4,698 items has been classified in the index under several headings so the reader who is seeking a quotation, epigram, or humorous story to illustrate even a particular word or a relatively restricted idea may find it by using the index.

THE BOOK OF WIT AND HUMOUR

A Public Speaker's Treasury

This book has been compiled as a source of usable humour for speakers, company directors, comperes, amateur entertainers, party wags, travelling salesmen, or simply for dipping into when you feel overwrought. Here is the ammunition that combats tension, for a good burst of laughter is as good as a tonic. **The book contains a wealth of items, including gags, wise-cracks and witticisms; jokes and jests; terse verse; humorous definitions; humorous book and song titles. A comprehensive index at the back enables quick and easy location of a witty reference to any subject. Here indeed is material in abundance for 'softening-up' any audience.** It will be invaluable for many people outside professional show business who are elected to speak in public — or who like to be the life and soul of the party whenever folk congregate for relaxation, be it a dinner function, or a celebration, or a company meeting. The items are original extracts from entertainment scripts, not merely collections of humour edited from various books, or quotations from other sources. **Somewhere and at some time the material has been successfully performed before audiences and has proved that it works.** Those who have profited from Cagney's script-writing include such notable performers as Ken Dodd, Tommy Cooper, Harry Worth and Les Dawson.

THE TOASTMASTER'S TREASURE CHEST

5,000 Indexed Items!

Herbert V. Prochnow & Herbert V. Prochnow, Jr.

The Toastmaster's Treasure Chest

The long-awaited companion volume to the Prochnows' classic public speaking book, *The Public Speaker's Treasure Chest* (over 500,000 copies sold).

For toastmasters, businessmen, politicians - or anybody who is called on frequently or occasionally for brief remarks. 5,000 items, all indexed, none duplicates the material in companion volume.

In view of the gratifying sales (over 5000,000 copies) of *The Public Speaker's Treasure Chest,* the authors believed that a companion book might be equally helpful to toastmasters and those who are required to lead discussions, conferences, seminars, or preside at luncheons and other functions. This book is the practical, valuable result. **Here are over 700 humorous stories, more than 1,300 epigrams, almost 725 examples of the wit and wisdom of world political leaders and famous persons, 200 inspirational quotations and illustrations, 240 toasts and sentiments for special occasions, more than 300 amusing and unusual definitions, over 200 unusual facts, stories, and quotations from biography, 350 proverbs of many nations, and hundreds of other items.** This book has been written for those who preside at dinners and meetings of various types; those who must make brief speeches; and those who enjoy reading humorous material, illustrations from biography, inspiring quotations, and anecdotes. There are quotations about business, education, medicine, government, and so on, to help the toastmaster when he introduces speakers in these specific areas. There are also quotations on inspirational topics such as faith, courage and character. A selection of English, French, German, Irish, Italian, Swedish, Chinese, Mexican, and many other national proverbs combine humour with wisdom. All this material is timely and useful!